FISHER
ANNOTATED TRAVEL GUIDES

Wilma Pezzini

Edited and Annotated by
Robert C. Fisher

Italy

83/84

Fisher Travel Guides
New York / Easton, Maryland / Champaign, Illinois

Library of Congress Cataloging in Publication Data

Pezzini, Wilma.
  Italy 1983/84.

  (Fisher annotated travel guides)
  Includes index.
    1. Italy—Description and travel—1975–   —Guide-
books. I. Fisher, Robert C. II. Title. III. Series.
DG416.T43   1983   914.5'04928   82–20985
ISBN 0–8116–0004–1

Maps and city plans by Pictograph

Text and cover design by Parallelogram/Marsha Cohen

Editorial production services by Cobb/Dunlop Publisher Services, Inc.

The Fisher travel guides include:

Bahamas	**France**
Bermuda	**Germany**
Best of the Caribbean	**Greece**
Britain	**Italy**
California and the Desert West	**Japan**
Canada	**Mexico**
Europe	**Spain and Portugal**
Florida and the Southeast	**Texas and the Southwest**

Distributed in the U.S.A. and Canada by
New American Library, 1633 Broadway, New York, N.Y. 10019

Distributed in the United Kingdom by
Columbus Books, 24 Red Lion Street, London WC1R 4PX

Distributed in Australia and New Zealand by
Doubleday Australia Pty., Ltd., 2A Woodcock Place, Lane Cove, N.S.W. 20066

Distributed in Continental Europe by
Feffer & Simons, B.V., 170 Rijnkade, Weesp, Netherlands

Distributed throughout the rest of the world by
Fleetbooks, c/o Feffer & Simons, Inc., 100 Park Ave., New York, N.Y. 10017

Printed in the United States of America

Contents

If ever there was a country to seize the romantic imagination, it is Italy. Italy the golden, Italy the magnificent, Italy the tragic, Italy the vast museum. No one can be indifferent to Italy who has seen any part of its mainland, especially its northern and central portions, where so many of the fine arts reached their highest form in Western man's path to the present.

This land of outstanding art, amazing churches, and a brilliant and optimistic people is, moreover, relatively cheap these days. The strength of the American dollar in the past two years has made the country more popular than ever, a flood of American citizens joining their fellow tourists from Britain, Canada, Germany and Scandinavia to swamp, at times, the primary sights. In the Sistine Chapel when it is filled with a polyglot of travelers, the tourist cacophony can be maddening, for example.

If I were forced to choose only one country on the European continent which I could visit, it would be Italy. The food, excellent as it is, lacks some of the sublety of the French cuisine. The people, while hospitable, aren't as warm as the Greeks. Things don't work, as they do in Germany. But the magical combination of architecture, painting, music and sculpture can be matched in no other place.

Italy has beaches, horse racing and every other form of entertainment known to most countries, but I believe you will want to come here for the visual experience, the pleasing assault on your eyes and ears of color, form, design, sound, and the sensuous flattering of your palate with food and wine.

About this Book

Over many years of writing and editing guidebooks, I have concluded that what the busy modern traveler needs is a concise listing of the best of certain categories ... the best in hotels, restaurants, museums and the like. The experienced traveler, in particular, wants sure guidance without having to wade through irrelevant information. The sophisticated traveler already knows how to pack, how to apply for a passport, how to buy an airline ticket, how to use a travel agent, and so forth. What he or she may want to know, however, is: What are the best and second best hotels in Rome; which of the museums in Florence should be visited if time is limited; and what can be seen in Venice in one day?

With the star rating system employed in this book, I think you'll find what you want, and quickly. The stars are awarded by the author and myself in consultation, and after discussing them with an ad hoc committee of friends (of mine and of Italy) acquired over 22 years in the travel publishing business.

Italy 1983–84 and 15 other titles published within the last nine months launched the new Fisher annotated travel guide series. These will be the first American guidebooks to attempt the classification of hotels, restaurants, museums, and even points of special interest in foreign countries. I do not believe for a moment, however, that everyone is going to agree with all our selections or the ratings that go with them. The annotations are intended to provide handy cross-references, some explanations, and, I hope, a bit of amusement. The books will be revised each year, and more new titles are planned for 1984–85.

About the Author

Wilma Pezzini is a well-traveled resident of Camaiore, a lovely village between Pisa and Florence where many American and British families have established summer residences. Born in Poland, and educated in Italy, Brazil and the United States, she brings a cosmopolitan outlook to this book, her second creation, following hard on the heels of the very popular Tuscan Cooking (Atheneum). Further insight on Italy was obtained when her husband was elected mayor of Camaiore, but her unique contribution to this series is her categorization of tourist highlights by artistic period rather than the simple points-of-the-compass description.

About the Editor

My qualifications to edit and annotate this book, as well as the others in the series, are based mostly on my 20 years experience with the Fodor guidebook organization, where I was chosen by Eugene Fodor to be his successor as editor-in-chief and president of the company. During my work with that firm, I lived for eight years in Europe and eight in Asia, both happy and productive periods. In the course of my work, I helped create more than 62 titles in the series of 75 books, and supervised all of them to ensure their proper revision from year to year. This led to constant traveling around the world, as the series eventually covered all or parts of 120 nations. Italy was my favorite, and frequent, destination on the continent.

Some further experience in sizing up the international scene was gained from my education, as, after graduating from Harvard College (where I studied international relations), I studied international law at the Columbia University Law School and at Tokyo University's Graduate School of Law.

On the professional side, I am currently vice-president of the Society of American Travel Writers, and a former president of the New York Travel Writers' Association, as well as being a director of the charitable foundation, the International Association for Medical Assistance to Travelers (IAMAT), a group whose services I recommend highly.

If you have read this far, you must be a friend or a relative, possibly a reviewer, or even as I am, a hopeless addict of travel books and guidebooks. Thanks, anyhow. I hope this book fills the bill for you.

On Using This Book...

It has been said that the Italian countryside was molded by history, and there can be no doubt that it would be difficult to understand Italy without some knowledge of its history. But alongside history there was another force that helped to move the mountains, drain the marshlands, terrace the stony hills and build the villages and towns: the effort of humans.

Neither topography nor climate was as clement toward this land as is commonly thought. A large portion of it is covered by mountains, some too harsh to be cultivated, others made of pebbly earth that tends to slide and is subject to erosion. Some parts of Italy are sitting on an underground volcano, other parts have an active volcano for background. Most of the country is earthquake prone. Coastlands are often sand and *argilla,* unfit for agriculture. And the one large Italian plain, the Val Padana (the Po River Valley), was originally a flat swampy surface, of little or no use for settlement until massive drainage dried it out.

argilla = clay

There is more. The Mediterranean climate is not as friendly as you might think. The dry, hot summer is often followed by a sudden overabundance of rain, causing floods and damaging crops. There is fog in fall and winter, especially in the north and on the Val Padana. Many places are afflicted with high humidity, and every region has unique climate problems, such as the hot African winds that sweep up into Sardegna or the cold Alpine frosts that hit the Trentino–Alto Adige at all times of the year.

Yet, in spite of all this, or perhaps because of it, Italy is a country with some of the most inspiring scenery in the world, which has produced some of the best artists and which attracts, now as ever, all those who love beauty, have a highly developed esthetic sense or are blessed with a particularly sensitive eye, ear and palate.

There is something to be seen, learned and enjoyed in every corner of Italy, whether your interest lies in history, art or music, if you love scenic beauty, food or wine. There's an abundance of material for nearly everyone: for the architect and city planner, for the painter and the graphic designer, for the gourmet and restaurant owner, for the fashion writer and the knitwear buyer, for the make-up artist and the movie fan, for the musician and the perfume expert.

Someone once said that Italy is an ancient land of eternal youth. This charming sentence is another way of saying that the countryside is old and mellow, the population full of fun and song. Reality is slightly more complex. The Italy of the eighties is a serious country, fighting with the same problems with which the rest of the Western world is fighting, plus the added burden of exchanging the old agricultural pattern for the new industrial system.

But a tourist is hardly aware of these changes; for a tourist, Italy is as charming as ever. The waiters are pleasant, the young men still ogle the attractive women, music is in the air and hot *cappuccino* is served at outdoor tables in Roma (Rome), Firenze (Florence) or Venezia (Venice).

This book cannot possibly cover all the facets of this small, crowded country. It is crowded not only with human beings—somewhere between 55 and 60 million locals plus the several million tourists that mill around most of the year—but also with cities, towns, villages, houses, churches, museums, monuments, panoramic views, roads, highways, mountains, hills, valleys, rivers, lakes, bays, hamlets, islands, restaurants, hotels, bars, stores, markets, piazzas, fountains, trees, flowers, cars, motorscooters, bicycles, tractors, boats, factories, campers, tents, football fields, beaches—anything and everything. We hope to give you a concise Italy, with enough description to make it interesting. We have included the important things, both old and new. The material to choose from was huge, so we've written of what we know best, trying to be as objective as we could. Bear with us if something you particularly like was overlooked.

Before 1970 the administrative procedures in Italy were handled by *comuni* and *province,* plus the central government. Then a new law created the regions in an attempt to make larger administrative units. After 1970 these larger units became a reality.

For centuries the regions have existed in Italy as a result of natural, ethnic and linguistic differences and the fragmented history of the country's different areas. But by becoming a political fact the regions are a step toward the modernization of the country.

There are 20 regions, including the two large islands of Sicilia (Sicily) and Sardegna (Sardinia), with some having special statutes that allow for such differences as linguistic ones. Each region is subdivided into provinces, for a total of 95 in all Italy. Each province is then subdivided into comuni, which can be as large as Roma and Milano (Milan) or so small that the administrators work only part-time. There are almost 10,000 comuni.

The following is a list of the regions and the provinces that make up each region. The first province listed is the *capoluogo,* equivalent to the capital of the region.

Each province has a *sigla,* a two letter symbol—except Roma, which uses the whole word. This sigla appears on automobile license plates and is used for all other purposes when identification of a province is necessary, such as mailing addresses. The name of a province is also the name of a city within that province, for example, Milano and Firenze are each the name of both a province and a city. In these cases, the city is mentioned *without* the *sigla,* for example, Salerno, and the province is referred to by saying the province of Salerno. Other cities within the province are followed by the sigla. For example, Amalfi (SA) means the city of Amalfi in the province of Salerno.

Except for Rome, which is described in an independent section, the itineraries in this book are by region. In a few cases, an itinerary may go from one region to another, but this will be clearly stated. Within each region, however, the directions will be from one province to the next. When such is the case, the first city or town of the new province will be followed by the sigla in parentheses. For example, when going from the city of Firenze to the city of Prato, only the names of the cities will be listed since the province is always that of Firenze. If, on the other hand, the itinerary were to be from the city of Firenze to the city of Montecatini, then the listing would read Montecatini (PT), indicating that Montecatini is in another province, Pistoia.

In each hotel or restaurant section there is an alphabetical listing of some of the cities mentioned. The cities that are provincial capitals will not be followed by the sigla. Every other city will be listed with its sigla in parentheses, for example, Volterra (PI).

NORTHERN OR EUROPEAN ITALY

Piemonte (Piedmont)

Torino (TO)
Cuneo (CN)
Novara (NO)
Alessandria (AL)
Asti (AT)
Vercelli (VC)

Valle D'Aosta

Aosta (AO)

Veneto

Venezia (VE)
Verona (VR)
Padova (PD)
Vincenza (VI)
Treviso (TV)
Rovigo (RO)
Belluno (BL)

Trentino—Alto Adige

Trento (TN)
Bolzano (BZ)

Lombardia (Lombardy)

Milano (MI)
Pavia (PV)
Como (CO)
Brescia (BS)
Varese (VA)
Sondrio (SO)
Bergamo (BG)
Mantova (MN)
Cremona (CR)

Friuli—Venezia Giulia

Trieste (TS)
Udine (UD)
Gorizia (GO)
Pordenone (PN)

Liguria

Genova (GE)
Imperia (IM)
Savona (SV)
La Spezia (SP)

CENTRAL OR ITALIAN ITALY

Emilia—Romagna
Bologna (BO)
Modena (MO)
Reggio Nell' Emilia (RE)
Parma (PR)
Piacenza (PC)
Forli (FO)
Ravenna (RA)
Ferrara (FE)

Toscana (Tuscany)
Firenze (FI)
Pisa (PI)
Livorno (LI)
Lucca (LU)
Pistoia (PT)
Massa-Carrara (MS)
Arezzo (AR)
Siena (SI)
Grosseto (GR)

Umbria
Perugia (PG)
Terni (TR)

Marches
Ancona (AN)
Ascoli Piceno (AP)
Pesaro e Urbino (PS)
Macerata (MC)

Lazio (Latium)
Roma (ROMA)
Frosinone (FR)
Viterbo (VT)
Rieti (RI)
Latina (LT)

SOUTHERN OR MEDITERRANEAN ITALY

Abruzzi
Aquila (AQ)
Teramo (TE)
Pescara (PE)
Chieti (CH)

Molise
Campobasso (CB)
Isernia (IS)

Campania
Napoli (NA)
Salerno (SA)
Avellino (AV)
Caserta (CE)
Benevento (BN)

Puglia (Apulia)
Bari (BA)
Brindisi (BR)
Taranto (TA)
Lecce (LE)
Foggia (FG)

Basilicata

Potenza (PZ)
Matera (MT)

Calabria

Reggio de Calabria (RC)
Catanzaro (CZ)
Cosenza (CS)

Sicilia (Sicily)

Palermo (PA)
Catania (CT)
Agrigento (AG)
Trapani (TP)
Siracusa (SR)
Ragusa (RG)
Caltanisetta (CL)
Messina (ME)
Enna (EN)

Sardegna (Sardinia)

Cagliari (CA)
Sassari (SS)
Nuoro (NU)
Oristano (OR)

This book is divided into five parts: hard facts and four areas of Italy. The first area is Rome. The next is northern, or European Italy, for all of its seven regions border on one or more European countries. The capital of this area is Milano, and it contains some of the most famous, important and beautiful towns in the world, such as Venezia (Venice), Genova (Genoa), Torino (Turin), Verona and Padova (Padua). The third area is central Italy, the very heart of the country—Italian Italy. Its nerve center is Firenze (Florence), but it contains all of Toscana (Tuscany) and Umbria, plus the rich towns of Emilia-Romagna, the rest of Lazio (Latium) and Le Marche (Marches). The last area is southern Italy, which we have named Mediterranean Italy. It includes the regions south of Rome, and the islands.

IMPORTANT NOTE ON PRICES, ETC.

Prices mentioned in this book were accurate at time of writing, but as all experienced travelers know, nothing in life is forever, particularly costs, hours and days of closing, and the ambience of a hotel or restaurant. Please phone ahead to obtain reservations, confirm price ranges, or check closing times in order to avoid being disappointed. We will be delighted to hear from you, whether it be a recommendation, complaint, or both at: **Fisher Travel Guides, Suite 2300, 401 Broadway, New York, N.Y. 10013.**

The Hard Facts

PLANNING AHEAD

Costs

Italy is a moderately priced country for travelers these days, though cheap is not the word. Thanks to the strength of the dollar, it is possible to enjoy a good meal in a first-class restaurant for about $15 per person. Rome and Milan are the most expensive cities, naturally, while Florence and Venice are only moderately so. The South is cheaper except for such rarified spots as Capri and Ischia.

Here are some typical costs:

	Rome and Major Cities	Elsewhere
Moderately-priced hotel. (per person in double room)	$30 (39,000 lire)	$20 (26,000 lire)
Lunch, moderate	$ 7 (9,000 lire)	$ 4 (5,200 lire)
Dinner, moderate	$13 (16,900 lire)	$10 (13,000 lire)
Total	$50 (65,000 lire)	$34 (44,200 lire)

Climate

Italy has a moderately warm climate, with spring and early autumn the best seasons. The winters can be cold and damp, while July and August can be too hot. In August, the Italians go on holiday, so best to avoid this month.

AVERAGE MAXIMUM DAILY TEMPERATURES (°F.)

	Winter (Jan.)	Spring (Apr.)	Summer (July)	Autumn (Oct.)
Milan (North)	41	64	84	63
Rome (Central)	46	64	84	68
Naples (South)	54	64	84	72

Holidays and Special Events

January.   Epiphany Fair. Roma (Rome). On January 5th, the eve of Twelfth Night, there is an outdoor display of gifts, toys and sweets around the grand Bernini Fountains.

February/March.   Carnival. Viareggio. A parade of spectacular floats is the glittering high point of the festivities.

March/April.   Scoppio del Carro, Explosion of the Cart. Firenze (Florence). On Easter Sunday, the success of the First Crusade is celebrated by igniting a pyramid of fireworks during mass.

Lowest APEX fare, New York - Rome round trip, was $699 at time of writing

You'll see the Befana, the toy-bearing witch, at Piazza Navona

May. Festival of St. Efisio. Cagliari. The festival runs from May 1st to 4th and includes a huge procession of pilgrims wearing 17th-century costumes as they accompany the statue of the saint.

Race of the Candles. Gubbio. On May 15th there is an unusual day-long pageant in which three tall shrines are hurried along the hilly streets by people in local costumes.

Palio dei Balestrieri, The Palio of the Archers. Gubbio. Medieval arms and outfits add authenticity and color to this crossbow contest between Gubbio and Sansepolcro, held on the last Sunday of the month. If Gubbio wins, stay for the celebration and parade.

Sardinian Cavalcade. Sassari. On May 23rd, thousands of people wearing traditional Sardinian styles take part in this long-established pageant.

June. Battle of the Bridge. Pisa. This combat, held on the first Sunday of the month, includes a medieval parade and, yes, a contest for possession of a bridge.

Gioco del Calcio. Firenze. This wild reenactment of a 16th-century soccer match—in authentic costumes—takes place twice, on June 24th and 28th. There is also a fireworks display on the twenty-fourth, the feast of St. John the Baptist.

The Lily Festival. Nola. On the last Sunday of the month a procession of allegorical towers is accented by pomp and colorful costumes.

July. Horse Race. Siena. Held on July 2nd, this is not your Kentucky Derby–type of event. For one thing, the horses are ridden bareback. For another, they careen around the mattress-padded campo. The medieval festivities also include flag throwing and a procession.

Festa dei Noantri. Roma. Trastevere, on the right bank of the Tiber, erupts in a carnival of folk dances, floats, fireworks and song that some nights may get downright Bacchanalian. Runs the week of July 19th–26th.

The Feast of the Redeemer. Venezia (Venice). On the third Sunday of the month there is a parade of gondolas and other craft that highlights the celebration of the feast.

August. Joust of the Quintana. Ascoli Piceno. In this exciting historical spectacle, held on the first Sunday of the month, the Piazza del Popolo overflows with people in medieval costumes.

Palio of the Gulf. La Spezia. On the second Sunday of the month there is a 2,000-meter rowing contest on the "gulf of the writer." (The poet Shelley drowned off the coast of San Terenzo, south of La Spezia.)

On August 16th, Siena has a replay of its July 2nd medieval horse race.

Feast of the Redeemer. Nuoro. To honor the Savior, beautiful local costumes are worn from August 27th–30th.

September. Joust of the Saracens. Arezzo. On the first Sunday of the month, you can see knights in armor tilting as in days of old.

Historical Regatta. Venezia. Also, on the first Sunday of September, watch richly decorated ceremonial boats sweep along the Grand Canal, followed by an exciting gondola race. Eye-filling period costumes add to the authenticity of this traditional competition.

This race (palio) in Siena has free admis- sion in the very center of the square

Piedigrotta. Napoli (Naples). Two days (September 7th and 8th) of fireworks, floats, illuminated boats and a song competition.

Joust of the Quintana. Foligno. On the second Sunday of the month, hundreds of knights in costume reenact a 17th-century pageant.

Travel Agents and Tour Operators

Here we are dealing with the retail and wholesale aspects of traveling, meaning that the tour operator is the wholesaler whose product can be bought through the travel agent. If you already have a favorite agent, you're lucky. You can give him or her a sketch of the trip you have in mind, and the travel agent can fill in the details. Other prospective travelers will have to do more homework before contacting an agent. With the help of a guidebook, brochures and other reference material, you should list where you want to go, the hotels in which you want to stay and as many other details as possible and give the list to an agent.

You could go directly to a tour operator, but we recommend using a travel agent with whom you feel comfortable. They should be aware of the latest travel packages and seasonal air or cruise fares, and they will contact the airlines or tour operators who can help realize your plans. And remember that the agent will charge you—and should tell you in advance that you will be charged—*only* if you ask for special services such as last-minute bookings or changes that involve telegrams or overseas phone calls. Their regular income is the commissions received from the airline, hotel or tour operator when a reservation is made on your behalf.

All reputable agents are members of the American Society of Travel Agents (ASTA) or, in Britain, the Association of British Travel Agents (ABTA). If you don't know an agent you can write for recommendations. In the USA to American Society of Travel Agents, 4400 MacArthur Blvd. N. W., Washington, D.C., 20036; in Canada to ASTA—Canada, 130 Albert St., Suite 1207, Ottawa, Ontario; and in the U.K. to Association of British Travel Agents, 53 Newman Street, London W1P 4AH, England.

Directory

There are many ways to obtain information, either before you leave or after you arrive.

In the USA and Canada

Italian Government Travel Office
New York
630 Fifth Avenue, New York, NY 10011
Tel. (212) 245–4822
Chicago
500 North Michigan Avenue, Chicago, IL. 60611
Tel. (312) 644–0990
San Francisco
360 Post Street, San Francisco, CA. 94108
Tel. (415) 392–6206

Canada Store
56, Plaza, 3 Place Ville Marie, Montreal, Quebec
Tel. 855–7667

In the UK

201 Regent Street, London W1R 8AY, England
Tel. (01) 439–2311

The Home Office

Via Marghera 2, 1-00185 Rome, Italy
Tel. (06) 4 95 27 51

British airways flies between several cities in either country

The airlines flying to Italy are excellent sources of information. Besides the national airline of Italy, Alitalia, there are TWA and Pan Am, and all of them should be able to provide you with schedules and brochures.

If you already are in Italy and want maps, lists of hotels or answers to specific questions, visit one of the Provincial Tourist Boards (*Ente Provinciale per il Turismo*), which you'll find located in the principal towns of a province, or one of the Local Tourist Boards (*Azienda Autonoma Soggiorno*), which are prominent at points of tourist interest.

Packing

Though Italy has a great diversity of climate, during the summer you should be comfortable in lightweight clothing. Pants suits are acceptable almost everywhere, but remember that for a Papal audience women must wear long-sleeved dresses and men must wear a jacket and tie.

For spring and fall, lightweight woolens are best, while for winter heavier clothing is needed. A light raincoat is practical at any time of the year, as are comfortable walking shoes.

Documentation

You must have a passport, but a visa is not required if you are a British, U.S. or Canadian citizen and plan to stay in Italy for less than 90 days. This regulation also applies to citizens of Australia, Ireland and New Zealand, among other countries.

A U.S. driving license is valid if you are driving your own car. However, the license must be accompanied by a translation, which you can get free of charge from offices of the Automobile Club of Italy or from the Italian State Tourist Office. Be sure to bring the car's registration.

Health certificates are not needed for entry into Italy or for return to the USA, Canada or Britain. However, be aware that a smallpox vaccination certificate is necessary for entry into the USA if, within the preceding 14 days, you have visited a country reporting a smallpox-infested area.

Handicapped Travel

If you or anyone in your party is disabled, before starting your trip you may want to refer to one or more of the books on traveling and the handicapped. Two that may be available in your library are: *Travelability* by Lois Reamy, published by Macmillan Company, and *Access to the World: A Travel Guide for the Handicapped* by Louise Weiss, published by the Chatham Square Press, Inc., 401 Broadway, New York, NY 10013.

Other sources of information include:

The Society for the Advancement of Travel for the Handicapped
   26 Court Street, Brooklyn, NY 11242

Travel Information Center, Moss Rehabilitation Hospital
   Tabor Road at 12th Street, Philadelphia, PA 19141

The Royal Association of Disability and Rehabilitation
   25 Mortimer Street, London W1, England

Tours for the disabled are offered by:

Flying Wheels Tours
   148 W. Bridge Street, Box 382, Owatonna, MN 55060

Kasheta Travel
   139 Main Street, East Rockaway, NY 11518

Rambling Tours
   P.O. Box 1034, Hallandale, FL 33009

Escorted tour packages are available, and the trips are different only in that they are more slowly paced. Of course, all services involved—hotel, transportation and so forth—are ready to assist their guests.

GETTING THERE

Many people agree that getting there is not the fun it used to be but are consoled by the fact that since the deregulation of trans-Atlantic fares, getting there at least is cheaper. Inflation and fuel costs are pushing the rates back up, but the range of special fares has widened. Your travel agent or the airline can explain what is currently being offered.

Direct flights to Italy from the USA are provided by Alitalia, Pan Am and TWA. Alitalia flies from New York and Boston to both Rome and Milan (Milano), and from Chicago to Milan. Pan Am has flights from New York to Rome. TWA flies from Boston to Rome and from New York to both Rome and Milan.

If you wish to travel to Italy by boat, there are two possibilities. You can sail directly via one of the three or four freighter lines with passenger service to Italian ports. Or you can take Cunard's *QE 2* to England or France and then make further connections. In either case, book well in advance.

FORMALITIES ON ARRIVAL

Customs

Italian customs officials are fairly lenient, but there is the usual crackdown on drugs.

Alitalia and British Airways serve several routes between cities in each country

Ford's Freighter Travel Guide lists all cargo ship possibilities

In addition to the regular personal effects, items that may be imported duty-free provided they are for personal use and are not to be sold, given away or traded include two bottles of wine and one bottle of hard liquor per person, 400 cigarettes and a quantity of cigars or pipe tobacco not exceeding 500 g. (grams) (1.1 lb.), a portable radio set (subject to a small license fee), and a maximum of 2.2 kg (4.4 lb.) of coffee, 3 kg. (6.6 lb.) of sugar and 1 kg. (2.2 lb.) of cocoa.

Italy still allows you to import firearms for sporting purposes, *provided that* you get a hunting permit from the Italian consulate *before* you leave home. If you have the permit, which is good for 30 days, you may import one rifle with 200 cartridges or two shotguns with 100 cartridges each.

Money

There are no restrictions on the amount of foreign currency you may bring into Italy. However, the government asks that you declare the amount you are carrying. This helps them to establish the amount of foreign currency that may be taken out of Italy.

When you exchange your dollars or other currency, you receive *lire* (L) (singular, *lira*) in return. At this writing, approximately L.1,200 = $1.00. There are bills (paper notes) in denominations of:

L.100,000	approx. $83	approx. £49
L.50,000	approx. $42	approx. £25
L.20,000	approx. $17	approx. £10
L.10,000	approx. $8	approx. £5
L.5,000	approx. $4	approx. £2.30
L.2,000	approx. $1.70	approx. £1
L.1,000	approx. $ .83	approx. 50 p.
L.500	approx. $ .42	approx. 25 p.

at presstime, the lira had sunk to a rate of 1,440 to the dollar, good news for american travelers

There are coins for 10, 20, 50, 100 and 200 lire. Do not be surprised if you are offered a postage stamp or other token in place of some of the lesser-value coins. Sometimes there are shortages of small change.

As we said, there is no ceiling on how much foreign currency you may import. Regarding Italian currency, however, you can neither enter nor leave Italy carrying more than L.200,000.

Getting into Town

Most travelers will arrive in Italy at Rome's Leonardo da Vinci Airport (usually referred to as *Fiumicino*) 25 km. (25 kilometers) (15 mi.) (15 miles) southwest of the capitol. To reach Rome you have a choice of an expensive taxi or an air-conditioned bus with ample room for your luggage. The latter, called an *Acotral*, for L.1,500 will take you in to Rome's Termini Station (*Stazione Centrale Roma Termini*), from where you can easily get to any part of the city.

a taxi to rome center should cost approx. 18,000 lire (approx. $13)

Travelers arriving on a charter flight may land at *Ciampino* Airport, which is closer to the center of Rome. The Acotral buses are available here, too, or you can take a train to Termini Station.

If you arrive by train it will probably be at Termini Station. However, if Rome is not the train's last stop, you may find yourself at the edge of the city. There should be no problem getting a train or bus connection from there to Termini.

Milan has two airports, and at both of them you again have the choice between an expensive taxi or a bus. From Malpensa Airport to the city's air terminal, the bus fare is L.2,000. The fare from Linate Airport into the city is L.1,000.

SETTLING DOWN

Choosing a Hotel

Italy controls the price range of its hotels (*alberghi*) and pensions or guest-houses (*pensioni*), setting a maximum and minimum rate for each category from deluxe to fourth class. As in most countries, the rates vary according to season and location. Prices will be lower in the smaller cities and towns and throughout Italy in the off-season months. Remember, too, that accommodations in the remoter areas will often be more modest.

The hotel costs listed below are for an average double room with bath/shower, the price mentioned is for two people in a room. These figures represent the general price range available for that hotel and pension category. The price includes taxes, services, heating, air conditioning and IVA Tax (added value tax, the Italian version of sales tax). The figures do not represent the price range of any specific hotel or pension. For that information, you or your travel agent may contact one of the Italian government travel offices whose addresses are listed in the **Sources of Information** section.

OFFICIAL PRICE RANGE

HOTEL	PENSION	LIRE	FISHER GUIDE CATEGORY
Deluxe		L.85,000–200,000	Very Expensive
First class		L.50,000–130,000	Expensive
Second class	First class	L.35,000–60,000	Moderately Expensive
Third class	Second class	L.25,000–35,000	Moderate
Fourth class	Third class	L.20,000–30,000	Inexpensive

Hotels in the higher categories offer the usual international standard of comfort. The differences between a deluxe and first- or second-class hotel can sometimes be hard to detect. Size might be a factor, or location or the level of service and amenities. As for the lower categories, it still is possible to discover a charming, slightly out of the way bargain.

Whatever your choice, we strongly advise you to book all hotels in advance. If for some reason you arrive without a reservation, there are hotel information desks located at most airports, railway stations and bus terminals. You may encounter long lines at them, especially during peak seasons.

STAR RATING SYSTEM

Hotels

★★★★★   5 Stars. Super deluxe establishment, BEST of the best.

★★★★   4 Stars. Deluxe. As comfortable as your own home, and better service.

★★★   3 Stars. Superior. Has the facilities that make it stand out.

★★   2 Stars. Excellent. There is nothing to complain about at all.

★   1 Star. Good. One or two things may be missing, but an o.k. place.

0 Stars. Recommended. (And look how much money we're saving!)

This is our rating system, not the Italian government's

Restaurants

★★★★★   5 Stars. Out of this World!

★★★★   4 Stars. Fantastic!

★★★   3 Stars. Superb!

★★   2 Stars. Excellent.

★   1 Star. Good.

0 Stars. Recommended.

Sightseeing, Museums, Etc.

★★★★★   5 Stars. You should make a trip to Italy if only to see this.

★★★★   4 Stars. You should plan your trip to Italy around this.

★★★   3 Stars. You should plan your day around this.

★★   2 Stars. You should detour a mile in order to see this.

★   1 Star. You should detour a couple of blocks to see this.

IMPORTANT NOTE: The Star Ratings for each country's hotels, restaurants and points of interest are based on each country's merits alone, and are not to be compared with ratings given to places in any other country. Standards and attitudes in each country vary, and so, therefore, must our ratings.

Choosing a Restaurant

Unlike the hotels and pensions, restaurants in Italy are not officially classified. The categories below are based on prices charged and represent the cost range for either a complete lunch or dinner, without wine or cocktails, for one person. Taxes and service charges added to your bill will vary from 12% to 20%, and there may also be a cover charge (*coperto*).

Restaurant Costs

For example: expensive = approx. $14 to $21

Very expensive	L.30,000–40,000
Expensive	L.20,000–30,000
Moderately expensive	L.15,000–25,000
Moderate, reasonable	L.10,000–20,000
Inexpensive	L.8,000 –15,000

Tipping

Although a service charge is added both to hotel and restaurant bills, it is customary to give an additional tip.

In hotels, give the porter L.500 or more per bag, depending on its size and the distance carried; L.300 to L.500 to the doorman when he gets you a taxi; L.500 to L.800 a day to the chambermaid, and a bit more per day for the concierge, with an additional tip for extra services.

If you have room service, give the waiter at least L.500, depending on the amount of the tab, and tip at least the same amount if you have valet service. At the hotel bar, tip 15% of your drink bill.

In restaurants, give the waiter 5%–10% of the check, or however much you wish if the service was extraordinary. If you have wine, you may tip the steward 10% of its cost.

Perks for the Experienced Traveler

BTLC are the Italian "go anywhere" train tickets that allow only the purchaser unlimited and unrestricted travel in Italy for a flat fee for a chosen duration. Their use is strictly limited to permanent residents of all countries except Italy. You may purchase the tickets in the USA at offices of the Italian State Railway representatives, or you may purchase them at main rail terminals in major cities in Italy.

If you plan to travel a great deal by train only within Italy, check the BTLC tickets. They are available for 8, 15, 21, and 30 days, first or second class. If you have a first-class ticket you are not charged a supplement, even on the Rapido or TEE trains. BTLC tickets also entitle you to make free seat reservations upon request at railway stations.

The Kilometric Ticket is another option. Although there are some restrictions as to which trains it can be used on without paying a supplement, this ticket has other advantages. One of them is that, unlike the BTLC, it can be used by more than one person. As many as five people, even if they are not related, may use the Kilometric Ticket at the same time. The conductor simply multiplies the distance by the number of adults. The Kilometric Ticket is good for a distance of 3,000 km. (1,875 mi.), or for a total of 20 trips, and is valid for two months. Like the BTLC, it can be purchased in the USA or in Italy.

The Eurailpass is similar to the BTLC, except that it offers unlimited first-class train travel not only in Italy but also in any country of Western Europe except Finland and the United Kingdom. The Eurailpass cannot be bought anywhere in Europe. You must purchase it before you leave North America. To do so, check with your travel agent or with railway agents in the larger cities. If the Italian, Swiss, French or German national railroads have an office near where you live, you may purchase a ticket from them.

There are passes available for periods of 15 or 21 days or one, two or three months. Of course, those on extensive trips benefit the most. With the pass you are also entitled to discounts on numerous ferries and buses.

The Eurailpass may only be used by one person, and he or she will be asked to present a passport when using the ticket.

Senior citizens and those 23 years of age and under are entitled to certain privileges with Inter-Rail and Inter-Rail Senior train passes available in Europe.

Travelers under 26 years of age can benefit from the BIGE-Transalpino discount tickets. Transalpino has offices in Milan, Rome and most major European cities.

a 15-day pass is $260, 21-day pass $330

Business Hours and Holidays

Banks are open Monday through Friday from 8:30 A.M. to 1:30 P.M. and remember that many Italian businesspeople close for the afternoon *siesta* but work later into the evening. With some variations, shop hours are from 9 A.M. to 1 P.M. and from 3:30/4 to 7:30/8 P.M.

The public holidays on which offices and shops are closed include January 1st (New Year's Day); Easter Monday; April 25th (Liberation Day); May 1st (Labor Day); August 15th (Assumption of the Virgin Mary); November 1st (All Saints Day): December 8th (Immaculate Conception); December 25th (Christmas); December 26th (Saint Stephen).

Many businesses are also closed on January 6th (Epiphany); the feasts of the Ascension and Corpus Christi; and on the Saturday following November 4th, National Unity Day.

In various cities, offices and shops are closed on the feast day of their patron saint: Venezia (April 25th, St. Mark); Firenze, Turin, and Genoa (June 24th, St. John the Baptist); Palermo (July 15th, St. Rosalie); Napoli (September 19th, St. Gennaro); Bologna (October 4th, St. Petronio); Cagliari (October 30th, St. Saturnino); Trieste (November 3rd, St. Giusto); Bari delle Puglie (Bari, for short) (Deceber 6th, St. Nicola); and Milano (December 7th, St. Ambrose).

Electricity

If you plan to travel with an electric razor or hair dryer, bring along a transformer. American appliances are made to operate at 120 V. (volts), but the voltage in most Italian cities and towns is either 115 or 220 V. To be on the safe side, check with the hotel before trying to use that electric iron.

You will also need an adapter plug because Italian sockets are built for prongs that are round, not flat like the ones on U.S. plugs.

Water and Drink

The water is safe in all major towns and cities

The quality of Italy's water varies. If you have the slightest doubt, don't drink it—and don't use ice cubes made from it. There is a wide enough variety of bottled waters, with or without carbonation, so that you don't have to risk Nero's Revenge.

Communications

The use of telephones in Italy is slightly more complicated than their use in the USA. In Italy there are two types of phones. For one type, you purchase a L.100 token (*gettone*) and insert but don't release it. Dial your number and when the party answers, release the token. You probably will have to insert a few *gettone,* even for local calls, to avoid being disconnected in the middle of a conversation. If you push a button when you are through, any gettone that were not used will be returned.

The other type of phone involves a *scuta* call, made from a booth in a restaurant or bar through an operator who may be the bartender. A meter keeps track of the call, and you pay the cost—and perhaps a service fee—when you finish and leave the booth.

If you're calling long distance between major Italian cities (*interurbano*), you can dial direct on public phones by using the area code of the city you're calling. Be sure to have plenty of gettone at hand. You can also direct dial calls to the USA. If calling the USA from your hotel, try to have the call charged to your phone at home rather than added to your hotel bill. Hotels often add a charge of their own that can double the cost of the call.

Most other international calls must be made from the phone company's offices.

Internal and international telegrams may be dictated over the phone to *Italcable.*

Stamps can be bought at the post office or at tobacco shops. If you don't want to beat your mail home, use an aerogram or send letters and even postcards via air mail. These services cost more but will get your mail home in a week to ten days, as opposed to a month or more for surface mail.

As for receiving mail while you're in Italy, it can be sent to a hotel where you have reservations or care of American Express in the larger cities. For general delivery service in smaller cities and towns, mail should be addressed to the local post office in your name, with the words *"Fermo Posta"* added after the name of the town. You can then claim the mail by presenting your passport at that post office.

Language

English is spoken, or at least understood, at most hotels and shops, but you may be more comfortable if you do a little homework. You may find you know more Italian than you realize. And you certainly will find that Italians are pleased by your attempts to speak their language.

For tours in English, check with American Express or your hotel. They should also be able to help you in case you need an interpreter or secretary or wish to arrange for a private tour with an English-speaking guide/driver. Your travel agent may also be able to help you secure these services.

Business Tips

As noted earlier, banking hours are from 8:30 A.M. to 1:30 P.M., Monday through Friday, and business hours generally are from 9 A.M. to 1 P.M., and from about 4 P.M. to 8 P.M.

If you plan to be meeting with Italian businesspeople, it might be diplomatic to learn a few phrases of greeting in their language and perhaps some words that pertain to the matters you'll be discussing.

Museums

Italy is a country of museums; almost every city has one, most have several. The South has an abundance of archaeological material; the North has many museums of wine and wine making; the Center has splendid art galleries and painting collections. There are many museums dedicated to specialties such as textiles, cars, umbrellas, spaghetti or World War I. Also, every large cathedral has its own museum, known as *Museo dell'Opera del Duomo.* We have listed the ones in Firenze and Siena, but they exist in almost every city.

The listings in this book are far from complete. They contain the 100 largest and best known museums and galleries and the ones we know and love. Furthermore, many collections are under revision and are closed to the public. As soon as we get news of their availability, our list will be brought up to date.

Note. It wasn't possible to obtain accurate prices of admission for every museum, and not all schedules were available as of publication. The prices and schedules given are accurate as of late 1982.

Medical Assistance

United States visitors to Italy are responsible for their medical bills, so you may want to take out insurance before traveling.

Most cities have English-speaking doctors and dentists. The British or U.S. consulate can give you the appropriate names and phone numbers. They can also give you the address of the hospital closest to where you are staying; you can also get this information through the personnel at your hotel or pension.

Stop in a drugstore (*farmacia*) at your leisure and pick up a list of those that are open nights and Sundays. You'll probably never need it, but it could prove valuable.

For emergency service (ambulance, fire, police) dial 113. Should an emergency arise while you are traveling, look for the first-aid service (*pronto soccorso*) at the airport or railway station. There should be a doctor on duty. Of course, this service is also found at all hospitals.

Finally, before traveling you may wish to join the International Association for Medical Assistance to Travellers (IAMAT), a nonprofit charitable organization that sponsors studies of the effects of travel on health standards. There is no fee to join, but contributions to help further the association's important work are most welcomed. One of their major achievements in recent years is a Worldwide Malaria Chart. Contact them at 736 Center St., Lewiston N.Y. 14092; 95 Norfolk St., Guelph, Ontario N1H 4J4, Canada; St. Vincent's Hospital, Victoria Parade, Melbourne 3065, Australia; or Gotthardstrasse 17, 6300 Zug, Switzerland.

IAMAT will give you a list of English-speaking doctors (and their clinics) in Italy

Metric System

United States citizens can take this opportunity to study metric measurements and become more familiar with them. Italy and most countries of the world use them, and eventually they may replace the current U.S. system (including using the Celsius rather than the Fahrenheit thermometer).

1 centimeter (cm.)=4/10 inch (in.). 1 in.=2.55 cm.
1 meter (m.)=3.28 feet (ft.) or 1.1 yards (yd.). 1 ft.=0.31 m.
   and 1 yd.=.93 m.
1 kilometer (km.)=.62 miles (mi.). 1 mi.=1.51 km.
1 gram (g.)=.035 (ounces) oz. 1 oz.=28 g.
1 kilogram (kg.)=35.27 oz. or 2.21 pounds (lb.). 1 lb.=450 g.
1 metric ton (t.)=1.1 t U.S.
1 liter (l.)=.26 gallon (gal.). 1 gal. U.S.=3.75 l.

As you can see, a liter is close to a quart, a meter to a yard, and a centimeter to a half-inch.

GETTING AROUND

By Air

Because of its shape, Italy lends itself to north–south air travel. Luckily, the country's domestic air service is excellent, with numerous regular flights from Milan and, especially, Rome to airports throughout Italy. Fares are reasonable and in some cases can be lowered—for young people or on night flights. For schedules from Rome and Milan, check with Alitalia, ATI or Alisarda. Alitalia also provides air service from other Italian cities and resort areas.

By Train

Train travel in Italy is generally comfortable and surprisingly inexpensive compared with rates in other European countries. Considering how the charm of the countryside can enhance your stay, trains deserve serious consideration when you're deciding how to travel.

Understanding the different classifications of trains is important to help you avoid unexpected and unnecessary delays, detours and crowds.

Trains listed as *rapido* connect main cities and are indeed rapid. Some of them are all first class, and it may be necessary to reserve a seat in advance. Be sure and check. In some cases, you must reserve seats at least five or six hours before departure. It can be done through a travel agent, but we recommend you do it yourself at the station. This is true for all trains on which you want to or have to reserve seats.

Express trains are just that, and they travel long distance. They offer both first- and second-class accommodations, as do the express *diretto* trains.

Trans-European-Express (TEE) trains that travel inside Italy are all first class. A supplement is charged, and you must reserve your seats in advance.

Best and fastest route – is Rome – Florence

Dining or buffet cars are attached to most long-distance trains; and you usually can stop at the platform at many stations and buy a snack for the next part of the trip. Another alternative is to pack some of your favorite foods so you can nibble and sip when you feel like it.

Sleepers are available on many long-distance internal and international trips. The supplement price varies according to the accommodation (single or double compartment for first class; tourist compartments with three berths for second class) and the length of the journey. *Couchettes* (seats that convert into couches) are available on some trains.

When deciding which train to take and when, and what class to travel, remember that second class can get crowded, especially on weekends. Also be sure to ask about special rates for senior citizens and young people and the various rail passes and excursion rates mentioned earlier in the section on **Perks for the Experienced Traveler.**

By Car

Flexibility is the key word here. When you drive you can go when you want, where you want, without worrying about timetables, and to places that trains and even buses don't reach.

Those are the benefits. What are some of the disadvantages? Well, there's the price of gasoline, probably $3.50 or more a gallon—so if you're going to rent a car, if possible rent a small one. Then there's the traffic in the larger cities and the problem of finding somewhere to park. And don't forget that you need a translation of a U.S. driving license, mentioned earlier in the **Documentation** section.

If you decide to rent a car you'll find the usual Hertz and Avis Offices in most big cities, airports and railway stations. Also check Europcar. And remember that you can arrange for a car before you start your trip. Ask your travel agent or your automobile club. (The Italian Automobile Club, ACI, is the equivalent of the Automobile Association of America, AAA.) If you're not using a travel agent, ask your airline's personnel for information about any fly/drive packages they may have.

Once on the road in Italy, keep your eye out for the following: high speed —they drive *fast* on their superhighways (*autostrade*); tolls—they vary according to the distances traveled on the autostrade and can mount up; unmarked local roads—they can be primitive and tough on a car.

Should your vehicle have a breakdown on any Italian road, dial 116 and the ACI will arrange for assistance. Another phone number to remember is 4212, area code 06. This number in Rome connects you with the central information office of the ACI, where you can learn about road and weather conditions and the location of spare parts, hotels and other ACI offices in areas you plan to visit—all in English.

Italy has zones (zona disco) where you park only after displaying a disc purchased at gas stations

By Bus

This may be your best—and only—choice for traveling between the smaller cities if you are not driving. Buses are seldom taken on long trips between major cities because they are slower and stuffier than trains and not always cheaper. However, if you love bus travel, Europabus has express service between most major cities, and it is only one of a large network of motor-coach companies. Again, your travel agent or Italian Government Travel Offices should be a source of more information.

By Boat

Capri, Ischia (or Isola D'Ischia), Sardegna (Sardinia), Sicilia (Sicily), Lake Como, the Aeolian Islands—don't forget that, ideally a trip through Italy, includes traveling by sea, lake or canal to some of the country's outlying districts. You may also sail to them by passenger steamer, car ferry or hydrofoil. Check locally for costs and schedules.

GOING HOME

Getting to the Airport

If you're staying in a major hotel in Milano or Roma, ask if it provides transportation to the airport. And be sure that you still have enough Italian currency to cover tips, to pay for public transportation, and for duty-free shopping.

Italian Customs

You may not carry more than L.200,000 out of the country. The only restrictions on gifts are on antiques and works of art, which require authorization of Italy's export office—the Ufficio Esportazione di Oggetti d'Arte e d'Antichita, Ministero Pubblica Istruzione, Via Cernaia, 1, Roma.

L. 200,000 = approx $140 at presstime

United States Customs

If you haven't taken advantage of the exemptions within 30 days previously, U.S. citizens returning to the USA from abroad may claim as exempt purchases up to a total $300 retail value (keep your receipts)—provided you have been out of the country for at least 48 hours. Above your exemption, the next $600 worth of goods will be assessed at 10% of the retail value. After that things get more complicated.

Every family member is allowed the same exemptions, and they can be pooled, but exemptions for alcohol and perfume can't be claimed by children under 18.

Don't try to bring in fruit, plants, soil, meats and so forth. If you plan to acquire foods abroad, you should write for the following pamphlet available from the U.S. Department of Agriculture, Federal Center Building, Hyattsville, MD 20782: "Traveler's Tips on Bringing Food, Plant and Animal Products into the U.S." It's pamphlet number 1083.

You may mail home small packages valued up to $25 without paying duty, provided they don't include alcohol, perfume or tobacco.

British Customs

If you return to Britain from a Common Market (EEC) country such as Italy, you get EEC allowances, which are 75 gr. of perfume, .375 liter of toilet water and gifts up to the value of £50 plus the following: 300 cigarettes (or 150 cigarillos, or 75 cigars, or 37.5 gr. of tobacco); 1.5 liters of strong spirits (or 3 liters of other spirits or fortified wines, such as sherry); plus 3 liters of still wine.

Canadian Customs

You may bring in duty free a maximum of 50 cigars, 2 lb. of tobacco, 200 cigarettes and 40 oz. of liquor, with a total exemption of $150. You may mail home unsolicited gifts up to $15 each.

Italy

Rome

If you are planning a trip to Italy, you will find that most roads still lead to Rome. At one time the capital of the world, it later became the goal of religious zesto and pilgrimages. Still later it was embellished by some of the world's best artists and fought over by the world's greatest kings. But now it's mainly an appetizer to the Middle East, a crossroads for anyone going from West to East and, recently, from East to West. More and more, Middle Eastern travelers going to London or New York stop for a few days in Rome. As a result, Rome, now as before, is a cosmopolitan city where tourists, foreign and Italian visitors, and the local population mix with no apparent difficulty, enjoying the special climate of luxury and lazy living, fashionable people and beautiful store windows, old mellow ruins and good, hearty meals.

La Dolce Vita is alive and well, but not at the same old stand

Some History

It wasn't always like this. The small town that started from the merging of two villages on two of the legendary seven hills and that slowly grew to be an empire that controlled most of the world became, in the 9th century, a village of only 20,000 souls.

The history of Rome is much like the economic rises and falls of a large corporation. First came the slow but stable successes of the republic, which reached a high point with the victory over Carthage in the Punic Wars. Then followed Caesar and the founding of the Roman Empire, with victories, conquests, slaves, wealth and power. After three centuries of this unquestioned world leadership, the great structure began to crumble. Savage tribes from the North got closer and closer to the heart of the empire, making Rome unsafe and undermining the social fabric. Slave discontent and a need for stronger spiritual guidance were some of the causes in the rise of a new religion that offered hope—Christianity.

The consequences of these changes were significant for the city and its structure. One result of the invasions was that the emperor and his court moved to Byzantium, which became Constantinople. The Eastern Empire was thereby created, leaving Rome with a shadow government and a military apparatus that wasn't capable of defending the city from invading hordes. But the seed of Rome's new power was planted. It became the seat of the new religion, and the new pontifex became the high priest of Christianity. *Pontifex* —keeper of the bridge—was an old Roman title and was always a position that stood for power and commanded respect.

But for the immediate future of Rome these changes bode ill. The hordes from the North attacked, and each new wave meant fire, destruction and disease. The struggle between the Goths—now masters of roughly half the Italian peninsula—and the Byzantine emperor involved Rome, besieged and finally taken. The food and water supplies got progressively worse, and the population dwindled.

But by the end of the 8th century the map of the civilized world had changed, and the church had found a strong secular arm in the Franks of Pepin and Charlemagne. Pepin defeated the Arabs, and his son defeated the Lombards—an enterprising northern tribe of central European origin that followed the Arian heresy. These victories were significant, the new Christian champion was crowned by Pope Leo III as Holy Roman Emperor.

Pippin (Pepin) was father of Charlemagne, the first Holy Roman Emperor

For a short period the city regained its vitality; new aqueducts were planned, and new buildings were put up. It did not last. From the port of Ostia came Saracen pirates, a new invading horde. In an attempt to protect the tomb of St. Peter, Pope Leo IV built a wall that isolated the Vatican grounds, creating the Leonine city. What was left outside became an easy prey to warring barons, for this was the medieval period, characterized in Italy by the great struggle between Guelfs and Ghibellines. It originated as a quarrel between two families of German nobles but developed into a fight for power that involved the pope on one side and the Holy Roman Emperor on the other.

All over Italy the cities, as well as the nobles and knights took sides. To be a Guelf meant to side with the church—equivalent to a conservative position; to be a Ghibelline meant to fight for the emperor. The division wasn't always that neat, and sides were changed again and again. But for the city of Rome this meant new bloodshed and turmoil since the local aristocracy became involved in the struggle.

Foreign kings and their soldiers took advantage of the confusion and once again descended into Italy and Rome. The pope, no longer safe in his walled citadel, allowed himself to be removed from the Vatican and took up residence in Avignon, France. Meanwhile, an adventurer named Cola di Rienzo, encouraged by Petrarch, the great poet, attempted to make Rome the capital of Italy. But the attempt was short lived.

The Avignon interlude was not a positive one for the papacy. The French popes weakened the church and, heeding the fervent prayers of St. Catherine of Siena, Pope Gregorio XI made a return to the Vatican in 1377.

After Avignon

The date 1377 can be considered the beginning of Rome's splendid new era. Not only because the pope was back in his traditional seat, but because times were, once again, changing. The decline of the feudal system and the rise of comuni all over the country had created new wealth. Many cities north of Rome were enjoying moments of greatness and prosperity. Firenze (Florence) began to bubble with new ideas in art, literature, the crafts, science and government. This new activity filtered down to Rome and, by the 15th century, the city became a meeting place for the greatest artists of Italy.

What the Renaissance did for Rome is material for more than one book. The new wealth, new means and new needs were used by a group of great popes and great artists. The results were the great art and architecture, sculpture and urban design that were created. Rome began to grow again, to acquire its monumental structure and to take its place among the European capitals, becoming once more, the capital of capitals.

The balance of power in Europe was continually changing in the struggles of the 16th century, and Italy was involved. The troops of Emperor Charles V (still a Holy Roman Emperor and, in this case, again enemy of the pope) entered and sacked Rome in 1527, causing the Holy Father to take asylum in the great fortress of Castel Sant'Angelo. The Reformation was disturbing Germany and the Roman church. But the city grew almost as if the difficulties and challenges were an incentive.

The Renaissance made room for the baroque period, and great artists continued to shape and mold the urban texture, attempting to match the great work of Michelangelo and Bramante. Bernini designed the magnificent colonnade and square before St. Peter's; Piazza Navona became the showplace of Pope Innocenzo XII; Pope Sisto V made changes that altered the very nature of the city, opening new streets and demolishing and reshaping the city. By now the population had reached 100,000, and economic conditions were improving.

The 18th century saw a partial slowing down of this process, but there were still several major works. The lovely Spanish steps (137 of them) that take us to Trinità dei Monti and the attractive Fontana di Trevi were built in this time.

Similarly to the rest of Europe, Napoleon was of major importance to Rome. He made Rome the second city of his empire, and his *prefetto*, Count Camille de Tournon, using a brilliant architect, Valadier, added his contribution to the monumental city. Thus were created the Pincio, the Piazza del Popolo and parts of Villa Borghese. But, in spite of good intentions, the French period was an economic disaster, the population dropped again and the city returned to a period of indifference.

During the much debated pontificate of Pius IX (1846–1878) the city regained life. The dates are significant because they span the period of Italian unification, which began in 1848 with the Milanese insurrection against Austria (called Milan's Five Days), proceeded with Piedmont's declaration of war, went through negotiations, plebiscites and military action and culminated with the fall of Rome in 1870.

At this point Rome entered still another, though not yet final, phase. While the population had leaped forward to an extent that even old, imperial Rome had not dreamed of, the monuments added after 1870 were not as impressive as those built before.

The greatest developmental changes of pre-World War II Rome came from the fascist regime. Mussolini, in yet another attempt at establishing a connection with ancient Roman power, tore down whole sections of the old city in order to open broad new boulevards. One example is Via dei Fori Imperiali, which takes us from the City Hall (Campidoglio) to the Colosseum, passing through the old Roman Forum and other splendid ruins. Close to the

Pius sealed himself in the Vatican in 1870, when Italy became a nation, and no pope left these walls until 1920

U. S. Embassy, Via Bissolati and Via Barberini are other fascist achievements. The buildings of that period are all over the city, their architecture easily identifiable by a massive lack of grace.

The last phase we will mention is the modern one after 1950. The broad avenue that leads up to St. Peter's Cathedral, Via della Conciliazione, was finished in 1952. Most of the buildings in the EUR area, residential as well as public, were built in the last 30 years. Some are attractive, others insignificant. But the growth of Rome in the last few years has been so great that most of what gets built is residential. Since the city is overcrowded, the expansion is at the edges, reaching towns that are 32–48 km. (20–30 mi.) away. This becomes of minor importance to the tourist. What is important is that the old wonderful works of art are maintained in the best possible condition, so that the greatest number of people can be exposed to that museum of museums called Rome!

ROMAN ROUTES

We will suggest several Roman itineraries, while attempting to follow the city's history. None of them are complete, for that would be impossible. They will, however, point out highlights of each successive period; you can choose those that interest you most. The periods are listed chronologically, but along each itinerary there will be monuments of other eras and styles. It is just as well that itineraries intersect, as this makes for variety. But the intention behind these indications is to provide a certain amount of historic continuity, and for those with an eye and ear for the sights and echoes of history, we hope it may prove worthwhile.

ANCIENT OR CLASSICAL ROME

Contemporary Rome has almost nothing in common with classical Rome. The two share a name, and the modern city has incorporated into its chaotic urban structure remnants of some splendid monuments of that past age and a unique distribution of streets and squares that cannot help but be influenced by the inherited design. *Before the 5th century A.D.*

It is not easy to understand the lay-out of the old city from the ruins that are left. One thing to keep in mind is that even ancient Rome grew slowly with varying intensity over a period of several centuries. For the sake of simplicity, let us assume two distinct periods: From the founding of the city to the end of the Republic is the first period: the Roman Empire is the second; and the death of Julius Caesar (44 B.C.) is the dividing line. The second period reached its peak under Trajan (A.D. 98 to 117) when the city's population was around 1,400,000 and Rome was literally the center of the world—*caput mundi.*

About 100 years earlier Caesar's nephew, Octavian Augustus, the great emperor who consolidated Roman power and "pacified the world" said: "I found a Rome of bricks and I leave a Rome of marble." We see, 2,000 years later, that this is not quite so since most of the marble has been removed. And many other changes have followed: the Middle Ages, the Renaissance, the

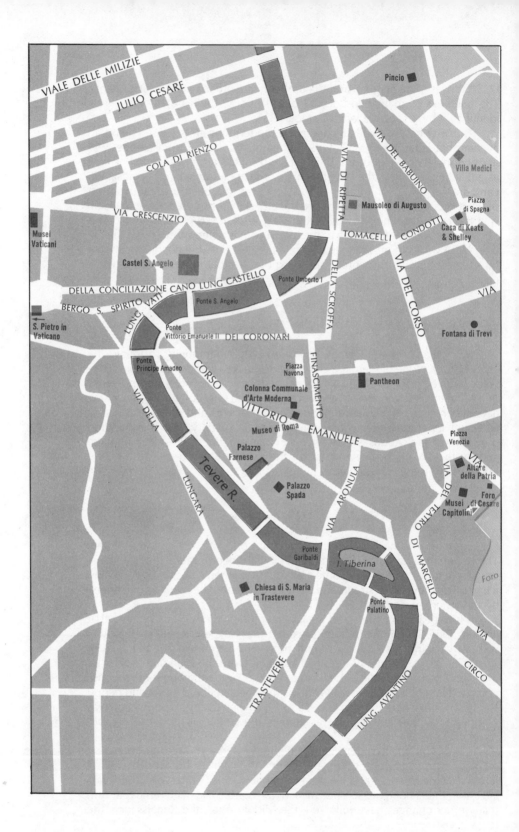

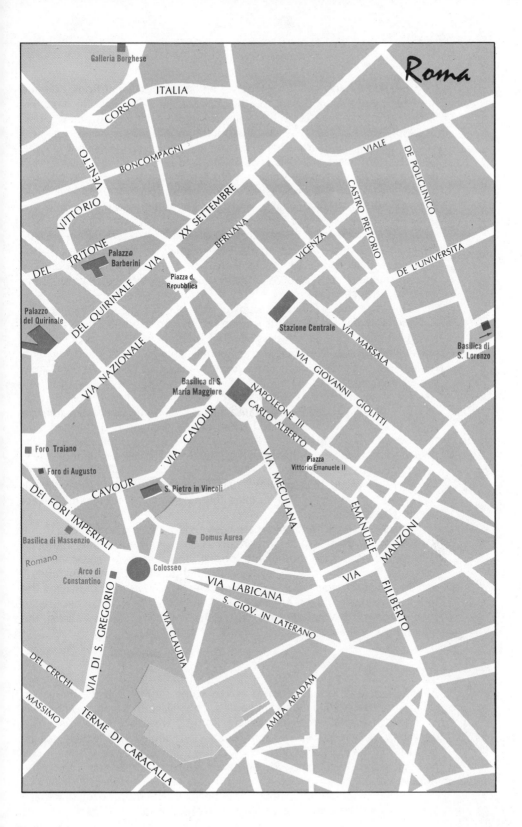

baroque period, and so forth. So when we speak of ancient Rome, we see Imperial Rome as a continuation of the old Republic of Rome, both character-ized by an impressive architecture that still generates enthusiasm and wonder.

Here we must say a few words about the style of ancient Rome. Classical Roman art originated from Italo-Etruscan art, modified by its contact with Greece. The former was primitive, with Asian overtones; the latter added refinement. They combined into one, in a style that became universal and reached its most perfect results during the Imperial Age. It should be noted that while the Greeks tended toward an ideal of esthetic beauty, their Roman offspring leaned toward a realistic and practical concept. Thus, the best examples of old Roman architecture are not temples—except for the unusual Pantheon—but the buildings that served Roma's citizens: palaces, baths, aqueducts, theaters and protective walls. The same can be said of ancient Roman sculpture, which served mainly to celebrate victories and to glorify emperors and generals.

There are two significant groups of Republican ruins still standing. The first and more important is at the Roman Forum, part of our first itinerary. This low-lying plain, located among several of the famous hills, was originally a marshy wasteland. Even before the Republic this area was dried out by a remarkable engineering feat: The *Cloaca Massima,* probably the first great sewer anywhere.

For many centuries most of the city's business whether commercial, religious, political or legal—was transacted at the Forum. Later it became too small, and other *fori* were added. The political situation had changed, and they were called Imperial Fori. As should be expected, the first one was dedicated to Caesar and the second to Augustus; the last and grandest was Trajan's Forum.

Another group of Republican ruins was found at Largo Argentina. It represents the remains of four temples; there is some debate as to their exact age and significance.

The suggestions listed below are designed for those who come to Rome with an strong interest in its past greatness but have limited time. Although far from complete, it is one of the longest itineraries given and cannot be accomplished in one day. It has been divided into three parts; itineraries 1 and 3 include the more spectacular monuments, such as the Colosseum, the fori, the Pantheon and the Ara Pacis. Itinerary 2 is a ride along an old Roman road, which takes you out of the city center and helps you to visualize the dimensions of the old capital.

Itinerary 1

Archaeology and legend seem to agree: Rome started with the merger of villages on two of the famous seven hills. The village of Romulus, known as *la Roma quadrata*, meaning "square Rome", was on the *Palatine*. This explains why, in later years, so many of the city's nobles wanted their palaces built on that very hill. The other hill was the *Capitoline*, where Rome's city hall still stands—*Campidoglio*. The area below, between the two, is the *Roman Forum*.

Our first itinerary of ancient Rome begins at the most beautiful Renais-sance *piazze*, the Campidoglio, one of Michelangelo's best Roman efforts.

*** Campidoglio

And here is our key to enjoying Rome: styles, great names, 26 centuries and their history, all of which cross again and again, blending and mingling in a harmonious design that forms a unique city.

Enjoy the perfection of the square, done by the great man in 1536. The center once held the bronze statue of Marcus Aurelius on a horse, the elegant base by Michelangelo, both of which were removed. On three sides the square is lined by noble palaces. The *Palazzo Senatorio* is City Hall and was built in the early 17th century over the ancient *Tabularium,* the old city's archive building. The twin palaces on left and right were designed by Michelangelo and built by Giacomo della Porta. They both house museums of mainly ancient art—mostly sculpture but also paintings at the *Pinacoteca Capitolina.* The same ticket, which costs L.400, or L.500 Saturday evenings, or free on holidays, will permit entry to both the Palazzo del Museo Capitolino and the Palazzo dei Conservatori. The hours are 9 A.M. to 2 P.M. daily, plus 5 P.M. to 8 P.M. on Tuesdays and Thursdays, plus 8:30 P.M. to 11 P.M. on Saturdays, plus 9 A.M. to 1 P.M. holidays; closed Mondays.

One of the best views of the *Forum* can be had by stepping down into the terrace at the right of *Palazzo Senatorio.* From there you can see the *Palatine* hill and the *Colosseum* (at a distance) plus the *Arch of Septimius Severus,* the remnants of the temple of *Saturn,* the *Curia,* the column of *Foca,* and so on.

Proceed down *Via del Tempio di Giove,* over old cobblestones, down to *Via del Foro Romano,* and enter the Forum. Admission ticket L.1,000, from October to May, 9 A.M. to 5 P.M. from June to September 9 A.M. to 7 P.M., closed Tuesdays. The entrance is on *Via dei Fori Imperiali,* and immediately to your right are ruins of the *Basilica Emilia,* built by two consuls in 179 B.C. and used for city meetings and merchant gatherings. There is little left but the colorful floor and bits of columns.

Next is the *Curia,* which is supposedly the oldest Roman Senate building, founded by Tullio Ostilio, one of the seven kings who according to legend, ruled the city before the Republic. The structure as we now see it was redone by Diocletian in A.D. 303 and became a Roman Catholic church in the 7th century.

In front of the Curia, note a small modern roof. Underneath is the *lapis niger,* a piece of black marble that holds the oldest Latin inscription in Roma, dated at about the 6th century B.C.. It is so old that the writing is bustrophedic, meaning from left to right then back from right to left and so on, like the pattern made by an ox plowing a field. (*Bustros* in Greek means ox.) The *lapis niger* is supposedly over the tomb of Romulus, but modern archaeology does not agree with that theory.

As you continue around the Forum you come upon the Arch of Septimius Severus, built to celebrate his victroy over the Parths and Arabs, A.D. 203. We cannot list every ruin that crowds the Forum. But to illustrate how important a place it was, even into the Middle Ages, note Foca's column. Foca was Byzantine or eastern emperor, and this last monument, placed in A.D., 608 was raised to honor him.

Next, go back to the entrance area where if you had turned left instead of right, stands the *Temple of Antonino and Faustina.* At the beginning of the *Sacra Via,* which here begins its uphill climb, this temple was dedicated to the memory of Empress Faustina in A.D. 141 and to her husband Antoninus

[handwritten margin notes:] Michelangelo was "the great man", of course

** The two museums of Capitoline

**** Roman Forum. Best photograph of this view is in afternoon, the sun at your back

You pass the Mamertine, where it is believed St. Peter was held prisoner

Pius after his death. It was transformed into a church in the 11th century and, in 1602, acquired the baroque facade it now has.

As you continue up the *Sacra Via,* you pass the *Temple of Romulus*—a round building that was supposedly dedicated to the son of Massenzio who had the same name as the founder of Rome. It later became a church. Past the ruins of the *Basilica di Massenzio,* you reach the *Arch of Titus,* built on the highest part of this road in A.D. 81 to celebrate his victory over the Jews, and the destruction of the Temple in Jerusalem. This arch was restored by Valadier in 1821; it is also called the "arch of the seven candles" because one of the sculptures on it shows the Menorah brought back from Jerusalem as spoils of war. Here, Roman and Jewish history intersect.

At this point there is a choice. One: double back down the *Sacra Via,* leave the *Roman Forum,* take *Via dei Fori Imperiali* and proceed—past the other side of the large *Basilica di Massenzio,* up to the *Colosseum.* Two: Go past the *Arch of Titus,* turn right and go past the *Ucceliera Farnese,* thus entering the *Palatine.* This will take you to the *Colosseum* from another direction, after having seen the Palatine hill, one of Rome's oldest inhabited areas. First you will stroll through the *Orti Farnesiani,* a large Italian-style garden, that was part of the 16th-century Farnese villa. It was built over the ruins of Tiberius' palace and, on a sunny day, is a charming sight.

As mentioned above, the Palatine was the best possible neighborhood in old Rome and a great favorite with emperors and nobles. During the Middle Ages it became a fortress of the Frangipane family and in the 16th century was taken by the powerful Farnese family who built the splendid villa and garden. The ruins on the Palatine are numerous and as important as those of the Forum. Many can be seen through guided tours only. Perhaps the most interesting is the *Antiquario del Palatino*—free admission, from 9 A.M. to 12:30 P.M.: closed Tuesdays. It contains selected and organized archaeological material from the hill.

As for the rest of the hill, choose from the House of Livia, the Flavi Palace, the Domus Augustana, Domitian's Stadium and the Baths of Septimius Severus. As you leave the Palatine, enter *Via di S. Gregorio,* proceed until you come upon the *Arch of Constantine* and, beyond, *the Colosseum.*

Whichever way you choose you will see that the Colosseum remains the most imposing symbol of Rome, of past power, of human capacity to build great things that neither time, natural calamity nor enemy wrath can destroy. It seems that the Venerable Bede once said: "as long as the Colosseum stands, Rome stands; when the Colosseum will fall, Rome will fall; but when Rome falls, the world will end." It is reassuring, then, to see how large and solid the Colosseum is.

The Colosseum's original name was the Flavian Amphitheater, for it was built by the first two Flavians, Vespasian and Titus. It was a gift to the Roman people, sorely tried by the sadism and insanity of the last two Julian emperors, Caligula and Nero. The location was the lake of the *Domus Aurea,* the magnificent palace Nero had wanted after the A.D. 64 fire. Old chronicles say it was so sumptuous and beautiful that it enchanted all visitors.

After the lake was filled and dried, in A.D. 72 the foundations for the gigantic amphitheater were laid. Titus inaugurated it just before the wars with the Jews in A.D. 80.

The Colosseum is elliptical: 188 m. (617 ft.) at its wider axis, 156 m. (512

*** Palatine. Tradition says Romulus lived here

There is a good view from the Palatine of the Circus Maximus

*** Colosseum. 5,000 wild animals were killed here on opening day

ft.) at its narrower one, with a circumference of 527 m. (1,729 ft.) It's as high as a 12-story building and has three levels of 80 arches each plus a last level with no arches. The 57/m. (187 ft.)-high northeastern outside is almost intact. It was originally covered with Travertine marble and equipped with machinery of great technical skill. A huge awning could be maneuvered into place to shield the 50,000 spectators from the sun; 32 elevators were able to bring wild animals from the underground; a special device could flood the arena with water in order to simulate naval battles. Its notoriety as a place of Christian martyrdom has been somewhat exaggerated. It was used mainly for entertainment, gladiator fights and wild animal fights. Admittance to the ground floor costs L.750.

On the busiest days, up to 1,000 pairs of gladiators would do battle

Itinerary 2

Itinerary 2 is a scenic ride (or walk, if you feel energetic) through a charming Rome, both old and new.

Begin at the *Terme di Caracalla,* largest public baths of ancient Rome; admission L.500; open from 9 A.M. to one hour before sunset on weekdays, 9 A.M. to 1 P.M. on holidays, closed Mondays. This impressive structure could accomodate more than 1,500 persons, who could choose among hot or cold baths, hot or cold showers or a steam bath. All of this was available in surroundings of walls and floors decorated with marbles, mosaics and other art. The baths, which were begun by Septimius Severus and finished by his son Caracalla, were inaugurated in A.D. 206. At present, one of the inside areas, the *calidarium,* is used for open air opera in the summer.

"Aida" is the favorite production here

After the *Terme,* continue down *Via di Porta S. Sebastiano,* an attractive, romantic street that leads up to the *Aureliano* walls. If you wish, there are stops along the way, such as, the little church of *S. Cesareo* in Palatio, 9 A.M. to 12 noon, 3 to 5 P.M., weekdays only; or the *Scipioni* family tomb, last resting place of one of ancient Rome's great families, June to September 9 A.M. to 1 P.M., 3 to 6 P.M.; October to May 10 A.M. to 5 P.M.; holidays 9 A.M. to 1 P.M., free admission. At the end of the street is *Porta S. Sebastiano,* considered the main entrance to the impressive walls of Rome. Many students of Roman antiquity feel that Aureliano's walls are the most outstanding, important and impressive structure of old Rome, more so than the Colosseum. They run 19 km. (12 mi.), were built between A.D. 272 and 278 by Emperor Aureliano and, at the time, enclosed most of the city within their solid circle.

The S. Sebastiano door itself is medieval since it was redone in the 5th century and again in the 6th by the great Byzantine general, Belisarius. Two crenellated towers flank the door, and inside there is access to a small museum, as well as to the walls themselves. You can take a lovely walk on the old structure; on Sundays there is a guide who takes you on three shifts —9 A.M., 10:30 A.M., 12 noon.

Just outside the walls is the church of Domine, Quo Vadis, where St. Peter turned back to his martyrdom

Outside the walls begins the Via Appia Antica, one of the oldest roads in Italy, in use since 312 B.C., built in order to connect Rome with the South. It runs all the way down to Brindisi at the heel of the Italian peninsula.

At the very beginning of the Appia Antica, after the second milestone, is the *Catacombe di S. Callisto* (Calixtus), admission free, from 8 A.M. to 12 noon and 2:30 P.M. to sunset, closed Wednesdays. These are the most important catacombs in Rome, dating back to the 2nd century. During the 3rd century they were used as official burying ground for the popes. The visit is made with a guide, stopping at *St. Cecilia's tomb* and the *Popes' crypt.* Note the important 3rd-century murals at the *Five Cubicles of the Sacraments.*

Continuing down the old road you will pass the *Jewish Catacombs* on the left and then reach a most imposing structure, the *tomb of Cecilia Metella,* daughter-in-law of Crassus, one of Caesar's partners in the first triumvirate. It's a large, cylindrical building decorated in travertine marble, the marble of Rome. During the Middle Ages the powerful Caetani family included the tomb inside a fortified castle. We can still see parts of the castle's crenellated walls.

After the Cecilia Metella tomb note the road itself. In some spots the old paving can still be observed, and the countryside is very attractive here, with old monuments and lovely pine and cypress trees alternating harmoniously. The road runs 12 km. (7.5 mi) and you are free to see as much or as little of it as you wish.

A variation of this itinerary will take you into Rome's most modern sections, EUR. Turn right after the catacombs, into *Via delle Sette Chiese.* This street is well known; on March 24, 1944, the Germans killed 335 civilians at the *Fosse Ardeatine,* just off to the left. A memorial ceremony is held here every year, and people often come in pilgrimage.

Further down, Via delle Sette Chiese connects with *Via Cristoforo Colombo,* which goes right into the EUR. This part of Roma was started under the fascist regime, meant to house a world exhibition (EUR = *Esposizione Universale di Roma*) in 1942, a project that didn't come about because of World War II.

Itinerary 3

Start out at the *Piazza della Rotonda,* the lovely baroque square that serves as foreground to the *Pantheon.* The two *caffès* with outdoor tables are among the busiest in Rome, and from March to November this is where most of Rome's golden and not-so-golden youth come for an after-dinner drink or cup of coffee. The Pantheon square is also known as *il salotto di Roma,* Rome's living room, and an itinerary of fashionable Rome would undoubtedly end here, around midnight, for a slice of watermelon in the summer and some extemporaneous jazz anytime, (often very good). A fun-loving, carefree, noisy crowd and lots of dogs rotate around *la Rotonda,* the pretty fountain.

During the day the *piazza* is full of buses with foreign license plates, bringing hundreds of eager tourists to see the Pantheon, an architectural masterpiece, as well as the ancient Roman monument in the best state of preservation. Originally built by Marcus Agrippa in 27 B.C. the building as you now see it is the result of Hadrian's manipulation. It was dedicated as a Catholic church in A.D. 609 and now contains the tombs of several Italian kings and queens, as well as Raffaello.

The Pantheon is a large brick structure with a cylindrical body capped by a hemispherical cupola that has an opening at the center—a brilliant engineering and architectural achievement. The portico front is a rectangle, decorated with 16 monolithic corinthian columns of pink and grey granite that hold up a triangular roof. There is only one entrance, made of two huge, old bronze doors that turn slowly on ancient hinges and are open every day from 9 A.M. to one hour before sunset. The admission is free.

The only metal left on the outside of the Pantheon is on its doors. The other ornaments were removed through the ages; the last ones were taken by order of Pope Urban VIII to be used for the famous Bernini canopy in St. Peter's. This pope's family name was Barberini, and the quick-witted Romans made a pun for the occasion: *"quod non fecerunt barbari, fecerunt Barberini,"* meaning "that which the barbarians didn't do, Barberini did."

One last comment about this beautiful old temple—the inside, even though simple and relatively bare, has a majesty and harmony that defies description. If you visit nothing else in Rome, see the Pantheon!

From the *Piazza della Rotonda,* with your back to the Pantheon, go straight ahead and either street will take you to *Piazza della Maddalena.* Still going straight ahead, you will find *Via della Coppelle.* Turn left and follow this narrow street until you reach *Piazza S. Agostino;* go past the steps and church, through the arch, and cross the busy street. This is the *Piazza delle Cinque Lune.* After that, again on the left, is a modern building that rests on the ruins of Domitian's stadium, which are worthy of a small detour. They illustrate how much a city can rise in 2,000 years and make an interesting contrast with the famous baroque square on the other side—*Piazza Navona.* Note the very narrow bricks, so typical of old Roman buildings.

In order to reach the next monument, you must go back a few steps, to *Piazza S. Agostino,* and turn left (north) onto *Via della Scrofa,* which will soon become *Via di Ripetta.* This is a pleasant walk, for the street is dotted with interesting shops—antique book binders, jewelers and old silver traders, stores that sell herbs, modern Danish pottery, exclusive letter paper.

The street widens and on the left-hand side you will reach what looks like a modern pavilion with large glass windows. It houses a very old monument, the *Ara Pacis Augustae.* This was originally built by Emperor Augustus between 13 and 9 B.C. in order to celebrate the peace that settled on the Roman Empire after his victories in Spain and Gaul. An *ara* is an altar, and in pagan times it was used as a place of sacrifice and worship.

The present arrangement was started in 1938, when the fragments of the original *Ara Pacis,* scattered throughout several museums, were brought together. The missing parts were added in cement. The monument itself isn't large. It's a marble enclosure, decorated with splendid sculpture representing various religious and secular Roman myths. At the center, the simple altar can be reached by climbing a few marble steps. The admission is L.200, and visiting hours are weekdays, 10 A.M. to 4 P.M.; Sundays, 9 A.M. to 1 P.M. closed Mondays, free admission.

Across the street from the *Ara Pacis,* again on *Via di Ripetta,* is the *Augustan Mausoleum.* One of the great monuments of old Roma, it was built to house the tombs of the Julian–Claudian family. It is a large, round structure, sliced off at the top and surrounded by cypress trees. There once was a statue of the great emperor himself at the center, but unfortunately, it perished of the same disease that decimates to many of Rome's outdoor statues. (A combination of climate and automobile exhaust cause marble and metal Roman statues to disintegrate slowly, begin to crumble, and have to be removed.)

*** The Pantheon is perhaps the best preserved of any Imperial buildings

* Domitian's stadium

* Ara Pacis Augustae

* The Augusteum shows definite Etruscan influence

The great mausoleum was a fortress during the Middle Ages, was used for various purposes in the centuries that followed and became a concert hall in modern times. At present, the city of Rome has closed it to the public.

The last monument in this itinerary is across the Tiber River. It is another famous symbol of Rome, the *Castel Sant'Angelo.* It can be reached in several ways. One way is a brisk walk from the *Ponte Cavour* (just below the Ara Pacis), along *Lungotevere Marzio* and *Tor di Nona,* then across the S. Angelo bridge. Another way is to cross the river at *Ponte Cavour* and turn left toward the *Palazzaccio* (the Palace of Justice) by taking *Lungotevere Prati.* The Palazzaccio, a huge ugly structure, which once housed the Ministry of Justice, is slowly sinking. Modern machinery in front of it is designed to give it shots of cement and other material, in an attempt to stop the sinking. Just before it note a little church in fake Gothic, which is unusual for Rome.

At this point the *Castel Sant'Angelo* is within sight. One of the most characteristic Roman buildings, this massive structure was originally Hadrian's Mausoleum, put up between A.D. 135 and 139. It suffered many changes, beginning with the name which, according to legend, comes from an angel that Pope Gregorio Magno saw at the top of the monument in 590. In that year, Rome was afflicted by pestilence and the pope was passing at the head of a procession, praying for a quick ending of the dreadful disease. At this point, the pontiff saw an angel that was putting a sword back into its scabbard at the top of Hadrian's mausoleum. When the disease began to recede, the monument acquired a new name. The main lines of the building are those of the original, and the most significant change is the Sangallo bastions, added under Pope Alexander VI. There were other changes under Pope Giulio II, and the statue of the angel sits on the base that held the original statue of the emperor. The building has been, at various times, a fortress, a prison, the papal residence and military headquarters. At present it houses the National Military Museum and a very good collection of offensive and defensive weapons that go from antiquity to the 19th century. There are a few famous paintings in the pope's apartments, including a Raffaello. The admission is L.1,000, and the hours are 8:30 A.M. to 2 P.M. weekdays, 8:30 A.M. to 1 P.M. holidays, closed Mondays.

*** Castel Sant' Angelo is a setting for Puccini's Tosca

MEDIEVAL ROME

This is a description of some significant buildings of a period that ranges from the 5th to the 14th centuries. During this time, Rome went from the greatness of the classical age, through the desolation of its worse era, to a rebirth of splendor known as the Renaissance. The length of time covered, the many changes that took place, the invasions, famines and diseases are too complex for a travel guide. The one significant fact that interests us is that out of the ruins of Imperial Rome another Rome arose. Through the difficulties of a turbulent period and in spite of great resistance, the embryo of Christianity brought to Rome by Peter and Paul survived, grew and generated another Rome—Catholic Rome.

5th to 14th centuries A.D.

The long centuries, which we call the Middle Ages, were mainly an age of strong religious feeling and ferocious fighting among local barons. A consequence of these two factors was that most of the structures built at the time were churches, restraining walls or towers.

The tower served a double purpose. It was tall, and could be used for long-distance observation; as a stronghold, it was difficult to take. When a feudal lord lived in the country, he could build himself a castle, surrounded by thick walls and moat, enclosed with heavy doors, provided with a draw-bridge to keep invaders out and with bastions for fighting them off. In the city, with space limited, the houses were thick walled and had narrow, barred windows, and the tower was important not only for protection but also as a symbol of power, a menace to all who might think of attacking. In medieval days, when a nobleman lost a battle, his life might be spared, but his tower was sliced in half or even razed to the ground.

After the 11th century, when warriors took up the colors of Guelfs and Ghibellines, the towers were built with different crenels. The straight ones were Guelf; the V-shaped ones were Ghibelline. Though there aren't many towers left in Rome (later you will understand why) and even fewer have been left full height, when you do find one standing whole, you can easily see whether the original owner was for the pope or against him.

The Guelph were pro-pope, the Ghibellines anti-pope

Other important elements of medieval architecture are the churches and the art inside them. Few men knew how to read and write in those days—those who could were either priests or scholars, so painting was used for information and illustration. Decoration was a secondary effect. Thus, the lovely medieval churches that remain are interesting not only from the exter-nal point of view but for the murals and mosaics inside. But only a few are well preserved. Many have been rebuilt. Some have been well restored.

While church architecture in the North acquired an upward tendency, in a style that is known as Gothic (though it has nothing to do with the Goths), Roman medieval churches, influenced by the massive presence of classical Roman structures, are mostly done in a style called, for that very reason, Romanesque. Furthermore, some of the loveliest medieval churches are old pagan buildings that were Christianized. A few show a marked byzantine influence, and some show signs of the Lombard passage.

Spread over a wider area than the more important ruins of old Rome or the best of Renaissance architecture, the Middle Age city is nevertheless contained within the walls of Aureliano. The significant buildings are in the areas of the Roman Forum, the Campidoglio, Quirinale Hill, the streets near S. Giovanni in Laterano, those on the way to St. Peter's and in Trastevere. If you are interested in seeing them, you will have to take a taxi, other public transportation or a car, preferably with driver. If you have a great deal of time and the weather is good, walk.

Vatican Walls. The 9th-century walls that surround the Vatican are an ex-ample of the architecture of that time. Ordered by Pope Leo IV to protect the tomb of the first apostle from invading infidels, they create the *Città Leonina,* Leo's city, a name often used by Romans to identify the Vatican.

* Vatican Walls

S. Maria Antiqua. At the Forum, S. Maria Antiqua is an important 6th-century structure, a rare example, especially for its 8th century frescoes, of byzantine art in Rome. It was opened to the public in 1900, after a 13th-century church built on top of it had been removed.

** S. Maria Antiqua

SS. Cosma e Damiano. Via dei Fori Imperiali. SS. Cosma e Damiano is a fine example of a pagan structure transformed into a Roman Catholic church.

** Cosma e SS. Damiano

Pope Felix IV had it built in the 6th century, using as its base the old library of the Peace Forum. Reconstructed in 1632 by Pope Urban VIII, this church was a great favorite of many popes, who often came here to say mass on the Sunday after Easter (in Albis).

Torre dei Conti.   Corner of Via dei Fori Imperiali and Via Cavour. Only the nobles could build towers. The Torre dei Conti, dating back to the 13th century, was built by Riccardo dei Conti di Segni, brother of Pope Innocent III. It's the second highest in Rome. An earthquake in 1348 brought down the two top levels. It was partially restored by Pope Urban VIII.

S. Maria in Cosmedin.   On the Palatine. S. Maria in Cosmedin is famous for the *Bocca della Verità,* which is still very evident under the portico. This old mask with a gaping mouth was used to frighten children during the Middle Ages and even later. It was said that if liars put their hands into the open mouth, they would have them bitten off. The inside of the church shows important works by the Cosmati, a family of artists that left many fine examples of mosaic art, sculpture and so on for over four generations. The structure is typical of 6th-century building, using an old Roman food storage house for a base—some columns are still inside. The 8th-century Pope Adrian I beautified it and later donated it to the fugitive Greek priests who were escaping from Constantinople (the old Byzantium) and surrounding areas due to difficulties with the iconoclasts.

S. Maria in Aracoeli.   At the Campidoglio. Placed at the highest point of the hill, the original basilica was built between the 4th and the 5th centuries. The spot is supposedly connected with the legend that it was here that Emperor Augustus was told by a Sibilla of the coming of Christ. In 1250 it was donated to the Franciscan order and rebuilt in a style that combines Gothic and Romanesque. The 13th-century floors are the work of the Cosmati. The main altar is baroque, and the church is a showplace of great art, including frescoes by Pinturicchio and a tombstone by Donatello. The lovely exterior is pure brick, which can be reached by an impressive stairway (124 steps) taken from the Temple of Quirino, on Quirinale Hill. This marble stairway was inaugurated by Cola di Rienzo in 1348, in thanksgiving for survival of an epidemic.

Torre delle Milizie.   Largo Magnanapoli, just east of Trajan's Column. The tallest tower in Rome, this large fortress was built around 1210 by Pope Gregory IX. Due to its height it was hit by lightning, and its crenels often had to be restored. The earthquake of 1348 reduced it to the present dimensions and caused it to lean.

SS. Giovanni e Paolo.   Not far from the Colosseum, at the foot of the Celio. This charming church is located in an equally charming piazza. Started in the 4th century over the house of the saints whose name it bears, the Romanesque bell tower was added in the 12th century. The interior was redone in the 18th century. Visit the underground level—from 8 to 12 A.M. and 3:30 to 6 P.M.—where you can see an old Roman house and a later Christian house, with frescoes of the 2nd, 3rd and 4th centuries.

SS. Quattro.   This truly medieval church is dedicated to four martyrs who refused to worship the pagan god Esculapio. They were marble workers, and

Emperor Vespasian built this forum.

★ Torre dei Conti

★★★ S. Maria in Cosmedin

The icono-clasts wanted to destroy all icons

★★ S. Maria dell' Aracoeli

★★★ S.S. Giovanni e Paolo. The piazza probably has not changed since medieval times

★★ SS. Quattro Coronati

their refusal consisted in not wishing to sculpt a statue of the god. Simpronio, Claudio, Castore and Nicostrato are to this day honored by other sculptors and marble artisans. The church is 4th century, and has been restored several times, but its appearance has remained that of a small fortress. The convent next to it had many illustrious guests, and the interior reflects the works of artists who knew how to work marble. It's still a favorite of local marble workers. Located midway between the Colosseum and St. John Lateran to the east.

S. Clemente.   Going toward S. Giovanni in Laterano, this medieval basilica is unusually well-preserved. Originally built in the 4th century, it was destroyed by the Normans in 1084 and rebuilt by Pope Pasquale II in 1108. Richly decorated with works of art of the same period, only a few additions were made in the 14th and 15th centuries. The "lower church" can be seen from 9 A.M. to 12:15 P.M., 3:30 to 6:30 P.M. with purchase of tickets. It is worth the visit to see murals that date back to the 6th century.

*** S. Clemente is owned by an Irish Dominican order

S. Pudenziana and S. Prassede.   Due north of the Colosseum at the Monti area, near the large Basilica of S. Maria Maggiore, are two medieval churches dedicated to two sisters. S. Pudenziana is said to be the oldest place of Christian worship in Rome, for here the father of these two sisters, Senator Pudente, gave hospitality to St. Peter. S. Pudenziana, the older church, has a precious mosaic (4th century) and a Romanesque bell tower. S. Prassede was built in the 9th century and has been restored several times. It has important mosaics and a 13th-century altar.

** S. Pudenziana and S. Prassede, for their mosaics

Torri dei Capocci e degli Arcioni.   Originally part of the same large castle, these large towers were recently restored. They are in Via Giovanni Lanza, near the Church of S. Martino. It was built with material taken from the nearby Trajan Baths.

S. Saba and S. Sabina.   Not far south from the Piazza Bocca della Verità, on top of the Aventine Hill, stands one of the best preserved medieval churches of Rome, S. Sabina. It has been restored with loving care, and the 5th-century structure and doors are almost intact. Inside you can see the serene charms of primitive Christianity, including colorful marble and old mosaics. S. Saba is a 7th-century church redone in 1205 and retouched several times since. It stands beyond the Viale Aventino, on a street that bears its name. The door and many of the inside works of art were made by the Cosmati family.

*** S. Sabina

** S. Saba

At this point we cross the Tiber River into the Trastevere part of town. Here live many old Romans who call themselves "romani de Roma," meaning they are the most Roman of them all. The area is full of narrow, tortuous streets and very old buildings in various states of repair or disrepair. Its charm is authentic, and the population is colorful and lively. New arrivals tend to be artistic, young and unconventional. The combination of locals (often owners of small stores, drivers of various types, waiters and such) and newcomers create the Roman version of La Vie Bohème, or as a Roman would simply say, *Trastevere.*

Torre degli Anguillara.   Of the many towers that once existed in this area, Torre degli Anguillara is the only one left. It is now known as the House of

Dante because it houses the scholars who dedicate themselves to interpretation of the *Divine Comedy*. This 13th-century structure belonged to a potent Guelf family and was formerly a prison.

S. Maria in Trastevere.   In the heart of the Trastevere district, this is one of the oldest churches in Rome and was the first one dedicated to the cult of Mary. The original was started in the 3rd century and completed in the 4th, but the building you now see was done between 1130 and 1143. The front is decorated with mosaics of the 12th and 13th centuries, and the Romanesque bell tower is one of the loveliest in Rome. The pavement inside is by one of the Cosmati family, and the ceiling is a masterpiece of 17th-century woodwork. Many important mosaics line the inside walls, dating from the 12th and 13th centuries, when the great mosaic layers of Rome did their best work.

*** S. Maria in Trastevere

Outside the Walls

The above is by no means an exhaustive listing of medieval structures in Rome, but unfortunately we have space limitations and most tourists have time limitations. Still, there are three other important churches of this period that cannot be overlooked. They are located farther out of town than those listed above, each one in a different direction.

S. Paolo Fuori le Mura.   One of the four great basilicas of Rome, this large church is 1.6 km (1 mi.) south of the ancient walls on the Ostiense road. It is the largest basilica after St. Peter's. Originally built by Constantine in A.D. 314 over the burial Place of the Apostle whose name it bears, it was enlarged in A.D. 386 and later completed with some of the loveliest mosaics in Rome. It remained in its original form throughout the ages, but was destroyed by a fire in 1823. The reconstruction respected the old design, and the basilica today gives us a very good idea of what classical temples looked like. A central nave and four aisles, divided by 80 monolithic columns, and marble everywhere give this church a very special grandeur. Along the walls, over the arches, there are medallions with the pictures of every pope the church has welcomed, from St. Peter to John Paul II.

*** S. Paolo Fuori le Mura stands near where St. Paul is believed to have been beheaded at the Abbazia delle Tre Fontane

S. Lorenzo Fuori le Mura.   East of the railway station about 1 km.(0.5 mi) outside the ancient walls. This basilica, on Via Tiburtina, is one of the traditional seven Roman churches visited by pilgrims. Tradition says it was built by Constantine in A.D. 330. It has been enlarged and redone through the centuries and partly destroyed by bombs in 1943. The bell tower is 12th-century Romanesque. The interior is impressively bare. The mosaic of Christ and Saints is 6th century.

* S. Lorenzo Fuori le Mura

S. Agnese.   Northeast of the railway station, just less than 2 km. beyond the ancient walls. At the end of the Via Nomentana, an attractive wide road, lined with trees, that follows the path of an old consular road of the same name, is S. Agnese, built on top of the catacombs that contained the remains of the saint. This old basilica dates back to the 4th century; the stairway was added in the 16th century. After a visit to this basilica, do not overlook *S. Costanza,*

* S. Agnese

a small round church that stands just below. This was also built in the 4th century as a mausoleum for Costantina, the emperor's daughter, and is decorated with precious mosaics that illustrate pagan subjects, such as wine gathering and other Bacchic scenes.

RENAISSANCE ROME

The complex phenomenon known as the Renaissance has few dates, no precise beginning, no circumscribed geography. For the city of Rome, Renaissance means rebirth, a return to the greatness of straight, wide streets, a new concept in building, living quarters no longer meant for defense, palaces that reflect this new freedom.

In spite of the desperate resistance of Byzantines, Genoese and Venetians, Constantinople fell to the Turks in 1453. The end of the Eastern Empire brought many refugees to Rome, among them priests of the Orthodox church who brought the long-forgotten Greek texts. Ironically, the new greatness of Catholic Rome began with the rediscovery of secular philosophy.

There were other stimulating factors. As early as the 14th century, the humanists had already laid the foundation for a new attitude. The wealth of the North had created new premises. The age of the comuni—city states—was making room for the new aristocracy. Power became more centralized, and one by one the cities acquired a set of nobles, a court. This tended to bring out refinement and a renewed interest in poetry, art and science.

Brunelleschi, the great Florentine architect, came to Rome looking for models and ideas. Impressed by the old buildings, Nero's incredible *Domus Aurea,* the Pantheon with its open cupola, he returned to his city and designed the charming cupola we still admire on the Cathedral of Firenze.

And here is a paradox that helps define the Renaissance spirit. Much later, when Michelangelo was invited by Pope Paul III to do the cupola for St. Peter's, the largest church of Christianity, he wrote a poem to honor his teacher Brunelleschi:

Michelangelo designed the dome at 72, and died at 90 before it was finished

> Vado a Roma per far la tua sorella,
> Più grande di te, sì, ma non più bella.

> I go to Rome in order to make your sister,
> Bigger than you, indeed, but not more beautiful.

Thus, the Roman Renaissance is a result of the impressive presence of great artists such as Bramante, Raffaello and Michelangelo, stimulated and sustained by a series of great secular popes who were equal to the demands of the new situation.

Renaissance Itinerary

An itinerary of Renaissance Rome begins, or ends, at the Vatican. A purist may argue that the great cathedral is also baroque, and that would be true, but the ideas that inspired it were Renaissance ideas, and the pope who wanted it was Julius II, one of the first of the great popes to influence the city's changes. His was the courage that brought down the old basilica, and he blessed the cornerstone of the new one on April 18, 1506. Bramante, already a famous architect, was put in charge of the grandiose project. But neither of them saw the completion of their church.

Pope Leo X, Giovanni de' Medici, son of the great Lorenzo, summoned Raffaello, with Giuliano da Sangallo as a helper. Later, Pope Paul III invited Peruzzi and Antonio da Sangallo and finally, in 1546, the aged Michelangelo was asked to complete the enormous cathedral. Others followed, the job was immense. In 1586 Pope Sixtus V had Caligula's obelisk raised in the square that precedes the great church. It was such a difficult task that many houses had to be destroyed in order to make it possible.

The 17th century brought changes to St. Peter's. Maderno changed the design from Greek cross to Latin cross, and the great Bernini finished off the square by adding the immense colonnade, which opens in front of the church like two welcoming arms.

The *Vatican,* then, is one of the great sights of Rome and the beginning of our Renaissance Rome itinerary. Visit the great cathedral which is filled with splendid works of art such as Michelangelo's *Pietà,* Bernini's *Baldacchino,* Maderno's Chapel of Confessions, a lovely wood Crucifix of the 13th century and an infinity of other great masterpieces, some quite recent, such as a monument of John XXIII by E. Greco. Do not overlook the Vatican Museums (usually open from 9 A.M. to 2 P.M. during Easter and from 9 A.M. to 5 P.M. from June 15th to September 30th; closed Sundays and religious holidays; admission by ticket costing L.2,000, except last Sunday of each month, when admission is free.

The *Vatican Museums* include old Greek and Roman sculptures; an Egyptian collection; an Etruscan museum; galleries of candelabra, tapestries and old maps; an ethnological–missionary museum; the Vatican library; Raffaello's rooms and his loggia; the Chapel of Nicholas V, decorated by Fra Angelico; the Borgia apartments, with works by Pinturicchio and others; a collection of modern religious art and the Sistine Chapel—the pope's private official chapel where the cardinals gather when they elect a new pope. It was built 1475–1481 by Sixtus IV, has frescoes by many of the best artists of the time, and contains the beautiful ceiling by Michelangelo, who painted it between 1508 and 1512 under Julius II.

Now back to our Renaissance itinerary, which continues across the river from the Vatican and points in the direction of St. Peter's seat.

The 15th century witnessed a gradual transformation of the city. The popes, back from French exile with consolidated power wanted to give their city a new dignity and stature. So they took a renewed interest in the roads that led to the Vatican, and built new streets to show the way.

The most desolate areas of the medieval city are the ones that change most radically. Menacing, stark towers made room for splendid palaces; fortresses were swept away so that long, straight streets could give the city another perspective—all traces of the Middle Ages disappeared in order to allow space for the new concept.

Renaissance Triangle

As the Tiber River meanders through Rome, it forms an elbow just upstream of the Tiberine Island. The angle formed by this narrow curve forms a triangle if we close it with a few streets—namely Via Ripetta, which becomes Via della

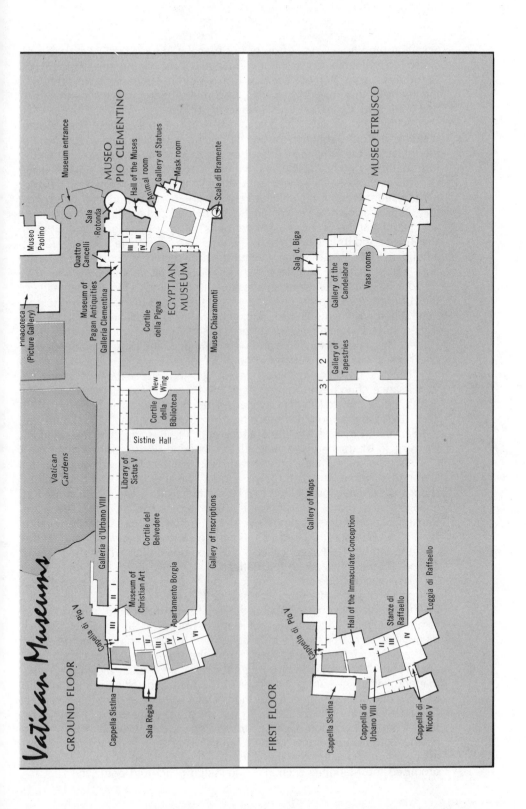

Vatican Museums

GROUND FLOOR

Vatican Gardens

Pinacoteca (Picture Gallery)

Museo Paolino

Museum entrance

Sala Rotonda

Quattro Cancelli

MUSEO PIO CLEMENTINO

Hall of the Muses

Animal room

Gallery of Statues

Mask room

Scala di Bramente

Museum of Pagan Antiquities

Galleria Clementina

Cortile della Pigna

New Wing

EGYPTIAN MUSEUM

Cortile della Biblioteca

Sistine Hall

Museo Chiaramonti

Galleria d'Urbano VIII

Library of Sistus V

Cortile del Belvedere

Gallery of Inscriptions

Cappella di Pio V

Museum of Christian Art

Apartamento Borgia

Cappella Sistina

Sala Regia

FIRST FLOOR

MUSEO ETRUSCO

Sala d. Biga

Gallery of the Candelabra

Vase rooms

Gallery of Tapestries

Gallery of Maps

Hall of the Immaculate Conception

Cappella di Pio V

Stanze di Raffaello

Loggia di Raffaello

Cappella Sistina

Cappella di Urbano VIII

Cappella di Nicolo V

Scrofa at the Ponte Cavour (top of our triangle), the Piazza S. Agostino and Corso Rinascimento, Corso Vittorio Emanuele II and Via Arenula, which leads to the river again. You will see that Corso Vittorio Emanuele II runs through the center of this imaginary triangle, becomes a bridge with the same name, and leads into Via della Conciliazione to St. Peter's.

Within this circumscribed area are many of the greatest Renaissance buildings in Rome—enough for one day's enjoyment and enough to illustrate the impact of the Renaissance spirit on the city. Many other excellent structures of the period lie outside, and we will note important ones. But the busy, very Roman area enclosed within the three imaginary lines drawn is a delightful adventure in itself, including lovely art, great architecture and much history, as well as being a very palpitating, crowded and exciting part of Rome.

Starting at the very top (northern point) of your triangle, go south down Via Ripetta and turn right at *Piazza Nicosia* into Via Monte Brianzo. Here is a building that's worth noting, even if the architecture is considered "transition" rather than the best Renaissance. The very fashionable *Hosteria dell-'Orso,* one of the most expensive restaurants in Rome, is located here where the *Albergo dell'Orso* once was. It was at the center of the city's traffic, the hotel where visiting noblemen, bankers, cardinals, artists and important foreigners stayed when they were in Rome to see Vatican dignitaries or the Holy Father. The stables were large and well equipped, and those who needed to hire horses, chaises or carriages could do so.

The next building worth noting is S. Agostino, one of the most charming Renaissance churches in Rome. It's at the Piazza S. Agostino (off Via della Scrofa, going toward Via dei Coronari). The church was built between 1479 and 1483. Outside note the imposing front; inside note the Raffaello fresco, the Sansovino marble Madonna and group, the Bernini altar, the splendid Caravaggio Madonna and a magnificent wooden Christ on the cross.

At this point, continue down toward the river by walking through Via dei Coronari. *Corona* in Italian means rosary, and this street was once full of shops that sold religious objects to pilgrims and visitors. The merchandise has changed, and this is one of Rome's best streets for antiques. There are Renaissance memories at almost every step. Raffaello supposedly lived in the house with numbers 122 and 123. Note the *Palazzo Lancellotti,* and, at the end, the famous little street called Via Banco di S.Spirito where money was coined. Again, this leads to the Vatican.

Two narrow side streets that lead off Via dei Coronari have two little churches that should be seen: *S. Maria dell' Anima,* on Via dell'Anima, built for the Germans living in Rome at the beginning of the 16th century, has a façade by Giuliano da Sangallo that is one of the purest Renaissance achievements. Furthermore, the beautiful bell tower is said to have been designed by Bramante. *S. Maria della Pace* across the street on Via della Pace, was an old church named *S. Andrea degli Acquarenari,* used by the workers who made a living by cleaning the water of the river and selling it for domestic use. On one of the entrance walls there was a painting of the Madonna with Child. Legend says that a child threw a stone at the painted Virgin and hit the face, from which blood began to ooze. Pope Sixtus IV (who is known for having commissioned the Sistine Chapel) went to the miraculous image, asking for an end of the conflicts started by the Pazzi conspiracy of 1478. He promised the Madonna a church and, since peace did come, he kept his

* Hosteria dell-'Orso

** S. Agostino is the favored church of expectant mothers

** S. Maria dell' Anima

** S. Maria della Pace

St. Peter's Basilica

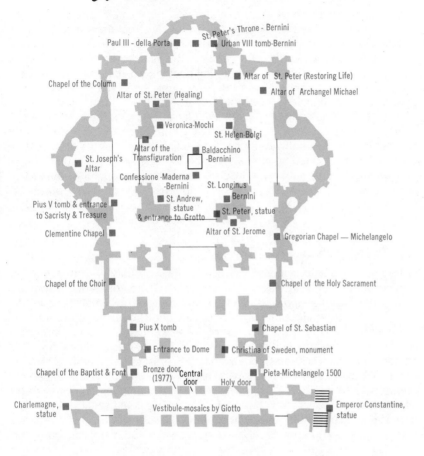

Paul III – della Porta

St. Peter's Throne – Bernini

Urban VIII tomb–Bernini

Altar of St. Peter (Restoring Life)

Chapel of the Column

Altar of St. Peter (Healing)

Altar of Archangel Michael

Veronica–Mochi

St. Helen–Bolgi

Altar of the Transfiguration

St. Joseph's Altar

Baldacchino –Bernini

Confessione –Maderna –Bernini

St. Longinus Bernini

Pius V tomb & entrance to Sacristy & Treasure

St. Andrew, statue & entrance to Grotto

St. Peter, statue

Clementine Chapel

Altar of St. Jerome

Gregorian Chapel — Michelangelo

Chapel of the Choir

Chapel of the Holy Sacrament

Pius X tomb

Chapel of St. Sebastian

Entrance to Dome

Christina of Sweden, monument

Chapel of the Baptist & Font

Bronze door (1977)

Central door

Holy door

Pieta–Michelangelo 1500

Charlemagne, statue

Vestibule–mosaics by Giotto

Emperor Constantine, statue

promise. It was restored in 1656, hence the baroque façade, but inside, over the arch of the first Cappella, note the famous Raffaello fresco, *le Sibille.* By the way, Via dei Coronari was also created by Sixtus IV, who was called *Restaurator Urbis,* city restorer. He called it Via Recta, straight street, and it was one of the first straight streets in the city.

Talking of straight streets, let us adjourn to another famous one, *Via Giulia,* named after Pope Julius II. This street starts at the river (Ponte Principe Amedeo) and ends at the river (Ponte Sisto), and it owes its greatness to two popes, the aforementioned Julius and Leo X, the Florentine who loved art and beauty almost as much as he loved God. He also loved his fellow citizens, and since many lived in the area, he had a church built to S. Giovanni since the Baptist is the patron of Firenze. At the northern end of Via Giulia is *S. Giovanni dei Fiorentini,* a very attractive example of Renaissance art.

One of the most impressive sights on Via Giulia is the back of *Palazzo Farnese,* considered one of the best examples of Renaissance architecture.

★ S. Giovanni dei Fiorentini

★★ Palazzo Farnese

Go around it, through the narrow Via Farnese and admire the whole piazza, with the two large granite tubs brought from the *Terme di Caracalla* and the splendid façade of the building.

A little further north up Via Giulia turn into the *Vicolo S. Eligio* and make a stop at the little church of *S. Eligio.* This lovely structure was planned by Raffaello and is living proof of his genius for balance and use of space.

Another building worthy of a detour is the *Palazzo della Cancelleria,* a master piece of the early Renaissance, built between 1483 and 1517, probably designed by Bramante. It's on the piazza (that bears the same name) off Corso Vittorio Emanuele II, north of the Farnese Palace. The *Palazzo Ricci,* on the square named after it, just off Via Giulia, is one of the best examples in Rome of a Renaissance building with a painted front.

Piazza Ricci lies halfway along Via Giulia's length, on its northeastern side. If you have more time after seeing the Vatican museum, you may wish to browse at the little squares, house fronts, shops and fountains; the area is full of Roman life. For example, take a morning walk through *Campo de' Fiori,* a large piazza near *Piazza Farnese,* where local residents buy their vegetables and fruit every day, midst loud Roman bartering.

Outside the Renaissance Triangle

Before ending your tour of Renaissance Rome, you may wish to see a few more outstanding achievements of those years that are not inside the triangle. Begin at the *Campidoglio,* the lovely square designed by Michelangelo (described in the beginning of itinerary 1 of Ancient Rome). Next, not far from it, is *Piazza Venezia,* with its *Palazzo Venezia,* made famous during the fascist years by the appearances of Mussolini. But the outstanding thing is the architecture, which is Renaissance with characteristics of a medieval fortress, such as the tower and the windows. The *portico* and its elegant *loggia* are reminiscent of the 15th century. The name of the building comes from the fact that it was used as an embassy of Venezia (Venice) from 1564 to 1797. There is a museum within the palace, with collections of textiles, tapestries, enamels, glasses and crystals, silverware, ceramics and majolicas, porcelain, terracotta statues, marble sculptures and other works of art. Admission: L.1,000; hours: 9 A.M. to 2 P.M. weekdays; closed Mondays.

The last monument on this list is *Porta Pia,* a gate in the ancient walls, which finishes off the straight line of Via XX Settembre. It was built by orders of Pope Pius IV by Michelangelo (his last effort) from 1561 to 1564. The great master gave this gate a simple grandeur, worthy of the last moments of the Renaissance. For Italians, it has another meaning as well: With the taking of this last gate in 1870, the unification of modern Italy was completed. Here then begins the contemporary history of Italy.

ROMAN BAROQUE

You may have already noticed that this itinerary is defined as Roman baroque, not baroque Rome. While other styles were described in terms of the city—its history, its development, its needs at a given time—the post-Renaissance changes that gave Rome some of its most beautiful sights deserves a different approach.

[Handwritten margin notes:]
Sr. Farnese later became Pope Paul III
* S. Eglio
** Palazzo della Cancelleria
** Palazzo Ricci
*** Campidoglio
** Palazzo Venezia
* Palazzo Venezia museum
* Porta Pia

Baroque, as a style, is connected with mannerism, a reaction to the classical, pure lines of the Renaissance. It aims at spectacular effect by use of curve, countercurve and scroll work. The word itself means involved, complex, circumvoluted and brings to mind florid, overdecorated rooms, churches or even cities.

In Rome, this description is only a part of the sensation produced by baroque art and architecture. The reasons are many, and we will discuss some of them.

The artists who came in the wake of the Renaissance geniuses were almost as brilliant as their predecessors; the popes of the late 16th and most of the 17th centuries were just as interested in beautifying their city, and the times were even more conducive to a desire for visual splendor.

The Roman Catholic church was faced with a new threat: the northern Protestant movements, the Reformation. Thus, the need for showing a strong, beautiful, overpoweringly impressive city was great. As in the Renaissance, this need could be met because the talent was available. The names of Bernini, Borromini and Maderno, alongside those of Popes Sixtus V, Paul V, Urban VIII, Innocent X and Alexander VII are present in almost every structure or design of those years. Therefore, while many cities saw a degeneration of baroque that led to an association of this style with bad taste, in Rome it attained such exquisite proportions and was handled with so much sense of balance that the results were uniquely beautiful.

Roman baroque is splendid because it enhances the beauty of a monument by placing it in an appropriate showcase. The tendency is not only to create a church or a fountain but its background (or foreground) as well.

Baroque Itinerary

Once again we must begin with St. Peter's. The design of the great cathedral was changed by Carlo Maderno, who substituted the original Greek cross design (four equal arms) with a Latin cross (three equal arms with the vertical lower one longer). This was done in order to incorporate the whole space that had been covered by the previous basilica. After that change, Maderno finished his work by adding the new façade, decidedly baroque, but measured and dignified, and always aware of the Michelangelo cupola above.

*****
St. Peter's

Inside the immense church is an infinite number of masterpieces, as mentioned earlier. Pay special attention to the black and gold Bernini canopy, placed over St. Peter's Tomb; it is one of the most aggressive and is impossible to ignore. In a lower key is the Bernini Altar.

***
Bernini's baldacchino

Outside, Bernini designed not only the colonnade, but the whole square. He gave it balance by moving the existing fountain over and adding another one, so that the huge obelisk towers between these two refreshingly soft sheets of water. Another Bernini achievement worthy of mention is the *Scala Regia,* a stairway that leads to the Vatican, just after the bronze doors of St. Peter's, at the right-hand side of the colonnade. These steps seem more majestic and deeper than they really are, just as the columns of the colonnade seem smaller when seen from a distance. Both are part of the charm offered by Roman early baroque.

Similarly to the Middle Ages, a coherent itinerary is impossible to plot here, for Roman baroque is almost everywhere. The most outstanding examples are Piazza Navona, the fountain of Trevi, the president's palace on the

Quirinale and S. Andrea della Valle, a large church that has the second largest cupola in Rome (after St. Peter's).

Piazza Navona.   This is the most beautiful and most famous square in Rome. Even the many odd types, drugged youngsters and stray dogs who lounge here have blended into the mellow scene. The sidewalk *caffès* are always crowded with tourists and others, all willing to pay L.2,000 for a lukewarm *cappuccino,* provided they can enjoy the view.

This piazza was originally Domitian's Stadium, hence the shape and the name. In medieval Latin it was called *Campus agonis,* meaning field of agony, and through several transformations—Nagone, Naone and so on—the word "Navona" was born.

Bernini and Borromini, two of the greatest names of baroque art, were closely connected with this square. It was originally planned by Bernini for Pope Urban VIII. Since this pope was severely critized for favoritism, his successor, Innocent X, dismissed all those who had been appointed before, including Bernini. Borromini, who had worked under the great master and was often at odds with his teacher, was put in charge of the completion. But the fountain that decorates the center of the square is a Bernini design. When the pope issued a public contest for the monument, Bernini made his little gem in miniature and showed it to Prince Ludovisi, a nephew of the pope. The latter, who had not been pleased with the Borromini offering, saw the model at his nephew's home, after having eaten an excellent lunch, and wisely changed his mind. He said that one should not see Bernini's works if one wished not to have them made. Thus, the *Fountain of the Four Rivers* (Nile, Ganges, Danube and Rio della Plata) was started in 1648 and finished in 1651 by the great man who, though past 50, was as vigorous as ever. The four rivers are meant to signify the universality of the church, and the obelisk that towers above comes from Massenzio's Circus. There are two more fountains on the square. One, depicting a man and dolphin, was made from another Bernini sketch. The other great monument that decorates the square is a Borromini design, the *Church of S. Agnese.* Legend has it that the Bernini statue facing the church recoils back in horror, as if the *maestro* were criticizing the unusual, graceful façade. But it's only legend. In all probability Bernini agreed with everyone else in saying that this charming piece of baroque art adds to the beauty of Piazza Navona. During the 17th century, the piazza was flooded in the summer, thus creating a small lake. Noble ladies watched from their windows; the less noble crowded the steps of the church; and eager youngsters bathed in the cool waters. This custom lasted well into the 19th century.

The interest of Pope Innocent X in *Piazza Navona* seems justified by the fact that his family's house faces the square. *Palazzo Pamphili,* to the left of the S. Agnese church, is among the most attractive palaces in Rome. It was acquired by the Brazilian government during the fifties, and now houses that country's embassy.

One of the most interesting buildings done by Borromini is the *Galleria Spada* in the *palazzo* of the same name. At the very end of Via Giulia, a few blocks below the *Palazzo Farnese,* it now houses a four-room museum with the private collection of the Spada family. It's worthy of a visit mainly because of the architect's interesting use of perspective and columns which causes it

*** Piazza Navona

Urban VIII even held Bernini's mirror so the artist could paint a self-portrait

*** Fountain of the Rivers

** S. Agnese

The most festive time here now is during Epiphany, in January

* Palazzo Pamphili

** Galleria Spada

to look longer than it is. Admission is L.500; the address is Piazza Capo di Ferro 3; the schedule is 9 A.M. to 2 P.M. on weekdays, 9 A.M. to 1 P.M. on holidays, (free admission); closed Mondays.

Just to the west of the *Pantheon,* there is a whole square that shows the charm of Roman baroque. The square, *Piazza di S. Eustachio,* is also famous for its caffè and its delicate balance of the period. Note the back of a church, *S.Ivo,* and the Borromini cupola. To the southeast of the Pantheon, you will find the *Piazza della Minerva* and will note the adorable marble elephant that decorates the square. The obelisk on its back is Egyptian, from the 6th century B.C., but the little *pulcino della Minerva* is made from a Bernini drawing. By the way, the church behind the little statue is *S. Maria sopra Minerva,* which was originally built over the ruins of a temple dedicated to the goddess of Wisdom and redone by the Dominican order in 1280; it is the only genuine gothic church in Rome. The simple, red-brick front is decorated with three Renaissance marble portals (1453). The interior, worthy of a quick visit, is rich with art and monumental tombs.

S. maria sopra Minerva

A wide street, which has been mentioned several times in our itineraries, houses three important baroque churches in Rome. The Corso Vittorio Emanuele II which, as we have seen before, leads to the Vatican, begins as the Via del Plebiscito at *Piazza Venezia.* Just off the square, to the left, is *Piazza del Gesù,* famous all over Italy because it houses the headquarters of the Christian Democratic Party. It also has the largest Jesuit church in Rome, *Gesù,* considered a prototype of baroque churches, done between 1568 and 1575.

** *Gesù church*

The most impressive part of the church is reserved for S. Ignazio, the founder of the Society of Jesus. In fact, his body rests under the altar of the chapel named after him. Another thing worthy of notice is the trinity group over the statue of the saint: It has the largest globe of *lapis lazuli* in existence. From the square, at 45° north, the rooms where the saint lived can be visited.

S. Andrea della Valle.   Further down Corso Vittorio (as the Romans call it). past *Largo Argentina,* on the left, is the grand church of *S. Andrea della Valle,* started in 1591 from drawings by Giacomo della Porta and finished in 1625 by the same Maderno who finished St. Peter's. He also designed the large cupola. Inside are the tombs of the two Piccolomini popes, Pius II and Pius III.

* *S. Andrea della Valle*

Continuing down the street, this time on the right, you will find another church with a Roman baroque front, *Chiesa Nuova,* meaning new church. Built between 1575 and 1605, it is very characteristic of its period, and the interior boasts paintings by many artists of the time, even a Rubens. To the left of this church is the *Oratorio dei Filippini,* designed by Borromini, with a typical curved front.

* *Chiesa Nuova*

* *Oratorio dei Filippini*

Most likely you will have already noticed that even though Rome is a city of museums—there are more than 80—the real museums of Rome are the churches. More than in any other city, the churches here are deposi-tories of some of the best works of art. Whenever a church is described, for the outside design itself or otherwise, it is impossible not to list some of the treasures inside. If you are an attentive tourist, almost every church in Rome can be a discovery, and the surprises are around each column and corner.

North of the Renaissance Triangle

One of the more interesting monuments of the baroque period is the *Porta del Popolo,* which is at the end of *Piazza del Popolo.* This great gate was built in 1561, and the original Renaissance design was by two students of Michelangelo. But the inside was redone by Bernini in 1655 when Queen Christina of Sweden came to Rome. This great gate is, therefore, a good example of how two styles can cohabit with dignity.

Several Roman villas were built at the height of the baroque period. First is the *Villa Borghese,* commissioned by Cardinal Scipione Caffarelli Borghese, nephew of Pope Paul V, and a great patron of the arts. He was also a collector, and his family has continued being so. Their collection is now the nucleus of the *Galleria Borghese,* where you can enjoy the sight of such splendid works as Bernini's *David* and *Apollo and Daphne,* paintings by Caravaggio, and sculptures by Antonio Canova. This small but very good collection is one of the "musts" of a visit to Rome. The admission is L.1,000; the visiting hours are weekdays, from 9 A.M. to 2 P.M. holidays, from 9 A.M. to 1 P.M. closed Mondays.

At the beginning of Via del Quirinale is a tiny church, *Chiesa di S. Carlino* (officially S. Carlo). This is a Borromini masterpiece, which could fit into one of the pillars that holds the cupola of St. Peter's. Here, the inventive artist gave free reign to his imagination, and the result is charming.

But Roman baroque is at its best in some of Rome's loveliest fountains. Just north of S. Carlino, or perhaps after you have walked down Via Veneto, you will reach *Piazza Barberini.* At the center of this large square is the famous *Fontana del Tritone.* This is also by Bernini. He did not have much water at his disposal here and invented this Tritone with his face turned to the sky, his arms raised holding the seashell that spews bubbly liquid, as if it were champagne. The *Fontana delle Api,* which is now at the beginning of Via Veneto, was designed by Bernini using the bee, a Barberini family heraldic symbol.

La Fontana di Trevi.   The most famous and most monumental fountain in Rome is not exactly baroque, but we include it in this itinerary because its inspiration came from Bernini. *La Fontana di Trevi,* one of the most beautiful creations of the 18th century, done by N. Salvi in 1762, is just southwest of the Tritone in the heart of Rome, off Via del Corso, leaning against the back of *Palazzo Poli.* This oasis of color and coolness represents the ocean, riding a chariot swiftly drawn by sea horses, led by Tritons. The water here is plentiful, refreshing and greenish blue, in striking contrast to the whiteness of the statues. The water that gurgles in this fountain is brought through pipes that go under the elegant *Via Condotti,* which gets its name from these conducts. It has been said that this fountain is the "fairy tale epilogue of Roman Baroque." Whether you throw in your coin or not, it's certainly one of things to see in Rome!

Quirinale.   Before we conclude this itinerary, two large buildings must be mentioned. At the top of the highest of the original seven hills of Rome is the *Piazza del Quirinale,* one of Rome's loveliest squares. At the back is the *Quirinale* itself, once the pope's summer residence, then the king's palace, now the president's official home. This stately building, with its long uniform

[handwritten margin notes:]
* Porta del Popolo
Christina is one of only 5 women buried in St. Peter's

*** Villa Borghese

* Chiesa di S. Carlino

** Tritone Fountain

* Api Fountain

** Trevi Fountain
Your luck is said to be best if you toss the coin over your left shoulder

* Quirinale

front and Bernini portal, is important because of its meaning and of the harmony of the entire square.

The other building, which is in the very center of the city, is also closely connected with the government. Just off *Via del Corso,* halfway between the northern and southern ends, is *Piazza Colonna.* It is noticeable by the tall column of Marcus Aurelius, which towers almost 30.5 m. (100 ft.) over the street and is made of 28 huge blocks of marble. In the column, a 2nd-century artist depicted, in a spiral that rises up and up, episodes of the Germanic wars won by the great emperor. In 1589 Pope Sixtus V changed the base and added the statue of St. Paul at the top. As you continue up the square, past the arcades to the left, you reach *Piazza Montecitorio,* full of cars, with a 6th century B.C. Egyptian obelisk at the center and the Italian Parliament to the right. *Montecitorio* was started by Bernini in 1650 and finished by Fontana in 1694. The huge *Chamber of Deputies* behind goes all the way to another square, called *Piazza del Parlamento,* where a new front was added in 1918. It was originally meant to house the courthouse of Rome. The Bernini side is curved, in a typical baroque movement that enhances the grandiosity of the building.

Finally, as you walk through Rome, remember that many other structures, some very old, some old, some Renaissance, were retouched during the 17th century. If there is one period, one style that can be said to predominate in this kaleidoscopic city, it's baroque.

*[margin annotation: * Piazza Colonna]*

NEOCLASSICAL ROME

The title of this itinerary should not mislead you. The style it describes, "neoclassical" which literally means "classical again" or "new classical," was a product of the Napoleonic era and a reaction not only to the preceding baroque, but even more so to the rococo that followed baroque in most of Europe. Rome did not have a rococo period, and most of Roman architecture in the 18th century seems to be an announcement of the elegant lines that became fashionable elsewhere only at the very end of the century and at the beginning of the next one. Thus, this itinerary will list both 18th- and early 19th- century monuments, as well as the streets and gardens that were added to Rome during that time.

Neoclassical Itinerary

S. Maria Maggiore.   This basilica, which is the largest church in Rome dedicated to the worship of St. Mary, stands on the Esquiline, the hill that was considered a "bad neighborhood" in the days of old Rome. (The original seven hills were Palatine, Capitoline, Aventine, Esquiline, Celio, Quirinal and Viminal.) The original church was built by Pope Sixtus III in 431, and its basic structure is still paleochristian. In the 13th century the apse was redone, and in the 17th century the back was restorated. The excellent front, with its *portico* and *loggia,* is the work of architect Ferdinando Fuga, done in 1750. The upper *loggia* hides the medieval facade, decorated with interesting mosaics. The interior is that of an ancient basilica with three naves divided by classical architraves and columns. The outstanding floor in the central

*[margin annotation: *** S. Maria Maggiore]*

nave was done by the same Cosmati family so often mentioned in our medieval itinerary. The wonderful ceiling is intricate woodwork done in the early 16th century, and thus Renaissance flavored. The mosaics, depicting scenes of the Old Testament (lives of Abraham, Moses and Joshua) are 5th century. The precious mosaics over the triumphal arch at the bottom of the church, showing the coming and childhood of Christ are also 5th century. Many important statues decorate this lovely basilica, our personal favorite among the larger churches of Rome. The two chapels that may strike you most are the *Sistine* and *Paoline*. Two popes—Paul V and Clement VIII—have their tombs here, and there is a very attractive chapel done for the Sforza family by G. della Porta.

S. Giovanni in Laterano.   This is the cathedral of Rome and of the world. It was started by Pope Melchiade, who was on St. Peter's throne from 311 to 314 and was built on land donated by Emperor Constantine for the very purpose of giving the city its own great church. It was destroyed and rebuilt several times; the present arrangement, dating 1646–1649, is by Borromini. It belongs in this itinerary because the majestic facade was added later, in 1735, from a drawing by architect Alessandro Galilei. (By the way, the 18th-century neoclassic style is also known as neo-Renaissance. The reason is obvious: the Renaissance was a rediscovery of the old classics, and the neoclassical period was a double rediscovery, for it took inspiration from old Greek beauty and couldn't help but emulate the greater masters of the first rebirth.) To the uninitiated eye, the grand front of *S. Giovanni* might look Renaissance.

The solemn, luminous interior has five naves and, like *S. Maria*, a Cosmati floor and a magnificent wooden ceiling. Note the large 18th-century statues of the apostles. Many valuable works of art decorate the walls of the external naves and the pillars. From the last chapel at the far left you can go into the exquisite cloister with the mosaic-encrusted columns done by Vassalletto in the 13th century. Remnants of the original basilica, inscriptions, tombstones and other material are visible along the walls.

Do not overlook the baptistry, which is considered the prototype of all baptistries, redone in the 5th century under Pope Sixtus III. Its octagonal interior with a central area formed by two series of columns that hold the cupola is very characteristic. One of the four chapels has an old bronze door that makes a pleasing sound when it turns on its hinges. The other three chapels are decorated with interesting mosaics, wooden ceilings and bronzes.

Piazza S. Giovanni in Laterano.   A large square, which houses not only the basilica and its baptistry, but the *Palazzo Laterano* and the tallest obelisk in Rome. It was the papal residence before the Avignon exile, and it was from the *loggia* of the old structure—the present building was done in 1586—that Pope Bonifacio VIII blessed the crowd that came for the first Holy Year in 1300. It is said that Dante and Giotto were present for the occasion.

The building in front of the palace houses the *Scala Santa*, which, according to tradition, are the steps of Pilate's *pretorio* in Jerusalem, climbed by Jesus on the day of the crucifixion. It is made of 28 marble steps, is wood covered and the faithful climb them on their knees.

***
S. Giovanni
in Laterano

**
Palazzo
Laterano

The other famous monument on the square is the 31-meters high *Theban Obelisk*, the highest in Rome. Originally carved 15 centuries B.C., it was brought from Egypt in A.D. 353 by Emperor Costanzo II on a ship specially built for the task, meant to decorate the *Circo Massimo*, from where it was moved to its present location in 1588.

The Spanish Steps.   Probably the most famous spot in Rome bearing a neo-classical touch is the charming *scalinata* (stairway), leading from *Piazza di Spagna* up to the little pink church of *Trinità dei Monti*. This church was built in the 16th century by the French king Louis XII and has a characteristic front with two small bell towers. The grandiose stairway that leads up to it was added in the 18th century and consists of 137 steps that make several harmonious curves. The view from the top is one of the best in town, for it dominates the straight line of *Via Condotti* and several of the grand cupolas of Rome, such as *S. Carlo al Corso* and *St. Peter's*. From here, a short and scenic walk takes you to the *Pincio*, a beautiful park built by Giuseppe Valadier in order to complete the design of the *Piazza del Popolo*.

Valadier is the great name in early 18th-century architecture. Napoleon had taken Rome, and had made it one of his capitals. The city was not at its best, and a new design was needed. Thus, the great Piazza del Popolo was built between 1816 and 1820. Valadier's handling of this space is similar to Bernini's handling of St. Peter's, with an oval that opens up on the sides. The center is decorated with another Egyptian obelisk taken from the *Circo Massimo*, with four tubs and marble lions at the base, done by Valadier. At the entrance of *Via del Corso* are two lovely baroque churches—*S. Maria dei Miracoli* and *S. Maria in Montesanto*. Their cupolas add to the overall beauty of the square.

The *Pincio* is particularly beautiful at sunset on a clear spring or autumn evening. Stroll from the *Trinità dei Monti*, along the *viale* of the same name and then along *Viale A. Mickiewicz*, which passes the *Casina Valadier*, a neoclassical jewel. The view is spectacular with several of the hills in full splendor at your feet.

Behind the *Pincio* begins the park of *Villa Borghese*, created during the baroque period. This green oasis can be entered from several directions: from *Via Veneto*, through *Porta Pinciana*; from *Via Flaminia*; and, as above, from the *Pincio*. The park houses three important museums in Rome, one smaller museum and the zoo and offers a refreshing landscape on a hot summer day.

The *Galleria Borghese*, contained in the *Casino Borghese*, was described in the preceding itinerary. But here we will note in greater detail the work of Antonio Canova, whose statue of Paolina Bonaparte as *Venere Vincitrice* stands out in the first room of the gallery.

Canova is to the neoclassical period what Bernini was to baroque and Michelangelo to the Renaissance. Each of these three men was representative of the essence of his time, each in his own way.

Pompeii and *Herculanum* had been discovered a few years earlier, and the young Canova was influenced by the classical beauty of the sculptures that were excavated. His handling of marble reflects this emulation, but the early 19th century modified classical perfection and the stone became flesh and fabric, almost moving and breathing.

The other two museums within the park are the *Galleria Nazionale d'Arte Moderna* and the *Museo Nazionale di Villa Giulia*, both on the *Viale*

*** Spanish Steps

** Pincio

* S. Maria dei miracoli

* S. Maria in Montesanto

** Canova's statue of Pauline Bonaparte

** Galleria Nazionale d'Arte Moderna

*
Museo
Nazionale
di Villa
Giulia

* S. Rocco

** Apostoli
SS.

**
Palazzo
Braschi

di Belle Arti. Near the *Piazza di Siena* is a small building that imitates a medieval fortress, *Fortezzuola.* It houses the *Museo Canonica*, dedicated to a sculptor of the same name.

Two small churches, three buildings and two important streets conclude this itinerary. The church of *S. Rocco,* at the end of *Via Ripetta,* has a facade by Valadier, inspired by the great Venetian architect of the 16th century, Andrea Palladio.

On the *Piazza dei SS. Apostoli*, south of the Quirinale Palace, is the 6th-century church bearing the same name. Its facade was made by Valadier, and inside there are works by Canova. Not far from this square, going to the *Quirinale* up *Via della Dataria* we reach on the Piazza del Quirinale itself the *Palazzo della Consulta,* an admirable piece of architecture by Ferdinando Fuga. This building was commissioned by Pope Clement XII, destined to be the *Sacra Consulta*, the Vatican's Supreme Court.

Another typical example of neoclassicism in Rome is the *Palazzo Braschi* on the *Corso Vittorio Emanuele II,* near *Piazza Navona.* This palace is noteworthy especially because of its stairway, *lo Scalone.* considered one of the loveliest in Rome. It is also the last palace built for the family of a pope —Pius VI—and attached to its back is another symbol of Rome, the old Greek bust known as *Pasquino*. This statue is famous because underneath it, at various times in Roman history, short poems written by anonymous authors were placed. These poems were critical, ironic, prophetic, bitter or amusing, depending on the time and situation. They are known as *Pasquinate* and are a living part of the last four centuries of Roman history.

The last building that truly represents the neoclassical spirit is on the *Via Salaria*, somewhat out of town. *Villa Albani,* built by Cardinal Alessandro Albani between 1746 and 1763 from a design done by Carlo Marchionni has elegant gardens that reflect the new mood.

Architectural Shopping Streets

You may not wish to venture out to the Salaria to see the lovely villa, but you will most likely walk through the most fashionable streets in Rome: *Via Condotti* and *Via del Corso.* The former, already mentioned several times, is the most elegant and exclusive shopping street in the city. Most of the stores that line the sides of this short stretch are old and traditional: There is *Bulgari,* the best-known jeweller of all Italy; *Gucci,* the most famous leather goods manufacturer; *Valentino,* Italy's foremost fashion authority and designer; *Ginori*, the first in the field of china and porcelain; and many others of lesser fame.

One of the oldest landmarks of this street is the *Caffè Greco,* a coffee shop open in 1760 by a Greek named Nicola da Maddalena, who prepared such an excellent cup of coffee that soon most knowledgeable Romans were his faithful clients. Between the 18th and early 19th centuries this *caffè* was patronized by famous men such as Chopin, Bizet, Liszt, Goethe, Gogol and Wagner, not to mention the Italians who made it their meeting place.

Via del Corso, the straight line that joins *Piazza del Popolo* to *Piazza Venezia,* is remembered for a different reason. The name itself comes from the fact that from the end of the 18th through the first half of the 19th centuries the Roman carnival was celebrated on this street, with richly dressed ladies and gentlemen parading up and down, acting in the most extravagant way, for during carnival all is allowed except violence. At the end, the street was cleared for a horse race, an unusual event since the horses ran without a rider: these were the *corse,* thus *Corso.* The Romans loved this wild fun, but it was stopped at the time of King Umberto, because of an accident that took place in front of his queen.

Now *Via del Corso* is a busy street lined with stores. A little less elegant than *Via Condotti* it represents the favorite shopping area of the average young Roman. Many bargains can be had here. The streets that radiate to the right, when going from Piazza Venezia to Piazza del Popolo, lead to *Piazza di Spagna,* and represent the best shopping area of Rome. Via Frattina, Via Borgognona, Via della Vite, Via della Croce are all lined with boutiques, shops of various types, caffès and restaurants. With a crescendo of extravagance and audacity, these shops become both extremely "out" and extremely "in" by the time you reach Piazza di Spagna. Here, where both tourists and Romans mingle, the stores cater to every taste.

If your trip to Rome is geared toward shopping and fun, this is the area to choose. Here you'll see them all: the elegant ones, the funny ones, the eccentric ones and, of course, the other tourists.

MODERN ROME

From the date of Italy's unification—1870—to the present, the changes in everyone's way of life have been immense. In the case of Rome, modernization was superimposed onto the basic novelty that followed unification—Rome was, once again, the capital.

Since then, the once quiet, provincial city of 200,000 inhabitants, which concentrated only on its position as seat of the papacy and other religious institutions that gravitated around the Curia, has developed into a metropolis of about 4 million inhabitants and not only the capital of Italy, but the door to the Middle East, the largest city on the Mediterranean and the crossroads of the world. In the last 100 years the city has expanded well beyond the old Aurelian Walls, going in every direction.

Modern Itinerary

We will describe the changes by following chronology and topography. But it is important to keep in mind that this city is alive and moving. At present it covers a surface of about 1,500 square kilometers (sq km.), (579 sq mi.) and many corners will have to be left out of our narrative.

The first major change after 1870 was represented by the opening of the *Via Nazionale* and the building of the railroad station, *Termini.* Then came the need for bureaucratic space, which generated the huge *Palazzaccio*, built on the right bank of the Tiber, as well as other, less-cumbersome ministries.

From the end of the 19th century to World War I, the monuments added to the already well-endowed Eternal City are noteworthy for their bulk rather than their beauty. The immense, white *Vittoriano* (built 1885–1911), also called *Altare della Patria,* the *Typewriter* or *the Wedding Cake,* stands out and hits your eye as you approach the *Piazza Venezia,* hiding the elegant *Campidoglio* with its chalky curlicues.

Fortunately, not all modern structures strike this harsh a note. Fairly unobtrusive are the *Palazzo delle Esposizioni* and the *Palazzo della Banca d'Italia,* both on Via Nazionale. There is also the lovely *Passeggiata Archeologica*, a straight, oleander-lined street that goes from the *Colosseum* to the *FAO* building.

Fountain of the Naiads

But let us return to the end of the 19th century, to one of the loveliest monuments in Rome, the *Fontana delle Naiadi.* Like the *Vittoriano,* it straddles the two centuries, for it was started in 1885 and finished in 1901. At the height of Victorian puritanism, the decorations added represented four naked nymphs and were the object of much turmoil and discussion. The vigorous group at the center was added ten years later. The magnificent fountain, located at the center of the large *Piazza Esedra,* is particularly attractive at night, and you may, as have many travelers, cherish the memory of your first impact with Rome when you get off a train at *Stazione Termini* and glimpse the fantastic sight of the *Fontana delle Naiadi.*

The 20 fascist years were also called the years of the demolishing pickax. The most important example of architecture of this period is *Via dei Fori Imperiali,* which though it gives no archaeological understanding of this richly endowed area, is of spectacular proportions. Nearby, *Via Cristoforo Colombo, Via S. Gregorio* and *Via Terme di Caracalla* unite the center of old Rome with an area that represents the most ambitious fascist attempt at urban development, *EUR.* Done with academic rigidity, this large area was meant, first, to house an exposition and, then, to become a model of modern living. Thus, marble buildings with columns and arches, huge porticoes, wide avenues and large statues attempt to be a classical impression. Some of the buildings are architecturally outstanding, such as the *Palazzo dei Congressi* with its flat, scarflike cupola. The *Palazzo della Civiltà del Lavoro* is noteworthy for its simple structure of nothing but rows of arches and is justly called the square Colosseum.

Of the streets and avenues opened in the last years of the 19th century, you should note *Corso Vittorio Emanuele II*, frequently mentioned in other itineraries. It was opened in 1886, using part of the old *Via Papale,* which the popes used to go from the Vatican to *S. Giovanni in Laterano.* Also from this period are *Via Arenula* and *Ponte Garibaldi,* which represent the easiest and fastest way of reaching Trastevere. And since you are on the right bank of the Tiber, just before reaching *Castel Sant'Angelo,* there is a structure to see that does not constitute one of Rome's proudest achievements. It's the aforementioned *Palazzo di Giustizia,* or *Palazzaccio,* built between 1888 and 1910, and meant to be one of the first buildings of a new area, the *Prati,* still one of Rome's most elegant neighborhoods. From the beginning, the large structure ran into technical trouble. The river bank wasn't solid enough to withstand its bulk, and the height had to be limited. The architect, Guglielmo Calderini, died of a broken heart, and the ugly monument is still empty, getting new blood in the form of cement injections and spoiling the view.

The restraining walls built on the river banks, as well as several of the bridges that connect the higher parts of Rome, such as Ponte Margherita (1891) and Ponte Cavour (1901), are also from this period.

The destruction and paralysis brought on by World War II was followed by a period of lethargy, but the 1950s saw new needs, and the first one was for a new railroad station. *Termini,* as you see it today, was a product of that time. By the way, the name of the Roman railroad station comes from old Rome. The Baths of Dioclecian— *Terme di Diocleziano*—are nearby, thus *Termini* from *Terme.*

To see the last important achievement of contemporary Roman construction, you must go all the way to the other end of town, following Via Flaminia upriver. Here, on the occasion of the 1960 Olympic games, a series of new structures were added to the city. The area is called *Villaggio Olimpico* and is composed of several buildings, all meant for sports: the *Palazzetto dello Sport,* the *Stadio Olimpico,* the *Stadio dei Marmi* and the *Stadio del Nuoto.*

This is no simple itinerary because, as we said earlier, modern Rome has expanded so much beyond the original Aurelian walls that it would be impossible to describe it well without going far out, in several directions. We have ignored, with regret, many of the larger new structures, but it is the fate of monuments, especially in a city like Rome. Perhaps another guide, written after the year 2000, will include the large Hilton Cavalieri Hotel on Piazzale Clodio as one of the new symbols of Rome!

FASHIONABLE, ROMANTIC, FRIVOLOUS ROME

Rome is a city of many moods. We've dedicated the previous pages to its history, its art, its urban changes. But there is also a fun side to this city, a sentimental side, a shopping and bargain-hunting side. Why not spend a day just enjoying the frivolous side of Rome!

Fashionable Rome's center is *Piazza di Spagna.* The square itself is full of lovely shops and boutiques, crowded with the latest clothes, shoes, books, anything. Peek into *Alexander's,* where the young Romans buy their outrageous outfits; check on *Camomilla* for odd things and odd types; or look into *Krizia,* owned by the wife of one of Italy's most talented movie directors, for the best in design. *Simon* is a fascinating place with household items such as coffee tables and mirrors; *W.M.F.* has interesting glass and ceramic objects; *Salato* has fabulous shoes.

From the *piazza* a series of streets go to *Via del Corso.* We've already seen the allure of *Via Condotti,* but this itinerary puts it in its natural place, for no street is as fashionable, as frivolous or as romantic. Even if you buy nothing but coffee at *Caffè Greco,* you'll have fun. Our suggestion is to see it on a sunny day, facing the *scalinata* of *Trinità dei Monti.* The other streets, *Via Frattina, Via Borgognona* and *Via della Vite* are equally full of new enticing merchandise, crowded with shopping tourists and Romans.

At 1 P.M. the stores close, and the Romans adjourn for lunch. You can choose among the restaurants in the area or take advantage of the peace and quiet—by 2 P.M. the traffic is down to a minimum and most of the people are gone from the streets—and take a walk through the *Pincio,* or sit on the Spanish Steps, or go to the *Pantheon* (walking briskly, it's less than 15 minutes from Via Condotti) or go see the *Fontana di Trevi* (same distance as the Pantheon, on the other side of Via del Corso). Everywhere you will pass bars with outdoor tables, where a *cappuccino* and *toast* (pronounced "tost" and meaning a grilled ham and cheese sandwich) will cost you no more than $2.00. True Italians, however, crowd the restaurants, eat well and go for their *siesta* until 4 or 5 P.M.

If you decide to do as the Romans, have a panoramic lunch at the *Hassler-Villa Medici Hotel.* Their rooftop restaurant has one of the loveliest views of Roma and the food is very good and very digestible. Or, for authentic Roman living, have lunch at *Ranieri's,* where the view is of elegant people and silent waiters.

If you wish to continue shopping, *Via del Corso* is another important artery. Here, rather than tourists you'll find young Romans. The boutiques are geared toward modern tastes, and the fashion-conscious secretary, young housewife or student shops here for sweaters and skirts.

For the moderate, popular taste, *Via Nazionale* is the street to see. Here the stores cater to the average Roman.

Finally, there is *Via Veneto.* Lined with famous *caffès,* grand hotels and elegant buildings, the most famous of Roman streets attracts the attention of many foreigners in Rome and is worth a few hours of your time. Though no longer lined with the best shops, it still boasts a few notables, such as *Fontana* for jewelry, *Albertina* for fancy knitwear and *Roux* for the craziest, most unusual shoes. Again, stop at *Cafè de Paris* or *Doney* for a midafternoon drink or coffee and to watch the people go by. If you like walking and the day is beautiful, go to the top of Via Veneto, through *Porta Pinciana,* where you can walk midst green lawns on the *Viale di Muro Torto* and reach the *Pincio* by sunset. Here is the most appropriate place to be if the sunset is lovely, and no Roman sight—dare we say, no sight anywhere—will be as inspiring.

After sunset it is probably time to go back to your hotel for a bath, a rest, a pause. Dinner, in Rome, is not early. You can try at 8 P.M., but most places begin serving after 9 P.M. Choose from the good restaurants in Trastevere or go to the *Pergola,* on the roof of the Hilton Cavalieri for a different view of Rome or try one of the trattorie near the *Pantheon* and end up at the *Piazza della Rotonda* for your after-dinner coffee. During the summer, *Piazza Navona* is also fun, for there are crowds of all types of people.

As an alternative, a drive through Rome at night can be exciting. The monuments are lit, and some are spectacular. The Colosseum, Castel Sant-'Angelo, Campidoglio, St. Peter's, Fontana di Trevi are as different by day as by night, as well as a new experience by moonlight. Choose your favorite and enjoy it.

If you like soft music, there are several good Piano Bars where you can stay into the wee hours over a glass of *spumante,* one of the last nostalgic reminders of the Rome that used to mean *dolce vita.*

Inside Information

Hotels

★★★★★   **FIVE STARS**

★★★★★   **1. LE GRAND HOTEL ET DE ROME**
Via Vittorio Emanuele Orlando 3, tel. 4709, 175 rooms with bath, single
L.125,000, double L.172,000, suite prices on request. Even if the location is
not as perfect as it might be, this is one of the most luxurious hotels in Italy
and certainly among Rome's very best. Each room has its own decorative
scheme with bathrooms that are refined and beyond description. Two excellent restaurants serve hotel guests and some of Rome's most important citizens as well. There is also a snack bar, Le Pavillon. There are conference
rooms available.

*** Le Rallye and Le Maschere restaurants*

★★★★★   **2. CAVALIERI HILTON**
Via Cadiolo 101, tel. 3151, 400 rooms with bath, single L.90–120,000,
double L.120–180,000, suite prices on request. Everything you'd expect from
a Hilton, plus a view of Roma. La Pergola's an absolutely marvelous rooftop
restaurant: Trattoria del Cavaliere is a very good downstairs restaurant. Other
facilities are a barbershop, souvenir shops and discoteque. The main attraction is the double pleasure of being in Roma but not quite out of the U.S.A.

***** La Pergola*
* Trattoria*

★★★★★   **3. HASSLER–VILLA MEDICI**
Piazza Trinita dei Monti 6, tel. 679.2651, 100 rooms with bath, single
L.105,000, double L.150,000, suite prices on request. Great luxury, great
reputation, famous guests, adequate service. Splendid view from the roof-
garden restaurant. Definitely the hotel to choose if what you want is a romantic, fashionable Roman weekend. Make reservations a few days ahead.

The Villa Medici, near the hotel, is now the Académie Nationale de France

★★★★★   **4. HOTEL EXCELSIOR**
Via Veneto 125, tel. 4708, at present 372 rooms with bath, single L.110,000,
double L.157,000. One of the largest in Rome, the best on Via Veneto, its
large, luxurious halls always teeming with Arab sheiks, bejewelled Japanese
matrons and Eastern European diplomats. Some rooms are in the process of
redecoration, thus it's advisable to book in advance. Inside sauna, hair-
dresser, massages and so forth. Piano-bar available from 12 noon to 2 A.M.
Also an inside snack bar and La Cupola, a good restaurant. Four conference
rooms, with simultaneous translation facilities, if needed.

** La Cupola*

★★★★   **FOUR STARS**

★★★★   **1. HOTEL LORD BYRON**
Via de Notaris 5, tel. 3609541, 55 rooms with bath, single L.85,000, double
L.110,000, breakfast L.4,500. Charming location, beautifully decorated
rooms, good restaurant. A little off center, but restful; the perfect hotel for a
Roman honeymoon. There are seven suites, some with lovely views. Make
reservations a few days in advance.

** Le Jardin restaurant*

★★★★   2. HOTEL D'INGHILTERRA
Via Bocca di Leone 14, tel. 672.161, 105 rooms with bath, single L.77,000, double L.103,000, breakfast L.3500. A favorite with newspaper people and movie people, this extremely well-located hotel is now a bit more expensive —has become first class—but still a very good buy. Valentino's store is literally within hand's reach; Via Condotti just around the corner; Piazza di Spagna is 20 steps up the street. Make reservations well in advance and enjoy your stay in the heart of fashionable Roma.

★★★★   3. HOTEL MEDITERRANEO
Via Cavour 15, tel.464051, 300 rooms with bath, single L.56,000, double L.84,000, breakfast L.5,000. This is the largest of the Bettoja chain and is modern and efficient. The restaurant has an important name: "21." There are penthouse suites and conference facilities.

★★★★   4. HOTEL RAPHAEL
Largo Febo 2, tel. 656.9051, 100 rooms with bath, single L.46,000, double L.72,500, double with terrace L.88,000. One of the most charming corners in Rome, near Via dei Coronari and Piazza Navona. A tiny green square, an ivy covered hotel, a peaceful oasis—intimate and romantic. An extra bonus is the good restaurant, il Raphaellino. In winter, be sure to book 15 days ahead; summers are less crowded, so 7 days ahead will be enough.

Charming roof garden

★★★   THREE STARS

★★★   1. HOTEL FORUM
Via Tor dei Conti 25, tel. 679.2446, 81 rooms with bath, single L.60,000, double L.90,000, breakfast L.6,000. Fabulous location between Piazza Venezia and Colosseum, with a view on Via dei Fori Imperiali from almost every room. Friendly atmosphere, the Old World touch. Has a roof-garden restaurant that features international cuisine and a splendid view. Garage.

Near top of Spanish steps. a favorite of King Constantine of Greece

★★★   2. HOTEL DE LA VILLE
Via Sistina 67, tel 679.8941, 189 rooms with bath, single L.66,000, double L.102,000. Very close to everything. Duke Bar downstairs, with buffet, second-floor piano bar. Some rooms with terraces and view. Patio restaurant and, in summer, outdoor eating.

★★★   3. HOTEL METROPOLE
Via Principe Amedeo 3, tel. 475.1441, 285 rooms with bath, single L.43,000, double L.74,000, triple L.89,000. Good first-class hotel near the railroad station with the added attraction of an excellent restaurant, the Apicio. Snack bar open until 2 A.M.

★★   TWO STARS

★★   1. ROME AIRPORT HOTEL PALACE
Viale Romagnoli 165, Lido di Ostia, tel. 569.2341, 265 rooms with bath, single L.40,000, double L.70,000, breakfast L.4,000. Modern, attractive ho-

tel, 15 minutes from the airport, not far from the sea, and 40 minutes from the center of town. Restaurant, bar, parking, swimming-pool, discoteque.

★★   2. MASSIMO D'AZEGLIO HOTEL

Via Cavour 18, tel. 460646, 250 rooms with bath, single L.48,000, double L.73,000, breakfast L.5,000. Most important of the five Bettoja hotels, it has been recently redecorated and every room has a radio and refrigerator. The garage can hold 150 cars. The restaurant is one of Rome's oldest. There are two conference rooms, one for 200 persons, the other for 50.

★★   3. HOTEL ATLANTE

Via Vittelleschi 34, tel. 656.4196, 71 rooms and 42 in annex with bath, single L.49,000, double L.69,000. Near Vatican, this good, modern hotel has a roof-garden restaurant with a view of St. Peter's, as well as modern conveniences such as a TV set, air conditioning and frigo–bar in every room. Also solarium and American bar. Small congress facilities for 60 participants, with simultaneous translation booths and earphones. In August, free pick up at the airport.

★★   4. HOTEL GREGORIANA

Via Gregoriana 18, tel. 679.4269, 19 rooms with bath, single L.36,000, double L.62,000. New, very small, the rooms in this hotel have some of the loveliest views in Rome. It's located at the top of the Spanish steps. Very difficult to get a room so book well in advance.

★★   5. HOTEL CARDINAL

Via dei Bresciani 35, tel. 654.2719, 74 rooms with bath, single L.40,000, double L.66,000, breakfast L.4,000. Just off Via Giulia, this elegant hotel has air conditioning and a frigo–bar in every room.

★★   6. COLONNA PALACE HOTEL

Piazza Montecitorio 12, tel. 678.1341, 104 rooms with bath, single L.45,000, double L.80,000, breakfast L.4,000. Brand new, this hotel was meant for politicians and those who come to visit them; Parliament is just across the square. Tourists are also welcome, and the location couldn't be better. Bar, TV room.

The original Colonna Palace is now an art gallery, next door to SS. Apostoli church

★   ONE STAR

★   1. HOTEL COLUMBUS

Via della Conciliazione 33, tel. 656.5245, 120 rooms, 90 with bath, single L.38,000, double L.55,000. This is your chance to sleep in a 15th-century palace for a reasonable price. Very near St. Peter's, not far from the rest of Rome. A good buy. Restaurant and garage.

★   2. SHANGRI-LÀ CORSETTI HOTEL

Viale Algeria 141—EUR, tel. 591.6441, 52 rooms all with bath, TV, frigo–bar, single L.44,000, double L.63,000, breakfast L.4,000. This well-decorated, comfortable hotel is in the modern part of Rome, about 20 minutes by subway form the center of town. Quiet at night, surrounded by greenery, it has a decent restaurant on the premises and a small night club. Olympic-size swimming pool and two conference rooms, one with movie projection facilities.

★ 3. HOTEL NAZIONALE
Piazza Montecitorio 131, tel. 689.251, 90 rooms with bath, single L.38,000, double L.72,000. Not old, not new, the hotel of politicians and businessmen, with the Chamber of Deputies literally next door; Via del Corso, the Pantheon, Fontana di Trevi, all within stone's throw—one of the most centrally located hotels in Rome. Extra bonus: just around the corner Rome's best ice-cream place—Giolitti. Book well in advance; don't expect exceptional service.

★ 4. HOTEL PLAZA
Via del Corso 126, tel. 672101,6783364, 207 rooms most with bath, single, L.43,000, double L.67,000, breakfast L.3,000. A few singles without bathroom at L.28,000. Traditional, a little old, large and reasonably priced. The location is very central. Many politicians and businessmen stay here. Service friendly but a little sloppy.

★ 5. HOTEL GIULIO CESARE
Via degli Scipioni 287, tel. 31.02.44, 80 rooms with bath, single L.42,000, double L.69,000. Not in the central part of town, but in a good residential area, this nice hotel is close to the state TV studios. Inside restaurant.

a former villa

★ 6. HOTEL COMMODORE
Via Torino 1, tel. 485656, 65 rooms with bath, single L.35,000, double L.54,000, breakfast L.3,500. Nice, modern hotel, not far from the railroad station and near Sta. Maria Maggiore.

NO STARS

1. HOTEL DEL SENATO
Piazza della Rotonda 73, tel. 679.3231, 50 rooms, single, no bath L.17,000, with bath L.29,000; double, no bath L.24,000, with bath L.35,000; triple, no bath L.30,000, with bath L.42,000, breakfast L.2,500. Very central, overlooking the Pantheon, this friendly, clean, efficiently run hotel has comfortable rooms. It's also one of the few that offers triples—practically the best buy in town.

2. HOTEL FONTANA
Piazza Trevi 96, tel. 678.6113, 30 rooms with bath, single L.33,000, double L.53,000. Ancient monastery, older than the famous fountain that decorates the piazza in front of it. Some of the rooms look out on the beautiful monument. Roof garden for guests only; famous for the movies made here during the glorious fifties and sixties. As a bonus, the hotel provides a coin for the fountain. Make reservations at least one week in advance.

3. HOTEL ATLAS
Via Rasella 3, tel. 462.140, 45 rooms with bath, single L.29,000, double L.48,000. Small, pleasant, near Via Veneto and Palazzo Barberini. Roof garden for snacks and sun bathing. Small bar.

4. HOTEL CARRIAGE
Via delle Carrozze 36, tel. 679.5166, 24 rooms with bath, single L.30,000, double L.41,000, breakfast L.2,000. Small, pleasant, near Piazza di Spagna. Friendly service. Two rooms have a terrace—the single costs L.35,000, the double L.50,000. Make reservations in advance.

5. HOTEL VALADIER
Via della Fontanella 15, tel. 679.6966, 38 rooms with bath, single L.25,000, double L.44,000, breakfast L.2,500. Near Piazza del Popolo and Via Margutta, this attractive hotel lives up to its name. The neoclassical furnishings and the atmosphere are pleasant. Good service.

6. HOTEL BOLOGNA
Near Piazza Navona

Via S. Chiara 5, tel. 656.8951, 118 rooms, some with bath, single with bath L.30,000, double L.45,000, breakfast L.3,000. Centrally located, nice hotel. Make reservations in advance.

7. HOTEL GENIO
Via Zanardelli 28, tel. 654.2238, 61 rooms, most with bath, single with bath L.23,000, 5 singles without bath L.15,000, double L.38,000, 10 doubles that can become triples L.48,000, breakfast L.3,000. Just off Piazza Navona, this hotel is run like a boarding house. Restaurant serves meals for guests only, once a day, L.7,000. On request, meals can be had twice a day.

8. HOTEL TORRE ARGENTINA
Corso Vittorio Emanuele II 102, tel. 654.1604, 32 rooms, some with bath, single with bath L.27,000, double L.42,000, breakfast L.2,500. Well-located, small, inexpensive hotel.

9. ASTORIA GARDEN HOTEL AND HOTEL MONTAGNA
Via Varese 8, tel. 495.3653, 30 rooms, single L.20,000, double L.38,000. Small, pleasant hotel near railroad station, has a tiny garden and baths in most rooms. There are very cheap rooms with no bath—L.16,000 for a single, L.28,000 for a double. Some of the personnel speak English. Make reservations in advance.

10. HOTEL DEI PORTOGHESI
Near Piazza Navona

Via dei Portoghesi 1, tel. 656.4231, 27 rooms, most with bath, single with bath L.25,000, double L.45,000. On a side street, not far from center.

11. HOTEL CONDOTTI
Via Mario de' Fiori 37, tel. 679.4661, 21 rooms, single L.15,000, double L.25,000, double with bath L.29,000, breakfast L.2,500. Good shopping

location, near Piazza di Spagna. Most rooms have no WC (toilet), only sink and shower, thus low prices.

Restaurants

★★★★★   **FIVE STARS**

★★★★★   **1. PAPÀ GIOVANNI**
Via dei Sediari, 4, tel. 6565308, closed Sundays and August. This charming restaurant is one of the most romantic in town. Tables for two or four, lovely silver and china, excellent wine list. The food is very special, the result of careful thinking, testing and talent. Near Piazza Navona, two steps from the Pantheon, it should be tried, if at all possible. The price hovers around L.30,000 per person; well spent.

★★★★★   **2. LA PERGOLA**
Sulla terrazza dell' Hilton Cavalieri, Via Cadiolo 101, tel. 3151, only evenings. Most unexpectedly, this restaurant isn't the least bit "Hiltonian" or even American, but boasts a new, exquisitite, light cuisine of European inspiration. The result is very original, recommended for gourmets who love to explore new tastes. The wine list was put together by Italy's greatest experts. The view, dominating Rome from the top of Monte Mario, is very special— in summer the terrace is cool. The drive up is reminiscent of the French Riviera "moyen Corniche." High prices, about L.40,000 to L.50,000 per person.

★★★★★   **3. ALBERTO CIARLA**
Piazza S. Cosimato 40, tel. 588668, only evenings and closed Sunday. The best fish restaurant in Rome, decidedly worthy of a detour. Good white wine, produced by the family. Ciarla, a charming man who combines his work with his hobby—underwater fishing—says that the level of Roman cuisine has improved because Romans have learned how to eat well. The price is around L.25,000 per person, which is more than reasonable.

In Trastevere

★★★★   **FOUR STARS**

★★★★   **1. LE RALLYE**
At the Grand Hotel, Via V.E. Orlando 3, tel. 54709, closed Saturdays, Sundays and August. A very fine restaurant in a very fine hotel. The prices are high, but there is a sophisticated clientele.

★★★★   **2. LE MASCHERE DEL GRAND HOTEL**
Via V.E. Orlando 3, tel. 4709. If you want to meet the Hollywood crowd in Rome, here's where it can happen. Good quality meats; classical cooking; a wine list of an excellent hotel. Expensive, about L.30,000 per person, perhaps more.

★★★★   **3. EL TOULÀ**
Via della Lupa, tel. 678.1196, closed Sundays. Handled with professional experience, this restaurant has been imporving—decidedly worth a visit. Elegant, refined, expensive, the Roman branch of the Venetian "El Toulà"

One of Alfredo Beltrame's group of restaurants

chain is one of the most exclusive restaurants in the capital. Low lights, pale pink tablecloths, deep, soft chairs, the atmosphere is in tune with the sophisticated clientele, the splendidly stocked cellar, the marvelous food and, as should be expected, the price, about L.50,000 per person.

★★★   THREE STARS

★★★   1. D'ARTAGNAN
Via Frascati—Colonna, km. 4, Montecompatri, Roma, tel. 948.5293. This large *trattoria* is outside Rome, but worth the drive. Owner Sandro Fioriti, a blond giant is an inventive cook. He cheerfully doles out such novelties as pork with blackberries, spaghetti with lemon sauce, flower petal salad, fried olives, frogs' legs and apple slices and the best ice cream north of Sicily, moving among his waiters with the lightness of a ballerina. The wine is good, the prices reasonable.

★★   TWO STARS

★★   1. LA CUPOLA DELL' HOTEL EXCELSIOR
Via Veneto 125, tel. 4708. Change is in the air. As is, very competent, high-level hotel cuisine, good wine list. Prices are L.30,000–35,000 per person.

★★   2. CHECCHINO DAL 1887
Via di Monte Testaccio 30, tel. 576318, closed Mondays and mid-August. Woth the trip for those who are interested in tasting old- fashioned genuine Roman cooking at its best. Fascinating location—the Testaccio isn't a natural hill but the result of an accumulation of broken amphors, from the days when Rome used the area as a port. Now the hill provides excellent cellars, as air circulates among the pieces of crockery. The food is based on inexpensive cuts—tripe, tail, sweetbreads and brains. Good wine and a fair price, L.15,000.

Rome's abattoir was once near here

★★   3. L'EAU VIVE
Via Monterone 85, tel. 654.1095, closed on Sundays and March. The service is slow. At 10:00 P.M. everyone says the Ave Maria. The "sister" waitresses wear colorful costumes, there is nice classical music piped in and the dishes are very, very international (living proof of the universality of the church). The sister in charge of the cellar knows her Bordeaux and her Beaujolais.

Oriental and African dishes as well as European

★★   4. LE JARDIN DELL'HOTEL LORD BYRON
Via Giuseppe de Notaris 5, tel. 3609541. This charmingly decorated restaurant, in a very good hotel, serves excellent food, has a good wine list, is most pleasant. About L.25,000.

★★   5. DELL'HOTEL EDEN
Via Ludovisi 49, near Via Veneto, tel. 480.551, closed Sundays. This terrace restaurant offers one of the best views in Rome, plus good food and excellent service. High prices, but worth every cent.

★★   6. G.B.
Via delle Carceri, tel. 656.9336, closed Mondays and August. N ear lovely Via Giulia, this small restaurant offers an extremely good "revival" of old-fashioned Roman and Jewish–Roman dishes of the 17th, 18th and 19th centuries. The name stands for Gianna Bondi, the owner, who runs the place with the love and artistry of a true gourmet. A treat for food lovers, gastronomes and all those interested in the past. L.20,000–25.000 per person.

★★   7. PASSETTO
Via Zanardelli 14, tel. 65.43.696, closed Sundays. One of Rome's oldest. Good service, good choice of wines, good clients, good food; price as expected around L.15,000–20,000 per person.

Near Piazza Navona

★   ONE STAR

★   1. CHARLY'S SAUCIÈRE
Via S. Giovanni in Laterano 268, tel. 736.666, closed Sundays and August. For those who prefer French cooking, are tired of pasta or simply happen to be near S. Giovanni in Laterano, this place offers a charming change. Swiss owner, who lives up to the name—thus, very fine sauces. The price is around L.20,000 per person.

★   2. TRATTORIA DEL CAVALIERE–HILTON CAVALIERI
Via Cadiolo 101, tel. 3151.149, no closing. This is the simple, everyday eatery of the Hilton Cavalieri. Cheerfully decorated with orange tablecloths and such, it features good regional Italian food coupled with U.S. efficiency. The prices are what you'd expect, and the hamburgers are as authentic as can be.

★   3. TAVERNA RIPETTA
Via Ripetta 158, tel. 654.2979, closed Sundays. Sardinian and Arabian specialties in a small simple little restaurant. Everything cooked with meticulous, loving care. Good wines. Call ahead if you go in the evening. Very reasonable prices.

★   4. LEON D'ORO
Via Cagliari 25, tel. 861900, closed Mondays and August 10th–September 10th. Run by a very ambitious and talented lady, this is one of the best fish restaurants in Rome. New and imaginative cooking. Good wine list, decent prices, L.15,000–20,000 per person.

★   5. PINO E DINO
Piazza di Montevecchio 22, tel. 65.61.319, closed Mondays and August 5th–15th. Very small place, refined, talented cooking, the wine carefully matched to the dish, reasonable prices: L.15,000–18,000 per person. A nice, minigourmet experience.

★   6. ARNALDO
Via di Grotta Pinta 8, tel. 6561915, closed Tuesdays and one week in mid-August. Charming place run with peotic grace by a ballet lover. Soft lights and

piped-in classical music. The food varies according to the season, prepared
with creative good taste. Wines fair, so is price: L.10,000–13,000 per person.

NO STARS

1. DOMUS AUREA
Parco del Monte Oppio, tel. 7315325, closed Tuesdays and August. The food
is average, but the place is lovely and has music in the evening. L.20,000–
25,000 per person.

Good view of Colosseum

2. NIHONBASHI
Via Torino 34, tel. 47.56.970, closed on Sundays. The best Japanese restaurant in Rome. Great variety, and even Chinese dinners if ordered ahead. The
prices are high: L.25,000–30,000 per person.

3. RANIERI
Via Mario dei Fiori 26, tel. 6791592, closed Sundays and August 12th–30th.
The location is very central; the tradition, the reputation, the service, all first
rate. Go for the sake of curiosity, to see where the original Ranieri cooked
for Queen Victoria and to feel some of the glamour still in the air. Very
average food, high prices, L.15,000–20,000 per person.

4. TAVERNA GIULIA
Vicolo dell'Oro, tel. 65.69.768, closed Sundays. Nice atmosphere, good
Genoese cooking, good wine list. Many knowledgeable foreigners come
here, but the place is not what it used to be. Still, the service is good and the
location unbeatable. Reasonable prices, L.15,000–20,000 per person.

5. AL MORO
Vicolo delle Bollette 13, tel. 678.3495, closed Sundays and August. The
owner played a leading part in Fellini's *Satyricon*. Aside from that, this very
small *trattoria* offers good food, good wine, a noisy atmosphere and reasonable prices: L.12,000–15,000 per person. Phone ahead for reservations.

6. IL BARROCCIO "ER FAGIOLARO"
Via dei Pastini 13, tel. 679.3797, closed Mondays and August. Very central,
this Tuscan restaurant is open for lunch until 2:30 P.M., dinner as late as
midnight. The cooking is hearty, wholesome country food. Good house wine
and reasonable prices: L.8,000–15,000 per person.

7. CORIOLANO
Via Ancona 14, tel. 8449501, closed Sundays. Elegant, sober, not too expensive and the food is authentic Roman, each dish done with loving care. Good
wine list. L.13,000–19,000 per person.

8. OSTERIA DELL'ANTIQUARIO
Piazza S. Simeone 27, tel. 659. Closed on Sundays, Terrace. Small restaurant
with very good home cooking, lovely terrace, in the heart of Rome and near
Via dei Coronari, famous for its antique shops. Reasonable prices, about
L.15,000 per person.

ask the waiter or maître d' what he suggests

These Carciofi = tender whole artichokes deep fried, served crisp, golden and hot

9. AI TRE SCALINI
Via SS.Quattro 30, tel. 732695, closed Mondays. Don't ask for a menu, don't argue with the waiter, be patient, you may wait a bit longer than usual. If you are inclined to adventure, try this place. It may be rewarding in terms of good food. Prices reasonable. L.15,000–20,000 per person.

10. CHECCO ER CARRETTIERE
Via Benedetta 10, tel. 5817018, closed Mondays and August 10th–31st. Typical Roman cooking, true Roman atmosphere—this Trastevere place is authentic! Try the spaghetti "alla Carrettiera," the "carciofi alla giudia," the Roman tripe or grilled lamb. The atmosphere is local, the red wine is better than the white wine, the prices are fair: L.12,000–15,000 per person.

11. DA GEMMA E MAURIZIO
Via Marghera 39, tel. 491230, closed Saturdays. One of the best small *trattorie* in town, this one is near the railroad station. Always crowded, so phone ahead. The price is very reasonable, about L.8,000 per person.

12. NAMASKAR
Via della Penitenza 7, tel. 65.47.053, closed Sundays and August evenings. Only Indian restaurant in Rome, is located in Trastevere. Phone ahead. Good food from the Maharaska region, pleasant service and atmosphere, reasonable prices.

13. IL MATRICIANO
Via dei Gracchi 55, tel. 35.95.247, closed Wednesdays and 15 days in August. Run by a family from Amatrice, this place has a faithful clientele of actors, newspaper people, local people. Hearty, spicy, regional cooking; sometimes very good, sometimes not so good. The house Frascati wine is good as well as the price.

14. OTELLO ALLA CONCORDIA
Via della Croce 81, tel. 67.91178, closed Sundays and mid-August. Three things recommend Otello: the location, the nice outdoors and the prices. Otherwise, much noise; average food—fresh, but cooked without genius; average wine. It is two steps from fashionable Via Condotti and lovely Piazza di Spagna. Note: the white-haired Otello, a lovely man who fed most of Rome's movie neophytes in the fifties. Fellini, Mastroianni and Gassman, plus many with less familiar names are old friends who still remember this *trattoria*. The cost is L.8,000 or so.

15. CANNAVOTA
Piazza S. Giovanni in Laterano, tel. 775.007, closed Wednesdays and August 2nd–25th. This inexpensive place offers efficient service and good food made with very fresh ingredients. The wines are average, the owner is from Amatrice, as are many of Rome's good cooks.

16. ROMOLO ALLA MOLE ADRIANA
Via Fosse di Castello 19, tel. 65.61.603, closed Mondays and 15 days in August. An inexpensive, well-located *trattoria*; between St. Peter's and Cas-

tel Sant'Angelo. Thus, at noon it's full of hungry tourists. The food is okay; the price is very low: L.8,000 per person.

17. GIRARROSTO TOSCANO

Via Campania 29, tel. 46.42.92, closed on Wednesdays and July 20th–August 5th. New ownership. The food is Tuscan, with little room for imagination. The Chianti is reasonable, and so is the price.

18. GIOLITTI

Via Uffici del Vicario 40, tel. 679.4206, closed Mondays. One of the best—possibly the best—ice-cream parlors in Rome. Just off Piazza Montecitorio (the Parliament), two steps from the Pantheon, makes excellent *cappuccini,* pastries, snacks. In summer, there are a few outdoor tables. In winter there is a large indoor room that gets crowded around 5 to 6 P.M. If you like ice-cream, don't miss their staggering concoctions—not only are they good to the palate, but they are fascinating for the eye!

19. CAFFÈ GRECO

Via Condotti 86, tel. 678.2554, closed Sundays. Very traditional, very elegant, very central. Once, this was a meeting place for the Roman *intelligentia.* Now, tourists and elegant Italians mix freely, served by a few haughty waiters in tails. Gucci and Co. are just across the street, so if you want a quick snack midst shopping and sightseeing, this is the obvious choice.

Byron, Liszt and Buffalo Bill all had coffee here

Entertainment

The best entertainment in Rome is people-watching, preferably from a sidewalk café, but if it's more structured diversion you're after, look for some of the following, after consulting your hotel concierge and/or local brochures to ascertain dates, times, prices, and so on.

Opera

The *Teatro dell'Opera,* on Via del Viminale, has a regular season from November to May. Grand opera al fresco can be seen in the Baths of Caracalla during the summer months, *Aida* being an all-time favorite.

Tickets on sale 2 days before performances

Concerts

Concerts are held frequently at the Accademia Nazionale di Santa Cecilia (the patron saint of musicians), 7 Via dei Greci. The same management produces lovely outdoor concerts in summer at the Constantine Basilica.

Great sacred music by church choirs less these days due to demise of Latin in the mass

Theater

If you speak or understand Italian, the theaters can be very interesting. Try the Valle, Via del Teatro Valle, for some of the more imaginative productions.

Drinking

For a drink, there is a Harry's Bar, Via Veneto, cozy and chatty. Disco addicts should look in on Jacki-O of Via Buoncompagni, where you can also dine. A smart place is Gattopardo, Via Maria dei Fiori. If you are staying at the Hilton or don't mind traveling a bit from the city center, try that hotel's La Pergola nightclub.

Festivals

Here are the more important special events in Rome.

January 5–6.   Feast of the Epiphany, Piazza Navona.

January 17.   Feast of St. Anthony, St. Eusebius Church. Blessing of tbe animals.

January 21.   Feast of St. Agnes, St. Agnes-outside-the-Walls. Lambs offered to the pope.

March 19.   Feast of St. Giuseppe, Trionfale district.

Palm Sunday.   The Pope blesses palm fronds.

Holy Week and Easter.   Many events throughout city and in the Vatican, with special services including those in the Catacombs and at the Colosseum. Easter blessing by the pope.

April 21.   Anniversary of Birth of Rome, celebrated at the Campidoglio.

June–September.   Sound and Light performances at the Forum, in English as well as Italian.

June 24.   Feast of San Giovanni, Church of St. John Lateran.

July (about the 15th–31st).   Feast of Madonna del Carmine, Trastevere district.

Shopping

Rome has several fine shopping streets, and quite a few areas famed for one specialty or another. Here are the best.

Italian fashion and good taste.   Via Condotti and Via Frattina, leading from foot of Spanish Steps.

International fashion and taste.   Via Veneto, Via Sistina, Via del Corso.

Antiques.   Via del Babuino and Via dei Coronari.

Old books and prints.   Piazza Borghese.

Open-air markets.   Porto Portese on Sunday mornings.

The "befana" witch brings toys to good children

Also called Festa di noantri

New books in English. Economy Book Store, Piazza di Spagna, or Lion Bookshop, Via del Babuino.

Museums and Galleries

★★★★★   MUSEI E GALLERIE PONTIFICIE—VATICAN MUSEUM
Viale Vaticano, tel. 698–3333. The largest collection in Rome, one of the largest in the world, the Vatican Museums are a series of rooms that contain, among other things, a tapestry gallery, a collection of religious contemporary art, a medal collection, a Christian epigraph collection, an Egyptian museum, a museum of religious sculpture (old and new), an Etruscan museum, a museum of profane sculpture, an ethnological missionary museum, a gallery of Italian painting from the Byzantine period to the 18th century, various smaller collections and the Sistine Chapel. The summer schedule, from July 1st to September 30th, is as follows: 9 A.M.–4 P.M. from Monday to Friday, 9 A.M.–1 P.M. Saturday. Closed Sunday, except for the last Sunday of the month, with free admission 9 A.M.–1 P.M. The admission price L.2,500. A child that measure less than 1 m. pays half-price. The winter schedule from October 1st to June 30th is 9 A.M.–1 P.M., Monday through Saturday; Sundays as in summer. The museums are closed January 1st and 6th, February 11th, March 19th, Easter Sunday and Monday, Ascension and Corpus Domini, May 1st, June 29th, August 15th and 16th, December 8th, 25th and 26th.

You can choose from 4 routes, which take from 2 hours up to all day

★★★★   MUSEO E GALLERIA BORGHESE
Villa Borghese, via Pinciana, tel. 858577. One of the most important 17th-century Roman collections; represents the good taste and ambition of the Borghese family. Unfortunately, it was looted during the Napoleonic period, but some of Bernini's best statues are still there, such as his *Apollo and Daphne* and *David*. Closed Mondays, open 9 A.M.–2 P.M. Tuesdays to Saturdays, 9 A.M.–1 P.M. Sundays. Admission is L.1000.

★★★   GABINETTO NAZIONALE DELLE STAMPE
Via della Lungara 230, Villa della Farnesina, tel. 654–0565. A collection of about 20,000 drawings and 150,000 prints, ranging from the 15th to 20th centuries. Laboratories for the analysis of paper and inks, using microbiological techniques. Ample darkroom facilities, restoration experts and equipment, a large archive. The Villa is managed by the Lincei Academy. When there are shows, the winter schedule is 9 A.M.–1 P.M.; Thursdays and Saturdays 9 A.M. –5 P.M. In summer, open daily from 9 A.M.–1 P.M. Free admission. For consultation of the archive, the schedule is 9 A.M. to 1 P.M. Tuesday to Saturday.

★★   GALLERIA NAZIONALE D'ARTE MODERNA
Viale delle Belle Arti 131, tel. 802751. This collection, which started in 1915 with the intention of documenting the modern art movements in united Italy, probably gives the best overall picture of the history of 19th- and 20th-century Italian art. The gallery also has conferences, films and art documentaries. There is a photo library and a specialized library with 40,000 volumes. Closed Mondays. Tuesday to Friday open 9 A.M.–7 P.M. with shows and gallery 2 P.M.–7 P.M. Saturday and Sunday open 9 A.M. to 1:30 P.M. for shows

and gallery. Admission is L.750. Free first and third Saturdays and second and fourth Sundays of the month.

★★   GALLERIA NAZIONALE DI ARTE ANTICA

Palazzo Barberini, via 4 Fontane 13, tel. 475–4591; Palazzo Corsini, via della Lungara 10, tel. 654–2323. This gallery comprises several ancient art collections, distributed in two locations. There are also laboratories for restoration, carpentry, libraries and archives. The works of art are from the 13th to the 18th centuries. *Palazzo Barberini:* Closed Mondays. Open weekdays 9 A.M. –2 P.M., holidays 9 A.M.–1 P.M. Admission is L.750. *Palazzo Corsini:* Closed Mondays. Open Tuesdays and Thursdays 9 A.M.–7 P.M.; Wednesdays, Fridays and Saturdays 9 A.M.–1:30 P.M.; Sundays 9 A.M.–1 P.M. Admission is L.500.

★★   MUSEO NAZIONALE MILITARE E D'ARTE DI CASTEL SANT'ANGELO

Lungotevere Castello 1, tel. 655036. A collection of offensive and defensive weapons, from antiquity to the 19th century. Also uniforms and momentos of the various Italian armies before unification. Since this castle was also a papal residence, there are paintings by famous artists in the papal apartments. Ticket L.1,000; open 9 A.M.–1 P.M. weekdays; 9 A.M.–12 noon holidays; closed Mondays.

★★   CATACOMBE DI S. SEBASTIANO

Via Appia Antica 132, tel. 7887035. This museum can be seen by special permission from the Pontificia Commissione di Archeologia Sacra, via Napoleone III, tel. 735824. The catacombs can be visited everyday except Thursday, from 8:30 A.M.–12 noon and from 2:30 P.M.–5 P.M.; admission is L.1,000.

★★   MUSEI CAPITOLINI E PÍNACOTECA

Piazza del Campidoglio 1, tel. 6782862. This collection was started in 1471, with a donation by Pope Sixtus IV of statues from the Lateran Palace. Since then these museums have had a varied history. At the end of the 18th century the popes began to give their preference to the Vatican collections, and a little later the French took many valuable pieces to Paris. Still, this is one of the foremost museums of ancient art, especially Greek, Roman and Roman copies of Greek. Closed Mondays; open Tuesdays to Saturdays 9 A.M.–1:30 P.M.; Sundays 9 A.M.–1 P.M.; Tuesday and Thursday also open 5 to 8 P.M.; Saturday also open 8:30 A.M.–11 P.M. Admission is L.400; Saturday evening L.500; Sundays free.

★   MUSEO BARRACCO DI SCULTURA ANTICA

Corso Vittorio Emanuele II 168, tel. 6540848. A particularly fine collection of ancient Greek plus other ancient sculptures. Closed Mondays; open Tuesday to Sundays 9 A.M.–2 P.M.; Tuesdays and Thursdays also 5–8 P.M. Admission is L.500.

★   MUSEO DI ROMA

Palazzo Braschi, Piazza S.Pantaleo 10, tel. 655880. At the back of Piazza Navona, a collection of several thousand items that document the changes of Roma in the last two centuries. Open everyday except Mondays from 9

A.M.–1:30 P.M., on Tuesdays and Thursdays also from 5 to 7:30 P.M. Admission L.200.

★   MUSEO NAZIONALE ETRUSCO DI VILLA GIULIA
Piazzale di Villa Giulia 9, tel. 3601951. Pre-Roman material of central Italy well cataloged and well subdivided. A large library (6500 volumes) of books on etruscology. Ticket L.500. Open 9 A.M.–1 P.M. weekdays; 9 A.M.–2 P.M. holidays; closed Mondays.

★   GALLERIA SPADA
Piazza Capo di Ferro 3, tel. 6561158. A minor 17th-century collection that has the advantage of being almost complete and in its original site. But its importance lies in the charming baroque architecture of the building itself. Closed Mondays; opened Tuesdays to Saturdays, 9 A.M.–2 P.M.; Sundays, 9 A.M.–1 P.M. Free for those under 20 and over 60; free first and third Saturday of the month and second and fourth Sunday of the month; otherwise admission L.500.

MUSEO DI PALAZZO VENEZIA
Piazza Venezia 3, tel. 6798865. The museum is meant for the decorative arts, such as Italian ceramics, arazzi, wooden sculptures. The building, however, is as interesting as the collections, for it was built for the Venetian ambassador to Roma, was later used by the French, then by the Austrians and finally by Mussolini. At present, large parts of the palace are in the process of being restored. Closed Mondays, Sundays and holidays; open Tuesdays to Saturdays 9 A.M.–1:30 P.M. Admission L.1,000; free for those under 20 or over 60. Free admission first and third Saturdays and second and fourth Sundays of each month.

Tours

One way to see Rome is to take a guided tour. For a first visit this is probably the best approach, considering the size of the city and the vast amount of things to see. You'll leave with an overall impression of having learned a lot about Rome.

There are many good tours to choose from: the American Express, its old offices now redone in three striking colors, is still at Piazza di Spagna 38, tel. 6764. United States citizens feel very much at home here. Their mail can be forwarded to the American Express address, and all employees will try to be helpful. Then there is C.I.T., the Italian Tourist Company, one of the oldest operating in Rome, at Piazza della Repubblica 64, tel. 4751052/4750298, and several private organizations, all equipped with new motorcoaches. One of the newest is the Green Line Tours (GLT) located at Via Farini 5A, tel. 4751480/4744857. There are also the older Carrani Tours, at Via V.E. Orlando 95, tel. 4742501; Appian Tours, at Via Veneto 84, tel. 464151; or Vastours SRL, at Via Piemonte 134, tel. 4754309/6799697. The accompanying guides on all of these are multilingual and well versed in local history and lore. The American Express guide speaks English only, which more than doubles the amount of information you get and justifies the higher cost.

Your hotel desk will arrange everything if you wish. As of this writing the prices run from $10 to $12 (U.S. money) for a half-day tour, plus extras such as admission fees to museums, snacks, tips.

The itineraries on these tours are pretty standard. These first two listed are one-day tours, four hours in the morning and four in the afternoon. They show you the major highlights—what you might call a minitour of Rome.

Tour 1 or American Express (AE) C.   Villa Borghese and Gallery, Quirinale, Fontana di Trevi, Piazza Venezia, Pantheon, St. Peter's and Vatican.

Tour 2 or AE Tour B.   Roman Forum, Colosseum, S.Pietro in Vincoli (with Michelangelo's Moses), S. Paolo Fuori le Mura, Campidoglio and Piazza Venezia.

The next two are half-day tours that show you some important art and a panoramic trip on an ancient road.

Tour 3 or AE Tour A.   Piazza di Spagna, Piazza del Popolo, Vatican Museums and Galleries, with Raffaello's rooms and Sistine Chapel.

Tour 4.   S. Maria Maggiore, S. Giovanni in Laterano, Catacombs and Via Appia Antica (AE Tour D, with some variations).

Other tours take you to Tivoli, by day and by night. These are advisable only when the weather is good since they take you out of town to visit the lovely Villa d'Este, with its terraced Italian garden and its multitude of fountains. There are special Wednesday morning tours that go to the Papal Audiences; others go to Castelgandolfo, the Pope's summer residence in the Alban Hills. You can see Rome by night, with or without nightclub. Or you can go out of town by organized tour. There is a very good buy for a two day tour, including food, transportation and overnight stay at a Sorrento hotel. The itinerary is Rome–Napoli (Naples)–Pompei–Sorrento–Capri–Napoli–Rome, and the price is about $100 (U.S.), as of this writing. Unfortunately, part of the Pompei excavations were closed after the November 1980 earthquake, but there is enough left to satisfy most tourists, and the trip to Capri is a delight.

From May 1 to October 31st several other bus tours are available from Rome. They vary in itinerary and duration (usually either three or five days), and they touch the cities of Assisi, Perugia, Siena, Firenze, Pisa, Bologna, Ravenna and Venezia. As a rule the accommodations are good, the food mediocre, and there is lots of sightseeing. Prices vary, but tend to be reasonable.

Information

Several places provide information to the English-speaking tourist, such as the Italian Tourist Office (ENIT), at Via Marghera 2, tel. 491646 or the Provincial Tourist Office, at Via Parigi 5, tel. 463748. Information about the Vatican can be obtained by calling 698–4866 and 698–4466. For anyone coming to Rome on pilgrimage, there is an organization called *Peregrinatio Romana,* at Via della Conciliazione 10, tel. 654–0912, that will provide food and lodging at very reasonable prices.

Catholic pilgrims will, of course, consult home town church officials about papal audiences, etc.

Sports

Spectator sports abound, starting with horse racing at the Piazza di Siena track near the Villa Borghese, where an international horse show is held in April and May. Other horse tracks include Le Capanelle, Tor di Valle and Tor di Quinto. You can watch soccer nine months of the year at the Olympic Stadium or the Foro Italico. Polo may be watched, if you can wangle an invitation, at the Rome Polo Club, Via dell'Acqua Acetosa.

Golfers are probably better off playing rounds at a resort, but if you must play in Rome, try Circolo del Gold di Roma, Via Appia Nuova, near Santa Acqua. Tennis enthusiasts should ask their hotel concierges to recommend a club with visiting privileges. Ditto for swimming. And *don't* go into the water at Ostia.

Getting Around

It's easy to walk around the most important parts of Rome, but if you are in a hurry, by all means take the relatively inexpensive taxi cabs. There is a rate card (with English translation) in each cab, and you'll note there are extra charges for night trips, luggage, ordering by phone, and so on. You'll find cabs at taxi ranks; they can't be hailed just anywhere.

The subway (Metro) is fine, but it only runs to limited areas from the Termini Station (see map). Bus service is fine except in the rush hours, and you'll have to, at least, read the ATAC bus directory carefully before you jump aboard. (Director is available at ATAC booth in front of Termini Station.) Bus stops are marked "Fermata." You board the bus at the rear, purchase your ticket (or drop a coin in a machine) and leave by the front door.

For a touch of romance, book a horse-drawn carriage for a ride through the park surrounding the Villa Borghese.

Catch your carrozza and its driver at the top of the Via Veneto

Directory

Churches and Synagogue

Rome seems to be a city of churches, and you may want to know where English-speaking services are held. Catholic: Santa Susanna, Piazza di San Bernardo. (Don't forget that confessions in English can be heard in St. Peter's itself.) Protestant: St. Paul's Within the Walls, Via Napoli (Episcopal). Synagogue: 5 Via San Francecso Desales.

Embassies

American: 119 Via Veneto. British: 80A Via XX Settembre. Canadian: Via G.B. De Rossi.

Hairdressers

EVE OF ROME
Via Vittorio Veneto 116, tel. 485858. Centrally located and expensive; efficient; English spoken by some. Facials, manicures, pedicures, hair.

SERGIO VALENTE
Via Condotti 11, tel. 6791268. Magnificent building and decor. Does all the fashion models in Rome, some famous movie stars and so on. Expensive.

SERGIO RUSSO
Piazza Mignanelli 25, tel. 6781110. Charming and talented, Mr. Russo likes to cut hair and does it well. All other esthetic cures available.

OBERDAN
Via Frattina 126, tel. 6790292. Central location, a very Roman touch, moderately expensive.

MARIO AL PANTHEON
Piazza della Rotonda, tel. 6561257 and 6561984. Competent and quick, centrally located, moderate prices.

Northern or European Italy

Each Italian region has characteristics of its own, and grouping them is not simple. The seven regions that represent our idea of northern Italy have one thing in common: they each have a border or frontier with one or two other European countries. Thus, Liguria borders on France, Piemonte (Piedmont) on Switzerland, the Vale d'Aosta on Switzerland and France, Lombardia (Lombardy) on Switzerland; the Trentino-Alto Adige has a large fron-tier with Austria and a small one with Switzerland; the Veneto touches Austria at its very north; and Friuli-Venezia-Giulia borders on Austria and Yugoslavia.

Language, mentality, eating habits, even music, are influenced and molded by the neighboring country, and these regions are psychologically closer to the rest of Europe than the balance of the peninsula.

Northern Italy contains some of the country's most beautiful scenery. The major lakes are here—Lago di Como, Lago di Gerda, Lago Maggiore; the Alps are here, with their famous passes into Switzerland, Austria and France; the Ligurian Riviera is here, with the well-known resorts of San Remo, Rapallo, Portofino; and the Venetian lagoon is here, with its magnificent islands and the jewel of the Adriatic, Venezia (Venice). There are also the Dolomites, the Po River Valley and the splendid cities of the area.

Northern Italy is also the most industrialized part of the country. The progress of industry and technology is its most important element, and a rising middle class has made its votes count here more than anywhere else in the country.

In addition, tourism represents a large portion of the local income; agriculture is present and prosperous; and there are still some craftsmen to be found.

Milano (Milan) is the undisputed capital of northern Italy, and the most important city in the country after Rome. A short history of the city later in this section will help you understand the area. This history with those of Rome, Firenze (Florence) and Venezia will provide a foundation for the

Northern Italy contains well over half the country's population

interpretation of the Italian mind, as well as the country's culture and way of life.

Many delightful half-day, full-day, weekend, or longer trips can be taken in northern Italy. Unable to describe them all, we have eliminated many of the Alpine itineraries—mountain lovers will find these in specialized books; have listed only two lake trips; and have not dwelled on the Riviera, even though it represents one of the loveliest spots in the world.

We do focus on the splendid towns of this area and on the less well-known excursions that can be taken from some of these towns. We have listed many lovely monuments, including villas, castles, churches, palaces and squares, and the interesting museums that are scattered throughout the region.

PIEMONTE AND VALLE D'AOSTA

Piemonte, the largest region in territorial Italy, occupies the northwestern part of the country. Together with the small special statute region of *Valle d'Aosta,* Piemonte is the most alpine of Italian regions. The name itself says it: "pie" means "foot" and "monte" is self-explanatory.

Geographically, this region is extremely varied. Its northeastern corner is lake country, with several small lakes plus the western shore of *Lago Maggiore*. The south of Piemonte borders on *Liguria,* a narrow strip of land filled with lovely beaches and seaside resorts. And the center of the region are hills and plains; it is the beginning of the fertile Po Valley and is very suitable for agriculture. In fact, Piemonte is one of the best wine-producing areas in the country; all wine lovers have tasted (or heard of) Barolo, Barbera, Dolcetto and Nebbiolo. Another staple grown here is rice, which is a basic part of Piemontese cooking. And the city of Alba produces one of the best white truffles in the world, its splendid aroma attracts gourmets from everywhere.

The Piemontese are a proud and sensible people and pragmatic in their approach to life. This is the region that gave Italy its royal family, the Savoia. In addition, the independence movement that started in 1848 and culminated in 1860 with a unified Italy had its political and diplomatic leadership from the Count of Cavour—Piemontese aristocrat and Italian patriot.

The combination of mountains and abundant water provides the region with reasonably inexpensive electricity. This fact and the character of its people, makes Piemonte one of the most industrialized areas in Italy. Together with its neighboring *Lombardia,* it forms the most active industrial complex of the country.

In the last 20 years *Torino,* the capital of Piemonte, has attracted a large part of the labor force that has been emigrating from the South. It is the same labor force that came to the United States in the late 19th and early 20th centuries and that emigrated to Germany and Switzerland in the early post-war years. Now the large factories that make most of the "made in Italy" cars plus the other factories of Torino and nearby cities absorb these transplanted families, and for the region it creates all the problems connected with such massive changes in the lives of people.

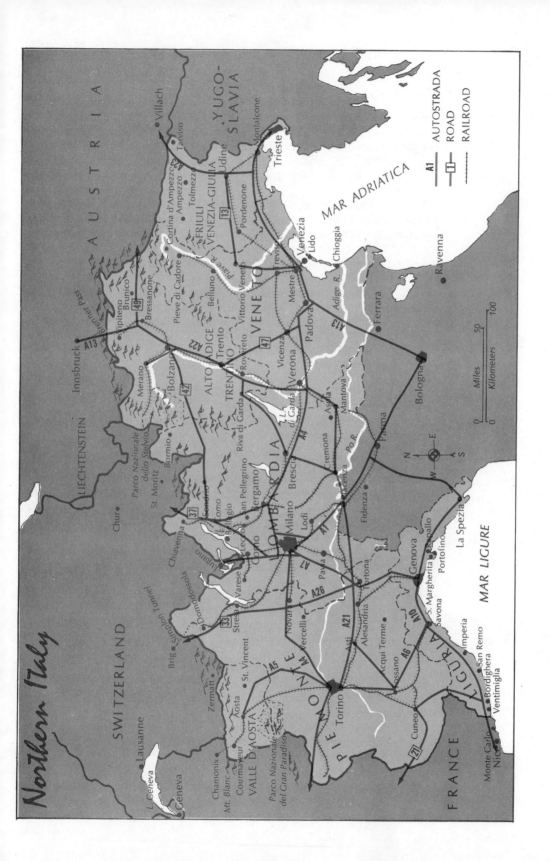

Northern Italy

Some History

Piemonte did not enter the mainstream of Roman history until the beginning of the Imperial Period. During the Middle Ages it was occupied by the Longobards and Franks, and its territory was divided into duchies and counties. As of the 10th century *Ivrea County* became important; it later subdivided into Ivrea and Torino and later still became a part of the Savoia domains.

During the free *comune* period, other areas of the region such as *Monferrato,* started to develop, but after the 15th century the history of Piemonte became identified with the history of the *Duchy of Savoia.* This family was involved in the supremacy wars that were being fought by France and Spain, but with Emanuele Filiberto and Carlo Emanuele I (1553–1630), it came into its own.

By 1743 the family of Savoia was ruling a state, and the whole region as we know it was a part of this state. After the short Napoleonic period, when Savoia was annexed into the French empire, it became the center of the political and military action that brought about the unification of Italy.

Some Thoughts On Art

Some Roman architecture can be seen in Piemonte, such as the *Porta Palatina* in Torino and the *Arco d'Augusto* at Susa, but the most important artistic manifestations in the region are either Romanesque–Gothic (11th–15th centuries) or Baroque (17th–19th centuries).

Bell towers and other structures done in Romanesque are scattered throughout the region, but there are few well-preserved, important remnants. The *Abbazia di Staffarda,* in the comune of Revello, province of *Cuneo,* is worthy of note as one of the most important Romanesque monuments in the area; the *Abbazia di Vezzolano,* in the comune of Albugnano, province of *Asti*, is an isolated monastery in southern Piemonte, built in the 11th century, with distinct Romanesque–Gothic influences.

At *Vercelli* look for the church of S. Andrea. Built between 1219 and 1227, it is one of the first examples of Gothic on the peninsula. The contrast in color—white, red and green—is unusual and striking. There are other Gothic structures in Piemonte at *Saluzzo, Chieri* and *Chivasso.*

Among the important structures to admire in Italy are the castles of *Valle D'Aosta.* Characteristic and multiturreted, these attractive structures dot the countryside. The most famous is *Fenis; Verres* and *Issogne* are also impressive and open to the public.

The Renaissance in Piemonte was felt mainly in the city of *Vercelli,* where a fine school of painting developed. It shows signs of the earlier contacts with the Longobards and is, therefore, somewhat different from the other styles of the time.

But the most important monuments in the region are in *Torino.* The Savoia family, in an attempt to give their capital a new look, invited numerous architects to work on a design for the city's urban improvement. As a result, Torino was embellished by many baroque additions, such as the Chapel of the Holy Shroud, at the cathedral, by Guarino Guarini, the *Palazzo Madama* by Filippo Iurvara, the *Basilica di Superga* by Iuvara and *S. Lorenzo* and the *Palazzo Carignano* by Guarini.

Torino

Torino can be easily reached by airplane, train or car, and while not a noted tourist center, it is certainly the center of one of the most important business areas in Italy.

Second largest city of the north (after Milano), this active and modern city is different from other Italian towns. It is the capital of the automobile industry and hub of one of the most important industrial systems of the country. From 1861 to 1865 Torino was united Italy's first capital. At present, it is still the first city of Piemonte. As we mentioned, it is the one that gave Italy the royal family, the *Savoia,* as well as today's industrial royalty, the *Agnelli*.

Torino, which was insignificant during the Middle Ages, became important after the 13th century when Savoia power solidified. Well located on the majestic Po River, the city's urban transformation began during the 17th and 18th centuries and reached its peak in the 19th century when it also became the center of political unrest. This is where the *Risorgimento* movement began, which led to the birth of the modern Italian state.

At present Torino is one of the largest immigration centers in the country; it is playfully called the third *southern* city of Italy because its workforce is composed mainly of transplanted Sicilians, Calabrians and Neapolitans. Its physical appearance is that of a noble 19th-century metropolis, with the old center surrounded by large squares and wide, straight, tree-lined avenues, creating a chessboard effect.

Any visit to Torino should begin around the area of *Piazza Reale* or *Piazza Castello,* where the most important monuments are. Begin by entering the *Duomo,* where the chapel of the *Sacred Syndone* is open daily from 7 A.M. to 12 noon and from 3 to 7 P.M.; holidays, mornings; closed Mondays. At piazza Castello is the most interesting building in town, *Palazzo Madama,* which by itself is a monument to the various styles the city contains. Its facade is baroque, done by Iuvara; the rest is medieval and partly incorporates an ancient Roman door. Within this large building is the *museo Civico di Arte Antica*, with interesting Piedmontese art from the Middle Ages to the early 19th century. Visiting hours are weekdays, 9 A.M.–7 P.M.; Sundays, 10 A.M.–6 P.M.; closed Mondays and holidays. *Palazzo Madama* also houses the *Armeria Reale,* one of Europe's best collections of arms and armour from the 16th to 19th centuries. There is a special room of Asiatic weapons that is particularly interesting. Visiting hours are weekdays, 9 A.M.–2 P.M.; holidays to 1 P.M.; closed Mondays.

The other building to visit is *Palazzo Reale,* a fine example of the luxury in furnishing and decoration that was popular from the 17th to 19th centuries. Note an interesting stairway, the *scala delle forbici,* leading from the first to the second floors; it was done by Iuvara. Still in the area, on piazza Reale, is the small church of *S. Lorenzo.* It was built by Guarini from 1668 to 1680 in the complex and busy baroque style that this talented architect favored.

Torino is a city of museums and galleries. Besides the two mentioned above there is a very good Egyptian museum, an excellent art gallery, *Galleria Sabauda,* a *Galleria D'Arte Moderna* and a *Museo d'Antichità.* There is also a *Museo dell' Automobile,* which documents the evolution and history of the automobile in Italy and the most important moments in the history of the

[handwritten margin notes:]
Agnelli, as in Fiat automobile

** Cathedral; the Santa Sindone (Holy Shroud) is very seldom on public display

* Palazzo Madama

* Museo Civico

** Royal Armory

* Royal Palace

* S. Lorenzo

**** Egyptian Museum

** Galleria Sabauda

automobile in the world. In this museum are the first Fiat (1899), "Itala," the car that won the famous Peking–Paris race in 1907 and many others.

For a refreshing break, visit the *Parco del Valentino,* a beautiful public park built in 1830. It contains a faithful copy of a Medieval castle and borough, as picturesque as the Valle d'Aosta originals. Or go shopping along *via Roma;* together with the parallel street *via Lagrange,* it forms Torino's elegant shopping area, full of boutiques and specialty shops.

For those with more time we suggest a walk along the wide and straight *via Po,* a street opened in 1675 to unite *Piazza Castello* to the large *Piazza Vittorio Veneto,* on the Po River. Off this street, along *via Montebello,* Torino's most characteristic landmark may be reached. The huge *Mole Antonelliana* was built in the 19th century, and from the top, reached by elevator, an ample terrace allows a nice view of the city. This building can be visited from 10 A.M. to 12 noon and from 2:30 to 7:30 P.M. and again from 9 to 11 P.M. in summer; from 8:30 A.M. to 12 noon and from 3 to 5 P.M. in winter.

For those who stay in Torino an extra day we suggest a visit to splendid *Basilica di Superga,* only 6 miles away; you can go by car, bus or small local train. From the tall hill (about 2,000 feet) there is a vast square with a view of the Alps, the plain and the city of Torino. The church itself was built by Iuvara in 1731; he used a neoclassical style that vies with many Renaissance buildings for balance and beauty. Another lovely Iuvara building is the *villa Reale di Stupinigi,* the hunting lodge of Vittorio Amedeo II, a frivolous rococo creation; one of the few in Italy. Stupinigi is also close to Torino, and can be reached by car or bus in about 15 minutes.

All of Italy offers lovely panoramic trips, and the Piemonte–Valle d'Aosta region is no exception. The major attractions of the region are twofold. On the one hand, are its splendid mountains and skiing facilities; on the other is the gastronomic appeal of its two fertile plains, *Langhe* and *Monferrato,* where the cities of *Alba* and *Asti* are the stages for fairs and shows of fine truffles and great wines.

For once, it is relatively easy to divide our weekend itineraries by season. We suggest a trip to *Lago Maggiore* in summer, one through the *Valle d'Aosta* or *Sestriere* in winter, a tour of the charming *Monferrato* in spring (equally nice in the fall, when *Asti* has its wine fair and *Moncalvo* its truffle fair), and a gastronomic tour in October through the magnificent Langhe, with a stop at *Alba* for the best truffle fair in Italy (first and second Sundays of the month).

Lago Maggiore

Lago Maggiore, one of Italy's loveliest lakes, has its northern tip in Switzerland and its eastern shore on Longobard territory. It can be reached from Milano in about 2 hours. The Piemonte side is reached from Torino by train or car. If you're driving, take the highway to *Novara,* then on to *Arona, Belgirate* and *Stresa;* return by way of *Monte Mottarone* and another lake, *lago d'Orta.*

Novara is at the far eastern border of Piemonte, and has many Lombard characteristics, but its architecture is primarily Piemontese. It has a cathedral done in 1869 by Antonelli in a style that can best be defined late neoclassical. The city on the whole is modern and active, with an energetic population and

[handwritten margin notes:]
* Mole = lit. pile, or huge structure. This was intended to be a synagogue, originally

*** Basilica of Superga

** Royal Villa of Stupinigi

Asti and Monferrato both produce great, dry red Barbera wine

** Novara Cathedral

** Baptistery

a prosperous economy. A short drive will bring you to *Arona,* a lakeside resort that has all the characteristics of its kind. You can take long walks along the water or a boat ride on *lago Maggiore* to other cities such as *Stresa* and *Locarno* (Switzerland). There is a colossal statue of S. Carlo and several 15th-century buildings. From Arona follow the lake in a northerly direction; head for Stresa, the best-known and most elegant city on the lake. Here the *Lungolago* is very attractive, lined with trees, hotels and luxurious villas and with a view of the *Borromeo Islands,* a group of three charming little isles that should be seen. *Isola Bella* is the most famous; it is occupied almost entirely by *Palazzo Borromeo,* a 17th-century residence of the well-known family that gave Milano two bishops and a saint. *Isola dei Pescatori* is, as the name implies, a fisherman's village, and *Isola Madre* is the largest and is occupied by another family palace and a splendid *Botanical Garden.*

*** Isola Bella

* Isola dei Pescatori

*** Isola Madre

Overlooking Stresa is *Monte Mottarone;* its marvelous view of the Alps and lakes attracts crowds of tourists. Go down on the other side and reach the city of *Orta,* on a lake that bears the same name. The little town is picturesque, with characteristic buildings dating back to the 11th and 12th centuries, the interesting *Palazzo della Comunità,* built in 1582, with a ground floor that is all arches and porticoes.

Valle d'Aosta and Monte Bianco—Skiing and Medieval Castles

From Torino a comfortable highway goes all the way to the city of *Aosta,* capital of the region that bears the same name. The drive will take you past *Ivrea,* a prosperous town that was originally Roman, then Medieval, and is now headquarters of the Olivetti corporation, Italy's electronic giant. From here continue to *St. Vincent,* a fashionable spa that has excellent waters for the digestive system and an active casino. It's the best place to visit castles *Verrès, Issogne,* picturesque *Ussel* and *Fènis,* the most spectacular fortress of the area, all within a few miles of St. Vincent. There are others, such as the attractive ruins of *Cly* or the 14th-century *Quart,* each with its own fascinating history. *Fènis* can be visited everyday except Tuesday, from 9:30 A.M. to 12 noon and from 2 to 5:30 P.M. It was begun during the 13th century by the Challant family and was used, like most Alpine castles, both as living quarters and as fortress. Its pentagon shape has been much copied, probably as a symbol of military strength and impregnability.

** Fènis Castle

Continue your trip on the highway to *Aosta* or, if you have time and love beautiful mountains, turn off toward the *Valtournenche* and *Breuil-Cervinia.* The drive is spectacular, and the famous *Cervino* (Matterhorn) will be your guiding light most of the way. It is a pyramid that rises over 12,000 feet.

Aosta is a famous city, with its history greatly influenced by its geography. It lies at the intersection between two Alpine landmarks—the *Monte Bianco* and *Gran San Bernardo.* The latter leads into Switzerland, the former into France, and both of these passes are busy with heavy traffic now as always.

The St. Bernard Pass is better known than the Mont Blanc route

Aosta has Roman monuments of great artistic value, such as the *Arch of Augustus,* erected 25 B.C., the date of the city's foundation. There is also a Roman Theater and a 1st-century door, *Porta Pretoria.* The medieval period is represented by *S. Orso,* a very old church and cloister with a charming priory attached later.

** Arch of Augustus

If you wish to ski, Aosta is only a quick stopover on the way to *Cour-mayeur*, one of the oldest and most famous skiing resorts in Italy. Here you can ski both winter and summer. There are two excellent establishments that are fully equipped to suit the most demanding skier. The area is also attractive to mountain climbers, not only because of impressive *Mont Blanc*, the highest Alpine peak, but for the many other surrounding climbs.

If you prefer excursions for scenic viewing, the area offers several cable cars that go to various peaks, including one that crosses Mont Blanc and goes to *Chamonix* in France. That crossing can also be made by car, driving through Monte Bianco tunnel opened in 1965; it is the longest in the world, about 6 miles (11.6 km).

*** View from cable car to Chamonix

Sestriere

Sestriere, one of the most modern best equipped ski resorts in Europe, is only a short drive west of Torino. Here you will find several good hotels and many excellent ski trails, with 25 comfortable ski lifts and cable cars, plus every other kind of equipment necessary for a pleasant and active winter vacation.

Le Langhe and Italy's noblest wines

Le Langhe is a double pleasure for wine lovers—lovely scenery and marvelous wine. It is enjoyable at any time of the year, and is especially perfect in September and October, when grapes are ripe and wine making is in the air.

The administrative and political center of this region is *Alba*, a city southeast of Torino, known for truffles and steeped in a pleasant 19th-century atmosphere. The wine-lovers' center will be two small communities, *La Morra* and *Grinzane Cavour*. But the trip begins at *Bra*, easily reached from *Torino*; take the *Autostrada* to *Carmagnola*, then continue on a smaller road, passing *Sommariva di Bosco*, to Bra.

At Bra, there is a charming baroque church, *S. Andrea*, and an attractive Gothic building *casa Traversa*. As you drive down to *La Morra* enjoy the neatness and simplicity of the surrounding country, which is almost Tuscan in its sobriety. At La Morra the view is lovely, and the greatest wine in Italy, *Barolo*, is made on the neighboring hills. *Nebbiolo*, the grape that is used to make the wine, probably comes from the oldest vineyard in the area. We find the grape mentioned in 1512 documents of the city council by its Latin name, *Nebiolium*. This grape is cultivated in the area around La Morra. The production of Barolo is limited to 81,000 tons per year, therefore, Barolo is not an overly abundant wine. Its deep red color and rich taste is responsible for its reputation: "a strong wine for strong men," ideal for roasts, game and strong cheese.

* S. Andrea

From La Morra go to the castle of *Grinzane Cavour*, where one of the richest wine collections in Italy can be admired. Only a few miles separate you from Alba, where a few modern hotels and a very good motel offer comfortable sleeping facilities.

** Grinzane Cavour castle

The other great wines of the area are Barbaresco, Dolcetto and Barbera. *Barbaresco*, is even rarer than Barolo; only 32,000 tons of grape are allowed per year. This is a slightly lighter red wine, elegant and discreet and loved by wine connoisseurs. It is made with the same Nebbiolo grape used for Barolo.

Dolcetto is produced in larger quantities from a hardy grape. It's a fragrant, fruity wine that is dry and lively. It's suited for pasta, fowl, cold cuts and cheese. The last one we'll list is *Barbera,* an extremely popular wine made almost everywhere in the area as well as in Lombardia. A bright, cheerful red and slightly bitter wine, it is suitable to drink with fried foods, boiled meats and hard cheeses.

This itinerary can be extended to include side trips to *Diano d'Alba, Serralunga d'Alba* and *Bossolasco,* all within wine-producing country.

LOMBARDIA

The central region of Northern Italy is not only the most densely populated (372 inhabitants per square kilometer, as opposed to 178 in Piemonte and 234 in Veneto), but also the most industrialized, richest region in the country. Its capital, *Milano,* is the most important city in Italy after Roma. All of its other provinces are well known, attractive and bustling with activity: *Pavia, Bergamo, Mantova, Cremona, Como, Varese, Brescia* and *Sondrio* are cities as full of history and art as they are of energetic people.

Lombardia is large; it ranks fourth in area, after Sicila, Sardegna and Piemonte. But in none of the other three regions is every square meter used to best advantage as it is here.

Lombardia is also very beautiful. It lies under the Alps and has the loveliest lakes. Its agriculture is the most modern and probably the most varied in Italy producing fruit, rice, corn, wine, grain and milk.

Favored by its central geographic position and with Milano as a natural magnet, this region is also the commercial center of the country. It is the area with the largest concentration of banks and where the subsidiaries of the large international corporations have their headquarters.

Lago Maggiore sits on its western border separating Lombardia from Piemonte, and *Lago di Garda* is on the eastern side. Lombardia's frontier with Veneto, *Lago di Como,* however, is the jewel of the region. It nestles under the Alps, just north of Milano and is the playground of the rich Milanese as well as the target of tourists from within as well as from without the country.

There are other attractions as well: villas and castles are scattered in the hills; winter sports are enjoyed in the Valtellina; and there is splendid art in Bergamo, Pavia, Mantova and Cremona.

Milano is one of the cities to see in Italy for shopping, for opera (the La Scala season opens on December 7th and offers some of the world's best), for sightseeing and for good food.

Industries are everywhere and cover every human activity: There is steel and mechanics, furniture and leather, textiles, chemicals and most of the important printing establishments.

While Campania (with Napoli) has the same population density as Lombardia, the latter is certainly the busier of the two, in fact, it is the busiest in the whole country.

Some History

The history of Lombardia is closely tied to the history of Milano, and both are tied to the history of northern Italy. When Emperor Augustus brought the frontiers of the Roman Empire to the Alps in 42 B.C., Lombardia became Rome's "Eleventh Region." During the 2nd century, when Rome was prospering under the Flavian rule, Milano acquired new buildings and baths and became a center of academic activity. During the anarchic 3rd century Milano was devastated by the *Alamanni,* a Germanic tribe that came through the Alps.

Other tribes continued to pour down the mountain passes, so Milano became an important strategic point. In the winter of 288–289 Diocletian and Maximinian met there in order to improve the defensive organization of the crumbling empire. It was the beginning of division, and Milano became the capital of the Western Empire, with Maximinian at the head of its political and military apparatus. He surrounded the city with impressive walls and built majestic baths and other structures.

For over a century (from 289 to 402) Milano was also the administrative center of the Western Empire, and the ups and downs of the newly born church were part of its life. During the years of the converted Emperor *Constantine,* Milano got its *basilica.* It also found itself at the center of the Arian heresy, and for 20 years it had an Arian bishop.

At the death of the Arian bishop in 374, a Roman consul took over religious power. *Aurelio Ambrogio,* a man both wise and just, was ordained bishop on December 7th, a date the city honors to this day. During the next few years the city was at the center of religious conflict: the Catholics and their bishop on one side, Empress Giustina and her Arian court on the other. Finally, in 386 the bishop got the upper hand. A Catholic king, *Teodosio,* had become sole master of the Italian peninsula. The doctrine so clearly expressed by Ambrogio became Milano's faith, and Ambrogio became its patron saint. But the centuries that followed brought changes, both for Italy and for Milano.

With the deaths of Teodosio and Ambrogio, the city's position deteriorated. New barbarian invasions came from the north, and the Western Empire moved its capital to Ravenna in 404. It was easier to defend and easier to reach from Constantinople, where Roman greatness continued, albeit with a new name: *Byzantium.*

Teodorico, a wise Goth, gave the country a few years of peace. In the first decades of the 6th century Milano once again became a center of intense intellectual activity. Unfortunately, *Giustinian,* the great Byzantine emperor, tried to regain the peninsula, and the Gothic War caused death and ruin for the northern provinces. Milano was put under siege and surrendered, and its citizens were massacred. The period that followed was not a happy one, with high taxes, famine and disease. But then an invasion changed the map of Italy.

The *Longobards* came into the country in 568. With this invasion the long and narrow peninsula, which had been unified by the Romans into a land with one language, one law and one administrative system, became divided into two parts, and this division lasted for over 1,000 years.

The immediate results were that while the bishop of Milano and the surviving nobles went to Genova, still a Byzantine possession, the Longobards settled in Pavia, where they established their court. At first they were pagan; when they finally became Christian, they embraced the Arian heresy.

The next centuries were marred by a series of wars that involved the then-settled Longobards, the Byzantines and, new on the scene, the *Franks.*

[handwritten margin note: Maximinian (Maximinus), later Emperor, began life as a shepherd]

There were occasional periods of peace, when the region continued to be a place of commerce and religion and Milano a city of scholarship.

The capital remained Pavia, which is the city that Charlemagne besieged and finally took in 774. The Franks were acting as the pope's strong arm, and the supremacy of the Church was re-established. It was an intelligent friendship. The Carolingian relationship with its bishops provided safe allies who looked after the king's interests in his absence. And the desire for renewal that characterized this period was positive for Milano, with the founding of a monastery dedicated to S. Ambrogio and a renewal of commercial and artistic activity.

In spite of the skirmishes that marred the Middle Ages, the region continued to grow and expand. The 10th and 11th centuries brought a new urban design for Milano, and many new buildings were added. These centuries also witnessed the growth of a conflict that eventually involved the whole peninsula.

Since the early centuries of Catholicism and the strong personality of S. Ambrogio, Milano had a tradition for "political" bishops who were the unofficial rulers of the city. This tradition brought about conflicts that led to the formation of two parties and to a civil war. This civil war led to greater conflict between the papacy and the emperor, with its first champions Pope Gregory VII and Emperor Henry IV.

The first round was won by the church, and the Gregorian reform prevailed. After many storms the pendulum swung back to a more disciplined approach, and 50,000 Longobards left with their bishops and went on the first Crusade. Much later, in the 19th century, this episode was beautifully put to music by Giuseppe Verdi.

Meanwhile, here as in the rest of Italy, free citizens united and formed associations that elected its members in order to administer their city. This was the beginning of the *comune,* an institution that still prevails, although somewhat adjusted to modern society. A coat of arms was created at the time of the first Crusade, similar to many others throughout the country. It showed a red cross on a white field; where red stands for the nobles and white for the common people. This color combination, also interpreted as red/Empire and white/Church, is still present in many Italian flags, shields and escutcheons.

The next champion of the empire that involved Lombardia was Frederick the First. He descended into Italy in 1154, and with the help of several other northern cities took Milano in 1158. The fighting lasted for many years. Milano's allies were the cities of Bergamo, Brescia, Cremona and Mantova; its enemies were Lodi, Como and Pavia. The Lombard League finally defeated the red-bearded emperor at *Legnano* on May 29th, 1176. This date is significant because it meant the end of the feudal era. After the peace of Costanza (1183) Milano, once again, began to thrive. The *Naviglio Grande* was built in 1179, an amazing achievement for its time. It brought water from the Ticino River into the city and helped irrigate the countryside. The growth of Milano in the early 13th century was so swift that it was difficult to govern. Wars between towns were still rampant, and the Guelf and Ghibelline conflict continued even after the last emperor, *Frederick II,* died in 1250.

The *comuni* made way for the *signorie,* and Milano was no exception. The archbishop elected in 1262, *Ottone Visconti,* was well within the city's tradition. More soldier than priest, he entered the city after a victorious battle

[handwritten margin note:] The parties were Guelphs, loyal to the popes, and Ghibellines, favoring imperial rule

[handwritten margin note:] Verdi's opera, I Lombardi, first staged in 1843

[handwritten margin note:] Frederick, also known as Barbarossa

[handwritten margin note:] Signorie = lords

Vipera = viper

Sforza, "the strong," rose from peasant boy to Duke of Milan

against the then signori and established a ruling house that held power well into the 15th century. The *vipera* of their coat of arms can still be seen on many Milanese buildings. The Visconti, interested in improving their city, left it with paved street, lovely churches and the first striking clock in Italy. One of them donated a mountain of white marble to the *Fabbrica del Duomo.* Most of the white marble used to repair the Cathedral still comes from this cave, which is on the western side of Lago Maggiore.

But the Visconti were an aggressive family, and eventually Firenze and Venezia, united against them and defeated them. When the last Visconti died in 1447 leaving no heirs, his captain, *Francesco Sforza,* became the new signori. This family held power for a period that coincided with the splendor of the Renaissance, and under their influence Milano got some of its loveliest buildings and works of art.

Lodovico il Moro made the city into a meeting place for the greatest names in architecture and art, such as *Bramante* and *Leonardo.* At the time of his rule *Castello Sforzesco* housed about 800 persons, all of whom served the duke: secretaries, treasurers, historians, scientists, astrologists, servants. The court was magnificent and luxurious, sparkling with jewels worn by lovely ladies and handsome gentlemen and richly decorated with velvets, embroideries, inlaid furniture, statues and paintings.

Such wealth and splendor was bound to attract attention. Louis XII of Orleans, the new king of France, was a nephew of Valentina Visconti, and on this pretext declared himself Duke of Milano in 1499 and descended into Italy. The castles of Milano were emptied and great carloads of precious art and jewelry were sent to France. The French took a fabulous collection of handwritten books from Pavia.

During the 16th century, Europe was dominated by the long conflict between Francis I of France and Charles V of Spain, Holy Roman Emperor. Most of this war was fought on Lombard soil; the Spanish army were the victors in Pavia on February 24th, 1525. The Sforza family regained Milano, but in reality the city remained under Spanish rule, a situation that lasted for almost 200 years.

The Spanish governors encouraged the traditional crafts and commerce and kept the city quiet. New defenses were built, enclosing more acreage and greenery, but two terrible plagues (in 1576 and 1629–1632) reduced Milano to only a few souls and marked the Spanish occupation as one of the sadder periods of its history.

The war of Spanish succession opened the 18th century, with the Austrians favored by the Milanese aristocracy. After years of struggle, the Austrians became firmly established and a long and stable period began for the great northern center of Italy.

But before the end of the 18th century *Napoleon* entered Milano, and on May 26th, 1805, after several attempts at forming an Italian Republic, the great Corsican was crowned King of Italy in the Duomo.

Napoleon's reforms were substantial, but for Lombardia they meant heavy taxes and 20,000 Italian young men for the French armies. Still, this moment marks a rebirth of Italy's military history.

After Napoleon's defeat, the Italians hoped for an independent state. Instead they became a part of the Austrian Empire. The kingdom of Lombardia and Veneto was only fiction; northern Italy was still a colony.

This period coincided with industrial progress and technical growth. The first Italian railroad, *Milano–Monza,* was inaugurated in the summer of 1840. Five years later gas lighting was brought to the streets of Milano. Times were ripe for change; and political activity, which had been secret and clandestine, began to come out into the open. Pope Pius IX was elected in 1846; Toscana's Granduke introduced new legislation; Milanese patriots demonstrated against the Austrians; and the patient diplomacy of the Count of Cavour, helped by French Emperor Napoleon III, finally brought about the creation of the kingdom of Italy. The year was 1859.

At this point the city of Milano had 250,000 inhabitants. The new nation needed goods, and Milano's textile industry, as well as its glassworks, iron mills and mechanical factories grew. The city's energies were infinite, and it provided the struggling new state with intelligent and hard-working citizens. All of this has earned for Milano the title *moral capital* of Italy, and for Lombardia its economic supremacy.

Some Thoughts On Art

There are few remnants of Roman civilization in Lombardia, the most conspicuous can be found in Milano, Brescia and Sirmione. But the region has been active and creative as far back as the early Middle Ages, especially where building is concerned, and the style known as Romanesque can be said to originate here.

The Longobard builders, intent on covering their houses adequately, devised the massive and compact structures that were then finished off with a low vault. The system was devised around the 8th century, and continued evolving until the 12th century, becoming more and more complex and spreading into the rest of the country and across the Alps. Many remarkable buildings in this style can be admired in Milano, Pavia, Como, Cremona, Brescia and other large cities, as well as in smaller centers such as S. Pietro a Civate, S. Vincenzo a Galliano, S. Tommaso ad Almenno and S. Salvatore.

Even though the Gothic style was present in most of Europe and Italy from the 13th to 15th centuries, Lombardia still built Romanesque structures. The addition of acute arches, however, allowed for a lighter appearance. The one notable exception was Milano's great *Duomo.* This complex church drew its inspiration from northern European models.

Renaissance architecture in Lombardia accepted the Tuscan models with some reluctance, and turned them into decorative channels rather than structures as such. The taste for lively color and picturesque appearance can be admired in the *Certosa di Pavia* or *Cappella Colleoni* in Bergamo. Other Renaissance art can be seen in Mantova and Milano; it always done by artists from other regions.

Lombard painting was influenced by the great Venetian painters, as well as by Leonardo. Only *Brescia* developed a school of its own, with *Savoldo, Moretto* and *Romanino.*

Towards the end of the 16th century *manierism,* encouraged by both cardinals *Borromeo,* became the dominant style, both in painting and architecture; it lasted well into the 17th century.

At the beginning of the 19th century neoclassical architecture added some remarkable buildings to Milano and provided that city's urban structure.

Milano

[handwritten margin note: Linate is closer to town, but transatlantic planes use Malpensa]

You can arrive in Lombardia by plane; flights go directly to Milano's two airports, *Malpensa* or *Linate.* Milano, the second busiest area in Italy, has daily flights to all large European cities and many U.S. and Asian ones. Train connections, either from other Italian cities or from abroad, are also excellent, and highways connect the large center to every corner of Italy.

The most European of Italian cities, Milano has always been a crossroads of commercial traffic, the "middle land" of Italy's greatest valley. Founded about 400 B.C. by Celtic tribes that came down through the Alpine passes, it owes its name to these ancient pioneers, who called it *Midlàn,* later Latinized to *Mediolanum.*

In spite of its centuries of history and great monuments, Milano has a basically modern appearance. Its urban structure is that of a wheel with many spokes, with *Piazza del Duomo* at the center. The central area includes famous *Galleria Vittorio Emanuele* and the various streets that go off from there, such as *Via A. Manzoni, Via Dante* and *Corso Vittorio Emanuele,* which becomes *Corso Venezia.* Within this area there is the exclusive *Via Monte Napoleone,* off *Piazza San Babila,* one of the fanciest shopping streets in the world. Advice to women who enjoy fashion: If you have only one day in Milano, take a walk up and down this street. You'll see next year's styles in jewelry, shoes, handbags and clothes. Enjoy a day of exciting window shopping and perhaps even real shopping.

Aside from *Via Monte Napo* there are other shopping streets in Milano, including the *galleria,* famous department store *Rinascente* and *Piazza San Babila.* Without detracting from the charm and elegance of Roma's *via Condotti* or Firenze's *via Tornabuoni* and *Palazzo Pitti,* Milano is undoubtedly *the* fashion center of Italy and vies with Paris for European priority.

[handwritten margin note: ★★★★ Milan Cathedral]

During your visit to the city, there is no question that the *Duomo* is the one monument you should see. It is not only Milano's most important, but also Italy's biggest and most complex, Gothic structure. Unlike the linear and elegant Italian Gothic of Toscana and Umbria, this is northern Gothic with vertical lines and a multitude of needles all pointing to the sky. Documents tell us that it was started in 1386 under Gian Galeazzo Visconti from drawings by an unknown architect. In order to appreciate the grandiosity of this church, take a short walk to nearby *Piazza del Palazzo Reale* and look at it from there. Your eye will take in the huge marble mass, the infinite pillars and the 135 needles, with the highest one crowned by a statue, the *Madonnina,* considered the city's symbol and protectress. Other statues decorate the sides and pinnacles; there are a total of 2,245. The facade, the big church's least interesting part, was finished off in a mixture of baroque and Gothic that is not harmonious. Do not overlook the back with its transept and polygonal apse enlightened by three huge windows.

The five 16th-century portals have modern bronze doors, each telling a different story. Beginning at the left, the first one tells of Constantine's Edict, the second of the life of S. Ambrogio, the third and central one of the life of Mary, the fourth the story of the city of Milano and the last one, installed only a few years ago and done by one of Italy's foremost sculptors, *Minguzzi,* tells the story of the Duomo itself.

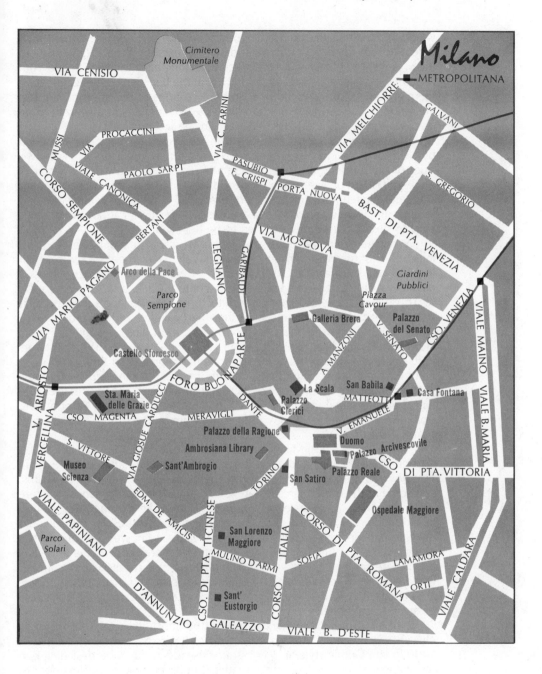

The large interior is divided into five naves, with colossal pillars acting as curtains and continuing the vertical feeling of the whole. But as in every Gothic church, the lion's share of beauty goes to the splendid stained glass windows covering the area that goes from one pillar to the other, each different from the next and done in different years from the 15th century to the present. The oldest and most precious, dating back to the 15th and 16th centuries, are along the two naves that are at the beginning of the Latin cross; there are some 16th-century ones in the two arms of the transept; the rest are modern. The World War II bombings destroyed many of these very large glass windows, and they were changed in the last 35 years.

The terraces of the Duomo are worthy of attention. They can be reached by elevator or by climbing 166 steps. The entrance is outside, from the two sides of the transept. It is open in summer, 8:30 A.M.–5 or 6 P.M., winter, 9 A.M.– 4 P.M.. Not only is there a very good view of the city and of the Lombard plain and Alps, but the terraces themselves, full of unbelievable needles and statues, almost a jungle of frills and furbelows, create an atmosphere that is hard to describe and must be seen to be believed.

**
Galleria

***
La Scala and its museum

While in the area, also visit the *Piazza Mercanti,* one of the last remaining corners of medieval Milano. Note the lovely *Palazzo della Ragione,* built in 1233 and used as the City Hall up to 1770. Also in the area, almost a passageway to *Piazza della Scala,* is 19th-century *Galleria Vittorio Emanuele II.* This fine example of Victorian architecture is also Milano's most popular spot, full of *caffès,* restaurants, bookshops, art galleries and fancy boutiques. At the other end is the *Scala*, one of opera's most illustrious temples, built along neoclassical lines by Piermarini in 1788. It holds about 3,000 spectators in its six levels and for many generations has represented the best starting point for a promising singer. Next door to the theater is the *Museo Teatrale,* with an important collection of objects and souvenirs of the theater itself and lyrical art in general. It can be visited in winter from 9 A.M. to 12 noon and from 2 to 6 P.M. and from May to October from 9:30 A.M. to 12:30 P.M. and from 2:30 to 6 P.M..

***
Castello Sforzesco – Michelangelo's last sculpture, the Rondini Pietà, is here

Like all large cities, Milano can be seen in one day or in one year. Good shopping, good eating and good theater are permanent attractions that can be enjoyed during all times of the year. There are several important museums, and some of the most interesting are located in a large Renaissance structure worth admiring—the *Castello Sforzesco.* Built on an existing 14th-century base, this impressive castle was the residence and fortress of the splendid dukes of Milano, and reminds us of their wealth and power. As we now see it, the square structure is a valid restoration of the original, and the museums it holds are among the best in Italy. The *pinacoteca* (art gallery) has paintings by *Mantegna, Filippo Lippi, Correggio, Tintoretto* and many others. There are important Egyptian furnishings and ceramic sections and a rich collection of musical instruments.

****
Pinacoteca di Brera

****
Da Vinci's Last Supper

***
Sant'Ambrogio

Not far from the castle is one of the most important Renaissance churches in Milano—*S. Maria delle Grazie.* It was built between 1466 and 1490 in late Gothic style; in 1492 Bramante added the apse, designing it in the shape of a large cube and decorating it in his elegant style. Next door to the church is *Leonardo's* famous *Last Supper,* done between 1495 and 1497, on the wall of the Dominican convent dining room. Another Milano landmark, the lovely church of *S. Ambrogio,* is not far from either the castle or S. Maria delle Grazie. Just off *via Carducci* and next to the *Università Cattolica,* S. Ambrogio is the most important medieval church in town, with a 9th-century apse. *S. Lorenzo Maggiore,* on *corso di Porta Ticinese,* is the most important monument to testify Milano's early Christian vocation. The original goes back to the late 4th–early 5th centuries, with much redone in the 16th century. Inside, entering on the right, the *Cappella di S. Aquilino* is intact as it was done in the 4th century. Another interesting church is *S. Satiro,* on *via Torino.* Unlike the previous one, this a Renaissance jewel, done by Bramante in 1478. *S. Eustorgio* is another Medieval church worthy of note; it contains masterpieces of painting and sculpture that go from the 11th to 15th centuries.

San Satiro

San Satiro baptistery

Sant'Eustorgio

But Milano is primarily a modern city, with theaters, museums, restaurants and good shopping facilities. You can choose from many art galleries from the *Pinacoteca di Brera* to *Museo Poldi-Pezzoli* or the *Galleria d'Arte Moderna.* There are other museums, but for most visitors Milano is a city for shopping, for business or for the great *Fiera Campionaria.* The fair is held every year from April 14th to 23rd in a huge area specifically designed to allow as many products and as many visitors as possible. Other shows are held here during the year, but the Fiera Campionaria is the most diversified, most interesting and largest.

Modern Art Gallery

Through Monza to Como

If you have 1 day to spare and desire to escape Milano and the big city, a visit to charming *Como* is our first suggestion. The drive will take you through *Brianza,* one of the softest, mildest, most delightful areas in Lombardia.

Just a few miles north of Milano, the city of *Monza* and its famous park. The attractive Gothic cathedral in the city holds the *Iron Crown,* used throughout the Middle Ages to crown the many "kings of Italy" and in 1805 to crown Napoleon. Legend has it that it was made from one of the nails used to hold together Christ's cross.

Monza Cathedral

The other Monza attraction is *Villa Reale,* a group of neoclassical buildings designed for Archduke Ferdinand of Austria in 1777 and later a favorite residence of Napoleon's stepson Eugene Beauharnais. The park behind, added in 1806, is a vast green area, part wooded, part cultivated, crisscrossed by avenues and streets, dotted with cottages and stables, with two golf courses and the famous *Autodromo,* a racing course for automobiles and motorcycles.

Villa Reale

From Monza proceed to *Carate Brianza, Inverigo, Alzate Brianza* and *Cantù.* The whole area produces excellent furniture and is dotted with attractive 18th-century villas. Cantù is especially interesting because of *Galliano,* where an 11th-century basilica, *S. Vincenzo,* contains a splendid group of *affreschi.*

S. Vincenzo and its frescoes

After Galliano head directly for *Como* and the lake. The city is lively and beautifully situated, with the lake at one end and the green mountain of Brunate as a backdrop. Do not miss the center of town with its elegant cathedral, one of the most significant Renaissance churches in Lombardia. *Broletto,* is the old city hall built in 1215 in Romanesque–Gothic. For those interested in Lombardia Romanesque there is an 11th-century basilica, *S. Abbondio,* which some consider a masterpiece. But a visit to Como means a walk along the lake, a glass of wine in one of the outdoor *caffès* or a boatride. And remember that much of the world's silk is made here.

Como Cathedral

Sant'Abbondio

Pavia

Just south of Milano is the interesting city of *Pavia* and the large and famous *Certosa di Pavia.* A visit to both is pleasant and relaxing. Take the *Autostrada* out of Milano; at *Binasco* turn onto state road 35 (SS 35) to the Certosa and proceed on that road to Pavia.

Take your time visiting the great Certosa di Pavia, one of the Lombard Renaissance masterpieces. Founded in 1396 by Gian Galeazzo Visconti, it was meant to be his family mausoleum. The large structure was finished in several stages: by 1452 the monastery was done, from 1462 to 1464 the cloisters followed, and finally in 1473 the church itself was completed. The rich facade, an excellent work by Mantegazza and Amadeo, was added from 1473 to 1499. To the left of the main building is a small baroque building, the *Foresteria,* now used as a souvenir shop. The interior of the church, divided into three naves with pillars, is an example of the transition between Gothic and Renaissance design. Both sides are lined with chapels. Note the second left with a splendid *Perugino* and the sixth left with S. Ambrogio and other saints painted by *Bergognone.* On the right, the fourth and fifth chapels hold some lovely Bergognone paintings, and the transept on the left has his famous *affreschi.* Also noteworthy are two magnificent bronze candelabras by *Fontana* in front of the altar and the statues of Beatrice d'Este and Ludovico il Moro done by *Solari* in 1497, at the center of the nave. Visiting hours of the Certosa are in winter, 9–11:30 A.M. and 2:30–5 P.M., and from May to October, to 6 P.M. It's closed on Mondays, except when Monday is a holiday. The interior is visited in groups; if you come alone, there is a wait until a group is formed. You will be guided by a monk. There is no admission fee, but an offering is expected.

Leave the splendid Certosa and proceed to Pavia. This noble city was famous even in Roman times, and reached the peak of its power during the Lombard reign from the 6th to 8th centuries. It was a prosperous comune and in 1359 was taken by the Visconti and incorporated into the Duchy of Milan. Though not very large, it offers several splendid monuments of Romanesque and Renaissance art.

There is only one itinerary to follow in Pavia; it is on foot through the old center of town. Begin at the Ticino River, near *ponte coperto,* and take *via Diacono* to *S. Michele,* a Longobard basilica considered one of the best examples of Romanesque architecture in the region. Then take *corso Garibaldi,* turn left into *strada Nuova,* and go into the Renaissance *Duomo,* where great artists such as *Bramante* and *Leonardo* (among others) worked. Proceed along the same street, the city's main street, and go past the theater, the university (very old, made famous by the experiments of *Volta,* the physicist who gave his name to the *volt*) and other interesting buildings. At the end of the street is the city's largest building, *Castello Visconteo,* a grand square brick structure with towers at the front corners; it now contains several museums. To the left is a lovely church, *S. Pietro in Ciel d'Oro,* another Romanesque building of beautiful proportions, a smaller, more contained version of S. Michele. The big attraction here is a Gothic arch, placed over the main altar, containing the remains of *St. Augustine.* The bones were transferred from Ippona to Cagliari and from there to Pavia in the 8th century. The *Arca di S. Agostino* is a complex marble coffin, full of statues and other decoration, the achievement of several 14th-century Lombard artists who

*** Certosa, lit. = "charter house," of Pavia

Don't forget to taste the liqueur

*** San Michele

** Pavia Cathedral

* Castello Visconteo

** San Pietro

were influenced by Tuscan models. Furthermore, the crypt of this church holds a sarcophagus with the bones of *Severino Boezio,* the Roman philosopher and adviser to Teodorico, who had him killed for treason in 524.

Since this is one of the largest and most interesting regions in Italy, there are many possibilities for charming weekend trips, as well as for visits to splendid cities. Cremona, Mantova, Bergamo and Brescia are all interesting and important. It would be difficult to decide whether to take a refreshing trip into the *Val Camonica* or a trip to Mantova where art, history and good food are the order of the day. We'll tell you about both; the choice is yours.

Bergamo, Lago d'Iseo and the Val Camonica

The trip from Milano to Bergamo is about one hour on one of Italy's busiest highways. If you're in a hurry (otherwise this city is worth a trip by itself), go straight to *Bergamo Alta* for a look at *Piazza Vecchia* and *Piazza del Duomo.* Here, in one small area, are some of the most significant buildings in Lombardia, and you'll find a harmonious blending of Romanesque and Renaissance architecture that has few parallels in the whole peninsula.

The upper town of Bergamo is more interesting than the lower

Leave Bergamo and head northeast, along the banks of the river Serio. You'll pass the populated and busy centers of *Albino* and *Ponte Nossa* before reaching *Clusone,* a pleasant mountain resort. The scenery that will distinguish the next part of the trip begins here; there are charming mountain villages and lovely pine covered woods. From Clusone you will reach *Passo della Presolana,* which is over 3,900 feet high. The area is populated with skiiers in winter, and is a charming place for an excursion in the summer. It's located between two valleys. As you continue the scenery changes again and begins to resemble the Dolomites. From here you will reach *Dezzo;* go toward *Boario Terme* where good hotel accommodations are available. The short ride from Dezzo to Boario Terme is interesting but not very pleasant if you dislike mountain roads and narrow passes.

On the following day, drive to *Breno* and from there to *Capo di Ponte.* Here is the center of an area that has more than 40,000 primitive etchings on rock (graffiti). These fascinating findings represent a living testimony of the prehistoric culture that existed in these mountains. The etchings cover about 25 centuries of human adventures, from the Neolithic, through the Iron Age, up to the early Roman conquest, about 16 B.C. The most important drawing is the *Roccia di Naquane,* with about 900 figures, done mostly during the period when humans used iron weapons and utensils.

* Rock of Naquane

On the way back stop at Breno, located under the ruin of a Frankish castle. Continue on the east side of the Oglio River and pass *Darfo* and *Pisogne.* Here the scenery changes again since you've reached the lake. Curve around the top, head for *Lovere,* then go down the west bank to *Sarnico.* The trip is not easy; it's full of tunnels and curves but is worth the effort. Sarnico has an interesting old center; the *lago d'Iseo* is small but charming and contains *Monte Isola,* the largest lake island in Italy. From here take the highway back to Milano or, if you wish to continue your trip eastward, to Brescia, Verona and Venezia.

** Monte Isola is largest island in any Italian lake

Mantova

Located at the southeast corner of Lombardia, the medium-size town of

Mantova is called "a small Venezia" because the Mincio River surrounds it on three sides. *Mantova* is in fact a peninsula encircled by water on all sides but one.

When the great poet *Virgil* was born in nearby *Piétole*, in 70 B.C., Mantova was only a small rural center, but by the 12th century it had gained some importance, and in 1273 it was a *signoria* under the Bonacolsi family. In 1328 it passed to the Gonzaga family, and its political and economic importance grew. Thus the city has some splendid medieval and Renaissance monuments plus the quiet, earthy charm that comes from being located in the large Po Valley.

Mantova is an excellent stopover if you are driving west from Venezia or east to Venezia. Last but certainly not least, Mantova boasts an interesting gastronomy that began during the rich Renaissance period and has been influenced by the Longobards from the north and by the Emiliani from the south.

Begin your visit at *Piazza Mantegna,* which, along with its neighboring *Piazza della Erbe,* is the center of town. You will immediately note the harmonious *Basilica di S. Andrea,* a Renaissance masterpiece designed by a Florentine, L. B. Alberti, and built from 1472 to 1494; it was completed by a cupola designed by Iuvara in 1732. The façade has a classical appearance, almost a triumphal arch, followed by an arcade and crowned by a tympanum. On the left side is an elegant Gothic bell tower left over from 1413. The interior has the same classical proportions; there is one nave with transept and chapels alternating on the sides, some large, some smaller. The first chapel on the left holds the tomb of painter *Andrea Mantegna.*

Piazza delle Erbe is surrounded by medieval buildings. At the corner of Piazza Mantegna note a 15th-century house with *cotto* decorations. Then note the *Rotonda di S. Lorenzo,* a Romanesque structure that goes back to the 11th century. Its interior can be visited from 10 A.M. to 12 noon and from 4 to 6 P.M.

Continue on to *Piazza Sordello,* which was the old political and artistic center of this city and has maintained a medieval appearance. Off of it are the *Duomo* and splendid *Palazzo Ducale.* The cathedral is a composite— with Gothic parts on its right side, an 18th-century façade and a Romanesque bell tower. The interior the work of Giulio Romano (16th Century), is more balanced; its five naves separated by columns and arches give it a classical appearance.

The palace is one of the largest, most impressive structures of its kind in Europe. It is interesting for itself, as well as for the collections it houses. It can be visited weekdays, 9 A.M.–1 P.M.; holidays, 9 A.M.–2 P.M.; closed Mondays. A tour, with a guide, takes about one hour.

This palace, also known as the *Reggia dei Gonzaga,* has been restored in recent years. The two buildings that form the east side of Piazza Sordello are from the end of the 13th century; other parts were added later, century after century, until the 18th century. Note the *Appartamento degli Arazzi,* which contains nine tapestries done in Flanders from drawings by *Raffaello. Via S. Giorgio,* which runs from the palace to the river, also borders the *Castello di S. Giorgio,* a massive 14th-century fortress that is a part of the palace. From the bridge that runs off this street you can enjoy a lovely view of the city and of the two lakes it divides. Highlight here is the *Camera degli*

*** Mantua's Sant'Andrea

cotto = brick

* San Lorenzo

* Cathedral

*** Palazzo Ducale

*** Raphael's cartoons for these tapestries now hang in London's Victoria and Albert Museum

Sposi, which loosely translates as *Matrimonial Suite* and was decorated with frescoes by *Mantegna* in 1474. The paintings, which represent scenes from the lives of the Gonzaga, are superb.

At the other end of town is another Gonzaga residence, done in a style that may be called country Renaissance. Designed by Giulio Romano in 1525, the enchanting *Palazzo del Te* can be visited in winter, 9 A.M.–12:30 P.M. and 2–4 P.M.; in summer, 3–6:30 P.M.; holidays, 9 A.M.–1 P.M.; closed Mondays.

Palazzo del Te **✱✱**

Mantova, a city full of charming streets and interesting corners, is meant to be visited leisurely. At *Piazza d'Arco* you'll find one of the best restaurants in Italy, *Il Cigno,* where you will find a good meal and will discover a 16th-century building with an interesting ceiling.

Il Cigno restaurant **✱✱✱**

LIGURIA

At the top of Italy's western coast is *Liguria,* a small strip of land shaped like an arch that nestles between the Maritime Alps and the sea. Its capital, *Genova,* is a famous port; the rest of the region is also dominated by the sea, either for food and work or for beauty and pleasure. The contrast between green hills and blue sea, as well as a climate that usually gives dry sunny winters, makes part of Liguria's coast known as the *Italian Riviera,* one of the world's most famous seaside resort areas.

Economic activities in addition to those connected to the sea include industry and commerce and a very specialized agriculture, with some areas growing vegetables, other areas concentrating on flowers, and most areas producing wine.

Genova is the busiest Italian port, for it serves not only much of northern Italy but also Switzerland. In fact, it vies with Marseille for first port of the Mediterranean. Other sea towns of some importance are Savona—the city that gave French soap its name (*savon*) and La Spezia, one of Italy's most important military ports.

The flowers are used in manufacturing perfume

The Riviera is divided into *Riviera di Levante* (East Riviera) and *Riviera di Ponente* (West Riviera). Its most important city is San Remo, where lovely villas and fashionable hotels clinging to the hills are surrounded by lush vegetation and colorful flowers. The casino provides entertainment and sunshine warms the heart.

Some History

Ligurian history is similar to that of Lombardia. Inhabited by the tribe that gave the region its name, it became Roman during the 1st century; it then was taken over by the Longobards and later by the Franks. After the 11th century, Genova began to acquire naval power and attempted to colonize the whole area. The other cities resisted, but by the 14th century strength prevailed and Genova became the region's ruler. Still, there were difficulties, mainly wars with Venezia and Pisa and invasions by the French and Spanish. A great admiral, Andrea Doria, defeated the enemies of Genova and reestablished the republic (1528).

Liguria, invaded by Napoleon, was annexed by France, but with the Congress of Vienna it became part of Piemonte. During the period of planning and later of fighting for Italian national unity, this region was involved in the activities that preceded actual unification, largely as a result of the influence of men such as Mazzini and Garibaldi.

Some Thoughts On Art

There are few Roman ruins, but there is an interesting early Christian monument at Albenga, the 5th-century *Battistero*. The most active periods were the Romanesque–Gothic, from the 11th to 14th centuries, and the late 16th century of baroque. Medieval architecture was influenced by the Longobards, the French, the Byzantines and Pisa. Most interesting monuments of this period can be seen in Genova, Albenga, S. Fruttuoso di Portofino and Lavagna.

Early Renaissance sculpture is present in the chapel of S. Giovanni, inside the Genova cathedral. During the 16th century the capital became artistically independent, and the result can be admired to this day (see below).

Genova

The first itinerary of this region begins in Genova since this is the largest and most interesting city. We'll start from *Piazza S. Matteo,* the medieval part of town. The square is bordered by houses done in black and white stripes. They belonged to the Doria family, along with the Romanesque–Gothic church of *S. Matteo.* The church was started in 1125 and the striped front was added in 1278. The 16th-century inside is superimposed on the Gothic structure. The crypt holds the tomb of Andrea Doria, the greatest Genovese.

** San Matteo

A short walk takes you to the cathedral dedicated to *S. Lorenzo.* It's the most impressive medieval monument in the city; it was started in 1118 and finished after the 14th century. Here again the black and white marble stripes along with the three Gothic portals and the two towers create an unusual effect. The interior is solemn and severe. Note the *Cappella di S. Giovanni Battista,* with its very ornate front by Gaggini and the statues inside by Civitali and Sansovino. The altar, under a 16th-century *baldacchino,* is modern.

*** Genova's Cathedral

Walk down *via S. Lorenzo,* which goes to the port and cuts the old city in two. Look into the narrow little streets that are so typical of this part of town and known as *carugi.* Admire the large port, which can be visited by motor boat, leaving from the *Calata degli Zingari.* (For information about the ticket, call 265712.)

Genova is a city for walkers. Here the streets are as important as the monuments; the lovely buildings that line the impressive avenues are often just private homes and cannot be visited. From the port, walk down *via S. Luca,* turn at the church of *S. Siro* and you will reach *via Garibaldi.* Note the harmonious mingling of styles. The old church, Genova's first cathedral, was redone between 1586 and 1613. The front is neoclassical, the inside a good example of Genoese baroque. At the corner of *via S. Siro* and *via di Fossatello* is a lovely medieval palace with an impressive 16th-century portal.

* San Siro

Via Garibaldi is one of the most monumental streets in Italy. Designed in the 16th century, with both sides lined by impressive 16th- and 17th-century palaces, it gives an accurate idea of the city's wealth during that period. Note No. 11, the *Palazzo Bianco*, redone in 1712 along the lines of a style known as *barocchetto genovese*. At No. 18 is *Palazzo Rosso*, done in 1677 in baroque. Both of these palaces contain good picture galleries. Admission is free; hours are weekdays, 9 A.M.–8 P.M.; Sundays, 9 A.M.–12:30 P.M.; closed Mondays. The galleries offer a large number of very good paintings by local Italian and international painters.

The *Circonvallazione a Monte* is a different type of walk along the high part of town. At the end of *Corso U. Bassi* note *Castello d'Albertis,* surrounded by a large garden.

Behind the main railroad station is *Palazzo Doria,* a grandiose structure redone by the great admiral between 1529 and 1547. In front of the station is another important street, *via Balbi.* Following it you'll reach the largest church in Genova, *SS. Annunziata.* The original front was designed in 1522; the neoclassical front was added in 1893; and the present forms were done between 1591 and 1620. Unfortunately, it was damaged during the last war, but the baroque interior is characteristic of the Genoese taste of that period.

If you have extra time, visit the Romanesque church of *S. Donato,* and the simple but charming *S. Maria di Castello.*

[handwritten margin notes:]
★ Palazzo Bianco
★★ Palazzo Rosso, including the family Van Dyke
★ Palazzo Doria
★★ Santissima Annunziata

Sea, Sun and Sky

In addition to Genova, Liguria offers two very famous itineraries: the *Riviera di Ponente* or *dei Fiori,* which reaches the border of France and passes through some of the most famous Italian tourist attractions, and the *Riviera di Levante,* a shorter trip that includes *Portofino, S. Margherita* and *Rapallo.* A short side trip from *Albenga* into the Ligurian Alps is an interesting change.

Head west out of Genova by first taking the *Autostrada* and then leaving it at *Albenga* and continuing on the *via Aurelia.* Choose between Albenga or the next town, *Alassio.* We prefer Albenga, with its medieval monuments and better restaurants. Continue to *Imperia,* enjoying the winding coastline and crowded resorts. Pass this typical port and stop at *Taggia,* with its little group of 14th- and 15th-century houses. *San Remo* is your next stop, where there is much to see; the walk on *corso Imperatrice,* the *casino,* the old town at *Pigna.* This is a good place to spend the night; there are hotels for every taste and pocketbook. From here to the French border is a 30-minute drive passing *Ospedaletti, Bordighera* and *Ventimiglia.* Of these, Bordighera is the most interesting, but the whole area is full of flowers. For beautiful panoramas, follow the old *Aurelia* between Bordighera and Ventimiglia. After *Mortola* the road forks and the high one has a very good view of Menton (France). One last reminder: At *Mortola Inferiore* the *Hanbury Gardens* are a very special collection of plants and flowers.

East of Genova, on the way to Toscana and Roma, lies the other section of Liguria's Riviera. Although the area is to be avoided in summer, it is beautiful in spring and fall and splendid on sunny winter days. From *Nervi* take *via Aurelia* to *Recco,* then leave it and take the narrow, winding road to *Camogli* and *Ruta.* After a tunnel, you'll find yourself on the road that goes down to *S. Margherita;* when you reach it the charming Gulf of Tigullio will appear before your eyes. Enjoy this beautiful little town or drive a few more miles to *Portofino* or even further to *S. Fruttuoso.* This last part of the journey can also be made by boat, avoiding the crowded road and affording you good sea air. Go back to S. Margherita and on to *Rapallo,* the largest city of this area, albeit the least attractive. After Rapallo it is wise to get back on the via Aurelia in the direction of Chiavari, Lavagna and Sestri Levante. As you pass Lavagna, note the stone roofs and the slate grey stone that is everywhere. The word *lavagna* means *blackboard* in Italian, and this is where most of the dark stones for blackboards come from. Another interesting thing to observe as you drive is the vast assortment of styles in the architecture of houses and villas on this coast. Combinations of Mediterranean, medieval and art nouveau dot the hills, and the various pinks, yellows and blues shimmer gaily in the Ligurian sunshine.

The Gulf of La Spezia

The *Gulf of La Spezia* can be reached by driving north from Toscana or by coming over the *Cisa* pass from Milano. It can be also reached from the north by continuing the previous drive. The gulf is fairly large, with *Portovenere* on one side, *Lerici* on the other and the city and port of *La Spezia* in the center. If you come from the east or south, you will pass the city of *Sarzana* and head for Lerici. Here you will note the castle, and if you climb it the view will be rewarding. The gulf, also known as *Golfo dei Poeti,* was a favorite with Shelley and Byron. The latter, a formidable swimmer, stayed at Portovenere and took long swims across the gulf to Lerici. Shelley favored the small village of S. Terenzo. He met his tragic death while vacationing there is 1822; his sailboat overturned near Viareggio. From Lerici the drive to La Spezia is a short one, and here lovers of sea lore can visit one of the best naval museums in the world. An interesting, winding road takes you to *Portovenere,* another picturesque little Ligurian town with the island of *Palmaria* just beyond. From Portovenere a short boat ride takes you to the *Cinque Terre,* the five little towns that make the best wine in the area. *Riomaggiore* and *Manarola* are the largest of the five, but the whole area is really quite small, closely fitted between steep hills and sea and full of romantic corners, busy hotels and good restaurants. This area is a fitting and proper last place to be in this small and charming region.

[handwritten margin note: Shelley set sail on the fatal day from Lerici's Villa Magni]

TRENTINO-ALTO ADIGE

This double-named region occupies a part of the northeast corner of Italy, and its extensive borderline with Austria characterizes the outlook of its people and their language. It's an area that will attract you if you are interested in mountain climbing, hiking, and skiing or are coming from Austria.

Trento is the capital of the autonomous region, which sends the Italian parliament representatives that speak with a German accent and are voted in by a party called the *Sudtyroler Volks Partei.* The other important city is *Bolzano.* Both centers are charming, clean, active cities that provide the rest of Italy with excellent fruit, milk products and wood, plus wines that resemble the light, aromatic German ones.

The other important attraction of the region is represented by the *Dolomites,* a particular section of the eastern Alps known for its interesting irregular formations and splendid pink and red tones. These colors are a special effect created by the setting sun on the reddish rock, but the Dolomites are also interesting because of their fabulous pine forests and their magnificent valleys and lakes, alternating in such harmonious counterpoint that you are left breathless and enchanted. It is an unexpected corner of Italy, with abundant clean air and good food.

Some History

Both Trentino and Alto Adige were conquered by the Romans in the 1st century B.C. and later occupied by the Longobards. By the 11th century A.D. the local bishops become civil rulers, and Austrian nobles aspired to this northern portion of Italy. In 1803 this aspiration became reality, and for more than a century the area was part of Bavaria. With the end of the World War I the region was returned to Italy.

Some Thoughts On Art

The area has some Romanesque and much Gothic art, along with its own typical style that borrows from Austria, from Venezia, from the Longobards and from Bergamo. The Gothic goes well into the 15th century, then a late Renaissance produced some interesting baroque, both sumptuous and controlled. The most important artist of this region is *Michele Pacher,* a 15th-century painter–sculptor.

Trento

Noble looking and severe, *Trento* is the capital of the region and of its province. It lies, midst majestic mountains, on the banks of a wider portion of the Adige River, and its name brings to mind the famous council held by the Roman Catholic Church from 1545 to 1563, a last attempt at stopping the Lutheran Reformation. It also houses Italy's most modern and advanced university, with an active school of social studies.

The most interesting buildings in Trento are its *Duomo,* a 12th- and 13th-century church in Romanesque–Gothic with a 16th-century bell tower, and the *Castello del Buonconsiglio,* which housed the bishop–princes and is dominated by the medieval *Torre Grande.* This large structure contains multi-creneled *Castelvecchio,* done in the 13th century and modified in 1475 in a style that can be defined as Venetian–Gothic (note the attractive *loggia*). The castle is surrounded by walls that are interrupted by tower-shaped ramparts and houses the *Museo Provinciale d'Arte* and another museum dedicated to the *Risorgimento* (the movement that led to Italian unification). Visiting hours for both museums are in winter, 9 A.M.–12 noon and 2–4:30 P.M.; in summer, 2–6 P.M.; holidays, 2–5:30 P.M.; closed Mondays.

If you have time, take a walk along *Via Belenzani* and note the Renaissance palaces done in a Venetian style; some have frescoed exteriors. At the end of this street is *Piazza del Duomo,* surrounded by noble buildings and decorated with a lovely 18th-century fountain. Here are a few houses with external paintings, a charming characteristic of this northern town.

[handwritten margin notes:] *** "Alpine Glow" is seen only intermittently, a few minutes after sunset when there is haze between the viewer and the sun

** Trento Cathedral

*** Castelle

** Art museum

* Risorgimento museum

In Bolzano, star attractions are
*Dominican Church and
**Franciscan Monastery

*** Strada delle Dolomiti trip

Rifugio = mountain hut

*** View from Pordoi Pass

Bolzano and the Dolomites

Bolzano, basically a modern city and the capital of Alto Adige, is located at the meeting point of two rivers—the Adige and the Isarco—as well as at the imaginary meeting place of two cultures—Italian and German. Like Trento, *Bolzano* is an active city with a busy population and many tourists—the famous Brenner Pass, one of the best ways to cross the Alps, is only 12 miles away.

The most interesting trip you can take along the Dolomites begins at Bolzano and ends at *Cortina d'Ampezzo.* Only 70 miles of actual road, it can take anywhere from 3 to 6 hours, depending on the detours you make. We strongly recommend a chauffeur-driven car or bus so you can enjoy the scenery better and because the roads are winding and better driven by someone who knows them.

From Bolzano take the road that goes to *Ponte Nova,* and go past *Nova Levante* and *Carezza al Lago* to *Passo di Costalunga.* The small and very blue lake of Carezza is a lovely place to stop and admire the scenery; for those who love spectacular views, take the ski lift to *Rifugio Paolina.* Proceed to *Vigo di Fassa;* at *Pozza di Fassa* several side trips can take you, either by funicular or cable car, to *Buffaure* where more pretty panoramas can be enjoyed. For hardy souls with strong cars and even stronger legs we suggest a drive up the *Vaiolet* valley and a walk to the *Rifugio* of the same name. The reward is a view of the Dolomite mountain tops that you will never forget. There are ski lifts at *Campitello* or *Col Rodella* that will provide panoramas that are only slightly less spectacular and certainly worth admiring.

The trip continues to *Canazei,* where a new road to *Pian Trevisan* and *lago di Fedaia* can be taken. Here yet another cable car goes up and offers a view of the very heart of the *Marmolada* glacier. This is the very center of this splendid range, and for those who take the cable car at *Sass Pordoi* and reach the almost 7,000-foot-high *Passo Pordoi,* the reward is a view of unbelievable grandeur. If you forgo this daring ride you can continue your drive to *Arabba* and take a different cable car to *Porta Vescovo,* which is yet another balcony that looks out on the glacier of Marmolada. After Arabba the road goes around a valley, the *val Cordévole,* and from the road itself you can admire the lovely Dolomites and then go up again to the *Falzarego* pass, flanked by the vertical wall of *Lagazuoi* mountain. Then drive down to the foot of impressive *Tofane,* the mountains that serve as backdrop to the magnificent valley of *Cortina d'Ampezzo.* Before you reach Cortina stop at the charming wooded area of *Pocol,* where you can enjoy a view of the valley below.

Cortina, the most fashionable skiing resort in Italy, is popular both winter and summer, offering the beauty of its natural setting and the comfort of its many good and excellent hotels, restaurants and shops. The combination of Alps and social activity, of excellent skiing and fashionable *caffès,* render Cortina a unique town—the most popular and most populated resort of its kind in Italy.

Merano and Madonna di Campiglio

The region has two other resorts that cannot be overlooked; both are great favorites in their own way. *Merano,* almost on the Austrian border, is an elegant spa that draws crowds in spring and fall because its climate is unusually mild for its location and its radioactive waters cure many ills, from nervous disorders to rheumatic pains, from inflammations of the urinary tract to those of the respiratory apparatus. A city of lovely parks and pleasant promenades, Merano is popular with older people who enjoy the easy life and comfortable hotels of the Alpine pearl.

Madonna di Campiglio, closer to Trento and to the northern tip of *lago di Garda,* is an entirely different resort, catering to the young skiers and hikers who are always looking for new trails and challenges. The city itself is tiny; the local population is less than 1,000. But every winter sport and some others as well such as tennis, horseback riding and swimming are represented here. Mountain climbers can use this little town as a base for many interesting runs; the area is full of peaks that rise well over 6,000 feet. Less than 2 miles away is *Campo Carlo Magno,* where the famous emperor supposedly stopped on his way to Rome and his coronation in the year A.D. 800.

[handwritten margin note: Charlemagne became the first Holy Roman Emperor on Christmas Day; in St. Peter's]

VENETO

One of the most beautiful and best known regions of Italy, the *Veneto* is made up of two natural areas, each very different from the other. The first is a plain created by centuries of deposits from floods of many rivers. The plain culminates in the Adriatic Sea with a special lagoon and delta formation —the Po River delta. The other is a hill and mountain region, made up of pre-Alps and Alps, similar to nearby Trentino-Alto Adige and to the upper portions of Friuli-Venezia Giulia.

The delta region is undoubtedly the more interesting and varied area for it includes the splendid city of *Venezia* (Venice), that unique conglomerate of about 100 little islands separated by deep canals and united by many bridges, as well as lovely Verona, Padova and Treviso. Geologically, the area is of recent formation, with the present profile dating back anywhere between 3,000 and 5,000 B.C., when the level of the Adriatic became what it is today.

The region has a mixed economy, with both agriculture and industry well represented. Not only does it grow good corn and wheat—the local staple is *polenta,* which is made of corn flour—but it produces some of the best wines in Italy and Europe. Other products include fruit, sugar beets and tobacco. The industrial activities of Veneto are varied, going from textiles and knitwear—the famous *Missoni* clothes are made here—to shipbuilding and household appliances.

The population is pleasant, polite and industrious; they are very different from the hardy Longobards, the proud and somber Piedmontese, the suspicious and sarcastic Tuscans or the carefree, singing Neapolitans.

The region has given Italy many talented artists, some of its best musicians, excellent screen writers and actors and good politicians, as well as a gentle, charming approach to life that counterbalances a national tendency for the melodramatic.

From cultural and social points of view, the mountain area is closer to the other regions around it than is the plain area. The one exception is the eastern shore of the lovely *Lago di Garda,* which provides Veneto with a small but beautiful lakeside riviera. Up north, the fashionable winter resort of

Cortina d'Ampezzo attracts skiers in the winter and the fashionable people of Milano, Firenze, Torino and Bologna in the summer.

Some History

The early history Veneto is not important. Primitive settlers on the delta were unified under the Roman Empire, and the small cities were raised to the rank of "colony" in 89 B.C. With the barbarian invasions, the area deteriorated and from the 6th to 8th centuries there was a further separation from the peninsula proper as a result of the massive Longobard presence in the west and northwest. The lagoon area was then populated only by these invaders. But since the area could so easily be reached from the sea, the natural consequence was a connection with Constantinople and the Byzantines. Soon the settlers on the lagoon were no longer simply fishermen, but they began to transport materials and commodities to and from the eastern ports.

Thus, with the 6th-century Gothic War, ascent of the lagoon area began, which in turn led to the rise of Venezia. From a frontier Byzantine duchy Venezia became a sea state, a powerful *signoria* and, finally, the independent republic—*la Serenissima*.

Other cities followed a different pattern, and during the feudal period they become *ducati, marche* and, eventually, free *comuni*. Their history is similar to that of other Italian cities, with the communal period making way for small *signorie,* in some cases a throwback to the great noble families that controlled the area when the feudal system prevailed.

But Venetian power quickly reduced these small states to satellites, beginning with *Verona* in 1339, then *Padova* and finally the whole region, even *Friuli* to the east (in 1420). Even the Milanese Visconti were overthrown, and the unified territory was then ruled by the Venetian doges for four centuries. This illuminated government retained control in spite of local wars, hostility from several neighbors and strong coalitions that defied it.

With the upheaval of Europe that followed the Napoleonic Wars, the Venetian territory, together with Lombardia, became part of Austria. But the independence movement of 1848, felt here more than elsewhere, caused the region to declare itself an independent republic and, in 1866, to join the rest of Italy as part of the newly unified state.

From duchy to commune, to municipality, is a long political leap

Some Thoughts On Art

Unquestionably, the most outstanding structure left by ancient Rome in northern Italy is the *Arena of Verona.* During the Middle Ages the region was influenced by two very different cultures: the inland cities acquired Longobard tastes, while Venezia and the lagoon area were Byzantine. Thus, Verona's beautiful *S. Zeno* has a Longobard character, while Venezia's splendid *S. Marco* and other churches in the area favor Byzantine art and architecture.

The entire region was active and thriving during the 13th and 14th centuries, and many churches and palaces were built, most in a style that is a combination of Romanesque and Gothic. Meanwhile, Venezia was creating a Gothic style of its own, with a light and imaginative touch that rendered the colorful decorations as interesting as they were unique.

The 15th century brought the Tuscan influence to *Padova,* first with *Giotto* (who painted there in the previous century), then with *Donatello* and

Mantegna. But the overpowering presence of Venezia was felt, and all cities in its orbit became its artistic satellites.

Venetian painting, pervaded with poetic naturalism and based primarily on color, became the most important in the whole zone, and its architecture, even while adopting the Renaissance forms, retained the lightness and love of color that was present there in the Gothic period. The artistic splendor of Venezia came to full bloom in the 16th century. With *Sansovino* and *Palladio,* the classicism of the 16th century evolved into a splendid, luminous architecture that eventually influenced most of Europe. The paintings of *Giorgione, Tiziano, Veronese* and *Tintoretto* achieved a ripeness of form and an intensity of color that is still unmatched.

During the 17th century the visual arts came to a standstill in Venezia, with only some worthwhile architecture by *Longhena.* The 18th century, however, brought rebirth of the great tradition of color by painters such as *Canaletto* and *Tiepolo.*

Another Venetian contribution to the world of art was made in the late 16th and 17th centuries. The rich and pleasure-loving city attracted the best musicians, and Venetian baroque laid the basis for concert and symphonic music by bringing together instruments and voices.

Venezia

The splendid city of Venezia (Venice) has been described, illustrated and sung about by almost every writer, poet, painter and novelist during the past 400 years or more. It has been called a "museum of the imagination," "the most ethereal of cities," "pearl of the Adriatic" and, by no less an authority on the subject than Hemingway, "a tougher town than Cheyenne when you really know it."

[handwritten margin note: Well, Venice does have twice the population of Cheyenne!]

The 20th-century traveler comes to Venezia when it is no longer at its best; it's no longer powerful, no longer rich, no longer the commercial or political center of the area. Venezia is now mostly an artistic and cultural center that attracts millions of tourists and visitors with its unique charm, its magnificent buildings, its quiet beauty and its spellbinding allure.

For many centuries Venezia was the city that acted as a *trait d'union* between Europe and the eastern Mediterranean, and most of what we now see is a result of this situation. Art and architecture combine to remind us of both East and West, and this is why the city is like no other. The fact that it's formed by more than 100 islands united (or separated) by as many canals, with small bridges connecting the whole is, of course, another reason for uniqueness.

[handwritten margin note: Trait d'union = hyphen, lit.]

Venetian urban history began in the 9th century as a result of several factors. First, there was a large growth of commercial activity, with northern timber, iron, amber and slaves coming through the small port on their way to Constantinople. Second, the political situation changed on both sides, with the Moslems expanding in the East and Charlemagne and the Franks coming into Italy from the West. The newly rich merchants, feeling pressure from both left and right, had no choice but to unite and fight for their independence. One enterprising *doge* established Venetian supremacy by sending to Alexandria for the spoils of St. Mark. The apostle was believed to have preached in the area, and when his bones were brought back in 828, Venezia

[handwritten margin note: The thieves who stole St. Mark's bones hid them in pigskins, knowing that Moslem officials wouldn't touch them]

became one of Christianity's most important cities, even before it was fully built.

The city we see today took four centuries to build and another six to improve. As the strength, power and wealth of the *Serenissima* grew and stabilized, Venezia expanded and added islands, bridges and buildings to the original settlement and became the fabled city we see and admire.

Even the shortest visit to Venezia must begin at *Piazza S. Marco* and continue with a boat ride up the *Canal Grande.* Then, if you have more time you can take another boat ride around the lagoon and visit the islands of *Murano, Burano, San Michele* and *Torcello,* or you can stay closer to the center and visit the area around *Rialto* bridge, with its interesting little streets and *campi* (in Venezia the only *Piazza* is St. Mark's, all other squares are called *campo* or *campiello*).

S. Marco, considered by some the most beautiful piazza in the world, is paved in costly marble, enclosed by splendid buildings and inhabited by 1,000 pigeons. Without a doubt, the first building you'll notice will be the magnificent *Basilica,* different from all other churches, a triumph of Byzantine architecture and Venetian taste. The large church was built between the 9th and the 15th centuries to hold the remnants of St. Mark the Apostle, and the façade alone is worth a trip to Venezia. Five deep arches, the brilliant marble decoration, precious mosaics, columns and portals are all there as if to remind us that this was one of the most powerful cities in Europe.

Note the exquisite Byzantine bas-relief sculptures that decorate the spaces between one arch and another and the splendid bands that run over the main portal depicting the months, the virtues and the prophets. On the terrace that divides the two levels note the famous bronze horses (as of this writing three are being restored and only one is visible). They are supposedly the work of a Greek sculptor of the 4th or 3rd century B.C., brought over from Constantinople to decorate the center door. Within a short time identical copies will be installed, and the originals will be kept in the *Museo Marciano.*

The interior is a Greek cross, with three naves in each arm divided by rows of columns that sustain the galleries that were once meant for the women—the Oriental influence is clearly felt. Powerful arcades serve as bases for the five cupolas, but the general impression is that architecture and structure make way for decoration and detail, and most of you will probably be overwhelmed by the brilliance of gold mosaics, the light that filters through the windows and the intricate design of the 12th-century floor. The infinite mosaics that cover every corner of this basilica follow a complicated iconographic plan that can be understood only through lengthy studies of specialized texts. They are the work of Venetian and Byzantine artists of the 12th and 13th centuries. Some were damaged and redone later on the basis of drawings by famous artists such as Tiziano, Tintoretto and Veronese.

Behind the altar is a magnificent jewel of Venetian and Byzantine workmanship: the *Pala d'oro,* covered with enamels and precious stones. It was worked on from the 10th to 14th centuries. It can be visited weekdays, 9:30 A.M.–4:30 or 5:30 P.M.; on holidays, 2–4:30 P.M.

But Piazza S. Marco is more than the splendid church. Right next to the basilica is lovely *Palazzo Ducale,* built from 1309 to 1442 and considered the best example of Venetian Gothic. On the *piazzetta* are the two columns of S. Marco and Todaro; the *Libreria Marciana,* a Renaissance masterpiece,

[handwritten margin notes:]

Campo, etc. = field or camp, lit.

★★★★★ Basilica of San Marco

You enter the church under the arch of Paradise

★★ Museo Marciano adjoins the basilica

★★★★ Rear view of pala d'oro is best

★★★★ Doge's Palace

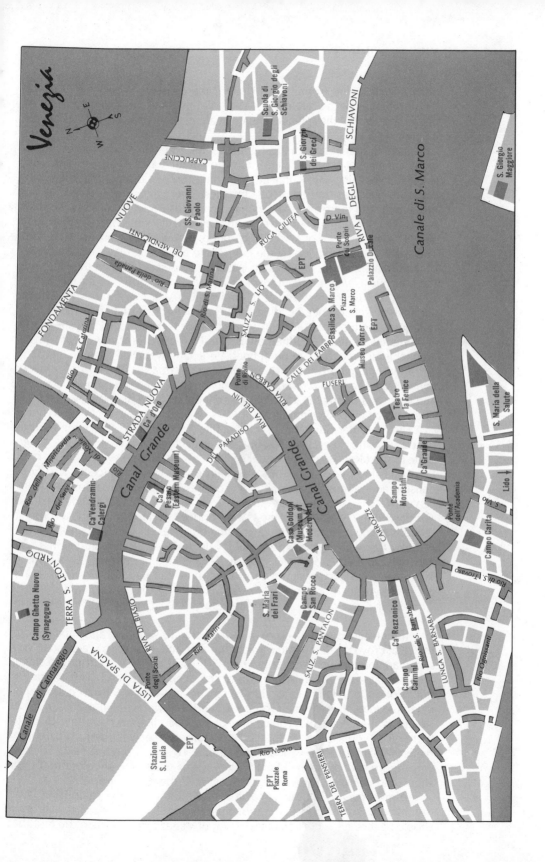

done by Sansovino from 1536 to 1588; the charming *Torre dell'Orologio* with its statues of the two moors. With all this there are also the masses of people that crowd the splendid square at almost every hour of the day almost 12 months a year.

From S. Marco turn to the *Canal Grande,* the widest and longest of the many canals that form the city. It has the double function of river and main street. Its two sides are connected by only three bridges and are lined by exquisite buildings and fabulous churches. The canal is almost 4 km. (2.5 miles) long and there are boats that go up and down with stops at important points. On the left (going upriver to the railroad station) note *S. Maria della Salute,* a masterpiece of Venetian baroque, built by Longhena from 1631 to 1681 with funds provided by the city senate because it was meant as a sign of thanksgiving for the ending of a pestilent epidemic. Also on the left, note the baroque *Gallerie dell' Accademia and Ca' Rezzonico* and the lovely Gothic *Ca' Foscari,* now site of the university. After the *Rialto* bridge there are several Renaissance buildings and, just before the station, another rich baroque structure, the *Ca' Pesaro,* which houses the modern art gallery and an Oriental museum. Further on is the *Fondaco dei Turchi,* built in an architectural style that can be defined Venetian–Byzantine, redone in 1869, and now occupied by the *Museo di Storia Naturale.* The word *fondaco* comes from the Arab *funduq,* which means emporium or commercial outlet and was used during the Middle Ages to indicate large deposits of merchandise with attached living quarters.

On the other side, coming back, after the *Canale di Cannareggio* (the next largest after Canal Grande), note the elegant *Palazzo Vendramin Calergi,* done in strict Renaissance, and once inhabited by Richard Wagner, who died there on February 13, 1883. A few canals down is the magnificent *Ca' d'Oro,* considered the most beautiful building on the canal, done in a flowery 15th-century Gothic. It now houses the *Galleria Franchetti.* You'll glide past the *Fondaco dei Tedeschi* and the *Rialto* bridge, which is one of the busiest sections in town. Some of the interesting buildings on your left will be large *Palazzo Grimani,* its three powerful levels designed by Sanmicheli in 1556 and *Palazzo Cornèr-Spinelli,* an early Renaissance masterpiece by Codussi. Then the canal curves, and a short time after you pass the *Ponte dell'Accademia* you can admire the *Prefettura* of Venezia, also called *Palazzo Cornèr* or *Ca' Grande,* a large three-story building done by Sansovino in 1537.

If time allows and if you're more addicted to shopping and mixing with the local crowd than to visiting great churches and museums, we suggest you spend an hour or two around the *Rialto.* The bridge itself is charming; a single arch contains three parallel stairways, the central one lined with shops on both sides. On the right hand side going upriver—on the S. Marco side and, in fact, leading to it—is the *Mercerie.* The Mercerie, with all of its little side streets, is the center of Venezia and of Venetian life, and strolling through them gives you a sense of the city's past and present, temper and people. Note the names of the various little streets. To mention but a few, *Spezia* was the street of spice merchants, *Orefici* was where the jewelers had their shops and *Narazeria* was once the center of the orange trade.

Almost every visitor to Venezia will take the trip to the main islands on the lagoon: San Michele, Murano, Burano and Torcello. And this is as it should be, because so much of the flavor of Venezia comes from the fact that

** Santa Maria della Salute
**** Accademia di Belle Arti
** Modern Art Gallery
Fondaco = lit.; "warehouse"
* Ca'd'Oro
Tedeschi = "German"
Prefectural headquarters, a modern term in an ancient building
Spezie = spice, orefice = jeweler and arància = orange

it lies on the lagoon. We suggest you take this little tour leisurely, with a possible stop at Torcello for lunch or in Murano for a visit to the Glass Works Museum—*Museo Vetrario.* Our favorite is the former, with its 7th-century cathedral that was redone in the 11th century. It has a powerful bell tower, lovely mosaics and a combination of classical (Romanesque) and Byzantine decorations that is as charming as any. Torcello is at the northern tip of the lagoon, about 10 km (6 miles) from Venezia. It was one of the first islands to be settled by the fleeing population, driven to the lagoon by the Barbarian invasions. It now has one enchanting little inn, the *Locanda Cipriani,* with a few rooms and a very good restaurant. It's the perfect place for a romantic weekend!

If you are fortunate enough to have a week or more in Venezia, there are many more things to see, places to visit, meals to enjoy. *S. Maria Gloriosa dei Frari,* a grandiose Gothic church, is one of the most important monuments in Venezia. The *Scuola di S. Rocco* is an impressive building decorated with large Tintorettos; nearby, the *S. Rocco* church has more Tintoretto paintings. On the other side of Venezia, visit *Campo SS. Giovanni e Paolo* and note the *Monumento al Colloni,* one of the best horse sculptures made during the Renaissance; it's the work of Florentine Andrea del Verrocchio who did the statue in 1488 and Leopardi who finished it by adding the elegant base in 1496. The church that gives the *campo* its name, *SS. Giovanni e Paolo,* also known as *S. Zanipòlo,* was built for the Dominican order. Begun in 1246 and completed almost 200 years later, it has Gothic lines and is filled with masterpieces. Not far from this large church is another, smaller one, *S. Maria dei Miracoli,* an early Renaissance jewel by Pietro Lombardo who built it from 1481 to 1489. It was meant to look like a precious box, symmetrical and compact, with its rounded front, marble decorations and lead roof all adding to this impression. A 19th-century commentator said it was "a Florentine thought that flowered on Venetian soil."

Venezia is a city of art and beauty, and there is something to do or see throughout the whole year. In August it's overrun with tourists, but the famous *Biennale d'Arte* is held at that time. One of Italy's best known literary prizes, *Il Campiello,* is given here in September, while the Venezia film festival, with its *Leone d'Oro* (the Italian equivalent of an Oscar), is held from the end of August into early September. Other important happenings are the Venetian Carnival, full of splendid noise and confusion, and the winter opera season at the *Teatro La Fenice,* one of Italy's most famous theaters.

Colli Asolani

Veneto is one of the most interesting and populated regions of Italy, and almost any road will take you to a quaint little town, to a splendid villa, or to the top of an enchanting hill. If you approach it for the first time, you will find pleasant relief from the visual orgy of Venezia in a little trip through the *Colli Asolani* just under the *Monte Grappa.* The area is not far from Venezia and can be reached easily from *Treviso.*

Colli Asolani is probably the most typical province of the Veneto in its atmosphere and character. Note the lovely *Duomo* and impressive *S. Nicolò* in late Gothic. Walk around the town; don't miss *Piazza dei Signori* and *Calmaggiore,* the city's animated main street. Come in May, when small

[handwritten margin notes:] ** Torcello Cathedral · **** Locanda Cipriani · *** Santa Maria Gloriosa · *** Scuola di San Rocco for its 56 big Tintorettos · Don't forget two Palladian masterpieces, the *** Redentore Church on Giudecca, and *** San Giorgio, on isle of same name · Colli Asolani = Asolani Hills · ** Treviso Cathedral · ** San Nicolò

planes can be boarded to view the most beautiful and interesting *villas* in the area, or in the fall, when so much of the good wine is made. When eating in Treviso, do not overlook the bitter, red *Radicchio Trevisano,* one of the best salads in the world.

For the relaxing trip mentioned above go to *Bassano del Grappa,* with its little wood bridge entirely covered by a roof; it's often redone, the last time was in 1948. From there go up the mountain that has given its name to one of Italy's best drinks, *grappa.* Drive down, past *Possagno*—birthplace of the great neoclassical sculptor Canova—and stop at *Asolo*—the center of these charming hills. This is a little town full of artists and scholars (Robert Browning stayed here for a few days and loved it) and has two of the best hotels in the area.

From Asolo drive to *Maser,* noting the villas and enjoying the country-side. At Maser visit the very famous *villa Barbaro* built by Palladio, (now Volpi) with its Veronese frescoes. It can be seen June–September on Tuesdays, Saturdays and Sundays from 3 to 6 P.M.; October to May from 2 to 5 P.M.

Head for *Valdoviàdene* by crossing the river Piave at *Ponte di Vidor.* Here, if you have time, take the panoramic route to *Pianezze,* a skiing resort that nestles in these lovely mountains. Otherwise go on to *Conegliano* by taking the so-called *Strada del Vino Bianco* through pleasant hills covered by rows of vines where some of Italy's best white wines can be tasted and some of Veneto's best food can be eaten. From Conegliano another road takes you into red wine country. By returning east, to *Oderzo,* you'll drive on the *Strada del Vino Rosso,* where some of the region's wonderful red and rosé wines are produced. The drive ends in *Roncade* at Castello Giustinian, now called *Ciani Bassetti.* If you have a chance, buy a bottle of Merlot, Cabernet, or Raboso.

Padova

Padova, one of the most interesting cities of this region, deserves a detour. Probably less monumental than Venezia or Verona, with an irregular topography and disordered street plan, it is the liveliest, most active city in this part of Italy. One of Italy's most discussed universities is in Padova. Founded in 1222, it attracted the greatest names of the 13th and 14th centuries, such as Dante and Petrarca, and continued to educate the best men of the Veneto even after the city fell into the hands of nearby Venezia. It still holds an important position and has gained some notoriety because several leaders of the Red Brigades were educated there.

The center of town is *Piazza Cavour,* and nearby is *Caffè Pedrocchi,* where much conspiring was done during the Risorgimento and where generations of students have enjoyed themselves. Not far is one of the main university buildings; in the other direction is the famous *Palazzo della Ragione,* with typical 14th-century *logge* and a characteristic roof of its time.

There are two important churches in Padova. One is the small and charming *Cappella degli Scrovegni,* in simple Romanesque–Gothic, decorated inside with some of the best *affreschi* Giotto painted. The other is the large and impressive *S. Antonio,* one of Italy's most visited sanctuaries, dedicated to the great saint who, though born in Lisbon, Portugal, in 1195,

You haven't had sweeter radishes anywhere

Grappa is like schnapps, liquid dynamite

Two hotels = ★★★ Villa Cipriani and ★★★ Duse

★★★ White Wine Road

★★ Red Wine Road

★ Palazzo della Ragione

★★★ Scrovegni Chapel ("Grotto Church")

★★★ Sant'Antonio ("Il Santo")

preached and died in Padova (in 1231). The façade is Gothic but its eight *cupolas*—little towers and minaret-like bell towers—and a mixture of Byzantine, Venetian and French Perigourdine Romanesque elements give it an appearance that is nothing short of fantastic.

Inside, the major altar is embellished by magnificent Donatello bronzes; countless other great artists are also represented in this fascinating basilica.

Walk around Padova and enjoy its atmosphere. *Via VIII Febbraio, piazza delle Erbe* (a vegetable market), *via S. Francesco, Piazza del Santo* are only a few of the interesting streets and squares that come to mind. In front of the basilica of St. Anthony is a statue that deserves a careful look— Donatello's *Monumento al Gattamelata*. The great Florentine sculptor created this splendidly heroic horse and rider in 1453, at the very height of the Renaissance. The subject is a Venetian general, Erasmo da Narni, known as Gattamelata, who lived from 1370 to 1443 and was famous for his leadership and courage. Since Padova fell to Venezia in 1405 and was a loyal and faithful subject, the connection is obvious.

*** Statue of Gattamelata

Verona

Verona, the most romantic city in the world, is also a part of Veneto and can be visited by anyone going from Venezia to Milano or vice versa. Close to Lombardia and to the lovely *Lago di Garda,* Verona was prosperous and important in the days of the Roman Empire. Of the numerous ruins that are still around to remind us of this fact, the famous *Arena* is by far the most significant. Built during the 1st century A.D., the Arena of Verona is one of the largest Roman amphitheaters to have survived in good condition. It has been restored to even further greatness in the 20th century by a very sophisticated redecoration. It's used as a theater for the grand and popular ballet and opera. If you come to Italy in July and August and are lucky enough to get tickets, the experience will be unforgettable!

*** Verona's Arena and don't forget *Juliet's house on Via Cappello

Verona is a city to tour leisurely; there is much to see and a charming atmosphere to enjoy. There are several charming *piazze* such as *Piazza delle Erbe* and *Piazza dei Signori;* several lovely old gates such as *Porta dei Borsari* and *Porta Palio;* several interesting bridges such as *Ponte Scaligero* and *Ponte Pietra;* many important buildings such as impressive *Castelvecchio,* attractive *Palazzo Pompei* and powerful *Palazzo Bevilacqua* (the last two by Sanmicheli, an architect of the late Renaissance). In addition, as is true of so many Italian cities, Verona boasts some of the loveliest Christian churches; *S. Anastasia, S. Bernardino, S. Fermo Maggiore, S. Giorgio in Braida,* the *Duomo.* The most beautiful of them all is *S. Zeno Maggiore,* a masterpiece of Romanesque architecture. It stands on a large and quiet square between a simple tower of the old abbey and its own slender, isolated bell tower. Its elegant façade is decorated by a single, large, round stained glass window and by a portal that contains the famous bronze doors, a 12th-century series of reliefs that tell stories from the Old and New Testaments and of the saint that gives the church its name. The equally simple and majestic interior is decorated with various 13th–15th century *affreschi,* 13th-century statues of Christ and the Apostles and a splendid triptych of the *Madonna and Saints* done by Mantegna in 1459. In addition, a trip to Verona won't be complete without a visit to S. Zeno.

** Piazza della Erbe

** Castelvecchio and its museum

** San Giorgio

**** San Zeno Maggiore

Lago di Garda

If you do go to Verona, a trip around the fabled *Lago di Garda* is almost inevitable. The largest and most visited lake in Italy, the Garda is also a *trait d'union* between the two types of Veneto territory mentioned earlier—the plain and the pre-Alps. A drive around the lake will take you through several lovely resorts, old centers and picturesque little towns; it will also include rolling hills, vines and olive trees, as well as rugged coastlines and woody areas. All of these sights have the lake's clear blue waters as background. Need we say more?

From Verona a short drive will take you to *Peschiera del Garda,* on the Mincio River. Note the 16th-century fortifications built by the Venetians. Take the road that goes north, following the lake. You'll pass *Lazise* and *Bardolino;* note the castle and walls of the former and the characteristic houses and churches of the latter. At *Garda* take a walk along the lake and be sure not to overlook *Punta di S. Vigilio,* the most romantic spot on the lake.

The drive then becomes a bit harsher, with typical Venetian houses and little ports clinging to the rocky coast. At *Malcesine* a few tunnels will signify a definite entry into mountain country. A stop here may be worth your while; there is an attractive castle to visit, an interesting Renaissance palace to look at and, for the hardier, a charming ride on a funicular that will afford splendid views of the lake and surrounding country.

You will pass another small center, *Tòrbole,* and then you'll reach *Riva del Garda;* you've now entered the *Trentino* and are past the boundaries of the Veneto region. But, as is often pointed out, the three regions that form northeastern Italy are very close to one another in culture, language and art. At *Rive del Garda* you may want to take the short ride to *Cascata del Varone,* where the view from the upper terrace is truly superb. This little town has an interesting race in March—a combination ski-and-sail—plus a giant slalom on the snows of nearby *Polsa di Brentònico.* After Riva head downward on the other side of the lake for the trip back. Your first stop will be *Limone sul Garda,* another picturesque resort. Then go on down to *Tremòsine, Maderno,* and *Gardone Riviera,* where the famous *Vittoriale* can be visited if you are interested in *D'Annunzio,* the famous poet and lover of the fascist period. Then on to *Salò, S. Felice del Benaco, Manerba* and *Desenzano,* which has the ruins of a Roman villa; then to *Sirmione,* beautifully located on a splendid peninsula that juts into the lake. The whole western shore is Lombard territory, a part of the province of *Brescia.*

Sirmione is a charming little town, famous in Roman days and sung about by poet Catullo. The archaeological area known as the *Grotte di Catullo* is at the tip of the peninsula and it affords a fascinating excursion. Also worth visiting is the *Rocca Scaligera,* a powerful 13th-century construction, with its original docks in very good condition. These are considered a rarity; very few medieval structures of its kind have lasted this long.

FRIULI-VENEZIA GIULIA

Friuli-Venezia Giulia, a small region on the eastern tip of northern Italy, is a composite of Alpine and sub-Alpine country, some plain, some lagoon and some seacoast, including the large port of Trieste.

[handwritten margin notes:]
Trait d'union = hyphen, lit.
Gabriele d'Annunzio (d. 1938)
Catullus (d. 54 B.C.) had a villa here

Blessed with an industrious population, the region has a florid economy that includes both agriculture and industry. It had the misfortune of a massive earthquake in 1976, but its citizens have already repaired much of the damage.

Somewhat similar to nearby Trentino-Alto Adige, the region is another special area for statues, influenced by neighboring Austria and Yugoslavia, as well as by being in the vicinity of Venezia.

Some History

Friuli-Venezia Giulia was Roman from the 2nd century B.C. It was included in the Tenth Roman Region, then called *Venetia et Histria,* with the city of *Aquileia* as its most important center. Because of its location, it was a natural passageway for the barbarians. From the 6th to the 8th centuries it fell almost entirely into Longobard hands, with the exception of *Grado,* which was held by the Byzantines. Like much of northern Italy, Friuli passed from the Longobards to the Franks, and the area prospered. *Aquileia* gained importance and, for a long period, it was the leading center of the northeast.

But just southwest of Aquileia a new city began to acquire strength and status. *Venezia,* strategically located on the delta of the large Po River, became a leading Mediterranean port, and by 1420 it conquered Friuli both militarily and commercially, extending its power as far as *Trieste.*

The situation remained relatively stable until the 18th century when Trieste was declared a free port in 1719. Then the advent of Napoleon caused a temporary change, and the area was divided between Venezia and Austria. Soon thereafter the Congress of Vienna created a new Europe, and Friuli-Venezia Giulia became entirely Austrian. In 1866, with the wars of Italian independence, some of the region returned to Italy, and after 1918, as part of the post-World War I settlements, the remaining portions, *Gorizia* and Trieste, were also incorporated into the Italian state.

Some Thoughts On Art

There are a few Roman ruins in *Trieste,* but the most important archaeological center in the region is *Aquileia,* with its remnants of late Roman civilization. At *Grado* there are several interesting buildings from the early Christian period (5th and 6th centuries) bearing a distinct Ravenna-like character, while *Cividale del Friuli* has a few reminders of the Longobard domination. There were some very good Gothic churches at *Gemona* and *Venzone,* but the 1976 earthquake left them in very bad condition, and reconstruction is slow, especially where restoration is necessary.

In the 15th century the area became a Venetian colony from an artistic point of view; this can best be seen in the city of *Udine,* which owes its central piazza to this particular style.

A characteristic trip through Friuli would have been to go from *Pordenone* to Udine, not in a straight line, but by going into the hills to *Spilimbergo, Pinzano, Osoppo* and *Gemona,* then going down to *Cividale del Friuli* and finally, going back on the plain to Udine. But we cannot recommend this itinerary now since this is where the earthquake did the greatest damage; the only reason for coming here now would be to see what the brave population is doing to rebuild and start anew.

Of more interest, especially if you like the lagoon, is a trip along the coast of Friuli with stops at *Palmanova, Aquileia, Grado, Monfalcone, S. Giovanni al Timavo, Sistiana* and, finally, *Trieste*. The best way to reach this area is by *Autostrada* from Venezia, which will take you directly to Palmanova through *Portogruaro*.

At *Aquileia,* now a very small town, note the splendid 11th-century basilica, the lovely *via Sacra* and the archaeological remnants that are all over, reminding us that 1,000 years ago this was an important city. Grado, on an island, is now a busy fishing village and resort, but 12 centuries ago it tried to rival Venezia.

*[margin note: ** Basilica of Aquileia]*

Trieste

Trieste, the most important city of this region, is also the most unusual city in Italy. Because of its geographic location (at the extreme northeastern tip of the country, on a strip of land that juts into Yugoslav territory), Trieste is very different from other Italian cities. Even though it existed in Roman times and was prosperous during the Middle Ages, the town we see today is a product of the late 18th and early 19th centuries. At that time it reigned over the northern Adriatic Sea, its most important port and a natural passageway for all merchandise going to the Danube basin. Today, when this is no longer the case, Trieste is still a fairly busy center. But it is also a dying city, with the highest percentage of retired persons in the whole country and a melancholy atmosphere.

[margin note: Trieste was the most important port of the Austro-Hungarian Empire (d. 1918)]

Culturally, the city has the U.N. International Theoretical Physics Center, a fairly modern university that boasts an active Economics Department and an energetic musical life that rotates around a good conservatory. Many busy *caffès* are known for their tradition in literature and history. During the early part of the century James Joyce lived here for many years.

Recently, with Yugoslavia on an austerity kick that has, among other things, reduced the quality of its coffee, Trieste has been serving as a shopping center for many Yugoslavs. Every Sunday thousands of them enter the city and stand in line outside bars that sell good Italian coffee, buying about half-a-million dollars worth of the precious black bean to take back home. For Trieste, this new source of income is an unexpected shot in the arm.

A visit may take about one day. City life revolves around *Piazza dell-'Unità d'Italia, Piazza della Borsa, Corso Italia, Piazza Goldoni, via Carducci* and *via Mazzini*. Walk along these streets and squares and look at the baroque and neoclassical buildings to get the feeling of what this town is like. The one outstanding monument is *S. Giusto,* located on a hill and considered the symbol of Trieste. The simple church is a result of a unification between two preceding Romanesque basilicas that took place in the 14th century. The older churches were from the 5th and 11th centuries—*S. Giusto* on the right and *Assunta* on the left. The squat bell tower includes the remnants of a Roman temple, and from its top there is a good panoramic view of the city.

*[margin note: ** Cathedral of St. Just]*

Not far from this church is the *Castello,* a structure that was started in 1470 over an existing Venetian castle which, in its turn, had incorporated a Roman rock. The ramparts were done in 1508, then in the mid-16th century; the last one was done in 1630. In this one case Trieste reveals itself as truly Italian, with one age superimposed on another and a final product that looks as natural as if it had been meant to look that way from the beginning!

*[margin note: * Castle and its museum]*

Note: The letters in parentheses in this section indicate the province. PD is Padua, for example. See "On Using this Book," at the beginning of this volume.

Hotels

ABANO TERME (PD), Veneto

Noted since Roman times for its anti-rheumatic mud baths, this spa is one of the most famous and best equipped in all of Italy. Approximate population: 15,000.

★★★★ FOUR STARS

★★★★★ GRAND HOTEL OROLOGIO
Viale delle Terme 1, tel. 669502. 152 rooms with bath, garden, sauna, *Closed winters* garage, seasonal. Expensive.

★★★★ FOUR STARS

★★★★ LA RESIDENCE
Via Monte Ceva 8, tel. 66833, 120 rooms with bath, tennis, garden, parking. Moderately expensive.

★★★ THREE STARS

★★★ HOTEL QUISISANA
Viale delle Terme 67, tel. 669299, 95 rooms with bath, golf, sauna, garden, parking. Reasonable.

★★★ HOTEL MIONI PEZZATO
Via Marzia 36, tel. 669338, 180 rooms with bath, tennis, garage. Reasonable.

★★★ HOTEL INTERNAZIONALE
Via Mazzini 7–Via Silvio Pellico, tel. 668000, 145 rooms with bath, tennis, garage. Moderate.

ACQUI TERME (AL), Piemonte

Important spa in southern Piemonte, this small town on the river Bormida was noted in Roman days. Approximate population: 23,000.

★★★★ HOTEL ANTICHE TERME
Borgo Bagni, tel. 2101, 95 rooms, most with bath, closed from October 15th to June 15th. Moderately expensive.

★★★   **HOTEL ARISTON**
Piazza Matteotti 1, tel. 2996, 35 rooms with bath. Reasonable.

ALASSIO (SV), Liguria

This elegant resort on the Ligurian Riviera is noted for its lovely beaches, which are some of the best in the whole region. There is a jazz festival in September. Approximate population: 14,000.

★★★★   **HOTEL DIANA**
Via Garibaldi 104, tel. 42701, 77 rooms with bath, sauna, indoor pool, beach, garage. Seasonal. Moderately expensive.

★★★   **HOTEL SPIAGGIA**
Via Roma 78, tel. 43403, 84 rooms with bath, beach. Reasonable.

★★★   **PARK HOTEL**
Via Madonna di Loreto 2, tel. 42681, 40 rooms with bath, terraces, swimming pool, parking. Reasonable.

ALBA (CN), Piemonte

Alba is an important town, located at the center of the Langhe area. It's noted for its exceptional wines such as Barolo, Barbera, Dolcetto and its white truffles. A fair is held in October. It still retains a medieval appearance. Approximate population: 32,000.

★★★   **HOTEL MONTEALBA**
Out-of town hotel. New and well furnished, garden, 44 rooms with bath. Parking. Moderate.

★★   **HOTEL SAVONA**
Older, 112 rooms, only half with bath. Reasonable.

ALBENGA (SV), Liguria

This historical city, which flourished during Roman and medieval times, is as an important fruit and vegetable market, as well as a seaside resort. Approximate population: 21,000.

★★   **HOTEL SOLE E MARE**
On the sea. tel. 52752, 28 rooms, half with bath. Inexpensive.

AOSTA, Val d'Aosta

Surrounded by the Alps, Aosta is an important tourist and industrial center of the region. Founded by the Romans, it came under the rule of the Savoia in the 11th century. It is a city of many Roman and medieval ruins and monuments. Approximate population: 40,000.

★★★   HOTEL VALLE D'AOSTA
Corso Ivrea 174, tel. 41845, 102 rooms all with bath, parking, garden. Moderately expensive.

★★★ Restaurant

On edge of town, as is hotel above

★★★   HOTEL NORDEN
Corso Btg. Aosta, 30, tel. 41947, 48 rooms, almost all with bath, garage, parking. Moderate.

★★   HOTEL JOCKEY
Via Promis 2 A, tel. 41000, 54 rooms, almost all with bath. Inexpensive.

ASOLO (TV), Veneto

A quaint little town located on a beautiful hillside. During the Renaissance it was host to Caterina Cornaro, Queen of Cypress, as well as to many scholars and artists. Approximate population: 6,000.

★★★★   VILLA CIPRIANI
Via Canova 298, tel. 52166, 32 rooms with bath. A 16th-century house, terrace, garden, garage. Moderately expensive.

Near Piazza

★★★   DUSE HOTEL
Via Browning 190, tel. 55242, 15 rooms with bath. Moderate.

★★   HOTEL BELLAVISTA
Via S. Martino 8 (on a hill at the east entrance to Asolo), tel. 52088, 13 rooms, half with bath, garden, view, parking. Moderate.

ASTI, Piemonte

A typical Piemonte city in the center of the Tanaro Valley, Asti is rich with monuments and medieval ruins. It flourished during medieval times and came under the rule of the Savoia in 1553. It is located in a zone famous for wines, vermouths and liqueurs. The third Sunday in September the *Palio d'Asti* is held (a horse race and a procession in medieval costumes). Approximate population: 80,000.

★★★   HOTEL SALERA
At the end of Via Fortino, tel. 211815, 49 rooms with bath, beautiful view, parking. Moderately expensive.

On town's edge

no restaurant

★★   HOTEL ALERAMO
Via Emanuele Filiberto 13, tel. 55661, 40 rooms with bath or shower. Moderate

★★   HOTEL PALIO
Via Cavour 106, tel. 34371, 29 rooms all with bath or shower. Moderate. *Ditto*

BELLAGIO (CO), Lombardia

Known as an elegant health resort, Bellagio has an ideal location on a promontory between the two arms of Lago di Como. Many beautiful parks and villas, notably *Villa Serbelloni* and *Villa Melzi.* Approximate population: 3,500.

★★★★★   **HOTEL VILLA SERBELLONI**
Seasonal, tel. 950216, 93 rooms with bath, garden, pool, beach, tennis courts, garage. Expensive.

Lakeside villa (16th c.)

★★★   **HOTEL DU LAC**
Seasonal (closed October 9th–April 9th), tel. 950320, 50 rooms most with bath, view of the lake. Moderate.

★★   **HOTEL BELVEDERE**
Seasonal, tel. 950410, 50 rooms most with bath, terraces, pool, beautiful view. Moderate.

BERGAMO, Lombardia

One of the most interesting cities in Lombardia and an active industrial center. Located to the north of Milano and to the south of Como and its lake, it acts as a natural outlet for the valleys above. Clearly divided into two cities: *Bergamo Alta,* a quiet medieval town on a hill, and *Bergamo Bassa,* a bustling, modern, industrialized city on the plain. The old city is charming; its monuments combine the Lombard and Venetian influences. Pope John XXIII came from a nearby village; his last living brother still receives many visitors. Approximate population: 125,000.

★★★   **HOTEL EXCELSIOR SAN MARCO**
Piazzale della Repubblica 6, tel. 232132, 81 rooms most with bath, garage. Moderately expensive.

★★   **HOTEL DEL MORO**
Largo Porta Nuova 6, tel. 242946, 25 rooms with bath, good restaurant. Moderate.

BOLZANO, Trentino-Alto Adige

The largest city in northeastern Italy, Bolzano is in a valley where the Italian-speaking population meets the German-speaking population. It is an active, modern center. Its position with respect to the Brenner Pass has been instrumental for its development since the Middle Ages. At that time it belonged to the Trento princes, but in the 16th century it was conquered by the Tyrolese and Austria, which held Bolzano until 1918. Approximate population: 107,000.

★★★★   **PARK HOTEL LAURIN**
Via Laurin 4, tel. 47500, 113 rooms with bath, garden, garage, warm-water swimming pool, near railroad station. Moderately expensive.

In large gardens

★★★   HOTEL GRIFONE
Piazza Walter 7, tel. 27057, 133 rooms, most with bath, garage, garden, warm-water swimming pool. Moderate.

★★   HOTEL ALPI
Via Alto Adige 35, tel. 26671, 112 rooms most with bath. Moderate.

BORDIGHERA (IM), Liguria

This small charming city is a health spa and seaside resort. It has lush vegetation and many hotels. Approximate population: 12,000.

★★★★   GRAND HOTEL DEL MARE
Via Aurelia, tel. 262201, 97 rooms with bath, pool, beach, garden, garage. Moderately expensive.

Well-sited over sea, very modern

★★★   HOTEL CAP AMPELIO
Via Virgilio 11, tel. 264333, 104 rooms with bath, pool, garden, garage, beautiful view. Moderately expensive.

★★★   HOTEL JOLANDA
Corso Italia 85, tel. 261325, 49 rooms, most with bath, garden, garage. Moderate.

★★   HOTEL ASTORIA
Via Tasso 2, tel. 262906, 24 rooms with bath, garden, parking. Moderate.

★★   HOTEL GARDEN
Via Roberto 10, tel. 260424, 24 rooms with bath. Moderate.

BORMIO (SO), Lombardia

Bormio is known for its thermal waters and as an important resort for winter sports. It's located in a valley, surrounded by magnificent mountains, just across the border from Switzerland. Approximate population: 4,000.

★★★★   PALACE HOTEL
Seasonal, tel. 903131, 83 rooms with bath, garden, sauna. Moderately expensive.

★★★   HOTEL BAITA DEI PINI
Seasonal, tel. 901385, 46 rooms with bath, garden. Moderately expensive.

★★★   HOTEL LARICE BIANCO
Seasonal, tel. 901193, 45 rooms with bath, garden, parking. Moderate.

★★   HOTEL ASTORIA
Seasonal, tel. 901012, 39 rooms with bath, garage. Moderate.

CAMPIONE D'ITALIA (CO), Lombardia

Located in the central basin of Lago di Lugano, this tourist center is entirely surrounded by Switzerland. (It is, therefore, advisable to have your passport within easy reach.) Noted for its gambling casino. Approximate population: 2,000.

★★★★ HOTEL LAGO DI LUGANO
At the entrance of Campione (in Switzerland), tel. 688591, 80 rooms with bath, garden, pool, sauna, beach. Expensive.

★★★ HOTEL CAMPIONE BISSONE
At the entrance of Campione (in Switzerland), tel. 686021, 50 rooms, most with bath, view of the lake. Moderately expensive.

CERNOBBIO (CO), Lombardia

A well-known resort on the lake of Como, Cernobbio has many magnificent villas. Approximate population: 8,000.

★★★★★ GRAND HOTEL VILLA D'ESTE
Seasonal, exit for Menaggio, tel. 511471, 162 rooms with bath, tennis courts, indoor and outdoor swimming pools, sauna, riding, garden, beach, discoteque, restaurant, large rooms, excellent service. One of the grandest hotels in Italy. Expensive.

★★★★ HOTEL REGINA OLGA
At the entrance to Como, tel. 510171, 67 rooms with bath, pool, garden, garage, on the lake. Moderately expensive.

★★★ HOTEL ASNIGO
At Asnigo, 2 km. north, Piazza Santo Stefano, tel. 510062, seasonal, closed November 1st–March 15th, 22 rooms, a few with bath, peacefully located in a garden on the hill of Como. Excellent service, terraces, beautiful views, parking. Moderately expensive.

CHIOGGIA (VE), Veneto

Known as a "miniature Venezia" with its canals and Venetian-style buildings, this charming city is located on an island at the extreme south of the Venetian Lagoon. It is an important fishing center and seaside resort. Approximate population: 53,000.

★★★★ HOTEL RITZ
Seasonal, Lungomare Adriatico 48, tel. 401900, 84 rooms with bath, garden, pool, seaside location, parking. Moderately expensive.

★★★ VITTORIA PALACE
Lugomare Adriatico 28, tel. 401820, 100 rooms with bath, seaside location, parking. Moderately expensive.

★★★ HOTEL ANZOLETTI
Lungomare Adriatico 30, tel. 400660, 50 rooms with bath, seaside location, garden, parking. Moderately expensive.

★★   HOTEL FLORIDA
Viale Mediterraneo 7, tel. 403505, 49 rooms with bath. Moderate.

COMO, Lombardia

Beautifully located city, on one end of the lake that bears its name. Was a prosperous comune during the Middle Ages, and from that time it has engaged in the industry and commerce of textiles, mainly silk. An important tourist center, it has attractive landscapes and lovely medieval monuments. Approximate population: 97,000.

★★★   VILLA FIORI
Seasonal, via Statale per Cernobbio 12, tel. 557642, 49 rooms, 41 with bath, garage, garden, view of the lake. Moderately expensive.   *private beach*

★★★   BARCHETTA EXCELSIOR
Piazza Cavour 1, tel. 266531, 50 rooms with bath. Moderately expensive.   *view of lake*

★★   ENGADINA HOTEL
Viale Rosselli 22, tel. 550415, 21 rooms with bath. Moderate.

CORTINA D'AMPEZZO (BL), Veneto

This town is the center of one of the most famous and elegant winter sports resort areas in all of Europe. It's set in the beautiful Dolomites; it has well-equipped hotels, modern sports facilities and a variety of trips and excursions within the surrounding area. It is also a primary mountain-climbing zone. Approximate resident population: 8,500.

★★★★★   MIRAMONTI MAJESTIC HOTEL
Seasonal, at Pezziè (exit for Pieve di Cadore), tel. 4201, 136 rooms, most with bath, garden, golf, tennis, covered pool, garage. Very expensive.   *Closed spring and autumn*

★★★★   CRISTALLO PALACE HOTEL
Seasonal, via Menardi 42, tel. 4281, 95 rooms with bath, garden, pool, tennis, ice skating rink, garage. Expensive.   *Ask for balcony room*

★★★   SPLENDID VENEZIA HOTEL
Seasonal, corso Italia 177, tel. 3291, 93 rooms with bath, parking. Moderate.

★★   HOTEL FRANCESCHI
Seasonal, via C. Battisti 86, tel. 2600, 42 rooms most with bath, tennis, garden, parking. Moderate.

COURMAYEUR (AO), Valle d'Aosta

This is the oldest and one of the most famous vacation spots of the Italian Alps. At the foot of Monte Bianco, it is an international summer and winter resort for skiing and mountain climbing. The cable car crossing of Monte Bianco (Mont Blanc) begins here and offers a spectacular view of the Alps. Many hotels. Approximate population: 3,000.

Closed November (handwritten)

★★★★   HOTEL ROYAL
Seasonal, tel. 83621, 80 rooms with bath, garage, swimming pool, garden. Expensive.

★★★★   HOTEL PAVILLON
Seasonal, tel. 82420, 38 rooms with bath, covered pool, garage. Expensive.

★★★   HOTEL PALACE BRON
Seasonal, at the Plan Gorret, tel. 82545, 29 rooms with bath, garden, parking, isolated. Moderately expensive.

★★★   HOTEL MODERNO
Tel. 82222, 30 rooms with bath, parking. Moderate.

★★   HOTEL CRESTA ET DUC
Seasonal, tel. 82585, 39 rooms with bath, garden, parking. Moderate.

GARDONE RIVIERA (BS), Lombardia

This elegant, first-class health resort is partly situated on a rolling hill and partly on the shore of Lago di Garda. It has many villas and hotels, all surrounded by luxuriant vegetation. It offers cultural and sport events, such as poetry readings, concerts, ballets, art shows and boat races of *bisse* (antique Venetian boats). Interesting to visit *Vittoriale,* last residence of poet Gabriele D'Annunzio. Approximate population: 2,600.

★★★★   GRAND HOTEL
Seasonal, tel. 20261, 203 rooms, most with bath, garden, pool, tennis courts, excellent location on the lake. Expensive.

On lake also (handwritten)

★★   HOTEL MONTE BALDO
Seasonal, tel. 20951, 44 rooms, most with bath, beach, garden, parking. Moderate.

★★   HOTEL DU LAC
Seasonal, tel. 20124, 30 rooms, most with bath, location on the lake. Moderate.

GENOVA, Liguria

The most important commercial port in Italy and one of the first ports of the Mediterranean, Genova is an active, thriving city. The entire city (Grande Genova), which is more than 30 km. (18.5 mi.) long, is tightly fitted between the mountains in back of it and the sea in front. But the hub of the original settlement clusters around the port and the streets behind it, which rise into the hills and are crowned by old fortifications and castles. Banking and commerce have always been Genova's forte, and, as of this century, it has added heavy industry to their shipping business. Its magnificent churches, famous for their characteristic stripes of black and white marble are partly responsible for the name Italians have given this lovely city: Genova, *la Superba.* Approximate population: 800,000.

★★★★   COLOMBIA EXCELSIOR HOTEL
Via Balbi 40, near the railroad station, tel. 201841, 171 rooms with bath, luxury hotel. Expensive.

★★★   SAVOIA MAJESTIC HOTEL
Piazza Acquaverde, tel. 261641, 115 rooms with bath, central location. Moderately expensive.

Also opposite rail station

★★   LONDRA e CONTINENETALE
Next door to and run by the same management as Savoia Majestic Hotel. Less expensive, equally efficient.

★★   BRISTOL PALACE HOTEL
Via XX Settembre 35, tel. 592541, 105 rooms, most with bath. Moderate.

★★   HOTEL ASTORIA
Piazza Brignole 4, near Genova's smaller railroad station, "Genova Brignole," tel. 873316, 74 rooms, most with bath. Moderate.

★★   BELLEVUE HOTEL
Via providenza 1, near main railroad station, tel. 262400, 38 rooms, most with bath, terrace, lovely view. Inexpensive.

Harbor views

★   HOTEL ORTI SAULI
Viale Orti Sauli 5, a little out of town, tel. 543354, 49 rooms with bath, quiet, modest but neat. Inexpensive.

★   PARK HOTEL
Corso Italia 10 (lungomare E), out of town, tel. 311040, 19 rooms, most with bath, garden, garage, on the shore. Inexpensive.

GRADO (GO), Friuli-Venezia-Giulia

Located on an island between the lagoon and the sea, this active fishing village is one of the most elegant seaside resorts and saltwater spas on the Adriatic. It was important from the 5th to the 9th centuries when it was often the residence of the patriarchs of Aquileia. Many hotels. Approximate population: 10,000.

★★★   ASTORIA PALACE
Largo San Grisogono 1, tel. 80016, 187 rooms with bath, covered pool, sauna, health club, garage. Moderately expensive.

IMPERIA, Liguria

Imperia is divided into two main centers: *Oneglia* (Imperia Levante) and *Porto Maurizio* (Imperia Ponente). They are connected by the *Via Aurelia* (Viale Matteotti), which runs along the sea. Besides being noted as a seaside resort, this active port is also an important industrial and oil trading center. An international chess tournament is held in September. Approximate population: 42,000.

In Oneglia

★★   HOTEL KRISTINA
Via Peri 8, tel. 23564, 24 rooms, half with bath, view of the sea. Moderate.

★   HOTEL CONCORDIA
Via G. Berio 41, tel. 20315, 16 rooms with bath, garage. Inexpensive.

In Porto Maurizio

Some rooms have view of sea
On beach

★★   HOTEL CORALLO
Corso Garibaldi 29, tel. 64691, 36 rooms with bath, garage, view. Moderate.

★★   HOTEL CROCE DI MALTA
Via Scarincio 142a, tel. 63847, 40 rooms, most with bath. Moderate.

IVREA (TO), Piemonte

Founded by the Romans, this small city is situated on the Dora Baltea River in a large rocky amphitheater. You may pass through on your way to Valle d'Aosta. It is an important industrial center for Olivetti products. Approximate population: 30,000.

★★★   HOTEL LA SERRA
Corso Botta 30, tel. 44341, 49 rooms with bath or shower, garage, covered pool, gymnasium, sauna, parking, best hotel in town. Moderately expensive.

★★   HOTEL RITZ
At Banchette (autostrada exit), tel. 2424148, 37 rooms with bath or shower, parking. Moderate.

★★   HOTEL SIRIO
At Lake Sirio, tel. 423646, 33 rooms with bath or shower, garden, beautiful views, restaurant, open all year. Moderate.

★★★ Restaurant

LA SPEZIA, Liguria

Situated at the end of a large and magnificent gulf, this active city is one of the most important navy strongholds in Italy. Also noted as a large industrial center with shipyards, mechanical plants, foundaries and refineries. Many small, quaint resorts are located within a short distance of this modern city; the most noted are Portovenere and Lerici. Approximate population is 121,-000.

★★★   JOLLY HOTEL
Via XX Settembre 2, tel. 27200, 110 rooms with bath. Moderately expensive.

★★   HOTEL ASTORIA
Via Roma 139, tel. 35122, 51 rooms, most with bath. Moderate.

★★   PALAZZO S. GIORGIO
Via Manzoni 60, tel. 33084, 68 rooms, most with bath. Moderate.

near shore

★   HOTEL FIRENZE e CONTINENTAL
Via Paleocapa 7, tel. 31248, 53 rooms, most with bath. Inexpensive.

LERICI (SP), Liguria

This small, picturesque city, located on a charming gulf, is a famous health and seaside resort. Approximate population: 14,000.

★★   HOTEL BYRON
Lungomare Biaggini 23, tel. 967104, 17 rooms with bath. Excellent location on the sea. Moderately expensive.

On town's main drag

★★   HOTEL SHELLY EL DELLE PALME
Lungomare Biaggini 5, tel. 967127, 53 rooms, most with bath, view of the gulf. Moderately expensive.

Ditto

★   HOTEL PANORAMIC
Seasonal, (above town), tel. 967192, 19 rooms with bath, parking. Moderate.

MADONNA DI CAMPIGLIO (TN), Trentino-Alto Adige

Surrounded by thick fir trees, this small town is a well-known vacation spot and winter sports resort. An important starting point for excursions, it also has three well-known ski areas: *Pancugolo, Spinale-Grosté* and *Pradalago*. Every year a race (Tre–Tre) is held to select skiers for the world cup competition.

★★★   SAVOIA PALACE
Seasonal, tel. 41004, 57 rooms with bath, garage. Moderately expensive.

★★   IL CAMINETTO
Seasonal, tel. 41242, 32 rooms with bath, garden, parking. Moderate.

★★   HOTEL OBEROSLER
Tel. 41136, 38 rooms with bath, garden, garage. Moderate.

★   HOTEL BONAPACE
Seasonal, tel. 41019, 41 rooms with bath, tennis, parking. Inexpensive.

★   HOTEL GRIFONE
Seasonal, tel. 42002, 40 rooms with bath, garden, garage. Inexpensive.

MANTOVA, Lombardia

On the southeastern corner of Lombardia, this prosperous city embodies the characteristics of three regions, Lombardia, Veneto and Emilia-Romagna. The Mincio river flows around it, almost like a lake; in fact, locally it is known as Lago Speriore, Lago di Mezzo and Lago Inferiore. Historically, it is famous as the birthplace of Virgil and for the enlightened rule of the Gonzaga family, responsible for most of the splendid Renaissance art that decorates the city to this day. Most of its inhabitants are occupied in agricultural, commercial and industrial activities. Approximate population: 65,000.

★★   HOTEL SAN LORENZO
Piazza Concordia 14, tel. 27153, 35 rooms with bath, central location. Moderately expensive.

★   HOTEL APOLLO
Piazza Don Leoni, tel. 23745, 35 rooms with bath, across the street from the railroad station. Moderate.

No restaurant

MERANO (BZ), Trentino-Alto Adige

Also called "la perla dell'Alto Adige," Merano is located in a large valley on the Adige River. This town is a famous and elegant vacation resort and spa. Its main seasons are spring and autumn. It offers a mild climate, a variety of mineral waters, horse races, many parks and hotels with excellent equipment. Approximate population: 35,000.

★★★★   HOTEL PALACE
Seasonal, via Cavour 4, tel. 23791, 102 rooms with bath, spa, covered and uncovered pools, sauna, parking. Moderately expensive.

Central location

★★★★   HOTEL CASTEL FREIBERG
Tel. 44196. Lovely medieval castle, splendid view, comfort. Closed from November to April. Advisable stopover when driving through the Brenner Pass. Moderately expensive.

★★★   HOTEL BRISTOL
Seasonal, via Ottone Huber 14, tel. 23361, 149 rooms with bath, heated pool, garage. Moderately expensive.

Ask for balcony room

★★★   HOTEL EMMA
Piazza Mazzini, tel. 47422, 150 rooms with bath, heated pool, parking. Moderate.

★★   HOTEL IRMA
Seasonal, via Belvedere 7, tel. 30124, 60 rooms with bath, covered and uncovered pools, sauna, tennis, parking. Moderate.

★★   HOTEL ADRIA
Seasonal, via Glim 2, tel. 26183, 41 rooms with bath, covered pool, parking. Moderate.

MILANO, Lombardia

Largest city in northern Italy, Milano is the most important commercial, industrial and banking center in the country. It is also the largest cultural and political community after Roma, and is often called the "moral capital" of Italy. It had a long, tormented history during the Middle Ages and Renaissance (see text) and contains a few splendid monuments that will remind you of its past. Basically, it's a modern, 20th-century city. Approximate population: 1,700,000.

★★★★★   HOTEL PRINCIPE e SAVOIA
Piazza della Repubblica 17, tel. 6230, 298 rooms with bath plus 78 suites. A luxury hotel geared for the big city. Garden, parking, excellent service. Expensive.

Furnished with many genuine antiques near station

★★★★   HOTEL MICHELANGELO
Via Scarlatti 33, tel. 2055, 285 rooms with bath, new, modern, parking, restaurant, even translating personnel available. Expensive.

★★★★   HOTEL PALACE
Piazza della Repubblica 20, near station, tel. 6336, 203 rooms with bath. Comfortable, excellent service. Expensive.

★★★★   HOTEL EXECUTIVE
Via Don Sturzo 45, near Alitalia Terminal, tel. 6294, 420 rooms with bath, very large, modern hotel. Conference room that can accommodate 1,200 persons, simultaneous translation facilities and other services. Moderately expensive.

★★★★   HILTON INTERNATIONAL MILANO
Via Galvani 12, tel. 6983, 340 rooms with bath. High international level. Mostly for businessmen who will be well served and pampered. Moderately expensive.

★★★ Da Giuseppe restaurant

★★★★   ET DE MILAN HOTEL
Via Manzoni 29, tel. 870757, 90 rooms with bath. The oldest and best-known hotel in town (Verdi died here), in a marvelous, central location. A favorite with show business people and very handy for shopping. Moderately expensive.

★★★★   HOTEL DUOMO
Via San Raffaele 1, tel. 8833, 160 rooms with bath, central location. Another favorite of businessmen passing through, lovely rooms, some with unusual arrangements. Moderately expensive.

★★★★   EXCELSIOR GALLIA HOTEL
Piazza Duca d'Aosta 9, tel. 6277, 260 rooms with bath. Was just completely redone and the service as attentive as ever. Attracts a sophisticated clientele, has conference rooms, garage, and decent restaurant. Expensive.

★★★   HOTEL FRANCIA EUROPA
Corso Vittorio Emanuele 9, tel. 708301, 135 rooms, most with bath. In the very heart of town, walking distance to shops and movies. Comfortable rooms, good service. Moderately expensive.

★★   HOTEL DEI CAVALIERI
Piazza Missori 1, tel. 8857, 170 rooms with bath. Traditional, well known, well located. Moderately expensive.

★★   HOTEL CAVOUR
Via Fatebenefratelli 21, tel. 650983, 113 rooms with bath, good location, old reputation, adequate service. Moderately expensive.

★★   HOTEL MARINO ALLA SCALA
Piazza della Scala 5, tel. 867831, 79 rooms, most with bath; just off the famous Scala Theater, ideal for opera lovers. Closed August 1st–20th. Moderate.

No restaurant

★★   FIERA MILANO HOTEL
Via Boezio 20, tel. 3105, 238 rooms with bath. For those who come exclusively for the Milano Fair, book well in advance. Small garden, restaurant, and everything else to make you comfortable. Moderately expensive.

★★   ANTICA LOCANDA SOLFERINO
Via Castelfidardo 2, tel. 632706, 11 rooms with bath. For those who come to Milano looking for romance or a "bohemian" atmosphere, this little inn is the ideal place. Charming, clean, casual service, it faces the streets of the Brera section, which is the Montmartre of Milano. Closed in August; be sure to book in advance. Inexpensive.

MONZA (MI), Lombardia

This historical city was very important during the 7th century, when it was under the Longobard rule. Noted for its famous park, where national and international auto and motorcycle races are held. Within this large park there are also a race track, two golf courses and a polo field. Monza is an active industrial center for felt and fabric. Approximate population: 120,500.

★★   HOTEL DE LA VILLE
Viale Regina Margherita 15, tel. 382581, 47 rooms with bath, garden, garage. Moderate.

★★   HOTEL DELLA REGIONE
Viale Elvezia 4, tel. 387205, 90 rooms with bath. garden roof. Moderate.

★   HOTEL DELL'UVA
Piazza Carrobio 2, tel. 23825, 12 rooms with bath. Inexpensive.

PADOVA (Padua), Veneto

One of the most interesting and important cities in northern Italy, Padova is at the eastern corner of the fertile Po River Valley. Noted since the days of the Romans, it had a lively communal period and an illuminated leadership during the 14th century. Thus, its cultural and artistic life flowered. During the next century it became the most active center in the area, with a university that attracted students from all Europe, splendid buildings and great artists. Particularly worthy of attention are Donatello's monument to Gattamelata, the *Cappella degli Scrovegni* with Giotto's "affreschi," the *Palazzo della Ragione* and the *Basilica di S. Antonio*. Approximate population: 242,000

★★★   PLAZA HOTEL
Corso Milano 22, tel. 656822, 150 rooms with bath, garage, restaurant open evenings. Moderately expensive.

Central location

★★   HOTEL MAJESTIC
Via dell'Arco-via Solferino, tel. 663242, 40 rooms with bath, good restaurant —Toscanelli. Moderately expensive.

★★   HOTEL AL CASON
Via Fra Paolo Sarpi 40, tel. 38439, 40 rooms with bath, garage. Moderate.

★   HOTEL MIGNON
Via Bellerdi 22, tel. 661722, 20 rooms with bath. Inexpensive.

★   HOTEL AL GIARDINETTO
Prato della Valle 57, tel. 656972, 18 rooms with bath. Inexpensive.

PAVIA, Lombardia

One of the oldest cities in the region, Pavia was capital of the Lombard kingdom during the 6th and 7th centuries. Prosperous during the communal period, it still retains the medieval urban design and two lovely 12th-century churches. There is a university and the Ticino River flows by. If you have time, do not overlook the *Certosa di Pavia,* a monument of Renaissance art, 10 km. from the city, which is one of the major tourist attractions near Milano. Founded in 1369 by Gian Galeazzo Visconti, it was meant to be a family mausoleum. In it you can admire the transition from Gothic to Renaissance, and the building of the Foresteria is an example of baroque. Approximate population of Pavia: 88,000.

★★   HOTEL ARISTON
Via Scopoli 10, tel. 34334, 60 rooms, most with bath. Moderate.

★   HOTEL PALACE
Viale della Libertà, tel. 27441, 47 rooms with bath, near the river. Moderate.

PORTOFINO (GE), Liguria

This small picturesque fishing village is justly known as one of the most famous romantic seaside resorts in the world. Approximate population: 800.

Ask for balcony room facing sea

★★★★   HOTEL SPLENDIDO
In the hills, tel. 69195, 67 rooms with bath, small pool, garden, tennis, garage, beautiful view. Expensive.

★★   PICCOLO HOTEL
Seasonal, via di Paraggi, tel. 69015, 26 rooms, most with bath, garden, garage. Moderate.

★★   HOTEL NAZIONALE
On the port, tel. 69138, 56 rooms, most with bath. Moderate.

PORTO VENERE (SP), Liguria

This small village is best known as a seaside resort. It is located near a small strait, with the Palmaria Island directly in front of it. Approximate population: 5,000.

★★★ HOTEL ROYAL SPORTING
At Cava degli Ulivi (1 km.), tel. 900326, 62 rooms with bath, air-conditioning, pool, beach, garage. Moderately expensive.

★★ HOTEL S. PIETRO
On the promontory, tel. 900616, 30 rooms, most with bath, view of the gulf. Moderately expensive.

★★ HOTEL BELVEDERE
On the street of La Spezia, tel. 900608, 19 rooms, most with bath, view of the gulf. Moderate.

Gorgeous views

RAPALLO (GE), Liguria

This town is a famous resort of the Riviera di Levante. Local craftsmen produce beautiful lace products, especially pillows. Approximate population: 30,000.

★★★ HOTEL BRISTOL
Via Aurelia Orientale 309, tel. 50216, 76 rooms with bath, garage, garden, pool, view of the gulf. Expensive.

★★ EUROTEL
Via Aurelia Occidentale 22, tel. 60981, 64 rooms with bath, garden, pool, garage, view. Moderately expensive.

All rooms with balconies

★★ HOTEL RIVIERA
Piazza 4 Novembre 2, tel. 50248, 26 rooms with bath, view of the sea. Moderate.

★★ HOTEL ASTORIA
Viale Gramsci 4, tel. 50680, 24 rooms, most with bath, view of the sea. Moderate.

SAINT-VINCENT (AO), Valle d'Aosta

This elegant resort is noted for its thermal cures and its casino. It also has facilities for tennis, indoor swimming, horseback riding and skiing. Approximate population: 5,000.

★★★★ GRAND HOTEL BILLIA
Viale Piemonte 18, tel. 3446, 134 rooms with bath, pool, tennis, garden, garage, parking. Expensive.

★★ Restaurant

★★ HOTEL ELENA
Piazza Zerbion, tel. 2140, 46 rooms with bath. Moderate.

Fine restaurant

★ HOTEL POSTA
Piazza 25 Aprile 1, tel. 2250, 40 rooms, most with bath. Moderate.

Central location

★ HOTEL DELLE ROSE
Viale IV Novembre 9, tel. 2237, 21 rooms, half with bath, garden, parking.
Inexpensive.

SAN REMO (IM), Liguria

During the second half of the 19th century, San Remo began to develop its
reputation as a health resort. Today, this modern city is one of the most
famous winter resorts in Europe. It is also a noted seaside resort during the
summer. More than 250 hotels and many cultural events, including the
well-known song festival. Approximate population: 64,000.

★★★★ ROYAL HOTEL
Corso Imperatrice 74, tel. 84321, 140 rooms with bath, pool, garden, beach.
Expensive.

Traditional elegance, overlooking sea

★★★ HOTEL MÉDITERRANÉE
Corso Cavallotti 76, tel. 75601, 70 rooms, most with bath, garage, garden,
pool. Expensive.

★★ HOTEL COLOMBIA MAJESTIC
Corso Nuvoloni 69, tel. 83322, 46 rooms with bath, garage. Moderately
expensive.

★★ HOTEL BEL SOGGIORNO
Corso Matuzia 15a, tel. 85480, 45 rooms, most with bath, garden, view of
the sea, parking. Moderate.

★ HOTEL BEAU RIVAGE
Corso Trento Trieste 49, tel. 85146, 30 rooms with bath, view of the sea.
Moderate.

SANTA MARGHERITA (GE), Liguria

Famous resort of the Riviera di Levante. Lush vegetation. Many hotels. Approximate population: 13,000.

★★★★ IMPERIAL PALACE
Seasonal, via Pagana 19, tel. 88991, 105 rooms with bath, garden, pool, view
of the sea, parking. Expensive.

Large, lush gardens

★★★ HOTEL MIRAMARE
Via Milite Ignoto 30, tel. 87014, 73 rooms with bath, garage, garden, pool,
beach, view of the sea. Moderately expensive.

★★   HOTEL LAURIN
Corso Marconi 3, tel. 89971, 41 rooms with bath, pool, located on the port.
Moderately expensive.

★★   HOTEL REGINA ELENA
Via Milite Ignoto 44, tel. 87004, 64 rooms with bath, garden, view of the sea.
Moderate.

★★   HOTEL LA VELA
Via Nicolò Cuneo 12, tel. 86030, 16 rooms with bath. Elegant villa with
garden, parking. Moderate.

SESTRIERE (TO), Piemonte

This resort has the most modern and the best winter sport's equipment in all
of Italy. Besides numerous ski trails and ice-skating rinks, it has tennis courts,
horse racing tracks and an 18-hole golf course. This tiny village is situated on
a pass between the Chisone valley and the Dora Riparia valley. Approximate
population: 750.

★★★★   PRINCIPI DI PIEMONTE
Tel. 7013, open only in winter. Best hotel in the area, 84 rooms with bath,
heated pool, garage. Expensive.

★   MIRAMONTI
Seasonal, tel. 7048, 36 rooms, most with bath, garden, garage. Moderate.

Open in summer

★   OLIMPIC
Seasonal, tel. 7344, 29 rooms with bath or shower. Moderate.

Ditto

STRESA (NO), Piemonte

Situated on the western banks of Lago Maggiore, below the forests of Matta-
rone and facing the basin of the Borromee Island, this small town has been
internationally known for centuries as a health resort. Many facilities for
tennis, swimming, boating, golf. Many hotels. Approximate population is
5,000.

★★★★   GRAND HOTEL ET DES ILES BORROMÉES
Corso Umberto 167, tel. 30435, 145 rooms, almost all with either a bath or
a shower, garage, garden, tennis, pool and beach. Baroque building with
towers, spacious rooms. Excellent service. Expensive.

★★★ Restaurant

★★★   REGINA PALACE
Corso Umberto 1, tel. 30171, 131 rooms, most with bath, garden, tennis,
beach, pool, parking. Moderately expensive.

★★   BRISTOL
Corso Umberto 73, tel. 30096, 181 rooms, most with bath, garden, garage,
pool and beach. Moderately expensive.

TORINO (TURIN), Piemonte

Second largest city of the north, this active city is the capital of Italy's automobile industry. Insignificant during the early Middle Ages, it became important after the 13th century, when the Savoia family consolidated its power. In the 19th century it led in the Risorgimento movement, which culminated in the unification of Italy with the Savoias as monarchs. Torino's large squares and wide avenues give it a very European appearance. Its main tourist attraction is the *Sacred Syndone,* preserved in a special chapel in the cathedral. Approximate population: 1,200,000.

Syndone = Holy Shroud of Turin

★★★★ TURIN PALACE HOTEL
Via Sacchi 8, near railroad station, tel. 548585, 125 rooms with bath, garage. Moderately expensive.

★★★★ JOLLY HOTEL AMBASCIATORI
Corso Vittorio Emanuele 104, tel. 5752, 197 rooms with bath, garage, lovely location. Moderately expensive.

One of Turin's newer hotels

★★★★ HOTEL SITEA
Via Carlo Alberto, 35, half-way between railroad station and city center, tel. 530512, 123 rooms with bath, garage. Moderately expensive.

★★★ HOTEL CITY
Via F. Juvarra 25, tel. 540546, 40 rooms with bath, garden, garage. Moderately expensive.

No restaurant

★★★ HOTEL ROYAL
Corso Regina Margherita 249, slightly out of town, tel. 748444, 65 rooms with bath, garden, tennis, garage. Moderate.

★★★ HOTEL MAJESTIC
Via U. Rattazzi 10, tel. 539153, 93 rooms with bath. Moderate.

★★ SUISSE TERMINUS HOTEL
Via Sacchi 2, near railroad station, tel. 542278, 76 rooms, most with bath, garage. Moderate.

★★ HOTEL LIGURE
Piazza Carlo Felice 85, tel. 512123, 149 rooms, most with bath, garage. Moderate.

★ HOTEL LANCASTER
Corso Filippo Turati 8, tel. 501720, 81 rooms with bath. Very moderate.

★ HOTEL PLAZA
Via Ilarione Petitti 18, tel. 632424, 55 rooms with bath, garage. Very moderate.

TRENTO, Trentino-Alto Adige

Severe and noble city, on the upper part of the long Adige River, surrounded by imposing mountains. Originally settled by the Romans, Trento became known because of the famous council held there from 1545 to 1563 in an attempt to stop Luther's Reformation. Now Trento is a florid town with small and medium wine, fruit and wood industries. It also has one of the most modern universities in Italy and is, like Bolzano, a meeting point for the two cultures of this area—the Italian and the German. Approximate population: 100,000.

★★★   GRAND ALBERGO TRENTO
Via Alfieri 1, tel. 26297, 94 rooms with bath, garden, good restaurant closed Sunday. Moderately expensive.

[handwritten: ask for balcony room]

★★   ALESSANDRO VITTORIA HOTEL
Via Romagnosi 16, tel. 80089, 50 rooms with bath, garage. Moderate.

★   EVEREST HOTEL
Corso Alpini 16, tel. 23180, 120 rooms with bath. Moderate.

TREVISO, Veneto

Charming and provincial, Treviso is one of the lesser known cities of the Venetian region. Most of its people are in various small industries, such as textiles or ceramic lamps, as well as agriculture and cattle raising. An interesting city to visit, it offers a variety of medieval and Renaissance buildings, externally decorated houses and two attractive rivers that intersect throughout the town, creating unusual corners. Approximate population: 20,000.

★★   HOTEL CONTINENTAL
Via Roma 16, near railroad station, tel. 57216, 81 rooms with bath. Moderate.

★★   HOTEL CARLTON
Largo Altinia 15, tel. 46988, 94 rooms, most with bath, snack bar. Moderate.

[handwritten: near rail station]

TRIESTE, Friuli-Venezia-Giulia

Main port on the Adriatic Sea, Trieste is a large, modern city. In the post-war years it has become an important industrial center, with such heavy industries as cement, steel, machinery, textiles and chemicals. While the original nucleus is Roman (1st century B.C.), Trieste began to develop only in the 18th century when it was used by the Hapsburgs as a free port. For over two centuries it had been expanding, and after 1918 it had become Italian again. Its commercial significance is great since it also acts as an entrance way for products that go to central Europe—the Jugolstadt oleoduct begins at Trieste. Culturally alive, it has a university, theaters and United Nations' International Center of Theoretical Physics. But the main city tradition is its *caffès,* always crowded, winter and summer, some famous for their literary habitués and for the lively discussions held in them. Approximate population: 265,000.

★★★   EXCELSIOR PALACE HOTEL
Riva Mandracchio 4, tel. 7690. 154 rooms with bath, central location, on waterfront. Moderately expensive.

★★★   HOTEL DUCHI D'AOSTA
Piazza Unità d'Italia, tel. 62081, 52 rooms with bath, good restaurant (Harry's Grill), closed Sunday. Moderately expensive.

★★   HOTEL COLOMBIA
Via della Geppa 18, tel. 69434, 40 rooms with bath. Moderate.

Near station

★   HOTEL SAN GIUSTO
Via Belli 3, tel. 764824, 46 rooms, most with bath, garage. Moderate.

VENEZIA (VENICE), Veneto

One of the world's most famous cities, Venezia is a series of small islands interconnected by numerous bridges that are woven into the waters of its lagoon. The city's population is around 100,000, an amazing number if we consider that they are often driven out of their houses by the merciless rise of the sea. Still, the splendid monuments, the luminous atmosphere, the regal aspect of this unique place are so spellbinding that they attract and hold people, no matter what the price. Words are not sufficient. This "pearl of the Adriatic" must be seen to be believed!

★★★★★   GRITTI PALACE
Campo Santa Maria del Giglio 2467, tel. 26044, 92 rooms with bath. One of the most famous hotels in Italy, with a view of the Grand Canal. A favorite with celebrities. Very Expensive.

★★★★ Restaurant was Hemingway's favorite

★★★★★   HOTEL CIPRIANI
Seasonal, isola della Giudecca 10, tel. 85068, 92 rooms with bath, garden, heated swimming pool, a lovely view of the *Isola di San Giorgio,* Expensive.

★★★★★   DANIELI ROYAL EXCELSIOR
Riva degli Schiavoni 4196, tel. 26480, 246 rooms with bath, just behind San Marco. Another of the splendid hotels in Venezia, larger than the *Gritti* but equally well staffed. Very expensive.

★★★★ Danieli Terrace, restaurant

★★★★   HOTEL EUROPA E BRITANNIA
Calle larga XXII Marzo 2159, tel. 700477, 206 rooms with bath, terrace on the Grand Canal. Expensive.

★★★★   HOTEL MONACO
Calle Vallaressi 1325, tel. 700211, 80 rooms with bath, good restaurant, closed Tuesdays. Expensive.

Near San Marco

★★★   HOTEL SATURNIA
Calle larga XXII Marzo 2398, tel. 708377, 96 rooms with bath. Moderately expensive.

★★★ Caravella restaurant

★★★   HOTEL GABRIELLI-SANDWIRTH
Riva Schiavoni 4100, tel. 31580, 110 rooms, most with bath, view of the San
Marco Canal. Moderately expensive.

★★★   HOTEL LA FENICE ET DES ARTISTES
Campiello Fenice 1936, tel. 32333, 68 rooms, most with bath. Moderate.

[handwritten: Near opera house]

★★   PARK HOTEL
Giardini Papadopoli, near railroad station, tel. 85394, 100 rooms with bath.
Moderately expensive.

VENTIMIGLIA (IM), Liguria

This city is in an important location near the French border. It is known for
its large flower market, and you should visit the Hanbury Garden, one of the
largest in the world. It has an interesting distribution of plants and flowers
along the steep coast that slopes down to the sea and many rare species of
plants. Approximate population: 27,000.

★   HOTEL BELSOGGIORNO
Via Asse 109, tel. 351286, 47 rooms with bath, parking. Moderately expensive.

★   HOTEL SEA GULL
Via Marconi 13, tel. 351726, 27 rooms with bath, view of the sea, restaurant,
Moderate.

Out of town

*[handwritten: * Restaurant]*

★   LA RISERVA
A Castel d'Appio, (5 km. to the north), tel. 39533, closed from September
15th to December 20th and from January to Easter, 21 rooms with bath,
garden, pool, parking, view. Moderately expensive.

VERONA, Veneto

After Venezia, Verona is the most important city of the region. Its location
is the main reason for its prosperity, which began in Roman times, continued
throughout the Middle Ages, with barbarian kings, as a free comune, and
finally under the powerful Della Scala family. In 1404 it passed into the hands
of Venezia, and remained so until 1796. There are monuments in Verona that
testify the different stages of its life, for example, the famous *Arena,* one of
the largest Roman amphitheaters that has survived in good condition (1st
century A.D.; lovely *S. Zeno,* with its precious bronze doors; *Castelvecchio,*
a lay medieval structure of the 14th century. A city of art and music—the
Arena is used for great opera performances during the summer—Verona is
one of the most attractive cities in northern Italy. It is also an important wine
growing center, producing some of the best wines in eastern Italy much as
Valpolicella and Amarone. Approximate population: 270,000.

★★★★   HOTEL DUE TORRI
Piazza S. Anastasia 4, tel. 34130, 100 rooms with bath, central location, lovely furniture. Expensive.

near cathedral

★★★   HOTEL ACCADEMIA
Via Scala 12, tel. 21643, 90 rooms, most with bath. Moderately expensive.

Central location

★★   HOTEL COLOMBA D'ORO
Via C. Cattaneo 10, near the Arena, tel. 21510, 55 rooms, most with bath, garage. Moderately expensive.

★   HOTEL S. LUCA
Volto S. Luca 8, tel. 591333, 34 rooms with bath. Moderate.

★   HOTEL SAMMICHELI
Via Valverde 2, tel. 23749, 15 rooms with bath. Moderate.

★   HOTEL FIRENZE
Corso Porta Nuova 88, tel. 590299, 60 rooms with bath. Moderately expensive.

VICENZA, Veneto

One of the most interesting cities in Italy from an architectural point of view, Vicenza has ancient origins and a Roman basis. After its share of battles with neighboring Padova and Verona, it gave itself to Venezia in 1404. Buildings done in Venetian–Gothic are followed by Renaissance ones, and during the 16th century the great Andrea Palladio adorned Vincenza with his neoclassical creations, a style that became a by-word all over Italy and Europe. At present Vicenza is an active industrial and commercial center. Approximate population: 120,000.

★★   HOTEL JOLLY CAMPOMARZIO
Viale Roma 27, tel. 24560, 35 rooms with bath. Moderately expensive.

near station

★   HOTEL CONTINENTAL
Via G. G. Trissino 89, tel. 505476, 52 rooms with bath. Moderately expensive.

★   HOTEL CITY
Viale Verona 12, tel. 45171, 23 rooms with bath, garden. Moderate.

Restaurants

ABANO TERME (PD), Veneto

★★★★   DELL'HOTEL TERME MICHELANGELO
2 km. west, toward Monteortone, tel. 524026, closed November 23rd–March 2nd. Full meals in evenings; cold buffet at noon. This new and modern

a good Veneto wine is valpolicella red

restaurant is noted for good food and service, plus a decent wine list. Call ahead. Moderate.

★★★   GASTON
Via Petrarca 25, tel. 669274, closed Mondays. Reasonable.

★★★   PICCOLO MARTE
At Torreglia, 6 km. from Abano, tel. 511177, closed Mondays, isolated, quiet location. Reasonable.

ACQUI TERME (AL), Piemonte

★★★   PARISIO
Via Alessandria 54, tel. 2232, closed Mondays and January. Good local cooking. Moderate.

ALASSIO (SV), Liguria

★★★   PALMA
Via Cavour 5, tel. 40314, closed Tuesdays (in winter) and from end of November to December 20th. Refined cooking and attentive service, plus good choice of local wines. Moderately expensive.

★★★   LA LIGGIA
Via Aleramo 3, tel. 469076, closed Mondays and from November to March. Simple restaurant that serves excellent Ligurian food and wine. Moderate.

ALBA (CN), Piemonte

The best Barbera red wine comes from Alba

★★★   DA BEPPE
Corso M. Coppino 20, tel. 43983, closed Fridays, one of the best in town. Moderate.

★★★   STELLA D'ORO
Good local restaurant, truffle specialties in season. Moderate.

Out-of-town

★★★   TRATTORIA DELL'ENOTECA
At Grinzane Cavour, in the castle that belonged to the family of the famous statesman. Tel. 62159, call ahead, closed Tuesdays. Moderate.

ALBENGA (SV), Liguria

★★★   C'ERA UNA VOLTA
A Villanova d'Albenga, tel. 58871. Closed Wednesdays from October to May. This restaurant has a good menu with new dishes added frequently; good choice of regional wines. Moderately expensive.

★★★   CASTELLO PUNTA SAN MARTINO
A Monte, tel. 51225. Closed Mondays and from first week of January to first week of February. Beautiful views of the sea, the countryside, the city and the island of Gallinara can be enjoyed while dining. Good food, adequate choice of Piemontese wine. Moderate.

AOSTA, Valle d'Aosta

★★★★   CAVALLO BIANCO
Via G. Aubert 15, tel. 2214, closed Thursdays. Always open from June to September. This restaurant has an antique wine cellar containing an excellent selection of wine, cozy, warm atmosphere, excellent food, drink, music and service, Moderately expensive.

★★★   BRASSERIE VALDÔTAINE
Via Xavier de Maistré, tel. 32076, closed Wednesdays and November. Its excellent location is the historical center of Aosta. Warm atmosphere, good service, food and wine. Moderately expensive.

★★★   DELL'HOTEL VALLE D'AOSTA
Corso Ivrea 134, tel. 41814, closed Tuesdays. Excellent music adds atmosphere to the already cozy dining room, good menu, wine selection could be better. Moderately expensive.

ASOLO (TV), Veneto

★★★★   CHARLY'S ONE
Via Roma 55, tel. 52201, closed Mondays. This restaurant with a pleasing and relaxing atmosphere has a large dining room and several outside tables. It is noted for its courteous and professional service, excellent food and vast wine list. Moderate.

One of the best local red wines is Bardolino

★★★★   VILLA CIPRIANI
Via Canova 298, tel. 52166, closed Mondays except April 1st–January 6th when it is always open. An elegant, refined restaurant noted for its precise and courteous service, excellent food and wine. Expensive.

ASTI, Piemonte

★★★   REALE
Piazza Alfieri 6, tel. 50240, closed Thursdays and July. Call for reservations. Housed in an old building, this restaurant has earned the reputation of being a restaurant of good wine where one eats well. Known for its Piemontese food, wine, and ice cream. Moderately expensive.

In addition to Asti Spumante, good local wines include Barbera, a dry red, and Moscato, sweet and white

★★★   FALCONE VECCHIO
Via S. Secondo 8, tel. 53106, closed Mondays and August. Seven centuries old (no kidding, we mean 700 years) you will find favorite dishes of that time on the menu today, good food and wine. Reasonable.

Out of town

★★★★   GENER NEUVO
Lungo Tanaro 4 (1 km. south of Asti), tel. 57270, closed Mondays, garden, parking. It's advisable to reserve a table as there is room for only 50 people. Special dishes can be ordered by telephoning at least two days in advance. Excellent food from antipasto to desert, good local wine. Moderate.

BELLAGIO (CO), Lombardia

★★★   LA PERGOLA
Seasonal, at Pescallo, tel. 950263, closed Tuesdays, excellent location on the lake, terrace, garden, parking. Moderately expensive.

★★★   IL PERLO-PANORAMA
(2 km. toward Asso), tel. 950229, closed Thursdays except during the season. Garden, beautiful view. Moderately expensive.

★★   BILACUS
Salita Serbelloni 32, tel. 950480, closed Mondays. Terrace, garden. Moderate.

BERGAMO, Lombardia

★★★★   VITTORIO
Via Papa Giovanni XXIII 21, tel. 218060, closed Wednesdays and August. This family-run place has the best food in town, even the fish is remarkable. Expensive.

★★★★   ANGELO
Borgo Santa Caterina 55, tel. 237103, closed Mondays and August. Elegant, mixing old and modern decor, this place serves very good food and good wine. Lovely garden in summer. Expensive.

★★★★   PERGOLA
Borgo Canale 62, tel. 223305, closed Sundays, Monday lunch and August. Classical, charming restaurant in the high city, excellent food that mixes Lombard and Tuscan cooking. Remarkable wine cellars and olive oil. Expensive.

★★★★   TRATTORIA DEL TEATRO
Via B. Colleoni 4, tel. 238862, closed Mondays and July. In the high city, this lovely old trattoria serves good local food, decent wine. Moderate.

BOLZANO, Trentino-Alto Adige

★★★★   DA ABRAMO
Piazza Gries 16, tel. 30141, closed Sunday evenings, Mondays and June 25th–July 20th. Good cuisine, with Italian bases and Mitteleuropean overtones, good wine list, polite and efficient service. Moderate.

[handwritten margin note: Lombardy's best red wine is Sassella, good up to 8 years]

[handwritten margin note: Famous Bergamo specialty is polenta, tasagna, made with milk, cheese and butter]

[handwritten margin note: Good local rosé here is Lagrein]

★★★★   CHEZ FREDERIC
Via Armando Diaz 12, tel. 41411, closed Tuesdays. In this city of Austrians and Italians, here is a good French restaurant. Adequate wines and service. It's advisable to reserve a table in advance. Reasonable.

Out of Town

★★★   CASTEL GUNCINÀ
2.5 km. in a northwestern direction. Charming hotel and good restaurant, splendid view of Bolzano and the Dolomites. Moderate.

BORDIGHERA (IM), Liguria

★★★   LE CHAUDRON
Piazza Bengasi 2, tel. 263592, closed Mondays and from the end of October until the first of December. Excellent food, service and selection of Ligurian wines. Moderately expensive.

★★   PININ-LA RESERVE
Via Arziglia 20, tel. 261322, closed Wednesdays. Moderately expensive.

★★   CHEZ LOUIS
Corso Italia 30, tel. 261602, closed Tuesdays. Moderate.

BORMIO (SO), Lombardia

★★★   CENDRE
Via Roma 20, tel. 903094, closed Mondays except from the middle of June until September, never closed on holidays. Small, 12-table, simple, and clean restaurant, home-style cooking, good wine, prices reasonable.

★★★   KUREC
Piazza Cavour 9, tel. 901219, closed Wednesdays. Valtellinese cuisine. Moderate.

CAMPIONE D'ITALIA (CO), Lombardia

★★★   DEL CASINO
Tel. 687921, on the lake shore, always open. This elegant restaurant offers a varied menu of international and regional food, good wine selection (mainly French and Swiss), the service depends on the waiter. Expensive.

★★★   TAVERNA
Piazza Roma, in front of the pier, tel. 687201, closed Wednesdays. Elegant restaurant, with courteous waiters, continuously changing menu depending on the season, mediocre wine selection. Moderately expensive.

Good choice for red here is Barbacarlo (Barbagallo), a bit sweet and tingling

★★   SPORTING
Beside the casino, good location on the lake, tel. 686131, closed Tuesdays, parking. Moderate.

CERNOBBIO (CO), Lombardia

★★★★   GRILL DI VILLA D'ESTE
Via Regina 40, tel. 511471, closed Mondays and Tuesdays at noon and from the end of October until the middle of November. This restaurant is located on the shore of Lago di Como in one of the most famous hotels of the world. Refined and elegant atmosphere, excellent, efficient service, good but limited wine list, average food. Expensive.

★★★★   VINO GIUSTO
Portici Hotel Regina Olga, tel. 512710, closed Wednesdays and August. Warm, cozy atmosphere, noted for its grilled and international dishes, good wine and discreet service. Moderately expensive.

★★★   HOSTARIA
Via Garibaldi 3, tel. 510151, closed Mondays and August. Reservations a must. Located in the main square of the city, this restaurant is extremely small with only 10 tables. Good, but slow service, as food is prepared upon ordering. Wine good but a limited selection. Moderately expensive.

★★★   TERZO CROTTO
Via Volta 21, tel. 510304, closed Sundays and January 10th–February 10th. The surroundings aren't very attractive, but the food is excellent. The wine is good, the service so-so. Moderate.

★★★   OLD ENGLAND
Via Regina 85, tel. 512693, closed Mondays and Tuesdays. Charming corner of England, almost a pub, this reataurant offers British and international food. Pleasant atmosphere, very good deserts. Moderately expensive.

CHIOGGIA (VE), Veneto

★★★   EL GATO
Campo S. Andrea 653, tel. 401806, closed Mondays and January 9th–25th. A fish restaurant, which offers traditional local dishes, good selection of wines. Moderately expensive.

★★★   LA PIAZZETTA
Piazzetta XX Settembre, tel. 403541, closed Mondays and January; open all of August. One of the best restaurants in the area. Simple, family-style atmosphere with the owner in the kitchen and his wife and children waiting on the tables. Excellent food and wine. Moderate.

COMO, Lombardia

★★★★   GESUMIN
Via 5 Giornate 44, tel. 266030, closed Sundays and August. Small, attractive place, serves best food in town, always crowded, call ahead. Very expensive.

Best Lombardy red is Gattinara, especially if over 5 years old

★★★★   DA CELESTINO
Lungo Lario Trento 11, tel. 263470, closed Wednesdays and two weeks in August. In the center of town, up a few steps, this pleasant restaurant offers good food. Reasonable.

★★★   IMBARCADERO
Piazza Cavour 20, tel. 277341, always open. Right on the shore of the lake, good food and plush surroundings. Moderately expensive.

CORTINA D'AMPEZZO (BL), Veneto

★★★★★   EL TOULÀ
Via Ronco 123, tel. 3339, closed Mondays, open from Dec. 8 to Easter and during the month of August. This is the most elegant restaurant in Cortina, with efficient and courteous service, refined hospitality, simple, but first-class food and excellent wines. Expensive.

★★★★★   RACHELE
At Salieto, tel. 60053, open or closed depending on the owner's health. Necessary to call ahead. Delicious home-style cooking, excellent service, unforgettable experience. Moderately expensive.

COURMAYEUR (AO), Valle d'Aosta

★★★★   LA MAISON DE FILIPPO
Località Entrèves, tel. 89968, closed Tuesdays and June. The most famous and characteristic restaurant of Valle d'Aosta. Wooden chests filled (almost overflowing) with cheeses, salami, sausages, breads and nuts. Excellent food. Moderately expensive.

Good local dish = trota alla Valdostana, poached trout

★★★   K2
Località Villair, via Val Sapin 19, tel. 82475, closed Mondays, November and from May to June. This rustic mountain restaurant has a good menu (typical of the region), good local wine and excellent service. Moderate.

★★★   BRENVA
Località Entrèves, tel. 89285, closed Mondays and some holidays. This newly restored mountain restaurant is an ideal place to relax after a day's skiing. Excellent service, good food, although menu lacks fantasy. Moderate.

GARDONE RIVIERA (BS), Lombardia

Good dry Lombardian red is Buttafuoco

★★   LA STALLA
Near Vittoriale, tel. 21038, closed Tuesdays, parking. Moderate.

★   SERENO
Near Vittoriale, tel. 20171, closed Mondays. Moderate.

★ EMILIANO
Corso della Repubblica 55, tel. 21517, closed Wednesdays. Inexpensive.

GENOVA (Genoa), Liguria

★★★★ DA SIMONA
Nervi, via Aurelia 50, tel. 328635, closed Sunday evenings, Mondays, and August 15th–September 10th. Nervi is not in Genova, but is nearby and worth the trip, especially for those interested in good food. The owner was a student of a great chef, Bergese, and it shows. Excellent wines and spirits. Moderate.

a good local white wine is Coronata

★★★★ CARDINALI
Via Assarotti 60/r, tel. 870380, closed Sundays and August. Probably the most elegant restaurant in town, offers classical cooking and appropriate wines. Moderately expensive.

★★★ TOE DRUE
Sestri Ponente, via Corsi 44, tel. 671100, evenings only, closed Sundays, Mondays and August. Be sure to call ahead, only 35 settings. An unusual *osteria* in an industrial area of Genova. The fish are caught the night before, the food is cooked by the owner's wife and is served by the owner at crowded tables. The whole experience is a treat, the wines superb. Very moderate.

★★★ ANTICA OSTERIA DEL BAI
Via Quarto 12, a Quarto dei Mille, tel. 387478, closed Mondays and August 15th–September 10th. Located in an old anti-Saracen fort (one of many built during the Middle Ages to defend the city against pirate attacks), this place offers excellent seafood, cooked the Genoese way. Advisable to call ahead, even if the premises are large. Good service and good wines. Moderate. *Note:* One of the truly historic places in Italy. Pope Pius VII stopped here during his forced trip to Avignon and exile. Then, years later, Garibaldi and some of his *Mille* ate here before going off to the famous Sicilian landing.

★★ DA FRANCO
Archivolto Mongiardino 2/r, tel. 203614, closed Sundays and August. In the heart of old Genova, this place isn't easy to find. Once found, do not shrink back in horror at the decorations, which please some more than others. Enjoy the good seafood and the choice of wines. Inexpensive.

★★ OSVALDO
Via Dellacasa 2/r, Boccadassa, tel. 310004, closed Mondays and August. The location on the little port, is charming. Truly a fisherman's restaurant, with only 20 place settings, where you eat what was caught the night before. Good wine. Moderate.

Good local bet = frittata genovese, spinach omelette

★★ ZEFFERINO
Via XX Settembre 20, tel. 591990, closed Wednesdays. This very good restaurant in the heart of town is a pleasant alternative to the many seafood restaurants. Enjoy the wide choice of pasta and meat dishes, and fish if you wish. Good wines. Moderately expensive.

★★   PICHIN
Vico dei Parmigiani 6/r, tel. 540554, closed Sunday evenings, Mondays and August. In an attractive, central location, serves good food and exceptionally good wines. Moderate.

Good local dish = cima alla genovese, cold stuffed beef or veal

★   CICCHETTI 1860
A Quinto, via Angelo Giannelli 41/r, tel. 331641. A bit out of town, serves genuine regional food, gives honest service, insignificant wine. Inexpensive.

★   GRAN GOTTO
Via Fiume 11/r, near Brignole railroad station, tel. 564344, closed Sundays and first 15 days in August. This place has a classical decor, old-fashioned regional food, good wine. Moderate.

GRADO (GO), Friuli-Venezia Giulia

★★★★   ANTICA TRATTORIA DA NICO
Via Marina 10, tel. 80470, closed Thursdays, always open on holidays. This restaurant is noted for its excellent food (dishes invented with what is available fresh in the local markets), excellent choices of wine and courteous service. Expensive.

★★★   COLUSSI
Via Roma 2, tel. 80110, closed Mondays and 20 days in December. Besides the main dining room, this restaurant offers a garden–terrace in the warm weather. Noted as a fish restaurant, good service and wine. Moderately expensive.

★★   ADRIATICO
Campiello della Torre 3, tel. 80002, closed Wednesdays and some holidays during the winter. Specializes in fish from the Adriatic, excellent selection of white wine, especially from the Friuli and Veneto regions, good service. Moderate.

IMPERIA, Liguria

At Oneglia

★★   CACCIATORI-DA SALVO
Via Vieusseux 14, tel. 23763, closed Mondays. Local specialties. Moderate.

★★   BEPPA
Via Andrea Doria, tel. 24286, closed Tuesdays. Specialty is fish. Inexpensive.

At Porto Maurizio

★★   NANNINA
Viale Matteotti 56, tel. 20208, closed Wednesdays and from the middle of November to the middle of December. Regional specialties. Moderately expensive.

★   LUCIO E PIERO
Lungomare C. Colombo 114, tel. 61062, closed Mondays. Specialty is fish. Moderate.

IVREA (TO), Piemonte

★★★   SIRIO
Via Lago Sirio 47, tel. 423646, closed Fridays from November until February. comfortable, relaxing atmosphere with a beautiful garden on the lake. Variety of traditional Piemontese food, excellent choice of wine. Moderately expensive.

★★   MORO
Corso d'Azeglio 41, tel. 2136, closed Sundays. Moderate.

★★   IL GAMBERO
Via Corte d'Assise 8, tel. 423763, closed Thursdays. Moderate.

LA SPEZIA, Liguria

★★   POSTA
Via Don Minzoni 22, tel. 34419, closed Saturdays. Moderately expensive.

★   CARLINO NUOVO
Piazza C. Battisti 37, tel. 32291, closed Thursdays. Moderate.

★   DA DINO
Via Da Passano 19, tel. 361557, closed Mondays. Tuscan cuisine. Inexpensive.

LERICI (SP), Liguria

★★★   CONCHIGLIA
Piazza del Molo, tel. 967344, closed Wednesdays and certain fall holidays. It's advisable to make reservations as the restaurant is small. Specialty is fish. Good service and good selection of regional wines. Moderately expensive.

★★   LE DUE CORONE
Via Mazzini 14, tel. 967417, closed Thursdays and from mid-November to mid-December. Advisable to make reservations. Excellent food, good service and selection of local wines. Moderately expensive.

★★   DA PAOLINO
Via San Francesco 14, tel. 967801, closed Mondays and one week in September. Excellent food and service. Adequate wine selection. Cozy, warm atmosphere. Moderately expensive.

[handwritten margin note:] Good local wine, yellow in color, is Cinqueterre

[handwritten margin note:] Local table wine, red/white, is Dolceaqua, not as sweet as you might think from name

MANTOVA (Mantua), Lombardia

Osso bucco is a Lombardian invention

★★★   IL CIGNO
Piazza d'Arco 1, tel. 327101, closed Mondays, Tuesday evenings and August. On a lovely square, this old building will delight the antique lovers. Excellent food, mostly local, done with loving care. Good wine selection. Moderately expensive.

★★   BRUSCHETTA
Via Cremona 3, tel. 20238, closed Mondays. Lively and gay, this unpretentious "pizzeria" also serves some good dishes and has good wine. Moderate.

★★   GARIBALDINI
Via S. Longino 7, tel. 29237, closed Fridays and July. Lovely, central location, good service, average cooking. Moderately expensive.

MERANO (BZ), Trentino-Alto Adige

★★★   ANDREA
Via Galilei 16, tel. 24400, closed Wednesdays and some holidays. Small, elegant restaurant with a reputation for excellent food (menu depends on the season and varies daily according to market's fresh products), wine and courteous service. Make reservations. Moderately expensive.

★★★   DELL' HOTEL VILLA MOZART
Via San Marco 26, tel. 30630, open all year. An elegant, refined and comfortable restaurant. Reservations necessary. It has a reputation for having the best quality of atmosphere, food, wine and service. Very expensive.

MILANO, Lombardia

★★★★★   GUALTIERO MARCHESI
Via Bonvesin de la Riva 9, tel. 741246, closed Sundays, Mondays at noon, Saturdays in July, August and December 25th–January 6th. Mr. Marchesi is considered one of the best cooks in Italy. His French training inspires his *nouvelle cuisine* masterpieces, but his genius is Italian. Be sure to call ahead. Very expensive.

★★★★★   SAINT-ANDREWS
Via S. Andrea 23, tel. 793132. Closed Sundays. Refined atmosphere, excellent food and wine, this is where the *Milano bene* meets, eats and exchanges sophisticated gossip. Advisable to call ahead. Expensive.

★★★★★   ANTICA OSTERIA DEL PONTE
Cassinetta di Lugagnano, tel. 9460222, closed Sundays, Mondays and August, out of town, 20 km. going west. An old country house in a tiny town on the Naviglio. The divine food is prepared with loving care and served with simple dignity. Limited menu, each dish a small masterpiece. Call in advance. Expensive.

Small and charming

★★★★   SCALETTA

Piazzale Stazione Genova 3, tel. 8350290, closed Sundays, Mondays and August. This delightfully decorated place serves excellent, imaginative food, offers a very good choice of wines, should be booked well in advance, as much as a whole week. Moderately expensive.

★★★★   PORTO

Piazza Generale Cantore, tel. 8321481, closed Sundays, Mondays noon and August. One of the best fish restaurants in Italy and Milano. Elegant location in an old Austrian castle. Call ahead. Moderately expensive.

★★★   PICCOLO GOURMET

Corso Italia 16, tel. 893819, closed Sundays and August. Elegant, lovely, centrally located, ideal for an important lunch or special evening. The food and wines are equal to the task. Moderately expensive.

★★★   PIERO

Via Nullo, Angolo via Goldoni, closed Sundays and August. In a new, large location, this simple tavern has always attracted Milano's VIPs because of its fresh, genuine food and its light dishes. The wines are excellent. Moderate.

Venetian-style cooking

★★★   TOULÀ

Piazza Paolo Ferrari 6, tel. 870302 or 8690575, closed Sundays and August. The Milanese version of this chain of excellent restaurants, dedicated to refined comfort and delicate cuisine. The wine list is long and well chosen, the atmosphere elegant and sophisticated. Expensive.

★★★   DA GIUSEPPE

At the Hilton Hotel, via Galvani 12, tel. 6983, open all year. As in Rome, the Hilton of Milano also boasts a good restaurant. Good traditional dishes and some successful attempts at *nouvelle cuisine.* As expected, plush surroundings, efficient service. Expensive.

★★   GIANNINO

Via Sciesa 8, tel. 5452948 or 5452765, closed Saturdays, Sundays and August. One of the traditional restaurants of Milano, has had its ups and downs in the kitchen, always elegant up front. Now the classical menu is good again, and the local rich are filling up the place. Be sure to call ahead. Expensive.

★★   GRAN SAN BERNARDO, DA ALFREDO

Via G. A. Borgese 14, tel. 389000, closed Sundays, Saturdays in July, three weeks from Christmas to January and August. Another of Milano's famous restaurants, old and noted for Lombard cooking. The setting is simple, the service cool, but the clients always come to taste the good food and see each other. Fair wines. Moderate.

★★   FRANCA

Viale Certosa 235, tel. 305238, closed Sundays, Saturday and Monday evenings and August. You eat what you get, but it's very good indeed. Tasty, hearty, Italian food, served in a simple *trattoria.* Good wine. Moderate.

★★   MALAVOGLIA
Via Giovanni da Milano 4, tel. 720664, closed Saturdays at noon and Sundays, 15 days in August, Easter and from Christmas to January. On the outskirts of town on a crowded corner of *Città degli Studi*. The cooking is simple, genuine and Sicilian. Leave room for the rich desserts and a small glass of sweet Pantelleria wine. Moderate.

★★   BERTI
Via Algarotti 20, near the railroad station and Hilton, tel. 6081696. Closed Sundays, mid-August and end of December. This is one of Milano's standbys. Lovely garden in summer, good food and excellent choice of wines, a serious approach to classical Lombard cooking. Moderate; if the wine is special, a little more expensive.

★★   BOCCONDIVINO
Via Carducci 17, tel. 866040, only evenings, closed Sundays and August. An unusual *osteria* that attracts cheese lovers. Also raw vegetables, cold cuts, and good wine. Moderately expensive.

★★   MALATESTA
Via Bianca di Savoia 19, tel. 5461079, closed Sundays, Saturday evenings and August. Elegant, slightly cool, serves good food, which sometimes is quite imaginative. The wines are few, but extremely well chosen. Expensive.

★★   GROTTA DA MARINO
Via Bergamini 13, slightly out of town, tel. 862917, closed Sundays, Mondays at noon and August. Warm, friendly, casual, this place serves very good fish, good meat, good wines and spirits. An elegant evening. Expensive.

★★   ELO WUE
Via Sabatelli 1, tel. 3185666, closed Sundays and August. The best Chinese restaurant in Milano, a good wine list, elegant surroundings; Peking duck available, provided you call in advance. Moderately expensive.

★   GAMBA DE LEGN
Via Elba 30, tel. 463091 or 490579, closed Sundays, Saturdays during the summer and August. An old-fashioned *trattoria* that serves traditional Milanese food. Tyrone Power once ate here. Moderate.

★   SAVINI
Galleria Vittorio Emanuele 11, tel. 8058343 or 8058364, closed Sundays and August. Part of the city's tradition, Savini is *the* Milano restaurant for decoration, silverware, location and overall class. But the food has been less than average, and the new management is working hard to regain the old reputation. We wish them well, but it's too soon to comment. Expensive.

In the galleria

★   TOPAIA
Via Argelati 46, a bit out of town, on the Naviglio, tel. 8373469, closed Sundays and August. A fun evening, a pleasant, friendly, cheerful atmosphere, occasionally, good guitar music, simple dishes prepared with loving care, some very special wines. Moderately expensive.

Minestrone alla milanese is prepared with pork fat

★   MICHELE E MARISA, ALLA SCALA
Via Marino 7, tel. 800197. At this time we don't know the closing day. In the heart of town, this Tuscan *trattoria* should continue to attract the show business crowd it was famous for at the old location on via Spiga. We also hope they'll keep the honest price and good wine.

★   LUCIANO
Via Ugo Foscolo 1, tel. 866818 or 870281, closed Mondays and August. Luxurious, centrally located, with excellent service. The food is valid, classical, old fashioned, the choice of wines is more than adequate. Moderately expensive.

★   BAGUTTA
Via Bagutta 14, tel. 702767, closed Sundays, in August and from December to January. Unfortunately, the food is no longer special, but the busy, attractive people still come here, and the location is as central as can be. Expensive.

★   VITTORIA
Via Anfiteatro 6, tel. 860726, closed Saturdays at noon, Sundays and mid-August. This small, new, pleasantly decorated place serves excellent food, a delicious bread, marvelous oil and some good wines. Moderate.

MONZA (MI), Lombardia

★★   CIGNO BLU
Via Cavallotti (angle of via Volturno), tel. 384932, closed Wednesdays and two weeks in June. This restaurant with two rustic dining rooms is *not* a place for calm, intimate dinners. During the day especially there is continuous comings and goings (rare exceptions). Average wine selection and good food; quick busy waiters. Moderately expensive.

★   ANTICA TRATTORIA
Piazza Carrobio 2, tel. 23825, closed Fridays. Moderate.

★   CORONA FERREA
Piazza Duomo 2, tel. 23637, closed Sundays. Moderate.

PADOVA (PADUA), Veneto

★★★   DOTTO
Via Squarcione 25, old center of city, tel. 25055, closed Sunday evenings, Mondays, and August. The best-known and most elegant restaurant in town, run with courteous efficiency. The food is fresh and seasonal, the wines chosen by a connoisseur. Moderately expensive.

★★   ISOLA DI CAPRERA
Via Marsiglio da Padova 11–15, tel. 39385, closed Tuesdays and August. Central location, good reputation, best choice is fish. Decent service and moderate wine list. Moderately expensive.

Good local dish = pollo alla padovana, roasted spiced chicken

Out of Town

★★★★   LE PADOVANELLE
Ponte di Brenta, via Ippodromo 4, tel. 625622, closed Sunday evenings, Mondays and August 1st–22nd. Charming location, at the race track, midst greenery; with hotel. The food becomes almost secondary, and in fact is. Good service. Moderately expensive.

★★★   BORDIN, AL CANCELLETTO
Camin, Zona Industriale IIa, via Corsica 4, tel. 760193, closed Sunday evenings, Mondays and August. Located in an area that was once rural and is now industrial, this excellent *trattoria* serves simple good food. The wine is made with family-grown grapes. The place is small, so be sure to call ahead. Worth the trouble of going out of town! Moderate.

PAVIA, Lombardia

★★★   CASTELLO DI COZZO
Cozzo Lomellina, tel. 74298, closed Tuesdays, January and August. Only with reservation. Fabulous old castle, accurately redone with taste. Refined table setting, excellent cellar. The vegetable garden on the premises guarantees home-grown delicacies. Waitresses will serve exquisite food of regional flavor. Expensive.

★★   BIXIO
Via Strada Nuova 81, tel. 25343, closed Sunday evenings, Mondays and August. A serious, professional place, good food, good wine list. Moderately expensive.

★   PIERINO
Viale Partigiani 141, tel. 466510, closed Sundays. A little out of town, this simple place offers good local food, a decent house wine. Moderate.

PORTOFINO (GE), Liguria

★★★   IL PITOSFORO
At the arcade, tel. 690268. Closed Tuesdays (from June to September) and from January 6th to the end of February. Excellent food and service. Large and varied menu and wine list. Expensive.

★★   DELFINO
On the harbor, tel. 69081, closed Thursdays. Expensive.

★★   STELLA
On the harbor, tel. 69007, closed Wednesdays. Moderately expensive.

★   BATTI
Vico Nuovo 17, tel. 69379, closed Mondays. Moderately expensive.

[handwritten margin note:] Garden dining in summer. Portofino has its own dry, white wine, Portofino

PORTO VENERE (SP), Liguria

★★★   ISEO
Calata Doria 9, tel. 900610, closed Wednesdays (except in the summer) and November. An excellent location on the harbor, where you can enjoy the view of the La Spezia gulf from the well-lit wooden veranda. Specialty of the house is fish. Moderately expensive.

★★★   AL GAVITELLO DA MARIO
Calata Doria 20, tel. 900215, closed Thursdays (except in July and August); open from April to October. An old fisherman's house, this restaurant has a very cozy and romantic atmosphere. Specialty is fish, excellent white wine from the surrounding hills. Moderately expensive.

★★   TAVERNA DEL CORSARO
On the promontory, tel. 900622, closed Thursdays. View of the gulf. Moderate.

RAPALLO (GE), Liguria

Pesto, basil, is a great Ligurian favorite. Try it on lasagne or with gnocchi, dumplings

★★★★   A CIGHÉUGNA
Via Sottocroce da via Savagna, tel. 61864, open Saturday evenings and Sundays or from Monday thru Thursday by reservation for a party of at least 15 people. Best restaurant in the area. There is no menu. Every dish, excellently prepared, is brought to you on a huge cart made by the owner (all the furniture of the restaurant is made by him). Wine is made by an uncle from Piemonte. Late at night the signora tells the story of her restaurant. Moderately expensive.

★★★   DA TONINO
Via della Vittoria 5, tel. 50745, closed Thursdays and November 6th–December 6th. Excellent home style cooking, good national and international (French, Yugoslavian, Hungarian) wine selection. Moderate.

★★   DA ARDITO
At San Pietro di Novello [3 km. (1.8 mi.) to the west], via Canale 9, tel. 51551, closed Wednesdays and January 15th–February 15th. Good food, excellent white wine from Liguria and Veneto. Moderately expensive.

SAINT-VINCENT (AO), Valle d'Aosta

★★★   BATEZAR
Via Marconi 1, tel. 3164, closed Wednesdays, for Thursday lunch in the winter and November. Located in the center of Saint-Vincent, this restaurant has a refined and warm atmosphere. Excellent, quick service, excellent food, good wine selection. Expensive.

★★   LE GRENIER
Piazza Zerbion 1, tel. 2224, closed Tuesdays, Wednesdays at noon, January 7th–24th and June. Warm atmosphere with soft lights and large beams of dark

wood. Large selection of dishes, some specialties of the region, selection of wine is not too good. Expensive.

★★ DELL'HOTEL BILLIA
Tel. 3446, always open. Noted actors, the jet-set and well-known business-men are among this attractive and spacious restaurant's clientele. It has a well-equipped kitchen, which can prepare for large numbers of people. It offers six types of local mineral water, as well as local wines. Excellent service and food. Moderately expensive.

SAN REMO (IM), Liguria

★★★ PESCE D'ORO
Corso Cavallotti 272, tel. 86641, closed Mondays and June. Reservations necessary. Excellent food, service and wine. Specialties of the house are fish and Ligurian dishes. A varied assortment of excellent regional and Italian wines. Expensive.

Have the local Vermentino, a dry white wine, with a pesto (basil) flavored dish

★★★ DA GIANNINO
Via Roma 47, tel. 70843, closed Mondays and June 20th–July 29th. Advis-able to make reservations. Most elegant restaurant of the area. Delicate balance of atmosphere, service and food. Excellent wine selection, specially Ligurian and Piemontese. Moderately expensive.

★★ U PISCI SPADA
Piazza Bresca 14, tel. 72985, closed Wednesdays and October. Characteris-tic fisherman's restaurant, genuine, home-style cooking, adequate wine selec-tion, good service. Moderate.

SANTA MARGHERITA (GE), Liguria

★★ LA CAMBUSA
Via Bottaro 2, tel. 87410, closed Thursdays (except July 15th–August 15th) and from January 8th to the middle of February. Pleasant atmosphere, excel-lent service. Specialty of the house is fish. Wine selection does not equal the quality of the food. Moderately expensive.

★★ ALL' ANCORA
Via Maragliano 7, tel. 80559, closed Mondays and January. Homelike atmo-sphere, courteous service, excellent food. Wine is barely acceptable. Moder-ately expensive.

★ DEI PESCATORI
Via Bottaro 44, tel. 86747, closed Wednesdays. Moderately expensive.

★ LA PARANZA
Via Ruffini 46, tel. 80686, closed Tuesdays. Moderately expensive.

★ FARO
Via Maragliano 24a, tel. 86867, closed Tuesdays. Moderate.

SARZANA (SP), Ligurin

★★   LA SCALETTA
Via Bradia 3, tel. 60585, closed Tuesdays. Moderately expensive.

★   LA CAPANNINA-DA CICCIO
(At Bocca di Magra–11 km. south), tel. 65568, closed Mondays. Moderate.

Out of Town

★★★★★   LOCANDA DELL'ANGELO
At Marinella, viale XXV Aprile, tel. 64391. One of the best restaurants in Italy, probably in Europe. This charming, modern inn offers comfortable rooms upstairs and a dining room full of light, with a view of the sloping lawn. The food is fresh, extremely well prepared, and exquisitely Italian. The cellar is stocked with the same good taste and the whole experience is one you will long remember. Expensive.

SESTRIERE (TO), Piemonte

★★   LA BRUA
(1 km. towards Sauze di Cesana), tel. 76000. Best to make reservations. Tuscan dishes. Moderately expensive.

★   LA BAITA
Tel. 7496, closed Tuesdays. Moderate.

STRESA (NO), Piemonte

★★★   IL BORROMEO DEL GRAND HOTEL ET DES ILES BORROMÉES
Corso Umberto 67, tel. 30431, open year round. Remodeled dining rooms in the style of the "Belle Epoque" when Stresa reached the peak of her splendor. Dishes from all regions of Italy with a predominance of Piemontese plates. Also a few international dishes. Adequate selection of wines. Moderately expensive.

★★   EMILIANO
Corso Italia, tel. 31396, closed Tuesdays (from October to May) and November. You can eat very well in this comfortable atmosphere. Special wine selection, excellent service, Moderately expensive.

TORINO (Turin), Piemonte

Turin is the birthplace of vermouth

★★★★★   CONT PIOLETT
Strada Santa Margherita 150, tel. 831028, open evenings only, closed Sundays and August. The most elegant in town, imaginative, well-chosen menu, good Piedmontese wines, lovely setting, beautiful garden in summer. Be sure to call ahead. Expensive.

★★★★   GATTO NERO
Corso Turati 14, tel. 590414 or 590477, closed Sundays, Mondays at noon
and August. Classical Tuscan cooking, considered the best of its kind in
Torino. Attentive service, pleasant atmosphere, good wines and other spirits,
excellent coffee. Moderately expensive.

★★★★   MONTECARLO
Via San Francesco da Paola 37, tel. 540412, closed Saturdays at noon,
Sundays and July. This classic, good restaurant is run by a Venetian with a
very good feeling for wines and food. Elegant, with good service, call ahead.
Moderately expensive.

★★★   SMARRITA
Corso Unione Sovietica 244, tel. 390657, closed Mondays. Fairly new, but
going strong. Good food, part Tuscan, part Piedmontese, part international.
Good wine. Expensive.

★★★   VILLA SASSI
Strada Traforo di Pino 47, out of town, tel. 890556, closed Sundays and
August. Interesting experience, not so much for the food but for the lovely
setting in an 18th-century villa. Expensive.

★★★   DEL CAMBIO
Piazza Carignano 2, tel. 546690, closed Sundays and August. This refined,
overdecorated, elegant restaurant is a classic with the city's aristocracy. The
food is regional, good, well served. Moderately expensive.

Owned by Cinzano vermouth people

★★★   IL BUCO
Via Lombriasco 4, tel. 442210, closed Sundays and ten days in July. This
charming *trattoria* has changed management and is now the closest thing to
a *nouvelle cuisine* offering available in Torino. A worthwhile trip for true
gourmets. Moderate.

★★★   IL CIOCOLON
Via XXV Aprile 11, tel. 630782, open only evenings, except on holidays,
closed Mondays and August. Excellent food, cheerful place. Mixture of Venetian and central European cooking, with a touch of genius and some surprises.
Good wines. Moderate.

★★   LA CAPANNINA
Via Donati 1, tel. 545405, closed Sundays and August. The owner has a
feeling for food and show business. Regional dishes, good wines. Moderate.

★★   ANTICA TRATTORIA PARIGI
Corso Rosselli 83, tel. 592593, closed Wednesdays and August. The name
derives from the road, which once led to Paris. The food is old fashioned,
simple, inspired. Each day is dedicated to a different specialty. Good local
wines. Inexpensive.

★★   AL BUE ROSSO
Corso Casale 10, tel. 830753, closed Mondays and August. Once a stable,

this restaurant is now one of the most attractive places in town. Very good food, excellent desserts and wines. Moderately expensive.

Good regional dish = peperoni alla piemontese, cold stuffed peppers

★★   OSTU BACU
Corso Vercelli 226, tel. 264579, closed Mondays and August. This small, warm and hospitable restaurant is run by a family foursome: father, mother, son and daughter-in-law. The food is regional, well thought out, delicious. Very good wine list, served by a sommelier. Be sure to call ahead, only 50 settings. Moderate.

★★   FERRERO
Corso Vittorio Emanuele 54, near the railroad station, tel. 546081, closed Fridays. This is an unexpectedly elegant restaurant that serves good food, offers good service, has a good wine list. Expensive.

★   TRE GALLINE
Via Bellezia 37, tel. 546833, closed Mondays and August. Good regional cooking by a native Piedmontese. The Barbera d'Asti wine is from the owners vineyards. Moderate.

TRENTO, Trentino-Alto Adige

★★   CHIESA
Via San Marco 64, tel. 985577, closed Mondays and 15 days in June. Good food served in an 18th-century building. Good choice of local wines. Moderately expensive.

Good local dish = lepre alla trentina, sweet-sour jugged hare

★★   PORT' AQUILA-DAI GIUS
Via Cervara 66, tel. 26139, closed Sundays and one month in summer. Genuine local cooking in traditional surroundings, regional wines. Moderate.

TREVISO, Veneto

★★★★   DA ALFREDO EL TOULÀ
Via Collalto 26, tel. 40275, closed Mondays and August 10th–25th. Unexpectedly, in this quiet provincial town is one of the best restaurants in Italy, the parent house of the El Toulà chain. A charming atmosphere is combined with the newest in Venetian, Italian and international cooking. The owner was a forerunner of the noted *nouvelle cuisine* theories. Good wine and service. Expensive.

★★★   BECCHERIE
Piazza Ancillotto 10, in the heart of the city, tel. 40871, closed Fridays, Saturdays at noon and the last 15 days in August. The most authentic and traditional restaurant in Treviso. Some dishes are revivals of old Renaissance fare. Excellent service, good wines. Moderate.

★★   L' INCONTRO
Largo di Porta Altinia 13, tel. 47717, closed Wednesday, Thursdays at noon and August 10th–25th. A modern, elegant restaurant located under a 15th-

century door. Charming service, simple and refined food, good wines. During the musical season—from October to December—open until 2 A.M. Moderately expensive.

TRIESTE, Friuli-Venezia-Giulia

★★★   SUBAN
Via Cornici 2, tel. 54368, closed Mondays, Tuesdays and August. Lovely view, excellent food. A remarkable combination of French cooking and Slav influences and the best cellar in town. Moderately expensive.

★★   AL GRANZO
Piazza Venezia 7, tel. 762322, closed Sunday evenings, Tuesdays, Wednesdays and February. A seafront eatery of old tradition, this is the place for fish in Trieste, especially the famous grauçeola. Good local wines and good service. Moderately expensive.

★★   SACRA OSTARIA
Via Campo Marzio 13, tel. 744968, closed Sundays, holidays and November. The chef is considered by some to be the most knowledgeable gastronome in Trieste. Moderately expensive.

★★   LE CAVE
Via Valerio 142, tel. 54555. A small fish place, expensive but very good. Be sure to call in advance. Expensive.

★★   HARRY'S GRILL DUCHI D'AOSTA
Piazza Unità 2, tel. 62081, closed Sundays. The most elegant in town, lovely atmosphere, cooking that represents the best of Trieste's great tradition. Some innovations as well. Expensive.

★   DANEN
Via Nazionale 194, tel. 211241, closed Thursdays and January 7th–February 7th. Typical Slav cooking, interesting and different. Good local wines, decent service. Moderate.

★   BUFFET BENEDETTO
Via XXX Ottobre 19, tel. 61655, closed Mondays and August. Combination of a delicatessen, cafeteria and restaurant, this is a worthwhile gourmet experience, even if the service is sometimes sloppy. Moderate.

VENEZIA, Veneto

★★★★★   DELL'HOTEL GRITTI
Campo S. Maria del Giglio 2467, tel. 26044, closed from mid-November to the end of February. In the most refined hotel, an intimate, quiet dining room and the best food in town. Very expensive.

★★★★   HARRY'S BAR
Calle Vallareso 1323, tel. 36797, closed Mondays. For the past 50 years this

Owned by Locanda Cipriani people

place has been a "must" for elegant people in Venice. The food is good, the atmosphere sophisticated, the wines excellent. expensive.

★★★★   LOCANDA CIPRIANI
Isola di Torcello, tel. 730150, closed Mondays, except in summer, and November 4th–March 15th. A beautiful, quiet inn with only a few rooms; simply prepared, exquisite food. Moderately expensive.

Catch the boat to Torcello from Harry's Bar at noon

★★★★   DANIELI TERRACE
Riva degli Schiavoni 4196, tel. 26480. The view of the lagoon, the quality of the service, the carefully prepared food all contribute to make a dinner here as memorable as any. If you have only one evening in Venezia and the weather is clear, this is the place to dine. Expensive.

★★★   ANTICO MARTINI
Campo San Fantin 1983, tel. 24121, closed noon on Tuesdays, and from December to March. Charming atmosphere, good international and Venetian food, wide choice of wines, an excellent house white. Expensive.

Summer garden dining

★★★   LA CARAVELLA
Calle XXII Marzo 2397, tel. 708901, closed Wednesdays. Refined, with a unique appearance that unites Venetian opulence and the English navy, this restaurant serves good food and offers the best wine list in town. Expensive.

★★   AL GRASPO DE UVA
San Marco 5094, close to the Rialto Bridge, tel. 23647 and 700150, closed Mondays and from end of November to Christmas. One of the better known *trattorie* in town, serves excellent fish and adequate wine. Moderately expensive.

★★   ANTICA BESSETTA
Calle Salvio 1395, Santa Croce, tel. 37687, closed Wednesdays and July 10th–September 1st. Simple, old-fashioned, very fresh and well-made Venetian food. Let the waiter–owner tell you what to eat, and remember that the best dishes are mentioned last. Moderate.

ask for fegato alla veneziana, calves' liver with onions

★★   AL CONTE PESCAOR
Piscina San Zulian 544, near S. Marco, tel. 21483, closed Tuesdays and from mid-January to mid-February. Simple and elegant seafood place. Uncomplicated, well-chosen food. Moderate.

★★   LIBERTY E PAGODA, DELL'HOTEL DES BAINS
At Lido, lungomare Marconi 17, tel. 76592, open from March to November. Delightfully decorated in art decò, this restaurant offers food that will remind you of the turn of the century. The *Pagoda* is done in *cinoiserie.* Moderately expensive.

★   ANTICA TRATTORIA POSTE VECE
Pescheria 1608, S. Polo, near the Rialto fish market, tel. 23822, closed Tuesdays and November 10th–December 12th. This place is nice for lunch.

The local intellectuals eat here, the food is good, the waitresses efficient, the house red wine adequate. Moderately expensive.

★   ALLA MADONNA
Calle della Madonna 594, San Polo, tel. 23824, closed Wednesdays from December 23th–January 20th, and the first week in August. This place was once among the best, is now adequate but uninspired. Moderately expensive.

★   ENOTECA AL VOLTO
Calle Cavalli 4081, San Marco, tel. 28945, closed Sundays and August. Almost unknown to tourists, this wine-tasting place is among the best in Italy, with an immense choice of local, Italian and international wines. Inexpensive.

VENTIMIGLIA (IM), Liguria

★   LA RISERVA ANTONIO
At Castel d'Appio, tel. 39533, open April until September and Christmas until New Year. Excellent panoramic view, good Ligurian food and wine. Also a hotel (see above). Moderately expensive.

★   RITROVO DEGLI ARTISTI
Via Cavour 79, tel. 33258, closed Sundays and November. Elegant atmosphere, Ligurian food and good wine selection. Moderately expensive.

★   LA MORTOLA
At La Mortola, tel. 39431, closed Monday evenings and Tuesdays. International cooking. Expensive.

VERONA, Veneto

★★★   I 12 APOSTOLI
Corticella San Marco 3, tel. 24680, closed Sunday evenings, Mondays and from mid-June to mid-July. The food is excellent, as are the wines, the service, the atmosphere. Expensive.

★★★   ARCHE
Via Arche Scaligere 6, tel. 21415, closed Sunday evenings, Mondays and last 15 days in July. Small and charming, located in the house next door to the Montagne palace (about to become a Shakespearian museum), this place serves excellent fish. Note the exquisite furnishings and ceramics. Be sure to call ahead. Expensive.

★★   MARCONI
Vicolo Crocioni 6, tel. 27472, closed Sundays, Tuesday evenings, and August 10th–25th. Elegant and refined, this restaurant specializes in Veronese cooking and serves mostly local wines. The service is pleasant. Moderately expensive.

[handwritten margin note: When in Verona, you must drink Soave, or better yet, drive to Soave and drink it there!]

★★   LA DIGA
Lungadige Attiraglio 33, outskirts of the city, tel. 563194, closed Mondays. A remodeled country house, this restaurant offers interesting food, using much fruit and creating new flavors. Good wine list and courteous service. Moderately expensive.

IL SEME
Via Cantarane 17, tel. 590850, closed Sundays, Saturdays also in summer and first 20 days in August. This new place is full of light and comfort, and the food is vegetarian and macrobiotic. A serene meal. Inexpensive.

VICENZA, Veneto

★★   DA REMO
Via Caimpenta, tel. 500018, closed Sunday evenings, Mondays and July 23rd–August 21st. On the way to Padova, in a Gothic villa, this large restaurant is considered the best in town. Venetian cooking, good choice of regional wines, decent service. Moderate.

★   TRE VISI
Contrada Porti 6, center of town, tel. 23964, closed Saturdays. Good local cuisine. Moderately expensive.

★   GRAN CAFFÈ GARIBALDI
Piazza dei Signori, tel. 230066, closed Wednesdays and November. In one of the most interesting spots of the city, this *gran caffè* is the meeting place of the best people in town. The restaurant in the back is elegant and serves good food. Moderately expensive.

Entertainment

Opera

Heading every list has to be La Scala in Milano, one of the world's greatest opera houses. Book well ahead, or try your luck with the hotel concierge. Opera runs from December to May (concerts in autumn, closed summers.) Opera can also be seen in Bergamo or Brescia starting in January. In Mantua, Cremona and Como, the opera season begins in February. You can see opera in Trieste from December. A gorgeous experience is opera in Venezia's elegant La Fenice opera house, December to May. Open-air opera in Verona is also a must if you are anywhere nearby.

Nightlife

For nightlife, Milano hotels are good; the Palace, Dei VaCavalieri and Hilton offer the best, whether it be roof gardens or discotheques. In Venezia, you should try the casino; it is the Palazzo Vendramin Calergi except in the summer when it moves to the Lido. Antico Martini, Campo San Fantin, is a nightclub as well as a restaurant; there are music and dancing.

Shopping

Milano may at times seem to be Paris or Rome, but while in Italy, look for the things this country makes best, such as fashions for men and women, leather items and fine printed silks. Milano's best shopping street is Via Montenapoleone. Every Saturday there is an antique and junk fair on the Via Calatafimi.

In Venezia you may want to buy glass since that's what the city is famous for. We recommend buying in town, not on the island of Murano where much of the glass is made, because the selection is better in town and the pressure less intense. Once famous for lace, Venezia no longer makes it, so you can ignore this item if you wish.

Museums and Galleries

CAPO DI PONTE (BS), Lombardia

PARCO NAZIONALE DELLE INCISIONI RUPESTRI
Tel. 42140. Contains ample documentation on prehistoric rock graffiti from the surrounding area, Valcamonica. Collections range from the Bronze Age to Roman times.

CHIERI (TO), (frazione Pessione), Piemonte

MUSEO MARTINI DI STORIA DELL'ENOLOGIA
Piazza L. Rossi, tel. 9470345. This private museum illustrates the story of wine, showing the objects used for making wine and for working the vines.

GENOVA (Genoa), Liguria

★ **GALLERIA NAZIONALE DI PALAZZO SPINOLA**
Piazza di Pellicceria 1, tel. 294661. Works of art by Ligurian, Italian and Flemish painters of the 16th–18th centuries are housed in this 15th-century palazzo.

★ **GALLERIA DI PALAZZO REALE**
Via Balbi 10, tel. 206851. Many fine works of the Bolognese, Genovese and Veneta schools of painting are exhibited in this museum.

★ **GALLERIA DI PALAZZO ROSSO**
Via Garibaldi 18, tel. 282641. Housed in this 16th-century palazzo is a noted collection of religious and profane works by Genovese artists of the 17th and 18th centuries. There are also many portraits by Van Dyck.

GIGNESE (NO), Piemonte

MUSEO DELL'OMBRELLO E DEL PARASOLE
Started in 1939, this private collection has a large number of umbrellas that go from the 17th century to the present. Ample documentation on the history of this useful gadget. Open in winter, and only by appointment.

LA SPEZIA, Liguria

★   MUSEO TECNICO NAVALE
Piazza Chiodo, tel. 36151. Material relating to the story of ships from various periods. An important Roman section with models; an excellent section of photographic documents.

MILANO (Milan), Lombardia

★★★★   CENACOLO VINCINIANO
Piazza S. Maria delle Grazie, tel. 4987588. For those who wish to see Leonardo's *Last Supper,* now being restored. Advisable to call ahead.

Cenacle = room of the Last Supper

★★★★   PINACOTECA DI BRERA
Via Brera, tel. 800985. In a 17th-century palace that used to belong to the Jesuits, this art gallery is connected to the Brera Academy, one of Italy's foremost art schools. Contains an important collection of Italian painting, especially of Lombard and Venetian artists, from the 17th to the 20th centuries.

★★★★   MUSEO NAZIONALE DELLA SCIENZA E DELLA TECNICA LEONARDO
         DA VINCI
Via S. Vittore 21, tel. 487034; 462709. A modern museum, opened in 1953, contains interesting sections on textiles, jewelry, information, acoustics, transports, physics, motors, agriculture and many other things. The building was a Benedictine Monastery from the 16th to the 18th centuries.

★★★ for da Vinci Gallery here

★★★   CASTELLO SFORZESCO
This large castle contains, in addition to the museum of modern art, several collections: *Gabinetto dei disegni* (design), tel. 62083943; *Museo degli Strumenti Musicali,* tel. 803071; *Civico Gabinetto Numismatico,* three sections: medals, prehistoric and Egyptian, tel. 62083119;62083944.

★★   CIVICA GALLERIA D'ARTE MODERNA
Via Palestro 16, tel. 702819. Contains paintings from the neoclassical period to contemporary times, with frequent exhibits. Incorporated with the museum housing the works of Marino Marini, one of this century's foremost sculptors.

★   MUSEO THEATRALE DELLA SCALA
Piazza Scala, tel. 893418. This museum contains objects and relics related to the theater and opera. It organizes conferences and shows and has an archive and record collection.

MUSEO DEL RISORGIMENTO
Via Borgonuovo 23, tel. 803549. Contains documents, relics and art of this period, one of the most important in Italian modern history. Organizes conferences and seminars and publishes a quarterly *Il Risorgimento.*

MUSEO DEL CINEMA
Via Palestro 16, tel. 799224. A collection of material that documents the history of this new art, cinema.

MONCALIERI (TO), PIEMONTE

CASTELLO REALE: APPARTAMENTI
This 15th-century castle was enlarged several times and contains objects and paintings of the Savoia. The royal apartments may be visited.

PADOVA, (Padua) Veneto

ORTO BOTANICO
Via Orto Botanico 15, tel. 656614. Founded in 1545, this is Europe's oldest botanical garden. Many examples of both local and exotic plants.

SAVONA, Liguria

PINACOTECA CIVICA
Via Quarda Superiore 7, tel. 26201. An important collection of Ligurian paintings of the 15th–18th centuries, as well as a collection of Savonese ceremics of the 16th–17th centuries.

TORINO (Turin), Pemonte

★★   ARMERIA REALE
(Royal Armory) Piazza Castello 191, tel. 543889. Started in 1837 by one of the Savoias and located in a wing of the *Palazzo Reale,* this excellent collection of arms and armour was completely reorganized between 1969 and 1977.

CENTRO STORICO FIAT
Via Chiabrera 20, tel. 670474. For those interested in cars, this private collection has every model ever made by the famous Italian house.

★★   GALLERIA SABAUDA
Via Accademia delle Scienze 6, tel. 547440.

★★★★   MUSEO EGIZIO
(Egyptian Museum) Tel. 537581

★ MUSEO DI ANTICHITÀ
(Antiquities) Tel. 535908 A great baroque building done in 1678 by Guarini, the *Palazzo dell'Accademia delle Scienze* houses an art gallery and two museums that represent the best of what Torino has to offer. The Egyptian Museum is among the best in the world, the gallery has some remarkable paintings of the Dutch and Flemish schools. Closed Mondays; open weekday 9 A.M. to 2 P.M.; holidays 9 A.M. to 1 P.M.

Palazzo Reale and Palazzo Madonna are interconnected

TRIESTE, Friuli-Venezia-Giulia

CIVICO MUSEO DI STORIA ED ARTE E ORTO LAPIDARIO
Via Cattedrale 15, tel. 741708. A museum that unites many collections, including prehistoric and medieval. There are interesting pieces in the Greek and Roman sections.

CIVICO MUSEO TEATRALE DI FONDAZIONE CARLO SCHMIDT
Piazza Verdi 1, tel. 61980. This museum has a fine collection of old Italian and foreign musical instruments, models of instruments made in Trieste, photographs and documents of past activities of the Trieste theater.

VENEZIA (Venice), Veneto

★★★★   GALLERIA DELL'ACCADEMIA
Dorsoduro, Campo della Carità, tel. 22247. Contains the most important existing collection of Venetian paintings from the 14th to the 18th centuries.

Also known as Accademia di Belle Arti

★★★★   MUSEO DI SAN MARCO
Piazza San Marco, tel. 25205. Noted for its 12th–14th-century mosaic decorations. Also contains 15th-century paintings and 16th-century furnishings.

★★★★   PALAZZO DUCALE
(Doge's Palace) Piazza San Marco. An important art gallery, with fine Venetian paintings from the 15th to 17th centuries.

★★   COLLEZIONE GUGGENHEIM
Dorsoduro 701, tel. 29347. A beautiful setting, the garden and palace of art-lover Peggy Guggenheim, houses a large and important collection of sculptures and paintings by great 20th-century artists.

★★   GALLERIA INTERNAZIONALE D'ARTE MODERNA
Ca' Pesaro Santa Croce 2078, S. Stae., tel. 24127. This museum contains modern Italian and foreign sculptures, paintings and graphics and an important collection of Venetian art from the 8th century to modern times. It also exhibits works from previous Venetian biannual art shows.

★   MUSEO ARCHEOLOGICO
Piazzetta San Marco 17, tel. 25978. Located in the old *Palazzo Reale,* this museum has a series of Roman or pre-Roman collections, such as Greek female statues from the 5th and 4th centuries B.C., a Roman coin collection dating back to the Republic (3rd to 1st centuries B.C.), pieces from the Napoleonic age, from the Bronze Age and from ancient Egypt.

The word ghetto comes from gettare, metal casting, after the foundries located here

MUSEO DELLA COMUNITÀ ISRAELITA
Cannaregio 2902, Campo del Ghetto Nuovo. This museum is located in an area of great historical significance for the Jewish people—the first ghetto. There are objects of worship and relics of various times, from various places. Open to the public; guided visits on request.

VIGEVANO (PV), Lombardia

MUSEO DELLA CALZATURA PIETRO BORTOLINI
Corso Cavour 84, tel. 70149. Models, prototypes and curiosities connected
with the shoe industry. Can be seen by request.

Tours

City tours are available in Milano by American Express, Cooks and CIT;
Venezia by American Express, Wagons-Lits, Cooks, CIT. The giant of Italian
tour operators, CIT, has tours covering all or parts of Northern Italy. They can
be reached at 600 Fifth Ave., New York, N.Y. 10019; 2055 Peel St., Montreal, Quebec; or 10 Charles II St., London SW1.

Sports

The sport of kings can be experienced at Milano's San Siro track. If you want
to ride horses instead of betting on them, you can do so, surprisingly enough,
at stables on Venezias Lido during summer. Soccer can be watched (not in
summer) at Milano's giant stadium, which houses one of Europe's best teams.

Participatory sports

Skiing is the reason people come here in winter, whether it be for the fabled
slopes of Courmayeur or Sestriere, the best organized of all resorts in Italy.
Skiing is also good at Breuil and Cortina d'Ampezzo, queen of the Dolomites.
In summer, swim at Venezias Lido, Portofino, San Remo, or Santa Margherita
Ligure. (You can also watch regattas off the Ligurian Riviera throughout sum-
mer; inquire locally for schedule.) Don't swim in Venezia itself or near Genoa.
  Golf is available on fine courses at Cernobbio (Villa d'Este), San Remo
(Degli Ulivi), Rapallo, Monza, and Varese. There is even a spectacular course,
18 holes (as all others listed here), at Sestriere.

Getting Around

The rail network can be used easily in northern Italy, but buses are tricky
unless you know enough of the language to ask for, and give, instructions. It's
pleasant to drive around, if you keep off the Autostrada and if you avoid the
month of August, when all roads are jammed. A combination of train and
self-drive may be the best. Careful preparations with a timetable from Italian
Railways, a good highway map from your automobile club and the location
of a few self-drive car agencies can make for a splendid journey.

Directory

Churches and Synagogue

In addition to the fabulous churches that you will go to see throughout this
region, you may want to know where to go to attend services. In Venezia,

the Anglican St. George's, Campo San Vio, is open during summer only. Confession in English can be heard in summer at San Marco. The Venezia synagogue, Tempio Israelitico, is in Ghetto Vecchio.

Consulates can be found as follows: American, Piazza della Repubblica, Milan; British: Via San Paolo, Milano and Accademia, Venezia.

Milano—Hairdressers

ANNETTE E MARIO
Via S. Andrea 2, central location, (corner via Bagutta), tel. 783245. The best clients in town; does everything from hair to face to nails. Expensive.

CONTALDO
Corso Monforte 9, tel. 7982247. Very capable, gives immediate service when requested. Expensive.

DINO AND CHARLES
Via Montenapoleone 8, tel. 791446. In the most fashionable part of town, a professional house of beauty care. Expensive.

Central or Italian Italy

Central Italy is the smallest of this book's sections in that it includes only five regions. But Toscana (Tuscany), Umbria, Emilia-Romagna, Lazio and Le Marche (Marches) are the very heart of Italy, as different from northern and southern Italy as they are from each other.

The most important city in this area is Firenze (Florence), in Toscana. Toscana has been called the garden of Italy, the heart of the country and a natural museum—it is all of these things. Umbria, one of the smallest regions in the whole country, is dotted with splendid monuments and blessed with a charming, green countryside. Emilia-Romagna has the lovely and well-known cities of Bologna, Parma, Ravenna and Ferrara. Its countryside is characterized by the flatlands of the Po River Valley. Its rich fields and large farms provide its good food. Lazio is a fascinating region, full of the memories of old Roma (Rome) and, even before that, of Etruscan settlements. The Marches is another small region. Its countryside combines mountains with water since it contains the southern tip of the Appennines and the Adriatic beaches.

Central Italy is the area in which St. Francis lived, before and after his conversion; the area that gave birth to Leonardo, Michelangelo, Dante and Giotto; the area where Shelley lived when he came to Italy; and the area where most visitors come today, looking for beauty, art and inspiration.

Not to mention the Medici!

TOSCANA

The central portion of Italy's west coast is occupied by Toscana (Tuscany), one of the largest and loveliest regions in the whole country. Its vast territory has been called a frontier between north and south; but for those who know it and love it, Toscana is very much its own place—an old harmonious land that offers the surprisingly easy interaction of harsh mountains with mellow hills, of beautifully tended fields with charming cities, of rivers and beaches, of peasants and artists.

Here nature and man have created a countryside that is unique in its esthetic soberness and continuity. The cities blend into the farms, the farms extend into the hills, the hills grade down to the coast; everything seems to

163

Tuscany's older towns were all built on high ground for better defense and to avoid malarial mosquitos

Drink your chianti when it is 2 years old (or more)

follow a pattern as if a design had been traced by an invisible hand. The evidence is everywhere: from the marble and stone mountains that display white scars from acquiring material for statues and houses, to the boggy swamps meticulously and scientifically drained in order to gain new fields; from the stony hills carefully terraced for planting olive trees and vines, to the rough, uneven rivers deliberately channeled to ensure waterways or to provide energy.

But no one planned Toscana on paper. This ancient land has absorbed many invasions and has survived many struggles; it has had moments of exciting creativity and power and moments of tragedy and famine. And out of this apparent disorder, out of this tormented history, out of this vital and skeptical population, we have been given the unbelievable beauty of Firenze (Florence), that splendid city that is a museum of museums, a showplace of masterpieces. We have also been given the excellence of Tuscan food and wine, the sober perfection of its many crafts, the harmony of its countryside.

Firenze is the unquestioned capital of Toscana. After Roma (Rome), it's the most visited and admired city in Italy. The lure of Venezia (Venice) and its lagoon is undeniable, but Firenze has always attracted the intellectual, the artist, the historian. There are many reasons for this magnetism; but the most important one is the Renaissance. It was born in Firenze, and it's still there, around every corner, in each splendid *piazza* or church. In spite of the more tranquil centuries that followed the Golden Age of the Republic and of Medici rule, this unique town, which has maintained its severe and beautiful appearance is almost a miracle of urban coherence. Next to the somber architecture of the 13th and 14th centuries, we can admire the elegant and measured Renaissance structures of the 15th and 16th centuries. Baroque has had little impact on Firenze, and the neoclassical and contemporary additions have respected existing patterns. Only a few heavy-handed 19th-century changes and the bombs of World War II have made small, ugly scars on this incredibly well-preserved city. The damage done by the November 1966 flood has been almost completely repaired.

Other Tuscan cities are equally worthy of note. There is *Siena,* famous for its lovely *Piazza del Campo* and for the *Palio,* a horserace lifted straight out of the Middle Ages; there is *Pisa,* with its old university and the most photographed landmark in Italy, the *Leaning Tower;* there is multitowered *San Gimignano;* charming *Pienza*, a small jewel built for a pope; *Lucca*, with its impressive walls and ramparts, considered by some the most perfectly preserved medieval city in Italy, certainly one of the best examples of urban planning of that time. There are *Arezzo, Prato, Pistoia, Montecatini, Massa, Volterra, Livorno* and many more.

Tuscan economy, originally built on agriculture, handcrafts and commerce, added industry after World War II. Textiles, shoes, leather goods, ceramics, glass and paper are some of the products made here. In line with its tradition of soberness and balance, factories tend to be medium or small, and labor is mostly local. Some of the old craftsmen such as the fine furniture makers, the alabaster carvers, the jewelers and the embroiderers are still operative. Knitwear is made on both levels—the fine handcrafted blending with the fine machine made—with enchanting and creative results.

But the proudest product of this land is wine, and Chianti is a byword, as well known as Coca-Cola and certainly older. The soft hills between

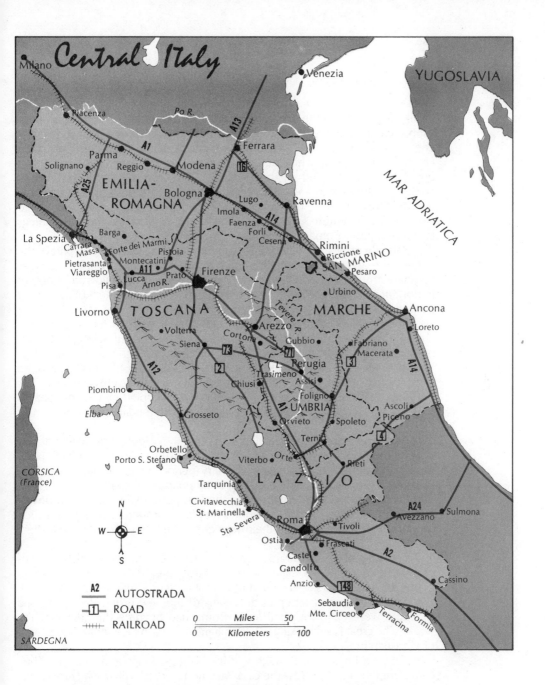

Central Italy

Milano
Venezia
YUGOSLAVIA
Piacenza
Po R.
A13
A1
Ferrara
Solignano
Parma
Reggio
Modena
16
A25
EMILIA-
ROMAGNA
Bologna
Lugo
Ravenna
Imola
MAR ADRIATICA
Faenza
Forli
La Spezia
Barga
Carrara
Forte dei Marmi.
Cesena
Rimini
Massa
Pistoia
Riccione
Pietrasanta
Montecatini
SAN MARINO
Viareggio
A11
Prato
Firenze
Pesaro
Pisa
Lucca
Arno R.
Urbino
Ancona
Livorno
TOSCANA
Loreto
Volterra
Cortona
Arezzo
MARCHE
Siena
Gubbio
Fabriano
73
Perugia
Macerata
A14
2
L.
A12
Chiusi
Trasimeno
Assisi
Piombino
UMBRIA
Foligno
Ascoli
Elba
Grosseto
Orvieto
Spoleto
Piceno
Terni
Orbetello
4
Porto S. Stefano
Viterbo
Orte
Rieti
CORSICA
LAZIO
(France)
Tarquinia
Civitavecchia
A24
St. Marinella
Sulmona
Sta Severa
Roma
Avezzano
Ostia
Tivoli
Castel
Frascati
Gandolfo
A2
Anzio
Cassino
148
SARDEGNA
Sebaudia
Mte. Circeo
Terracina
Formia

N
W E
S

A2 ——— AUTOSTRADA
1 ROAD
+++++ RAILROAD

Miles
0   50
0   100
Kilometers

Firenze and Siena are covered with thousands of vines, carefully chosen,
tended and sprayed, its fruit picked, pressed and blended to give a final
product that equals no other. When the research group led by great Italian
physicist Enrico Fermi accomplished its purpose and split the atom, they
drank Chianti to toast the achievement.

Some History

Parts of Toscana, some of the oldest inhabited areas of Italy, were highly civilized as early as the 6th century B.C. The Etruscans, a population both sophisticated and mysterious, were settled in a vast area that is roughly contained between the Tiber and Arno rivers. Some historians think they came from the East while others theorize that they were an indigenous population that acquired a higher level of culture because of their commercial contacts with Greece and Asia Minor. Whatever the truth, it is undeniable that the Etruscans were the first civilization on Italian soil, closely connected with the early centuries of Roman growth and responsible for many things later considered Roman.

After the total affirmation of Roman power, Toscana became part of the empire (the seventh region in the Augustean division), and most Tuscan cities originate from this period and the two centuries that followed. Another important result of the Roman occupation was the development of large rural properties. These properties were a dominating characteristic of this land that lasted for many centuries in a variety of forms, such as feudal property, church property or simply the *latifondo,* a large property belonging to one owner that has been modified through the ages and has lasted to this day.

After the fall of the Western Roman Empire (A.D. 476) Toscana was open to attack from the north (Germanic tribes) and from the sea (Byzantines). The northern attackers prevailed, and in 570 it was occupied by the Longobards who made Lucca their capital and established the feudal system in most of the area.

At this point it may be useful to stress that the Middle Ages were not one compact period, but were divided into three distinct parts: the feudal, land-developing period; the court and chivalry period, which includes the Crusades; and the city and middle-class growth period of the latter Middle Ages. The Longobards were present during the first period when land and power were neatly divided among the nobles and large properties had names such as *marche* and *contee*, with their respective overloads known as *Marchese* and *Conte*.

The advent of the Franks from the later 8th to early 9th centuries changed many things. Unlike the Longobards, they did not come as immigrants but as invaders. Thus much of the established situation remained with groups of armed men set up as guardians of the new order. Roads that led to Rome were built, for once again Rome had become the center of the world. The great Frankish king, Charlemagne, had won his victory in the name of Christianity.

Toscana became a throughway for bishops, kings and pilgrims. They came from the north, across the Cisa Pass along a road called *Via Francigena,* and continued south on their way to Roma. Monastic orders and other groups (such as the Templar Knights) built abbeys and hostels in order to accommodate these travelers; some still stand.

Around the year 1,000 there was a general improvement in the standard of living, an improvement that reached every corner of Europe, but was especially felt in Toscana. New techniques for working the land were found; for example, the *yoke*, which allowed two animals to pull the plow together and changed the leverage and fulcrum; the water mill, another form of energy; the large hay sickle; the beating of grain. All of this meant more food and population growth, resulting in an increase in the demand for goods and the consequent affirmation of the marketplace.

Tuscan cities felt these changes and became aware of a new importance. They gave birth to the first communal experiments and by the 11th century attempted economic freedom and political independence. So while, on the one hand, many aggressive young nobility heeded the pope's call to free the Holy Land and left their castles in search of glory and adventure, on the other hand, the cities began to grow and prosper making fortunes for the hard-working craftsmen and merchants. Tuscan cities fought each other often, greedy for markets, land and power. But there was a unity at the base, a similarity of language and culture, a spiritual bond that bound the region together.

In 1115, Firenze became a free *comune* and began to dominate the Tuscan scene. Its history has been a continuous crescendo of economic growth, political expansion and increasing prestige. It reached unexpected heights by the 16th century, with two great Florentine popes and two Medici queens of France.

Many factors contributed to the rise of the free, strong city-state, and in Firenze they were reinforced by the economic vitality of the city, rivaled only by Milano (Milan). There was a strengthening of the *arti e corporazioni*, associations of artisans who worked at the same trade. The bankers developed new ways for favoring exchange and opened branches of their banks abroad. The merchants increased the range of their market by shipping overseas. The golden *fiorino*, first coined in 1252, became the strongest currency of its time.

But this was also a period of violent internal strife, not only in Toscana, but in all of Italy. The struggle between pope and emperor, which involved all cities and all families, spilled over into minor feuds and became so generalized it is difficult to untangle the reasons for most fighting. When the Guelphs finally won in 1267, the habit was so strong that in Firenze they became divided again and were called White and Black—and fighting went on. The great Florentine poet, Dante Alighieri, was a White. When his faction lost he was expelled from the city; he died in Ravenna in 1321.

Guelph and Ghibelline supported pope and emperor, respectively

By the end of the 13th century the Middle Ages entered their final phase. For the Tuscan cities this also meant a change in urban structure. The tower, that most impressive medieval structure, was still being built, but a new tendency began to take shape. In front of the large cathedrals that began to appear there was an ample space, the *piazza*. It was a return to the old Mediterranean meeting place, which in ancient Roma was called *forum*. The *piazza* implied greater security, its open space and light gave a sense of freedom. The church emerged from the strenuous period of fighting the Empire with a new conception of its role in society, which was no longer purely religious but embraced all of life. The square in front of the cathedral became the center of town.

The last two decades of the century witnessed enormous building activity in Firenze. Many large monuments were planned, promoted by the city government and the *Arti* and executed by one of the great architects and city planners of all times—Arnolfo del Cambio. We will name only two of his great works. *Palazzo Vecchio,* now called *della Signoria,* and the Cathedral, *S. Maria del Fiore*.

The ruling fact behind this expansion was wealth, a growing financial strength that continued throughout the next century, with government becoming centralized and the stronger families concentrating power in their own hands. Thus Firenze and many other Italian cities became *signorie*.

The calamitous 14th century, with its terrible 1348 plague that reduced the population to one-third of its original number, did not prevent the continuing growth of Florentine commercial power and the advent and advancement of a family whose name became forever linked with both Firenze and the Renaissance.

The Medici became influential with Cosimo il Vecchio, who took over his father's bank, developed a currency exchange, accumulated an immense fortune, and took over the city government.

For the city of Firenze the years of *Cosimo il Vecchio* and his talented grandson *Lorenzo il Magnifico* were positive in every way. The Renaissance had reached its full maturity. Artists were at their creative best; science and literature were reaching a growing audience; music was experimenting with new forms; Toscana was leading the way into a new age. The pulse of life was beating faster and faster, but during that special, golden hour time seemed to be standing still.

With the death of Lorenzo in 1492 the Medici lost power. Charles VIII of France entered Firenze, collected a handsome ransom, and left; the old republic was brought back to life. But communal days were over, and the years that followed were chaotic. After much bickering and confusion, the Medici returned in 1529, and by 1537 *Cosimo I* was a worthy successor of his forefathers. He re-established a brilliant court, conquered most of Toscana and ruled with strength and dignity, winning the emperor's approval and the pope's blessing.

From the 17th century onward the history of Toscana was uneventful with ripples that did not greatly influence it. The Medici became grand dukes, and the region a grand duchy. *Galileo* built his telescope and discovered Jupiter's satellites in 1610. Florentine cooking was taken to France when *Caterina de Medici* married the Dauphin and the French court began its refined gastronomic adventure. The Medici dynasty extinguished itself in 1737 and was substituted by the Austrian House of Lorraine. They reigned with dignity and justice, and in *Pietro Leopoldo* gave Toscana its most illuminated ruler since Cosimo il Vecchio. The late 18th century was marred by Napoleon's conquest, then all returned to normal tranquility until the unification of Italy, when Firenze became a temporary capital from 1865 to 1871. The rest is modern history.

Some Thoughts on Art

Here again, we can only give a few highlights of this vast subject, for to write of Toscana is to think of art, and to write of art is to visualize Toscana.

It's important to remember that artistic styles do not begin and end with the regularity of seasons. They develop slowly and often coexist, with one style still reaching its maturity while the embryo of another is forming. Thus, the inheritance of classic culture is present in many medieval structures, the simple lines of Romanesque are contained in later buildings; and so on.

Etruscan ruins are present all over the region, from *Fiesole* to *Cortona*, from *Volterra* to *Populonia*. They are remnants of walls, doors and temples, but mainly of tombs. There are relatively few Roman ruins in Toscana, some in Pisa and Lucca, most at Fiesole; examples are a temple, a theater and baths. The oldest are at *Ansedonia,* near *Orbetello* (GR), dating back to 273 B.C.

Unexpectedly, the style that dominates the Tuscan landscape is Romanesque. It is highly representative of the feudal period and mirrors the ideological solidarity that existed between clergy and nobility during the early Middle Ages. The nobles were concerned with hunting and fighting; the church was concerned with the soul. This is the age of the *basilica,* a horizontally built structure that achieves incredible balance between round and pointed elements and uses sculpture to integrate the whole. We should keep in mind the fact that most of the population was illiterate, and thus the stone statues, alfrescoes and mosaics that line doors and interiors of churches were equivalent to the modern "cartoon," a visual story of the sacred family and other biblical characters. The splendid *Basilica di S. Miniato* in Firenze is one of the best examples of this approach, even if much of the material was added later.

Another structure that characterizes this period is the *pieve,* a country church that served as a gathering place for the peasants and their families. Many still stand on isolated hills.

There were two major types of Romanesque in Toscana—Pisan and Florentine. The latter spread to Prato, Pistoia, Volterra and Siena. The former was concentrated in Pisa proper and had a rich development in Lucca. The famous *Leaning Tower of Pisa* is an important example of the Pisan style, which incorporated classical, Longobard and Arab elements and produced the lovely, airy columns and arches that are so well illustrated by the spectacular tower. In Lucca, the Cathedral, *S.Martino* and the large church of *S. Michele* are most interesting and illustrate the *lucchese* variations of the Pisan style.

The 13th and 14th centuries witnessed the advent of Gothic, brought from the North especially from France, by the many travelers who cross the land. Gothic brought technical innovations, but its popularity was connected with a different approach to God, who was then worshipped with grandiosity by the rising middle class. Wealthy merchants and powerful nobles no longer satisfied with the small basilica or the modest *pieve,* began to build *cathedrals,* the most characteristic structure of the Gothic period.

The magnificent cathedral of Firenze, *S. Maria del Fiore,* is a good example of the new vision. But it must be noted that this is not northern Gothic, but a modified Tuscan version that added a very Italian sense of balance and limpid beauty to the large structure.

At this time Toscana became a lively laboratory of new ideas, and the language of art gained new freedom. Painters such as *Cimabue* and *Giotto,* sculptors such as *Andrea Pisano,* architects and city planners such as *Arnolfo del Cambio* changed the world of art and building and gave it new depth and meaning. They gave their art the new spirit that surrounded them and laid the foundation for the Renaissance.

By the beginning of the 15th century the change reached its full maturity, and Toscana became a new leader, a throbbing pulse that sent messages of rediscovered good taste and proportion to the rest of Europe. *Brunelleschi* and *Donatello* visited Roma and returned to Firenze full of new projects. The

[handwritten margin note: The leading Romanesque painter was Cimabue, late 13th century]

great architect added the splendid cupola to the Florentine Cathedral, the sculptor changed his style and did some of his best work. *Masaccio,* a friend of both, brought this new realism into painting, and together they brought about a revolution that characterized the early Renaissance.

The 15th century saw a growing number of painters who left a large number of magnificent works. It's the century of the *Beato Angelico,* of *Paolo Uccello,* of *Filippo Lippi* and *Andrea del Verrocchio,* of *Sandro Botticelli.* Their work, along with that of scores of lesser-known Tuscan painters, is present in many Italian museums, of which the *Uffizi Gallery* in Firenze is the largest.

By the 16th century the Renaissance had reached its peak. The giants who dominated the scene were Tuscan by birth and early formation, but their best work was done elsewhere. *Michelangelo Buonarroti* participated in the spirit of the rediscovered Republic, but when the Medici returned to power, he took his enormous talent to Roma. *Leonardo da Vinci* was formed under Botticelli and Verrocchio, but was tempted by the Milanese court and left.

Michelangelo left Florence for good in 1534

Now the Tuscan cities acquired their definitive faces, the ones they have maintained to this day with meticulous vanity and studied care. Baroque and rococo, the two ornate styles that dominated the 17th and 18th centuries in most of Europe left very few traces on the Tuscan landscape. But it should be noted that Florentine and Tuscan artists have greatly contributed to both styles in Prague, Vienna, Warsaw and Paris. Seen from the perspective of time, we could almost say that while they accepted these changes as natural and necessary, they preferred to leave Toscana pure, with the balanced lines of the Gothic, Romanesque and Renaissance periods—a living museum of its greatest age.

The short Napoleonic period brought some neoclassical activity, especially in Lucca. But that elegant style blends easily into the Tuscan landscape and does not greatly engage the eye. The 19th century was artistically static, with only one episode worth mentioning—the Florentine painting group known as the *Macchiaioli* who broke with tradition and cleared the way for French impressionism.

But not all of the arts are visual, and before we close this chapter we will say a few words about music. The 14th century witnessed a new musical, *Ars Nova Fiorentina,* which broke away from the "one voice" sound of Gregorian chant and introduced several voices, some even interpreted by instruments. This profane music used words by the greatest poets of its time, such as *Dante, Petrarca* and *Boccaccio,* and its technical and expressive maturity allows us to suppose that previous, undocumented experiences had been made. What we do know is that around the year 1000, a monk named *Guido d'Arezzo* gave a name to musical notes and started humanity on the "do, re, mi."

During the 16th century music became of major interest in Firenze and a group of friends met at the palace of Count Bardi del Vernio to experiment with new forms. The *Camerata dei Bardi* became famous, for out of its meetings the musical melodrama was born. In fact, the first preserved *opera* in history was *Euridice*, and its first performance was at *Palazzo Pitti* on October 6, 1600.

About one century later a harpsichord builder named Bartolomeo Cristofori, who worked at the Medici court, had an idea. He took one of his harpsichords, replaced the jacks with little hammers and began the age of piano music.

Itineraries

Toscana can be reached from north and south—that is, from Milano and Roma—by train, car or plane. The plane takes you to Pisa airport; the train to either Pisa or Firenze, with connections to the other cities. By car you can come on several roads; from Roma we recommend two: either *Autostrada del Sole,* the highway, or the *Aurelia,* an old Roman military road that going along the coast reaches France.

Our first itinerary follows the lovely Aurelia through the whole region, all the way to Massa and Carrara, which border on Liguria. At the beginning we go through several small resorts just out of Roma: *S. Severa* with its grandiose castle and *S. Marinella. Civitavecchia* should be passed quickly, unless you're interested in a busy port, then on to *Orbetello* and interesting *Monte Argentario* with *Porto S. Stefano.* This part of the drive takes you through the *Maremma,* Italy's equivalent of the American West, where cows and cowboys once could be seen and rodeos were held. From Orbetello to *Grosseto* and *Follonica* the countryside is flat.

If you are interested in visiting *Elba,* the first island of Napoleon's captivity, turn off at Piombino. *Portoferraio* is the point of arrival, and from May to October this island is the place for a lovely, quiet weekend. There are pretty little fishing villages, small museums, charming beaches, picturesque views, attractive walks, one tall peak that can be reached by cable car, moderate but pleasant hotels and a couple of good restaurants.

If you continue your trip along the Aurelia, after Follonica you'll pass *S. Vincenzo, Castagneto Carducci* (named for one of Italy' most famous poets), *Cecina,* a large resort town, *Vada* and finally *Castiglioncello,* a small but very fashionable resort that nestles on a rocky little promontory with the splendid sea below. In our opinion, the Italian Riviera begins here and from here to the end of this itinerary and through the first two itineraries of Liguria (which begins with *Sarzana* and ends at *Ventimiglia* on the French frontier) the lovely little beaches, the sea, the rocky hills and villas, the flowers and lush vegetation are all enchanting.

Castiglioncello is not the most convenient place for a stopover; it has many *villas* but few hotels. From here it's a fairly short drive to *Livorno,* the largest port in Toscana and one of its more modern towns. It was founded by the Medici in 1577, and was semidestroyed during the World War II. The reconstruction has maintained most of the original plan. There isn't much to visit, except for a statue on *Piazza Micheli* called *Monumento dei 4 Mori,* one of the best examples of 17th-century sculpture, done by Bandini to honor Ferdinando I, with four chained moors added by Tacca 27 years later. Nearby is the Medici port and the old fortress.

The most popular excursion out of Livorno is 9 miles up to the *Santuario di Montenero,* dedicated to the Patron Saint of Toscana, originally done in the 14th century, then redone in 1575 and 1721. The church has a very baroque interior—unusual for Toscana—and the *piazzale* affords a splendid view.

From Livorno the drive is uninteresting; the Aurelia deviates from the coast at Pisa, but you can avoid the city center and continue to *Viareggio.*

[handwritten margin notes:]

* S. Severa castle

In fact, Napoleon was given Elba for his exile, and was its ruler

Livorno = Leghorn is the birthplace of Modigliani (d. 1920)

** Sanctuary of Montenero

Molo = pier

A good place to eat is ★★ Montecatini, on the sea

If the weather is nice stop here and take a walk along the *molo* where some of the nicest boats in Italy lie at anchor. Or walk along the beach and enjoy the shops and cafés. The architecture in Viareggio is art deco. During the winter, on the four Sundays that precede carnival see Viareggio decked out in party clothes, for here is one of the liveliest carnivals in Italy. This is also a good place for a lunch break or to stay the night, provided it's off season. Avoid this city in July and August. All hotels and restaurants are crowded, traffic is difficult and the beach is full of chairs, umbrellas and humanity. But when June and September are warm they are ideal months to be in this area.

From Viareggio to *Lido di Camaiore, Marina di Pietrasanta* and *Forte dei Marmi,* it's all *Versilia*, the playground of Toscana's wealthy and not so wealthy, a beach lined with hotels, restaurants, nightclubs, cinemas and all the things that mean fun, fun, fun.

The rest of this itinerary takes you to *Massa* and *Carrara,* where you reach the Ligurian frontier. Along the way you pass the great marble deposits of Toscana, stocked with the marble from the mountains behind the *Apuan Alps.* Here great sculptors from Michelangelo to Henry Moore have been coming for centuries, picking and choosing their way through the enormous blocks of stone. At Carrara look for the *Mostra Nazionale del Marmo.* If you're interested in autographs, find the *Edicola dei Frantiscritti,* which has many famous signatures from Giambologna (1598) to Canova (1800). Carrara also has an important cathedral, in Romanesque-Gothic, and the *Palazzo Cybo-Malaspina* houses a valuable collection of paintings.

★★★ *Locanda dell 'angelo*

If, at this point, you are looking for a place to stay, within a few short miles from Carrara is a small place called *Ameglia di Sarzana,* which has a large and lovely inn, the *Locanda dell'Angelo.* Here you can spend a quiet, comfortable night and eat in one of Italy's best restaurants.

From Pisa to Lucca to Firenze

★★★ *Leaning Tower of Pisa*

For those who arrive in Toscana by plane, the visit to any parts of the region begins at Pisa. Even if you stay for just one hour, take a look at the *Campo dei Miracoli,* which contains the *Battistero,* the *Duomo,* the *Campanile* (otherwise known as *la Torre di Pisa,* the Leaning Tower) and the *Camposanto* (or cemetery). On a sunny day the spectacle is unforgettable, with blue skies, the well-kept green lawn, the special dark pink old brick and the creamy marble of the monuments. In 1173 the famous tower was started on an unfortunate spot that has a layer of water underneath. The result was that one side of the tower sank. The work was stopped at once; it was tried again in 1185, then stopped for almost a century; it was finally taken up again in 1275 and finished in the early 14th century. Although the possibility of a collapse is occasionally discussed by the local press, so far it seems to have held, with an inclination of more than 5 degrees, which is equivalent to about 7 feet of sinking on the south side. The tower has an elegant cylindrical shape, with seven levels of columns and arches and one smaller level on top, reached by climbing 294 steps. Admission is L.1,500; the Leaning Tower is open every day from 8 or 9 A.M. to sunset.

★★ *Pisa Cathedral*

The *Duomo,* or cathedral, is the most important monument in Pisan Romanesque. It was started in 1064 and completed about 100 years later. It presents an amazing architectural unity. Do not miss the bronze doors, especially the *Porta di S. Ranieri,* which has scenes of the life of Christ done by Bonanno Pisano in 1180.

The interior is solemn and large, livened by black and white marble stripes and many masterpieces that cover several centuries. Of the five naves, the central one has an impressive roof; at the end the famous *Pergameno di Giovanni Pisano,* done from 1302 to 1311 is considered the most significant Gothic sculpture in Italy. There are splendid paintings by Andrea del Sarto and a mosaic by Cimabue.

The Baptistry is a round Romanesque structure with a small brick cupola surrounded by a *loggia* with Gothic points. The building was started in 1152, continued during the 13th century by Nicola and Giovanni Pisano and finished in the 14th century. Note the four portals, especially the one facing the cathedral, and, inside, the *Pergameno di Nicola Pisano* (1260), the first Gothic sculpture in Italy. If you admired the *Pergameno* in the cathedral, compare it with this one, done by the father of Giovanni Pisano.

** Baptistry

The *Camposanto* is surrounded by a simple rectangular structure in marble with two doors that lead inside. It was badly damaged in 1944, and although much work has been done in the last 35 years, a complete restoration has not been achieved.

** Camposanto Cemetery has earth brought from Jerusalem in 1203

Another sight to see in Pisa is the *Piazza dei Cavalieri,* a short walk from *Campo dei Miracoli* and the center of the old medieval city. Here the atmosphere is clearly latter Renaissance, with the lovely *Palazzo dei Cavalieri,* decorated with 16th-century "graffiti" and the church of *S. Stefano dei Cavalieri,* designed by Vasari. Inside, the many Saracen flags captured by Pisan sailors.

* Church of S. Stefano

For those with more time, we recommend a walk along the Arno, which in Pisa is just as lovely as in Firenze, and the buildings are more colorful. Note the charming little church on *Lungarno Gambacorti, S. Maria della Spina.* It's a little jewel of Romanesque–Gothic art; a charming miniature worth admiring.

* S. Maria della Spina

From Pisa there are several ways of reaching Firenze, of which a short trip on the Autostrada is the fastest but least interesting. We will suggest two itineraries, both to be done by car. One will take you through some of the loveliest cities in Toscana, the other through the lower Arno Valley.

Our first Tuscan itinerary of some length goes from Pisa to Lucca, from Lucca to Pescia and Montecatini, from there to Pistoia, then to Vinci and Firenze. The road from Pisa to Lucca is a 20-minute drive upward on an attractively curved road lined with olive groves. After a short tunnel you arrive on the Lucca side. On your right, note the lovely villas that dot the landscape. The city itself is surrounded by thick brick walls and can be entered by several doors. If possible, drive along the lovely *mura,* lined with old trees and interrupted here and there by ramparts. The experience is unique, time seems to turn back and even if you're driving a modern car the feeling around you is positively medieval. Then park the car and walk around the city. Go down *via Fillungo,* down *via Guinigi,* down *via Elisa,* which becomes *S.Croce,* then *Roma* and finally *S. Paolino.* This walk will take you from one end of town to the other. Along *via Fillungo* be sure to note the *Piazza del Mercato,* an old Roman amphitheater, then *Piazza Guidiccioni* and then the 13th–century church of *S. Cristoforo.* On *via Guinigi* note the interesting tower with trees growing at the top. *Via S. Croce* begins with an old 12th-century door, *Porta S. Gervasio,* and a few steps later opens into *Piazza S. Maria Forisportam,* where an old marble column indicates a spot that was "out of town" in Roman days and even later.

Of the many churches that this closed and pious city contains, the two most important are *S. Martino* and *S. Michele in Foro.* Let us begin with the latter, a fine example of *Pisano–Lucchese* Romanesque, started in 1143. The front seems too large for the rest, with its four levels of arches and columns and the colossal statue of S. Michele at the top. Note the whole *piazza,* with its old iron chains and medieval stones. Also of interest is the street in front of the church, *via di Poggio,* where a plaque indicates the birthplace of Giacomo Puccini.

The next church to visit is *S. Martino,* which has a very unusual, asymmetrical front, three large arches, each of a different dimension, the same pisano–lucchese small arches and columns of S. Michele and a Romanesque tower of majestic simplicity. The interior, done later and therefore with a Gothic imprint, contains a lovely marble statue, the *Tomba di Ilaria del Carretto,* the best work of Jacopo della Quercia, and a small chapel called *L'Edicola del Volto Santo* with a wood statue of Christ that is most unusual, probably Oriental in origin. It was mentioned by Dante. Note the *piazza,* the fountain and the houses surrounding the *piazza.* If you have time before leaving Lucca, walk down *via del Battistero,* lined with antique shops and a *patina* that only time can bestow.

Leave Lucca by *Porta Elisa,* named for Napoleon's sister and the newest door of the city walls, and take the road called *Pesciatina,* which goes to *Pescia* and *Montecatini.* If you have time to spare, stop at *Collodi* and visit the park of *Pinocchio.* Otherwise, you'll reach Pescia in about 20 minutes; Montecatini is a few miles farther. This fashionable resort offers many out-door *caffès* and some good shops, plus the well–known waters that do wonders for the digestive system. For those who have time to spare there is *Montecatini Alta,* a picturesque little town that can be reached by going up 5 miles of winding road. On a clear day the view is most rewarding.

From Montecatini to Firenze the drive is short, and passes through Pistoia. If you have time make a detour to see Vinci. Pistoia is one of the smaller Tuscan provinces. During the Middle Ages it was squeezed between Lucca and Firenze, and in 1530 it became part of the Medici Duchy. It has an interesting *Piazza del Duomo,* representative of the Tuscan city piazza, with cathedral, bell tower, baptistry, city hall, medieval tower and other palaces. Note the *Duomo,* a 12th–13th-century structure in the Pisan style, with a few lovely Andrea della Robbia *terra cottas* in the vault over the central door. Inside, in a small chapel (*Cappella di S. Iacopo*) the altar contains a very important work in silver done by several jewelers of the 14th and 15th centuries. These jewelers came from Siena, Firenze and Pistoia, and they depicted stories from the Old and New Testaments and the life of S. Iacopo. The *Dossale di S. Iacopo* can be seen from 9 A.M. to 12 noon and from 3:30 to 7 P.M.

All other buildings on the piazza are interesting, especially the small Gothic *Battistero,* with its elegant octagonal shape dressed in green and white marble. On a side street that bears its name is a Pisan–Romanesque church of the 12th century, *S. Andrea.* The *Ospedale del Ceppo,* a 14th-

(margin notes)

** S. Michele has works by Della Robbia and Lippi

*** S. Martino Cathedral

A fine restaurant in a garden here is ** Le Panterоie

*** Pistoia Duomo

** Baptistry

** S. Andrea

** Ospedale

century building, is preceded by a lovely *portico* on columns decorated by Giovanni della Robbia.

At this point the trip takes on a different feeling, for we suggest you leave Pistoia bearing south, toward the Monte Albano and Vinci. The drive is charming, midst woods and beautiful panoramas. At Vinci visit the castle and Leonardo's birthplace. Continue toward Carmignano and stop at *Poggio a Caiano* for a tour of the grandiose *Villa* done by Giuliano di Sangallo for *Lorenzo il Magnifico*. The Medici had, like all great families, their share of famous love stories. *Poggio a Caiano* witnessed the epilogue of the most tragic, a complex affair between Francesco de' Medici and Bianca Cappello, a Venetian beauty. In 1587 they both died here within a few hours of each other, in circumstances that were never quite clear. Later, during the years when Firenze was capital of Italy and the Savoia monarchy had to move from its Piemonte home base, the Villa was a refuge for the lovely Rosina, beloved mistress of King Vittorio Emanuele II.

Continue your trip toward Firenze, but make a small detour toward Artimino, another 16th-century Medici villa. Just before you reach it, there is a picturesque little town, *Comeana,* and a very interesting Etruscan tomb. Back up to Poggio a Caiano and north to Prato, one of the country's big textile centers. Here, visit the *Duomo,* one of the loveliest churches in Toscana. Built in Romanesque style between the 12th and 13th centuries, it was enlarged with a Gothic transept in the 14th century. The elegant front was finished off with white and green marble stripes, work that took from 1385 to 1457. About 30 years later Andrea della Robbia did the glass terracotta over the front portal. At the right corner admire the *Pergamo del Sacro Cingolo* by Michelozzo, with Donatello's *Danza dei putti* around it (what you'll see is a copy, the original is at the *Museo del Duomo*). The interior, severe in its Romanesque simplicity, contains many lovely paintings; the apse is decorated with lovely frescoes about S. John the Baptist and S. Stefano done by Filippo Lippi. If you wish to stay longer, visit the lovely Renaissance church, *S. Maria delle Carceri,* by Sangallo, and the *Castello dell'Imperatore,* an imposing medieval structure that copies the famous *Castel del Monte* in Puglia. The emperor was Federico II.

On the way to Firenze pass *Sesto Fiorentino* for a visit to the *Museo delle Porcellane de Doccia;* it is of special interest for those who like porcelain and china. After that, waste no more time and head for the capital, for whatever time you have in Firenze will not be enough!

From Pisa to Volterra to Firenze

Before describing Firenze, here's another side trip to take through Toscana —the Toscana of the lower Arno Valley. By looking at the map you can see that the Arno River has three branches between Pisa and Firenze, all on the left or lower bank. Reading them down river (from Firenze to Pisa, where the river reaches the sea), they are the Pesa, the Elsa and the Era. We leave Pisa going toward *Ponsacco,* a small town on the Era. The first interesting place we reach is *Calci,* which has a remarkable Romanesque *pieve* in the center of town and the grand *Certosa di Pisa* just outside. This certosa, one of the largest monastic compounds in Italy, can be visited by appointment only

[handwritten margin notes]
** Vinci Castle and Museum

The King's mistress lived here from 1864-1871

*** Prato Cathedral

** S. Maria delle Carceri

* Castle

** Porcelain Museum

* Romanesque church of Calci

** Carthusian Monastery (Certosa) of Pisa

everyday except Monday. The schedule is: May to October, 3–6 P.M. weekdays, 2:00 to 4:45 P.M. holidays, from November to April, 2–5 P.M. weekdays,
1:30–4:15 P.M. holidays. From Calci continue to *Cascina,* a city of special
interest for furniture lovers, for here is one of the largest permanent furniture
shows in Italy; many artisans live and work here. Go on to Vicopisano, a small
picturesque town; then cross the *Arno* taking the road to Ponsacco. Pass
through this busy little center and continue to *Capannoli.* Note the large
Medici villa of *Camugliano* with towers and a lovely staircase.

At this point a choice is necessary. If your time is limited and you wish
to reach Firenze within a few hours, head north to S. Miniato, then Empoli,
Montelupo Fiorentino, Lastra a Signa. If you have time to spare, continue
south toward *Volterra,* one of the most interesting cities in all of Italy. The
drive is along small country roads and will take anywhere from 1 to 1 ½ hour.
The road winds through lovely farmlands and woods, and the last miles are
uphill. But it's worth the effort; you'll have something to talk about after
you've seen Volterra. On a clear day the view is splendid, and a walk through
this old city is a step back in time.

Piazza dei Priori, the center of town, is pure Middle Ages; if some of the
buildings were added later you won't notice, the imitation is perfect. As you
drive outside note the Roman Theater and, on the other side of the oval, the
Arco Etrusco, part of the original Etruscan walls. The street that leads into
town, *via Porta all'Arco,* is lined with small alabaster shops for working
alabaster has always been this city's main source of livelihood. Take a walk
along *Viale dei Ponti* and enjoy the view. Find the *Quadrivio dei Buom-
parenti* and note this most medieval spot in this medieval city, with its
house-towers (or tower houses) lifted straight out of the 13th century almost
intact. Take a walk 2 miles out of town, along the *Balze,* an impressive
precipice created by erosion, which has slowly swallowed Etruscan cemeteries, churches and monasteries, and which makes this city a likely candidate
for becoming a ghost town.

If you decided against this side trip to Volterra there is a short version
of this itinerary which goes from Capannoli to *Palàia:* You'll then see the
interesting 13th-century Gothic S. Martino church. This part of the drive is
on lovely, winding roads, and the next stop, *S. Miniato,* is a picturesque little
town perched on a hill. Visit the *Duomo* and enjoy the view. Walk around
this charming place. If it happens to be October, look for truffles; they are
sold on the streets and are among the best in Toscana. Then go on to *Empoli,*
an industrial city that will give you a good idea of how modern Toscana lives.
The main church was originally 11th century, but is now mostly redone and
of limited interest. Continue to *Montelupo Fiorentino,* with another multitowered Medici villa, the *Ambrogiana.* It cannot be visited because it is used
as a hospital for the mentally ill. Now you're almost in Firenze, but if you wish
to see two lovely Tuscan pievi with interesting *affreschi,* stop at Signa and
look for *Pieve di S. Giovanni Battista* and *Pieve Vecchia. Lastra a Signa*
still has part of the medieval walls, and the church of *S. Martino a Gan-
galandi* offers an abundance of 14th- and 15th-century paintings and
affreschi.

By the way, there are good restaurants all along this itinerary. *Miravalle*
at S. Miniato would be our first choice because of the view; *Da Carlo* at
Capannoli has good game.

Or you may prefer to wait until you get to Firenze to eat; the food will delight all of your senses, but mostly your eyes and palates.

Firenze

Florentine greatness goes from the 11th to the 16th centuries. There were 500 years or so of economic leadership, of intense political activity, of unequaled artistic vitality. The importance of Firenze, which has Etruscan origins and was a Roman colony, began during the Middle Ages.

One of the earliest experiments in city independence was achieved by this city. At the beginning of the 12th century it was already a commune with free artisans and had an active marketplace and a relatively mobile population. The Tuscan cities of the late Middle Ages were born of a necessity to mediate between public and class needs. For Firenze this rediscovered democratic bent was responsible for the vast changes that followed.

All itineraries of Firenze begin at the *Duomo,* or better, *Piazza del Duomo,* with the splendid cathedral, *S. Maria del Fiore,* the *Giotto Campanile* and the *baptistry,* one of the oldest monuments in town. Begin with the baptistry, dedicated to the Baptist himself, the city's patron saint, S. Giovanni. It can be visited in winter from 9 to 12:30 A.M. and from 2:30 to 5:30 P.M. and in the summer from 9 to 12:30 A.M. and from 3 to 6:30 P.M. Some say the original structure dates back to the 4th or 5th century, others say that it's 11th–12th-century Romanesque. The shape is octagonal, the outside is white and green marble—characteristic of Florentine–Romanesque —and the three bronze doors are one of the sights to see in this city. The door that faces south done by Andrea Pisano, is the oldest, showing scenes of St. John's life. The date is 1330. The northern door, by Lorenzo Ghiberti, is in late Gothic, showing scenes of the life of Christ. The eastern door, facing the *Duomo,* is also by Ghiberti but is done in a newer style and is considered his masterpiece. Michelangelo called it *Porta del Paradiso,* and the ten forms are done in a pictorial style with Old Testament scenes that shows you the new tendencies and gives you an idea of the changes brought about by the Renaissance.

✱✱✱✱ Baptistry

The interior is splendidly ornate, with an octagonal cupola decorated with Byzantine mosaics and lovely paintings and statues. Note Donatello's *Magdalen* and the inlaid floor depicting the Zodiac.

The famous bell tower, started by Giotto in 1334, is one of the best examples of Florentine Gothic; it is 276-feet high and dominates the square with its elegant shape and lovely marble colors. A 414-step staircase takes the enterprising visitor to the top terrace. The schedule for entering is: winter, 8:30 A.M.–12 noon and 2:30–4:30 P.M., closed Sunday afternoons; summer, 8:30 A.M.–12 noon and 2:30–6 P.M. From the top of this bell tower the view of the city is superb.

✱✱✱✱ Campanile

The *S. Maria del Fiore* cathedral is not only the largest of the three important monuments in this area, it is the most impressive religious structure in Firenze. Started in 1296 by Arnolfo del Cambio, its lines are typical of the simple and linear Gothic that characterize the use of that style in Toscana. As with so many churches, it had more than one "creator." Giotto was appointed director of the works in 1334, then Lapo Ghini and Francesco Talenti were appointed. Each added something to Arnolfo's original plan, and by 1421 the structure was completed as far as the drum. The one remaining

✱✱✱✱ Cathedral

problem was a cupola; it was brilliantly solved in 1418 by Brunelleschi. He studied ancient Roman architecture, especially the Pantheon, and tradition has it that he used a construction technique called "herringbone." Studies of this design have occupied specialists for centuries, but the details are still unknown. The cupola and its lantern were completed in 1461. The top can be reached by climbing 463 steps. If you are interested, look for a small door at the end of the left nave. The schedule for entering this stairway is identical to the one for the *campanile*. The top offers an interesting view of the city, as well as the possibility of admiring the inner structure of the cupola. As of 1982 this landmark of Firenze has been undergoing important repairs and the climb is temporarily not allowed.

The interior of the cathedral is full of important artworks, among them a splendid, unfinished Michelangelo *Pietà*, stained glass windows by Ghiberti, a Luca della Robbia terracotta depicting the Ascension, frescoes by Vasari and Zuccari (latter 16th century) and more stained glass by Donatello and Paolo Uccello. The cript of Santa Reparata is interesting; digging is still in progress in an attempt to unearth the original church that occupied the site.

There is a museum of important *Duomo* art. It's located at No.9 of the piazza and contains some of the best works done in Firenze during the 14th and 15th centuries. The schedule is: winter, 9:30 A.M.–4:00 P.M.; summer 9:00 A.M.–1:00 P.M. and 3:00–6:00 P.M.; Sundays, free admission 10:00 A.M. –1:00 P.M.

From *Piazza del Duomo* you can go in many directions. We will suggest a few but cannot indicate all possibilities because this is Firenze, where every street is an artistic itinerary.

For art lovers the first choice is to go down *via de'Calzaiuoli* toward *Piazza della Signoria* and the *Uffizi*. On the way you will pass *Orsanmichele*. If all things included here are visited with care, it's a full day's journey. The street itself is very attractive; it's full of lovely shops some of which sell, as the name implies, shoes. *Orsanmichele* is one of our favorite buildings, a fine example of Florentine Gothic. Originally built by the grain merchants, it became a church in 1380 with another floor added. While the inside of this small church is relatively simple, the exterior is lined with ornate "niches" containing statues of the *Arti's* patron saints. These statues, taken as a whole, offer an eloquent document of Florentine sculpture from the 14th to the 16th centuries. The most important sculptors of the period are represented. Inside note the famous *Tabernacolo di A. Orcagna* in marble, mosaic and reliefs; it's one of the most delicate creations of its kind.

When you reach *Piazza della Signoria* it is important to keep in mind that this was the political center of Firenze at the time it was built (13th–14th centuries). It remains important to this day for *Palazzo Vecchio* houses City Hall. Facing the magnificent palace to your right there is the *Loggia della Signoria*. Originally meant for city ceremonies, it now contains some of the most important late Renaissance statues—either copies or originals. At the center of the square is a plaque showing the spot where the reforming priest Gerolamo Savonarola was burned in 1498. There is also a bronze equestrian statue of Cosimo I by Giambologna and a large Neptune fountain by Ammannati, considered a better architect than sculptor.

Palazzo Vecchio or *della Signoria* is undoubtedly the most important nonreligious building in Firenze, as well as one of the most significant medi-

** Santa Reparata

Originals of works now copied in Campanile are here, for example

*** Orsanmichele

** Tabernacle

Botticelli destroyed some of his "sinful" works under Savonarola's influence

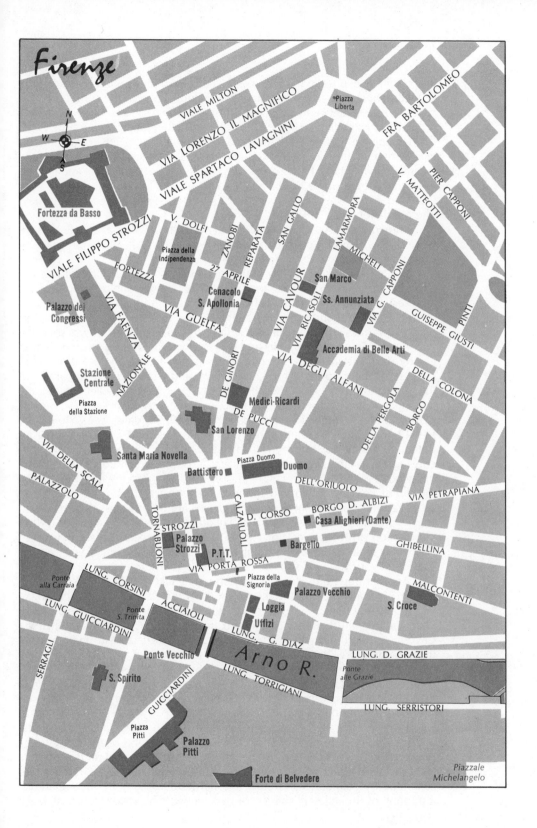

*** Palazzo Vecchio was the home of Cosimo I, who restored the Medici to the greatness

***** Uffizi Gallery

Don't forget da Vinci's Annunciation

** Medici-Riccardi Palace and museum

*** S. Lorenzo

eval public structures in Italy. Its tower, along with the Giotto campanile, the Brunelleschi cupola and Michelangelo's David, is one of the symbols of the city. It was built between 1299 and 1314 according to Arnolfo del Cambio's project and was enlarged in the 16th century by Buontalenti and Vasari. From the beginning it was destined for use as a public building; government meetings were held here during the Republican period. When Firenze became the capital of unified Italy, Palazzo Vecchio was the site of parliament and housed the foreign office. Since 1872 it has been the City Hall. Visiting hours are from 9 A.M. to 4 P.M. weekdays, 9 A.M. to 12 noon Sundays, closed on Saturday. The admission is L. 1,500.

Immediately following *Palazzo Vecchio* is the *Uffizi Gallery*. Before we write of this splendid collection, we'll say a few words about the space in front of it, *Piazzale degli Uffizi*.

While the irregular *piazza* of the medieval period was born with and as a result of the city, the Renaissance piazza was designed in order to perform a pre-established function. It is often as much of a monument as the palaces and churches that surround it or as the statues that stand in its center. This piazzale was designed and built by Vasari from 1560 to 1574. It was specially intended for Cosimo de' Medici and was meant to be the center of the Grand Duchy. It was flanked by the two wings of the large structure (the Uffizi) created for the purpose of housing the legal and administrative apparatus of the Medicean state. Now it houses the most important art collection in Italy. Its visiting hours are: weekdays, 10:00 A.M.–4 P.M.; Sundays, 9 A.M.–1 P.M.; close Mondays. Admission: weekdays, L. 1,250; Sundays, free. The gallery has 42 rooms, divided into three major galleries, and contains works by Botticelli, Leonardo, Mantegna, Correggio, Durer, Holbein, Raphael, Michelangelo, Titian, Tintoretto, Caravaggio, Rembrandt, Rubens and many, many others. At the end you find the *Corridoio Vasariano,* which runs across the top of *Ponte Vecchio* and connects the *Uffizi* with *Palazzo Pitti.* It can be visited by appointment only; small groups are taken across each morning, usually around 9:30 A.M. The Uffizi ticket office will be glad to give you further information on the subject, or call 218341 if you speak Italian. No trip to Firenze is really complete without a visit to the Uffizi, but if you see the *corridoio* your trip will also be considered a real success!

Another important Florentine itinerary will take you to *S. Lorenzo,* with *Palazzo Medici-Riccardi* and the *Cappelle Medicee.* The walk is short; take *via de'Martelli,* which is to your right when you face the Battistero and turn your back on the Duomo. At the end of the street, before it becomes via Cavour, turn left and you will reach *Piazza S. Lorenzo.* With your back to that church (more later about it) you will be facing one of the best Renaissance palaces in Firenze—the *Medici-Riccardi.* Built from 1444 to 1464, by Michelozzo for old Cosimo de' Medici, it was the court of *Lorenzo il Magnifico.* Its pure lines defy description; we can only say that some of the main floor windows are attributed to Michelangelo.

We will dedicate this part of the itinerary to the *piazza* and the beautiful *S. Lorenzo,* built by Brunelleschi 1442–1446; it is one of the outstanding religious buildings of the early Renaissance. The front was left unfinished. The inside is shaped like a Latin cross, with a wide transept and three naves separated by columns. Its serenity and harmonious lines are incomparable, a triumph of Brunelleschi's vision of perspective. The inside front wall has a balcony done by Michelangelo; this and its many other masterpieces make the church one of the most important monuments in Firenze. At the left of the transept note the *Sagrestia vecchia*— designed by Brunelleschi and decorated by Donatello—a jewel of Renaissance taste. To the left admire the splendid sarcophagus of Giovanni and Piero de' Medici, made in porphyry and bronze by Verrocchio in 1472.

The next important item on this itinerary (which is all Renaissance, from the early years to the latter ones) is the *Cappelle Medicee.* On the right of the transept is the new sacristy, which cannot be entered from the church. Worked on by Michelangelo from 1520 to 1524, it was finished by Vasari. The similarities and differences between these two chapels illustrate the changes that were taking place at the time.

Enter from *Piazza Madonna degli Aldobrandini* behind S. Lorenzo. From the vast crypt go up into the baroque *Cappella dei Principi,* shaped like an octagonal cupola. This is the Medici mausoleum where the grand dukes of Toscana are buried. Two are surmounted by huge bronze statues done by Pietro Tacca. From here you can enter the *Sagrestia Nuova* of S. Lorenzo, which contains the famous *Sepolcri Medicei* done by Michelangelo between 1524 and 1533. The tomb of Lorenzo, Duke of Urbino, father of Catherine de Medici, holds the *Thinker* and two figures, *Dawn* and *Dusk.* The tomb of Giuliano, third son of Lorenzo il Magnifico, holds a statue of the duke himself and two reclining figures that represent *Day* and *Night.*

*** Michelangelo's sculptures in the new Sacristy of S. Lorenzo. (Medici Chapels)*

When you leave the Cappelle Medicee, you have finished one of the shortest and most exciting Renaissance itineraries in all Italy.

Now return to the heart of Firenze, *the Piazza del Duomo.* The next itinerary is a bit longer and much more varied. There will be some interesting shopping, some interesting Renaissance palaces, and two Gothic churches. There is a little medieval street with houses and towers and, most surprising for Firenze, a church with a baroque front. You also get your first glimpse of the Arno River.

Begin by turning your back on the *Duomo* and go down *via de' Cerretani* on your right. It is one of the busiest streets in Firenze, full of traffic, pedestrians, and interesting shops. When the name chages to *via Panzani* bear left onto *via Rondinelli.* At *Piazza Antinori* you can admire a small church, *S. Gaetano,* one of the rare examples of Florentine baroque (1648). Then turn onto *via Tornabuoni,* the most aristocratic street in town, full of elegant stores from the *Rive Gauche* of Yves St. Laurent to the first *Gucci.* The best gloves, the best lingerie, the best object d'art can be bought on via Tornabuoni. If nothing else, window shop and have a good *aperitivo* in one of the fashionable coffee houses.

* S. Gaetano

The most important building on via Tornabuoni is *Palazzo Strozzi,* another great Renaissance structure. A few steps further is *Piazza S. Trinità* with a column that was brought from the *Terme di Caracàlla* in Roma and two attractive palaces. At the right, facing the river, is the church of *S. Trinità,* one of the loveliest Gothic churches in town. The front is baroque, added in 1594, but the interior is noble and severe and represents one of the first attempts at Gothic in Firenze.

** Palazzo Strozzi

*** Santa Trinita has beautiful Ghirlandaio Holy Family

For a step back in time, turn onto Borgo SS. Apostoli, a medieval street lined with old houses and towers; on a small square admire the *SS. Apostoli* church, an 11th-century Romanesque building with a portal added later. At this point you can see the river. A few steps back toward via Tornabuoni and you'll be just across from *Ponte S. Trinità,* the Arno's most majestic bridge, with three elastic arches, designed by Ammannati in 1570. It was destroyed by bombs during World War II and rebuilt exactly as before

After admiring the bridge, continue along *Lungarno Corsini,* one of the loveliest stretches of this long street. Passing *Palazzo Corsini,* note one of the few Florentine palaces done in baroque. At *Piazza Ognissanti* note the very baroque front of the church, redone in 1637; the slim bell tower, however, tells of Gothic origins. Now turn right and retrace your steps along *Borgo Ognissanti* until you reach *via de' Fossi.* Turn left onto this street lined with excellent antique shops. Continue until you come upon *S. Maria Novella,* one of the most famous churches in Firenze, a masterpiece of Gothic architecture, started by the Dominican order in 1246 and finished in 1360. Here again there is a lovely piazza with two marble obelisks and an elegant loggia across from the church. But the front of the church itself, inlaid with green and white marble, monopolizes the eye. On the left are the beautiful cloisters, a group of Gothic structures worth admiring. Open weekdays, 9 A.M.–4 P.M.; Sundays, 9 A.M.–12 noon. The inside of S. Maria Novella is a vaulted Gothic basilica, its nave and aisles divided by pillars. There are affreschi by Filippino Lippi and Ghirlandaio, crucifixes by Giambologna and Brunelleschi, a terracotta basin by Giovanni della Robbia and a painted crucifix by Giotto. Under the left nave altar there is a fresco by *Masaccio,* which is considered not only that painter's masterpiece but one of the most important works of the early Renaissance.

Just behind S. Maria Novella is the *Stazione Centrale,* done in 1935 and considered one of the best buildings of its kind.

Next we suggest a walk, which is the easiest way to reach the Arno River from Piazza del Duomo. Then cross over on the famous *Ponte Vecchio* and go to *Palazzo Pitti* and the *Giardini di Boboli.* Again from the *Battistero,* facing the *Duomo,* take the street to your right, *via Roma.* Soon you'll reach *Piazza della Repubblica,* the center of modern Firenze. Here are the fashionable *caffès* that fill up at noon, the larger stores and the lovely people. Note the imposing arcade that forms the background of this piazza. Our walk continues down the same street, which is now *via Calimala.* Soon you'll reach the *Loggia del Mercato Nuovo;* built in 1551, it was then a banking center and is now a picturesque straw market. At the bottom a statue of the *Porcellino,* a wild boar in bronze added to the fountain by P. Tacca in 1612, was copied from an older model.

Just behind the loggia is the *Palazzo di Parte Guelfa,* built in the 14th century and enlarged by Brunelleschi in the 15th century. Worth seeing is the splendid *Salone Brunelleschiano* inside, with a terracotta by Luca della Robbia and a wood ceiling by Vasari.

Now go back to the narrow street you were following, which has again changed name and is now *via Por S. Maria.* Even though it was almost completely destroyed during the last war, the reconstruction has respected the preceding pattern, and as you approach the river and the oldest and most famous bridge in Firenze, the Middle Ages will accompany you every step of the way.

Ponte Vecchio was the only bridge spared by the Germans, and it retains its 1345 appearance. Lined with jewelry shops on both sides, it represents one of the most pleasant promenades in Firenze, in Italy and probably in the

* Santi Apostoli has a della Robbia tabernacle

*** Santa Maria Novella

Il Porcellino is also the nickname of the market itself

** Palazzo di Parte Guelfa

** Ponte Vecchio

world. At the center both sides have a terrace with a view of the river, the *lungarni* and the other bridges.

After the bridge continue along *via Guicciardini* and you'll soon arrive at *Palazzo Pitti,* the largest building in Firenze, designed and built by Brunelleschi in 1458 and enlarged several times. After 1549 it became the residence of the grand dukes, and it now contains the *Galleria Palatina,* the *Museo degli Argenti* and the *Galleria d'Arte Moderna.* In recent years Pitti has also been the elegant scenario of many fashion shows, attracting the best in Italian high styling and large numbers of foreign buyers.

*** Palazzo Pitti, especially for its Raphaels*

The *Boboli* gardens are an enchanting break from the palaces, churches and galleries of Firenze. Here is one of the best examples of Italian gardening, where nature is influenced by imagination and surprises peek out from unexpected places. They can be entered from the left of Piazzale Pitti and extend all the way around the palace. Do not expect to see the whole garden in one visit, just enjoy a refreshing hour or two.

** Boboli Gardens*

We will present no more itineraries of central Firenze, even if its beauties do suggest another 20 or 30. If you've done the above you've seen the heart of town. Only the outskirts remain, and they are also full of spendid sights; we will mention the most important.

Take *viale dei Colli* to the *Piazzale Michelangelo.* It's the loveliest ride out of Firenze; the piazzale offers not only a large copy of the *David* but a view of the whole city below, with the Giotto *Campanile,* the Brunelleschi cupola, the Arnolfo tower and *Ponte Vecchio* all there together—the most beautiful picture postcard in the world!

*** View from Piazzale Michelangelo*

Just behind you, or just before the large piazzale, depending on the direction, is a small hill with a basilica on top. *S. Miniato al Monte* is the Florentine masterpiece of Romanesque architecture. This little church is almost a perfect theorem of programmed lines, from the symmetrical rhythm of its frontal arcades to the linear perfection of the green and white marble, to the balance of the inside steps and partitions. Built outside the city walls, it stands on the same spot occupied by a 4th-century chapel—still there at the time of Charlemagne—that had been dedicated to *S. Miniato,* the first Christian martyr of Firenze. The basilica we now see was started in 1018 and completed in 1207. The bell tower fell in 1499 and was rebuilt in 1524; the stairway that connects it with *viale del Colli* was added in 1868. The inside has a magnificent marble pavement, many enameled terracottas by Luca della Robbia, a chapel by Michelozzo and many other splendid sculptures, frescoes and mosaics.

*** S. Miniato al Monte*

Just behind the Boboli gardens is *Forte Belvedere,* built at the end of the 16th century by Buontalenti and offering another good view of the city. The city of Firenze holds its more important art shows inside the fort.

Do not leave Firenze without a visit to *S. Croce,* one of the great Franciscan churches in Italy and one of the masterpieces of Florentine Gothic. Designed by the great Arnolfo, it was built in 1294. The marble front and the bell tower are 19th century. The inside holds the tombs of Firenze's greatest sons from Michelangelo to Machiavelli. Dante, who died in Ravenna and was buried there, has a commemorative plaque. In one of the chapels are some memorable Giotto affreschi with stories of St. Francis.

*** Santa Croce
The death scene in these frescoes moved Michelangelo to tears*

To the right of S. Croce is the lovely *Cappella dei Pazzi,* with a charming cloister. Unfortunately, the whole area was badly damaged by the November

1966 flood, where the water reached almost 18 feet. The *cappella* is one of the best works of Brunelleschi, done between 1443 and 1446. The little terracotta cupola is by Luca della Robbia. The whole area has been painstakingly restored.

There is more to see in Firenze; other art galleries and museums are listed in the **Inside Information** section on museums. Hotels and restaurants are also listed in Inside Information.

Side Trips from Firenze

The first itinerary out of Firenze is almost a must—a fairly short trip to *Siena* that takes you through the *Chianti* country. First, take the road to *Galluzzo*, where you can visit an interesting *Certosa*. Then take the Autostrada to Siena for a short trip to *S. Casciano Val di Pesa,* where there is an interesting church. On the way to *Certaldo* are two castles and two churches worth admiring, all near and around *Fiano.* Stop at Certaldo to walk through the old town, which is the birthplace of Boccaccio.

The tiny borough of Certaldo is perfect, an intact little town with cobblestones and old charming and restful houses. Enjoy a Tuscan lunch at the *Osteria del Vicario,* an enchanting 13th-century palace turned into a small hotel and restaurant (one of the beams that holds the ceiling is almost 1,000 years old).

Proceed toward *S. Gimignano,* another medieval town, famous for its many towers. On the way make a short deviation in order to admire one of the loveliest pievi in Toscana, *Pieve di Cellole,* a jewel of early Romanesque.

S. Gimignano is a city to walk around in; the streets are lined with little shops, the churches are small but full of things to see; the walls are 13th century. Note the *Piazza della Cisterna,* a triangular piazza with herringbone paving. *Via S. Matteo* is the main street in town, and *Piazza del Duomo* is the main square.

Continue toward Siena by passing Poggibonsi, and you will drive through the heart of the Chianti area. After passing *Colle Val d'Elsa* and *Monteriggioni*—both picturesque and interesting—you will reach *Siena,* one of the most famous cities in Italy.

Siena's history is similar to that of Firenze, but since it is a rival history, it finishes at an earlier date. It was a free comune with Ghibelline leanings (as opposed to the Guelf loyalties of Firenze and Lucca), and throughout the 13th and 14th centuries its battles were often victorious. But the 15th century began to see a weaker Siena, which first become a signoria and finally a part of the Medici domain (1559).

Since the period of Sienese greatness coincided with the period of Gothic greatness, it should come as no surprise that most of Siena's remarkable buildings are in that style. Begin your visit of the city with *Piazza del Campo,* one of the most beautiful medieval squares, shaped like a scallop shell and surrounded by old palaces and towers. Continue with *Palazzo Pubblico* and the slender *Torre del Mangia* along the straight side and the monumental *Fonte Gaia* in the center. Twice a year (July 2nd and August 16th) the famous *palio* is held here; it's a medieval horserace that unleashes fierce rivalries among the various *contrade* of the city and gives you a unique spectacle of

[handwritten margin notes:]
* Pazzi Chapel

You can buy Chartreuse from the Carthusian monks at the ** Certosa

* Osteria

* Church of Cellole

Ghibellines supported nobility against the popes

Signoria = feudal fief

**** Piazza del Campo

Middle Age pageantry and color. Don't just come to Siena on the dates of the palio. Plan ahead. The city gets crowded beyond belief, and the best viewing places are booked months in advance.

The *Palazzo Pubblico* is considered the most elegant Gothic building in Toscana meant for secular use. It was built from 1297 to 1342 partly in stone and partly in brick, with the lovely tower del Mangia rising over 300 feet on its left. At the foot of the tower is the light *Cappella di Piazza*, which is finished off in Renaissance arches.

Inside the palazzo is the *Museo Civico*, which can be visited from 9 A.M. to 12 noon and from 2 to 5 P.M. The collection of paintings in the nearby Cathedral museum, is remarkable, probably the best in Toscana after the *Uffizi*.

Siena is another Italian town that can best be admired by walking. After you've enjoyed Piazza del Campo leave by way of *via di Città*, a charming street that climbs softly midst lovely medieval houses and palaces and that will take you to the other splendid monument of Siena, the Cathedral. As you walk along via di Città, admire *Palazzo Chigi Saracini* at No. 89 and *Palazzo Piccolomini delle Papesse* at No. 126, now housing the *Banca d'Italia*, done by Bernardo Rossellino in 1495 in the Florentine Renaissance style. Note the difference between this palace and *Palazzo Marsili*, done in 1458, with residual Gothic characteristics.

At this point you will reach *Piazza Postierla*, a small piazza with a column that is surmounted by the Sienese *lupa*—note the exquisite wrought iron flagpole. Turn right onto *via del Capitano*, and after a short walk you will reach *Piazza del Duomo*, dominated by the marble bulk of the *Duomo*. On your left is the *Palazzo Arcivescovile*, an unattractive imitation Gothic done in the 18th century. Note for art lovers: Inside this palace is a lovely Madonna on wood, the *Madonna del Latte* by A. Lorenzetti, which can be seen by request only.

The cathedral is one of the most splendid creations of Gothic architecture in Italy. It took more than 200 years to build, from mid-12th century to about 1382. The façade, especially the lower part, is considered its most interesting part; it was designed by Giovanni Pisano at the end of the 13th century. The upper part, done about 100 years later, is in a flowery Gothic that clearly shows the changed tastes of those years. Note the right side, somber and covered in two colors, and the romanesque bell tower in black and white stripes with six levels of windows.

The interior of the *Duomo di Siena* is one of the most striking you'll ever see. Not only does the black and white marble create effects of *chiaroscuro* that almost resemble op-art, but the pavement is the most precious of any church, with 56 scenes done by exceptional artists over a period of another 200 years from the mid-14th to mid-16th centuries. The most important of these are kept covered by wood planks and can be seen only from August 15th to September 15th.

Other art works crowd the Duomo; take a walk and look at the Michelangelo statue, the Bernini baroque chapel and much more. Do not miss the *Libreria Piccolomini*, an enchanting Renaissance creation that Cardinal Francesco Todeschini Piccolomini (later Pius III) had made for the purpose of housing the books of his uncle, Pius II. This jewel of Renaissance art can be visited 9 A.M.–1 P.M. and 2:30–6:30 P.M.; admission is L.500.

*** Palazzo Pubblico

* Piazza Chapel

* Chigi Palace

** Piccolomini Palace

** Madonna in Archbishop's Palace

**** Siena Cathedral

*** Cathedral Library

Another masterpiece can be seen in the transept—the famous marble pergamo of Nicola Pisano, done between 1266 and 1268 with the help of his son Giovanni and other students, one of whom was Arnolfo del Cambio (see **Firenze**). It stands on nine columns, the middle one is surrounded by allegoric statues, and the parapet is decorated with seven beautiful reliefs that tell stories of Christ.

The baptistry is under the apse of the cathedral, almost a crypt. It can be entered by going down on the right side of the duomo, after passing a rich 14th-century portal. Built between 1316 and 1325, it has a lovely Gothic façade, with an unfinished upper part and three harmonious portals on the lower part.

Note the well-known *Baptismal Font* by Iacopo della Quercia, done from 1417 to 1430, a representative masterpiece of Tuscan sculpture during the transition from Gothic to Renaissance. Some of the statues—*Faith* and *Hope*—that surround the hexagonal tub are by Donatello, and the six bronze reliefs are by della Quercia, Ghiberti, Giovanni di Turino, Turino di Sano and Donatello.

Other things to admire in Siena are its charming streets, *via Banchi di Sotto* and *via Banchi di Sopra,* the churches of *S. Francesco* and *S. Domenico,* a lovely Renaissance structure, the *Loggia della Mercanzia,* an interesting building in Gothic–Renaissance and the *Piazza Salimbeni* with its Gothic palace.

After Siena return to Firenze along the other side, a sweet and rippling drive through rows and rows of hills full of vines and an occasional olive grove. You'll pass *Castellina in Chianti, Greve* (there is also a small river by that name) and *Impruneta,* with a lovely basilica and the well-known factories of *cotto* (ceramic tile). For wine lovers, this trip offers many possible stops, with wine tasting every step of the way.

The last Tuscan itinerary we wish to suggest is both exciting and uplifting, a combination of lovely cities, splendid natural surroundings and religious mysticism. It takes you from Firenze to Arezzo by going through the hilly and mountainous country of the *Pratomagno* and the *Casentino.* If you wish to see only the city of Arezzo the autostrada will take you there in about 90 minutes, while this trip is a whole day.

Leave Firenze by coasting the Arno until you reach *Pontassieve,* a city where the Arno meats the Sieve. Proceed eastward into the hills and higher, through a scene that is enchanting and relaxing and different from the Toscana you've seen so far. If you have time, make a detour to the convent of *Vallombrosa.* If you like views from the tops of mountains, drive the extra few miles to M. Secchieta, almost 5,000-feet high. The panorama at the top is rewarding.

Before you took the detour to Vallombrosa you reached *Passo della Consuma;* from there you can begin the drive down into the large valley of the *Casentino.* Soon the view is dominated by the castle of *Poppi.* Cross the Arno—here in its higher part—and visit this city and its grand *castello dei Guidi.* Not far from the spot where you cross the Arno is the plain of *Campaldino* where on June 11, 1289, a famous battle was fought between Firenze and Arezzo, with Dante Alighieri on the Florentine side.

Leave Poppi and take the upward road to *Camaldoli.* The drive itself prepares you for the stark and solemn *Eremo,* with pine forests around you

*** Cathedral Museum across the street

* Poppi Castle

Dante, on the Florentine (Guelph's) side, won

as the road climbs to the old monastery and the baroque church. Beyond the church are 20 cells, some still inhabited by monks who are also hermits; women are not allowed in this area.

Drive down from this remote mountain top, pass the small town of *Bibbiena,* and stop at *Piazza Tarlati* and admire the view from the terrace. Then proceed to *La Verna,* one of the most famous Franciscan sanctuaries. The road is winding and the surrounding countryside is somber and grey, a fitting prelude to the famous convent. This is where St. Francis of Assisi received the *stigmata* and this is where he died. The mountain was donated to him in 1213, and the following year he started a few cells. On Septem-ber 14, 1224, he received the signs of his sainthood, and after that this mountain top became a shrine visited by thousands of believers every year.

** Mt. La Verna

The view from the convent is splendid, for it takes in both the Prato-magno and the Casentino. The small church of *S. Maria degli Angeli* has three lovely Della Robbia terracottas, and an affresco-decorated corridor leads to the *Chiesa delle Stimmate* where a glass-covered stone marks the very spot where the miracle occurred.

The drive down is not as pleasant as the rest of the trip, and unless something has changed in the last few months (which in Italy is always a possibility), the road is not in very good condition. But soon you will again be driving along the Arno and toward Arezzo, the eastern province of Tos-cana where great artists were born and lovely Umbria is a close neighbor.

Arezzo had Etruscan origins and a Roman period, but as in so many Tuscan cities, it really began its greatness as a commune around the 11th and 12th centuries. Even more than Siena, it was an early victim of Florentine power. But the leadership of Bishop Guido Tarlati brought the city back to a new splendor, and most of the impressive churches and palaces you will admire are from that period.

Tarlati died in 1327

If you come to Arezzo by car, leave it outside the city walls. This is definitely a city for walking. The most interesting and most famous thing to see in Arezzo is the cycle of *affreschi* by Piero della Francesca, known as *la Leggenda della Croce.* It can be admired in the Basilica of S. Francesco, in *Piazza S. Francesco.* The church itself is a Gothic structure of the 13th–14th centuries; it was later redone and is partly unfinished on the outside. But the interior is impressive in its naked simplicity; and the paintings, done from 1453 to 1464, are truly outstanding. They represent one of the highest achievements of the Renaissance, both for their rich colors and for their rigorous style.

*** The frescoes were painted 1452–66

After you finish your visit to the basilica turn right, then left onto *Corso Italia,* the Arezzo main street. You can walk the rest of it later; at this point just admire the short stretch that leads to *Pieve di S. Maria,* the loveliest medieval church in Arezzo and one of the most important examples of Romanesque in Toscana. Begun in 1140, it had Gothic motifs added at the beginning of the 14th century, was mishandled in the 16th century and was later restored. This lovely pieve (one of the few in-town Pievi) is on *Piazza Grande,* an irregular, large, picturesque square. It's one of the most charac-teristic squares in all Italy and is site of the *Giostra del Saracino,* held on the first Sunday in September. This piazza also holds the *Fiera Antiquaria* on the first Sunday of every month. Piazza Grande is also called *Vasari* because of the grandiose *Palazzo delle Logge* done by Vasari in 1573.

** S. Maria church

*** Saracen Joustry

* Antique Fair

The continuation of corso Italia is *via dei Pileati* where you'll pass, on your left, the impressive *Palazzo Pretorio.* Higher up, on via dell'Orto No. 28 is the supposed birthplace of poet Petrarch; it was rebuilt in 1948 and is now the headquarters of the *Accademia Petrarca di Lettere, Arti e Scienze* and other cultural institutions. It can be visited from 10 A.M. to 12 noon and from 5 to 6 P.M.

On your way to the Duomo you pass the *Passeggio del Prato,* Arezzo's public gardens, where the *Fortezza* stands. This fortress was rebuilt by the Medici during the 16th century on designs done by Giuliano and Antonio da Sangallo. Climb onto the fortress for an excellent view of the city and surrounding countryside.

Now you've reached the city cathedral, a large building done in 13th–14th century Gothic and finished during the early 16th century. The façade is a modern restoration, but note the interesting 14th-century door on the right. Inside the three-nave structure is majestic with its vertical look. The stained-glass windows, mostly done during the 16th century by G. de Marcillat, are particularly lovely. Note the Tarlati chapel (1334) and the Gothic tomb of Pope Gregorio X.

The last important church to visit in Arezzo is the *Basilica di S. Domenico,* a Gothic building started in 1275 that houses a splendid *Crucifix* over the main altar; it was done by Cimabue when he was quite young.

On *via XX Settembre* is the house of Giorgio Vasari, with some lovely *affreschi* by Vasari himself. It can be visited weekdays from 9:30 A.M. to 3:30 P.M.; holidays from 9 A.M. to 1 P.M.; closed Tuesdays.

There are two interesting museums, the *Galleria e Museo Medioevale e Moderno* at via S. Lorentino 8 and the *Museo Archeologico Mecenate* at the *Monastero S. Bernardo.* In front of this museum is the Roman Amphitheater.

As with most Tuscan towns, Arezzo can be enjoyed by walking through it and taking in the atmosphere, enjoying the caffès and shops and admiring the medieval houses and squares.

While we will suggest no other itineraries here it is difficult to leave Toscana without considering some of its other lovely cities that may be visited if time permits. South of Arezzo is *Cortona,* a charming town located on the eastern edge of Valdichiana, an area famous for its good beef. Cortona has Etruscan origins and is a small showplace of Renaissance art. Going west from Cortona, across the *Autostrada* is the city of *Montepulciano,* another Renaissance city, almost untouched and famous for its wine production. And very close by lies the city of *Pienza,* a small miracle of Renaissance urban planning built for Pope Pius II Piccolomini.

EMILIA-ROMAGNA

The two names of the region, Emilia and Romagna, indicate two distinct areas. *Romagna* is the southeastern part; most of it is on the Adriatic; and it includes the provinces of *Forlì* and *Ravenna,* parts of *Bologna* and *Ferrara,* and the republic of *S. Marino.* The rest of the area is *Emilia,* which includes the fertile Po River Valley and the east side of the Appennine Mountains.

One of the largest and richest regions in Italy, Emilia-Romagna is included in the central Italy section because it does *not* have a frontier with another European country. Otherwise, several aspects of its character suggest a unity with the North. Both its politics and its economy resemble those of the large northern centers of Milano and Torino, and its way of life is modern and progressive.

The food, unlike that of Toscana or Lazio, is rich with butter and cream, boiled and braised meats, and homemade pasta. The dialects spoken in the various cities are closer to French and Lombard than to Toscana's purer Italian or Umbria's quasi-Roman inflections.

Bologna is still Italy's gourmet Mecca

But geography is inescapable, and in spite of its similarities with the North, Emilia-Romagna is a central region. Its capital, *Bologna,* is almost in the middle of the peninsula; the area is influenced to a large degree by both the Po River and the Appennine Mountains, which give it its own peculiar character.

This region has the richest farmlands in Italy and leads in the production of grain, sugar beets and fruits. It runs a close second in tomato and wine production and a comfortable third in rice cultivation. Cattle breeding is also at its best here, with famous *parmigiano* and *prosciutto di Parma* (Parma cheese and ham) known everywhere in Italy and abroad.

Industry is another important part of the Emilia-Romagna economy. Some factories are connected to agriculture, others to the refineries of Ravenna. Among other things, the region is known for its ceramics, its shoe factories, its knitwear industry, its furniture makers, its electric appliances, its machinery and its graphics. In other words, almost every aspect of modern manufacture is covered.

But for the tourist, this is a region of interesting cities. *Bologna,* an opulent, lovely city to visit, has a famous university. *Ravenna* was a capital in the days of Byzantine power and has some of the most splendid mosacis in Italy. *Parma,* a capital at a different time, was given to young Maria Luisa of Hapsburg as a consolation after Napoleon's defeat; it has maintained its aloof, slightly aristocratic air. *Ferrara, Modena, Piacenza, Forli* and *Reggio Emilia* are the region's other provinces, each an active city with its own life and story.

Last but certainly not least is the fact that this is an opera lover's paradise, for here music is a serious part of life. To sing in the Parma Opera House means facing the most difficult and demanding public in the world. And one of the greatest living singers today, Luciano Pavarotti, is a native of Modena.

Some History

The Etruscans brought Emilia-Romagna to a high level of civilization and prosperity as early as the 6th century B.C. After the second Punic War it passed into Roman hands, and the *via Emilia* was built in 187 B.C. This great Roman road unified the region, and the cities we now visit were created alongside it. Later, the whole area was incorporated into the empire as the Eighth Region.

As the twilight set on the Western Empire, with the decadence of Roma and the increased importance of Constantinople, the city of *Ravenna* became a splendid capital. Thus, while most of the region was invaded by the Longobards in 568 and became a feudal state, which was continued by the subsequent invasion by the Franks (754–774), the Eastern part retained its Byzantine character for a long time.

As in the rest of Italy, the 11th and 12th centuries represent a period of free cities, rivalries and fighting. The pope and emperor were the dominating powers. The great Swabian emperor, Federico II, was defeated at Parma and Fossalta (1249), and the region was opened to the families that were establishing themselves in other areas. Parma and Piacenza, the closest areas to Lombardia, fell to the Visconti; Modena and Reggio were taken by the Estensi who were already established in Ferrara, and all of Romagna was broken up into small fractions that were fought over by Firenze, Venezia and, with particular insistence, by the church. Bologna became an especially strong *signoria,* first with the Pepoli family then with the Bentivoglio.

After the 16th century, largely as a result of the battling capacity of Cesare Borgia and the talents and ambitions of Pope Julius II and his successors, Romagna became a definite part of the church state.

For the next three centuries the situation remained stable, with the Farnese family (who entered the scene after the downfall of the Visconti) in control in Parma and Piacena; the Estensi in control in Modena and Reggio; and the Church in control in the remaining territory.

Napoleon unified the region under one name, the *Repubblica Cispadana,* which was later enlarged and became part of the *Repubblica Cisalpina* (1797). With Napoleon's defeat and the restoration, things went back to the way they were with the exception of Parma and Piacenza, which were given to Napoleon's ex-wife, Maria Luisa of Hapsburg.

The period of Italian unification was active in Emilia-Romagna, with much agitation and several deaths, but it finally ended on March 18, 1860, when the large region became part of the new Italian state.

Some Thoughts on Art

Except for the *Arch of Augustus* in *Rimini,* there is not much evidence of Roman art in Emilia-Romagna. But from the 4th to the 6th centuries *Ravenna* was the center of a new Christian–Byzantine style that left splended architectural achievements and beautiful mosaics.

Later, a few outstanding Romanesque cathedrals with a very distinct Longobard influence were built in *Modena, Piacenza, Parma* and *Ferrara.* In the Parma baptistry there are works by the greatest sculptor of his time, Antelami.

The city of *Bologna* owes its appearance to the Middle Ages, and examples of the best Gothic styles in the region are found here. Another very good example is in Piacenza, the *Palazzo del Gotico.*

Bologna dominated the artistic scene in the 14th century in ways other than through architecture. There was a very active school of painting characterized by its vigorous realism.

In the 15th century leadership passed to *Ferrara,* one of the liveliest Renaissance centers in the country. An extremely expressive school of painting developed, and the brilliant architect, Biagio Rossetti, left his mark. Other cities were also building at this time, but mostly with Tuscan artists and builders.

In the 16th century Parma was the most important painting center, with the refined sensuality of Correggio and Parmigianino, and Bologna regained leadership with important sculptors and painters of its own. By the end of the century, baroque entered the scene, and Bologna was among the first to adorn itself in that style.

There were several good painters in the 19th century, including one *Macchiaiolo.* The 20th century produced the great G. Morandi, a Bolognese, while Ferrara saw the birth of metaphysical painting with De Chirico and Carrà.

Bologna

There are very good trains to Bologna from all major cities in the north and south and airplanes from Roma and Milano. The *Autostrada del Sole* passes through the region, either from the north via Piacenza, Parma, Reggio, Modena, or from Firenze over the Appennine Mountains; this is a very lovely drive that takes about 1 hour. Another way of reaching Bologna is from the northeast via Venezia, Rovigo or Ferrara.

Whichever way you choose, Bologna is one of the most important cities in Italy and will not disappoint you. The reddish buildings and long streets bordered by *porticoes* are characteristic of this active and opulent town. It can be visited in one or two days, more if you wish to spend time in museums and picture galleries.

Any itinerary of Bologna begins at the *Piazza Maggiore.* It's the monumental center of city life, surrounded by medieval, Gothic and Renaissance structures worth admiring. Note the temple of *S. Petronio,* one of the most impressive buildings in Italian Gothic. It was built from 1390 to 1659 (that is not a misprint, it *really* took more than 250 years). The center portal is decorated with powerful sculptures by Sienese Iacopo della Quercia, done from 1425 to 1438, and considered masterpieces of early Renaissance art. The immense interior is divided into three naves, with many chapels on both sides. On top of the major altar is an impressive choir in wood inlay, with several organs, one of which—the one on the right—is probably the oldest in Italy (1470–1475). A careful visit of this very large church could take well over 1 hour, with stops to look at lovely frescoes, Gothic wood statues and beautiful *maiolica* floors.

Back on the piazza you can admire the *Palazzo Comunale,* part medieval and part early Renaissance. Do not miss the *Fontana del Nettuno,* one of the loveliest 16th-century fountains; its bronze statues were done by Giambologna in 1566. This is a city of interesting streets, and from here you can walk along one of the most picturesque, *via Rizzoli,* with sidewalk caffès lining both sides. At the end you'll find *Piazza di Porta Ravegnana* with the two leaning towers of Bologna. They are not as famous as Pisa's splendid Tower, but they do lean, and if you climb to the top there's a good view of the city.

Walk along *via Zamboni,* lined with porticoes and beautiful palaces. Gothic *S. Giacomo Maggiore* has an interesting Renaissance chapel, *Cappella Bentivoglio,* with an elegant cupola and lovely frescoes.

(marginal handwritten notes:)
** Piazza Maggiore
*** San Petronio
* Palazzo Comunale
** Leaning Towers
** San Giacomo Maggiore

Not far from this church is the main building of the University of Bologna, the oldest university in Italy. All other Italian universities originate from this one. Its fame is primarily a result of the rebirth of Roman law as well as from giving the first anatomy lessons in Italy. On the top floor is an interesting Museums of Ships with models of 17th and 18th century *galeoni,* maps and other material.

At the end of the street is the *Pinacoteca Nazionale,* one of Italy's best galleries, which is particularly important for knowledge of 14th- and 18th-century Bolognese paintings. Visiting hours are weekdays, 9 A.M.–2 P.M.; holidays, 9 A.M.–1 P.M.

Other interesting churches are the pure Gothic *S. Maria dei Servi,* one of the loveliest in the city; *S. Domenico,* a large church with a remarkable marble urn sculpted by some of the greatest 13th-century artists; *l'arca di S. Domenico; S. Francesco,* one of the most characteristic buildings in Bologna, done from 1236 to 1263, with French Gothic influences. This church was partly destroyed in World War II and later reconstructed. Note that Bologna, like so many large Italian cities, has important churches dedicated to the two saints who represent the strongest monastic institutions: St. Dominic and St. Francis.

Finally, there is the *Metropolitana,* Bologna's cathedral. This church, which has ancient origins, was dedicated to St. Peter. It was redone in 1605, has a majestic 18th-century façade by Torreggiani and a 12th–13th-century bell tower. The grandiose proportions of this church, its elegant and rich interior and the well-preserved old neighborhood behind it are all worthy of a visit.

Bologna is not a small city, but walking around can be fun. Besides the already-mentioned via Rizzoli, there are *via Ugo Bassi, via Indipendenza, strada Maggiore, via S. Stefano, via d'Azeglio, Via Manzoni* and *via Galliera,* one of the most monumental, lined streets with interesting and varied palaces —some Gothic, some Renaissance, some baroque. These streets offer infinite opportunities for window shopping, as well as for actual shopping. Like Roma, Firenze, Venezia and Milano, Bologna has a style of its own, and elegant pocketbooks, shoes, gloves, dresses and sweaters will enchant the knowledgeable shopper.

Ferrara and Ravenna

If you have one more day and wish to see another splendid city, there are two, totally different ones, from which to choose; each is a short ride from Bologna. If you go northeast for a short drive, you will arrive at *Ferrara,* one of the splendid Renaissance cities of Italy. If you go east you can spend a day in *Ravenna* admiring the best in early Byzantine art. We will begin by describing Ravenna.

Ravenna is almost on the Adriatic (originally it did reach the sea). It is of particular interest for those who study the early Middle Ages because it reached maximum splendor during the 5th and 6th centuries and represents a transition between the Roman and Byzantine worlds. *Galla Placidia, Odoacre* (476–493) and *Teodorico* (493–526) were the three barbarian rulers who lived here and adorned the city with superb buildings.

* University Museum

*** Pinacoteca Nazionale

* Santa Maria dei Servi

** San Domenico

* San Francesco

* Bologna Cathedral

Ravenna is not a large city, and one day of energetic walking should allow you to see all of it. Begin with *S. Vitale,* one of the purest early Christian basilicas in Italy. It shows the transition between classical and Byzantine architecture. It was built in 525 and consecrated in 547; it has a picturesque polygon-shaped exterior, a cupola and a cylindrical bell tower. The interior is richly decorated with marbles and mosaics representing Old Testament scenes, Christ and Emperor Giustinian and Empress Teodora. Right near the basilica is the *Galla Placidia Mausoleum,* built by the great queen about one century earlier. Its interior is a feast for the eyes, with one magnificent mosaic after another. A pleasant walk up *via Fanni, via Barbiani* and left onto *via d'Azeglio* will bring you to the *Duomo*—originally built at the beginning of the 5th century and later redone in baroque (1734–1743). To the left of the cathedral is the small, simple, octagonal *baptistry,* called *Battistero Neoniano* or *Degli Ortodossi.* It was started in mid-5th century and completed shortly thereafter with splendid mosaics under Bishop Neone (thus the name). A jewel worth visiting!

Backtrack a few steps; turn right onto *via Guerrini,* go past *Piazza Caduti per la Libertà* and enter the *Zona Dantesca.* Here are the church of *S. Francesco,* a 5th-century church reconstructed during the 10th century and restored after World War II bombings, and *Dante's Tomb.* Hours are 9 A.M. –12 noon; and in winter, 3–5 P.M.; in summer to 7 P.M. Dante, the greatest Italian poet, came to Ravenna in 1317 and died there on September 14, 1321. His tomb, shaped like a small temple, was built in 1480. An arc with a sculpture of the poet's head by P. Lombardo was added in 1483. There is also a small museum dedicated to Dante.

Take another short walk up *via Guaccimanni,* turn left onto *via Roma* and you come upon *S. Apollinare Nuovo,* a church built by Teodorico at the beginning of the 6th century. It was intended for the Arian cult but was consecrated to the Catholics by Bishop Agnello some 60 years later (anywhere from A.D. 557–565). Its simple brick façade has a portico in front. The interior is in three naves, with the center one lined in mosaics and divided into three areas. The two upper areas depict Christ, the saints and prophets in a classical style. The lower one is done in a 6th-century Byzantine style. It shows two splendid Martyr processions; one goes from Ravenna toward Christ on a throne surrounded by angels and virgins; it is preceded by Magii going from the city of *Classe* toward the *Madonna with Child.*

The last two monuments are a bit further away. *Teodorico's Mausoleum* is about 1.5 miles north and can be visited from 8:30 P.M. to 12 noon and from 2 P.M. to 5 or 6 P.M. in winter and 7 P.M. in summer. It was built in 520 by the great Gothic king. It is a single, massive polygonal structure on two levels, with a distinct barbarian character. It is a unique building, dignified and simple.

On the other side of town, going toward Rimini, about 3 miles out of town, there was a town called *Classe,* which was once Ravenna's port. Its only remaining building is a grandiose basilica, *S. Apollinare in Classe.* Note the lovely 10th-century bell tower and portico. This large church was consecrated in 549. The interior has precious Byzantine columns and capitals, sculptures and ornaments, and as with the other structures you've seen, interesting mosaics of the 6th and 7th centuries.

****
San Vitale mosaics

**
Mausoleum

*
Cathedral

***
Baptistry

*
San Francesco

*
Dante's Tomb exterior rebuilt in 1780

***
Sant' apollinare mosaics

**
Teodorico's Mausoleum

***
Sant' apollinare in Classe

A visit to Ravenna will not only show you Byzantine mosaics and buildings. It is a charming city that reflects the slow and easy provincial life in Italy, with nice shops, lovely squares lined with caffès, tranquil people enjoying wine. If you are interested in gourmet places in Italy, plan your drive back to Bologna in the early evening and stop at *Imola* (about 30 to 40 minutes out of Ravenna by the highway). Here is one the very best restaurants in the country, the *San Domenico*. It's closed Wednesdays and you should call ahead because there aren't many tables and it's usually full.

The other city we suggest that you visit is *Ferrara*. It has a very different look, partly reminiscent of the Tuscan towns, partly of the northern ones. Two of its most important buildings are in the center of town. You can, therefore, begin your visit at *Piazza Cattedrale*. Keep in mind that the history, as well as greatness, of this city are closely connected to the house of *Este*. They ruled there in mid-13th century, were officially endowed with it by the pope in 1332 and governed well into the 16th century, when Ferrara basked in the light of great artists and *literati* because of the liberality and generosity of its first family. This city was one of the centers of Renaissance culture and art. And while it was not as rich or as powerful as Firenze and Venezia, its smaller size will allow you an almost complete immersion into the period and into how it felt to live during that splendid moment.

Any city that was florid during the Renaissance was doing well at least two centuries before that, and here is an example. The Ferrara cathedral is a medieval building, done in Romanesque–Gothic style from the 13th–14th centuries. It has a solemn marble façade with three cusps livened by small *loggias* and interesting sculptures. The majestic, marble-covered bell tower, done along classical lines, was designed by L. Alberti and built from 1451 to 1596. The interior is large and impressive; it was restored during the 18th century and further decorated at the end of the 19th century. The loveliest art is from the 15th and 16th centuries; for example, there are two bronze statues by D. Paris and a large fresco of the *Universal Judgement* by Bastianino.

Not far from this piazza and the cathedral is the *Castello Estense,* an impressive fortress surrounded by a moat with four massive towers at the corners. It was built in 1385 and completed during the 16th century. Visiting is 9:30 A.M.–12:30 P.M. and 3–6 P.M. in summer; 2–5 P.M. from October to May; closed Mondays. Note the *Salone dei Giochi* (literally, playroom); it has beautifully decorated walls and ceiling.

Ferrara is a city of lovely palaces and wide streets. Walk along *corso della Giovecca;* admire the charming *Palazzina di Marfisa* at No. 174, the 17th-century church *dei Teatini;* and the *Palazzo Roverella,* with a remarkable Renaissance façade at No 47. Off this street is *via Savonarola;* it was opened during the early Ferrarese Renaissance and has houses and palaces worth admiring on both sides.

Via Scandiana is another important street. At No. 23 is the famous *Palazzo di Schifanoia.* It was built at the end of the 14th century, transformed by B. Rossetti during the Renaissance (1466–1493) and is now site of the *Museo Civico.* It is open to the public holidays, 9 A.M.–12:30 P.M.; summer, 9 A.M.–12:30 P.M. and 3–6 P.M.; October to March on weekdays, 2:30–5:30 P.M. Do not overlook the *Sala dei Mesi,* which is decorated with some of the best frescoes in Italy. Not far is another beautiful example of Ferrarese archi-

*****
San Domenico restaurant

**
Piazza of Ferrara

***
Cathedral of San Giorgio

**
Estense Castle

**
Palazzo Schifanoia and Civic Museum

tecture, *Palazzo di Ludovico il Moro.* It is on the corner of *via XX Settembre* and *via Porta d'Amore.* Both of these lovely palaces saw the lavish and entertaining d'Este court at its height, so the feeling of Renaissance luxury, good taste and pleasure runs throughout the splendid rooms and corridors!

Another lovely street is the *corso Ercole I d'Este,* with the *Palazzo dei Diamanti* at No. 21. This palace gets its name from the diamond-shaped decorations that line its façade; it is considered one of the most elegant Renaissance buildings in the world.

As you walk around this charming city and enjoy its medieval and Renaissance design, keep in mind that at one time it was considered the first modern city in Europe. Times do change!

Via Emilia-Romagna

The most interesting trip you can take in Emilia-Romagna is to follow the old road that gives the region its name—the *via Emilia.* Like all Roman roads, it's almost perfectly straight. It cuts across the fertile, southern plain of the Po River from Cattolica to Piacenza. The cities that formed alongside it, or that were bisected by it, are the main cities in the area. From *Cattolica* drive to *Rimini,* then to *Cesena,* then to *Forli* and finally to *Faenza.*

Faenza is worth a short stop to see its lovely cathedral and the *Museo delle Ceramiche.* The cathedral is one of the better early Renaissance buildings in Romagna. It was begun in 1474 from a design of Giuliano da Maiano; its majestic front was left unfinished. The museum is located at *via Campidori 2,* corner *viale Baccarini;* its visiting hours are in summer, 9:30 A.M.–1 P.M. and 3:30–6:30 P.M.; in winter, 2:30–5:30 P.M.; closed Mondays. It is a unique center of study and information on the history and art of ceramics from Italy, as well as other countries. The exhibits range from pre-Colombian to modern, from Turkish and Chinese to American, from Renaissance maiolicas to Picassos and Chagalls.

Drive through *Imola* (unless you stop for lunch there), and onto Bologna (see preceding itinerary). If you do not stop in Bologna, a short drive will bring you to *Modena,* a city that has grown around the old Roman nucleus and is still cut in half by the *via Emilia.* Make a short stop in order to admire the *Duomo,* a Romanesque masterpiece started in 1099 by a Longobard, Lanfranco, and finished in the 13th century by northern architects. On the façade are some of the finest early Romanesque sculptures in Italy, done by Wiligelmo in the early 12th century. An interesting bell tower with a pointy Gothic top completes the structure. Modena is the birthplace of the famous tenor Luciano Pavarotti.

Continue north on the Emilia, pass the city of *Reggio* and head for *Parma.* This enchanting city has Roman origins, but its present appearance is a result of its more recent history.

Parma flourished during the communal period (11th–13th centuries), and the 12th-century cathedral and baptistry are still there to prove it. The church is considered one of the best creations of its time; its austere façade and lithe bell tower are a study in sober harmony. The cupola interior bears a splendid fresco by Correggio—the *Assunzione della Vergine*—done between 1526 and 1530. Just outside the agile octagonal structure of the baptis-

Palazzo di Ludovico il Moro and its museum

Palazzo dei Diamanti and its museum

** *Faenza Cathedral*

** *Ceramics museum*

** *Modena Cathedral*

*** *Bell Tower*

*** *Parma Baptistry*

Handwritten margin notes:
** Cathedral and Tower
* San Giovanni
** Madonna
Arturo Toscanini (d. 1957) was born here
** Piacenza Duomo
**** Osteria

try is a Gothic–Romanesque building that rivals the famous tower of Pisa in beauty and proportion, lacking only the height and majestic setting.

The second period of Parmese good fortune was during the 16th century when the Farnese dukes made it their capital. During this time the Renaissance churches of *S. Giovanni Evangelista* and *Madonna della Steccata,* decorated by Correggio and Parmigianino, were designed in the elegant style for which that period is famous.

But the city's overall appearance, that air of a small 18th–19th century capital, comes from its last period of greatness when the Borbone family was on the throne and Parma's cultural and artistic life was lively and intense. In 1815 the duchy was given to Maria Luisa of Hapsburg, Napoleon's young wife, and French and Austrian noble ways became part of the city's heritage. If you happen to hear the local dialect, note how much it resembles French.

The *Galleria Nazionale* has many masterpieces of *Parmese* art, especially from the 15th to 18th centuries; visiting hours are weekdays, 9 A.M.–2 P.M.; holidays, 9 A.M.–1 P.M.; closed Mondays. For those who love music, a visit to *Toscanini's* house on via R. Tanzi 13 may prove interesting.

The northernmost city on the Emilia—before it enters Lombardia—is *Piacenza.* Here the old communal palace, *il Gotico,* is an admirable example of Longobard–Gothic architecture. Just in front of this lovely building are two equestrian statues of the Farnese, which are masterpieces of baroque sculpture. The *Duomo* and *S. Antonino* are two fine Romanesque churches, while *Madonna di Campagna* and *S. Sisto* are pure Renaissance. Piacenza is another city for dining. The *Antica Osteria del Teatro* offers excellent food in beautiful surroundings.

UMBRIA

La verde Umbria, the only region in Italy that has no connection to the sea, is located almost at the center of the Italian peninsula. It gets its name from one of the oldest Italian people, the *Umbri.* The territory today is only partially similar to the region it once was.

Umbria's geographic position has determined much of its history, as well as being responsible for the charm and beauty of its rolling hills, green plains, lovely cities and artistic treasures. The population, which is of Latin and Etruscan descent, speaks a language similar to the Roman dialect. It behaves in ways that are part Roman, part Tuscan for these are the two large regions that influence and surround Umbria.

Most probably you will remember this region for its saints because this is where two of Christianity's greatest spiritual leaders came from—*S. Benedetto di Norcia,* the 6th-century founder of monasticism, and *S. Francesco d'Assisi,* the 13th-century reformer. And while most of St. Benedict's monasteries are outside of the region and scattered throughout Italy, (*Montecassino* the greatest of all, is in Lazio), the Franciscan city of Assisi is all there.

Umbria is known for its animal and vegetable products, especially grain, vines, olives and small animals such as pigs and sheep. In fact, the word *norcino* in Italian means *pork butcher* and derives from the city of *Norcia.* The *Terni* area has mostly steel and mechanical industries, and *Perugia* is famous for its chocolate factories and its university.

Some History

The original inhabitants of the Umbria, Etruscans on the right and Umbri on the left of the Tiber River, were both conquered by Roma in 295 B.C. After that Umbria became the Sixth Region under Augustus and was joined to Tuscia (Toscana) under Diocletian.

The cities began to emerge and take sides during the 6th–7th-century Gothic Wars. These wars were mainly between Roma and Ravenna, with Goths, Byzantines and Longobards fighting over power on the peninsula. Centrally located Umbria was caught in the middle of things. Eventually, the *Duchy of Spoleto* emerged as the strongest feudal unit; the other power that influenced the area was the church. After the 8th century, as a result of various donations and conquests, the papacy became the virtual owner of this region.

The 11th and 12th centuries brought the *comunal* period to Umbria, and social forces here as elsewhere in Italy tended to solidify in the newly freed cities. *Perugia* soon emerged as the strongest among the various towns. Along with saints such as S. Francesco there were many soldiers of fortune such as Gattamelata da Narni and Braccio da Montone.

The next two centuries brought the *signorie* to Umbria, with strong families taking over in each city. By the 16th century the whole area was incorporated in the papal state. Then the agitated Napoleonic period generated a change, with the creation of a *Trasimeno* department and Umbria's capital once again was Spoleto.

With the winds of unification sweeping over the whole country, Perugia rebeled in 1859, and the plebiscites of the following year decided in favor of Italy.

Some Thoughts on Art

Ancient ruins in Umbria are either Etruscan or Roman. The former are concentrated in Perugia, Orvieto and Todi, while the latter are found in Assisi, Spoleto, Spello and Gubbio. Some interesting early Christian architecture can be seen in Spoleto and Perugia or in the charming little temple at *Clitunno,* but only in the 12th century did artistic activity really begin to blossom.

The cathedral of *Assisi,* the cathedral and S. Gregorio in *Spoleto,* and S. Silvestro in *Bevagna* are some of the Romanesque buildings to admire here. Also note the Longobard inspiration behind them. But the most impressive structures in Umbria are Gothic of the 13th and 14th centuries, and that is the style that left its imprint on the cities as well. Assisi built its two churches to S. Francesco and S. Chiara, and the greatest artists of the time such as Cimabue, Giotto and Simone Martini came to decorate them. *Orvieto* proudly erected its Duomo, done by the great Sienese artist, Maitani. This architecture is secular as well as religious. Perugia built its *Palazzo dei Priori;* Gubbio, built the *Palazzo dei Consoli,* and Todi and Città di Castello also have palaces.

The Renaissance did not produce many remarkable buildings in Umbria —only a palace in Perugia and a church in Todi. Under the influence of Tuscan artists, however, the region developed its own school of painting. The style was apparent in several small centers such as Gubbio, Spoleto and

Foligno, but Perugia was the most important for it produced great artists such as *Perugino* and *Pinturicchio* and educated the incomparable *Raffaello*.

Orvieto, Todi, Perugia

Driving north from Roma on the *Autostrada del Sole,* the long highway that connects Milano to Napoli, the first important Umbrian city to appear is *Orvieto.* Just over 1 hour from the capital, on the left side of the road, this picturesque city clings to its eroding piece of hill in defiance of gravity and time. Its simple history is divided into two distinct periods of greatness: Originally Etruscan, Orvieto was insignificant during the Roman period, then it reflourished in the Middle Ages, went through the usual ferocious fighting with other cities and was annexed by the church in 1450. As we now see it, the medieval period is what strikes us most, with the 12th and 13th centuries vividly represented.

One of the most important buildings in Italian Gothic style is the *Orvieto Duomo.* Started in 1290 by L. Maitani, it has a splendid façade with three impressive portals deeply embedded, a large round, central stained-glass window and extremely delicate and precious reliefs on the four columns that separate the three portals. The entire building achieves a harmonious balance of vertical and horizontal lines that is as breathtaking as any in Italy.

The façade is a masterpiece of geometry and color. It was designed to resemble a gigantic triptych, with architecture, sculpture and mosaics blending together to give an effect that is nothing short of triumphant. Other artists connected with it are Andrea Pisano, Andrea Orcagna (responsible for the round window) and possibly Arnolfo del Cambio.

The interior is simple and majestic with three naves supported by cylindrical pillars with beautiful capitols. It has a roof in uncovered wood beams and of Romanesque influence. Of the many works of art that fill this splendid church, note the magnificent *affreschi* by *Luca Signorelli,* done between 1499 and 1504 and considered one of the greatest and most significant painting cycles of the Renaissance. Make sure you put a coin in the machine that will light up these dramatic and energetic nudes.

Orvieto is also known for its pleasant white wine. Even if you don't have a meal here, enjoy sitting around *Piazza del Duomo* or *Piazza della Repubblica* and sipping some of the golden nectar. Not far from this latter square another outstanding building, the *Palazzo del Popolo.* This grandiose structure was built in the 12th century in Romanesque–Gothic style. Its majestic outer stairway and its elegant triple windows make it an interesting sight. Before leaving Orvieto note the *Pozzo di S. Patrizio* (St. Patrick's well), which can be visited from 8 A.M. to 8 P.M. It was built by Sangallo the Younger, between 1527 and 1537, by the wish of Pope Clement VII. It is a cylinder-like chamber about 36 feet in diameter and almost 200 feet deep, where two superimposed spirals go down, each with 248 steps lit by 72 windows.

About 1.5 miles out of town is the *Abbazia dei Ss. Severo e Martirio,* which is not only interesting to visit, but is now a rather good hotel and restaurant. Note the 12-sided tower.

The drive from Orvieto to *Todi,* one of Umbria's more charming cities, is a short one. This town was Etruscan, then Roman, then a flourishing *comune;* it still has its medieval appearance. While the *Duomo, Piazza del*

★★★★
Orvieto
Cathedral and
its frescoes

★★
Palazzo del
Popolo (or
Comunale)

★ Patrick's
St.
well

★
Hotel and
restaurant

★
Duomo and
piazza

Popolo and two other churches are lovely and enjoyable sights, we perfer to take in the city as a whole. Its tortuous streets, its arches and its dark houses are a step back into the Middle Ages.

If you love the Renaissance, we suggest a short walk to the outskirts of Todi to look at *S. Maria della Consolazione,* a building attributed to Bramante and done in the elegant, symmetrical style of its time. It was started in 1504 and finished in 1617. Its shape is a Greek cross, with three polygonal apses and a semicircle, lovely windows with curved and triangular fronts, a square terrace with four eagles at the angles and an exquisite, tall cupola that balances the whole design to perfection.

*** *Santa Maria*

From Todi a short drive on the new super highway takes you to *Perugia,* the region's capital and one of the most beautiful cities in Italy. *Piazza IV Novembre* is the artistic center of town, with the splendid *Fontana Maggiore* in the middle, the *Cathedral* at the north side, the *Palazzo dei Priori* on the south side and the *Loggia di Braccio Fortebraccio.* The fountain is interesting because of its period—the 13th century. At that time when most of the outstanding buildings constructed were either churches or city halls, Perugia was beautified by this elegant monument. It is adorned with two marble conchs, excellent sculptures by Nicola and Giovanni Pisano.

** *Maggiore Fountain*

Perugia's cathedral is 14th and 15th-century Gothic, with a simple, unfinished façade and the left side done in white and red marble. On the steps is the vigorous statue of Pope Julius III. The interior is the usual three naves, but of equal height and divided by tall pillars. At the beginning of the right nave, closed off by a 15th-century wrought iron gate, is the chapel of S. Bernardino. On the altar is the *Deposizione* by Baroccio. At the polygon-shaped apse note the wooden choir, beautifully carved and inlaid by Giuliano da Maiano and Domenico del Tasso.

** *Cathedral*

But the dominant structure on the piazza is the grandiose *Palazzo Comunale* or *dei Priori,* one of the most powerful and impressive Gothic structures in Italy. Built between 1293 and 1443, it is all done in squared-off blocks of stone, with narrow Gothic windows and battlements all around the top. Inside is the *Galleria Nazionale dell'Umbria,* an excellent art gallery that documents the development of Umbrian painting from the 13th to 19th centuries. Visiting hours are weekdays, 8 A.M.–2 P.M.; holidays, 9 A.M.–1 P.M.; closed Mondays. On the main floor of the building is the *Sala del Collegio della Mercanzia,* a large, rectangular room lined in sculptured wood, with benches and chairs for the *Consoli della Mercanzia.* It's style is late Gothic (first half of the 15th century). Visiting hours from 9 A.M. to 1 P.M.; weekdays also from 3 to 6 P.M. This room was a meeting place for the city's merchants, the equivalent of a medieval chamber of commerce.

*** *Palazzo Comunale*

** *National Gallery*

Now go toward *corso Vannucci,* the largest and most elegant street in town, and at the end of *Palazzo dei Priori* you'll find the *Collegio del Cambio,* built for the money changers in mid-15th century. Visiting hours are 9 A.M.–12:30 P.M. everyday, and 2:30–5 or 6 P.M. weekdays. Beautiful decorations, including frescoes by Perugino, render this building one of the best examples of Renaissance art.

** *Collegio del Cambio*

Perugia is a city that had two very distinct periods of prosperity and greatness, one Etruscan and another that goes from the 11th century to 1540 when Pope Paul III incorporated the city into the Papal state. Most of the admirable monuments we have described were built during the second pe-

(margin notes, left side)

** Arch of Augustus

** Oratorio di San Bernardino

* San Domenico

* Archeological Museum

** San Pietro

*** Tomb of the Volumni

**** Basilica di San Francesco Take a flashlight for lower church

*** Church of Santa Chiara

** Temple of Minerva

riod. The first period, however, also left interesting ruins. There are the walls that surrounded the hill and the doors that led into the citadel. Note the *Arco Etrusco* or *d'Augusto,* its lower part dating back to the 3rd century B.C. (Etruscan), its upper part a Roman addition of the 1st century—the inscription *Augusta Perusia* is responsible for its name, the loge and fountain of the left tower were added in the 16th century.

Not far from the arch is the church of *S. Bernardino,* a jewel of Renaissance architecture and plastic decoration. In another direction you'll find the university, one of the most unified campuses in Italy, known for its courses to foreign students.

A visit to Perugia is incomplete without a walk to *Piazza Italia.* From the *Giardini Carducci,* weather permitting, you can admire a valley that is the very heart of Umbria.

If you have extra time, another walk will take you to 10th-century *S. Pietro.* You will pass grand *S. Domenico* and the *Museo Archeologico Nazionale d'Umbria,* which can be seen weekdays, 9 A.M.–1:30 P.M.; holidays to 1:00 P.M.; closed Mondays. Between the two churches is a monumental double door, *Porta S. Pietro.* If you feel energetic, return by taking *viale Roma,* following the 15th-century walls, passing the railroad station and enjoying the view of the valley below. If you're driving, a very short trip (about 4 miles) will take you to the *Ipogeo dei Volumni,* an Etruscan 2nd-century B.C. tomb that contains seven lovely cinerary urns.

With Perugia as your base, visit other lovely Umbrian cities. First and foremost is *Assisi,* perched on its hill, dominated by the outstanding tributes to St. Francis, the great 13th-century saint and reformer. The famous *S. Francesco* was born to a wealthy merchant in 1182, had a lively youth, and in 1206 began his life of poverty and penitence. Recognized by the pope in 1209, he started his order of Minor Friars, followed by the *Clarisse* in 1212. After years of predication and travel (as far as Egypt in 1219), he received the stigmata in 1224, died two years later and was canonized in 1228. The small and beautiful city of Assisi is so permeated by this dazzling figure that any reference to other historic events or other personalities seems inadequate.

Enter Assisi through *Porta S. Francesco* and visit the large basilica dedicated to the saint. Prepare to spend the better part of a day here. You can then stop to admire the splendid Cimabue and Lorenzetti frescoes in the *Chiesa Inferiore* or the famous Giotto cycle in the *Chiesa Superiore.* Picture the life of St. Francis in 28 powerful *affreschi* begun by the great painter in 1296 and considered his maturest, most dramatic work.

This immense church was started in 1228 and consecrated in 1253. The church is actually two churches, one on top of the other. The lower one is the true sanctuary, its severe Romanesque–Gothic interior a place of meditation and faith accentuated by the absence of light. Many of the great artists who lived during the 13th, 14th and even 15th centuries worked in this city and the lower church contains some of the best work done at that time. The upper church is a pure and agile Gothic structure, contrasting vividly with the darker sanctuary below. Here the art is equally good, but there is less of it; the lighting, however, is better.

The rest of the city can be seen by walking up *via S. Francesco, via del Seminario* and *corso Mazzini.* Other churches are *S. Chiara, S. Pietro* and the *Duomo,* dedicated to S. Rufino, the city's forgotten patron saint. The

Piazza del Comune, in the center of town, is located where the old Roman forum used to be, and on the left-hand side is the ruin of an old temple, *Tempio di Minerva,* built during the empire period and later transformed into a church.

The visit to Assisi is so mystic and uplifting, that you will forget the other tourists, the crowded *caffès,* the unsophisticated hotels. For those of you who like religious manifestations, this is the city to visit Easter week, in early October for the St. Francis festivities, on August 12th for S. Chiara and from April 30th to May 10th for a charming return to ancient days during the *Calendimaggio* festivities.

Another short drive from Perugia will take you to *Gubbio,* one of the most genuinely intact medieval towns in Italy. After parking your car near *Piazza Quaranta Martiri* take a walk up *via della Repubblica* and up the steps to *Piazza della Signoria.* Here the view is lovely, and *Palazzo dei Consoli* is considered one of the most beautiful public buildings of its time in Italy.

Other things to admire in Gubbio are the cathedral and *Palazzo Ducale,* a Renaissance building done by the Montefeltro family and supposedly an imitation of the Urbino palace of the same name—note the inner court, *Cortile,* considered a magnificent piece of Renaissance design. Gothic *S. Francesco* is the church that faces the parking area, and the *Teatro Romano* is just a short walk away. During the summer classical theater is done here.

*[handwritten margin notes: Don't forget *** Convent of Santo Damiano, where St. Francis wrote his Canticle of the Sun   ** Palazzo dei Consoli   * Palazzo Ducale   * Roman theater]*

MARCHES

Marches, the Adriatic region, is an eastward extension of Umbria, with the Romagna at the north and Abruzzo at the south. It is neither a large nor a very populated area; it is composed of an attractive coast, some hills and some mountains.

Marches economy is mainly agricultural, including grain, vineyards—one of Italy's best white wines, the *Verdicchio,* is made here—vegetables and animals. Fishing and some related industries that derive such as canning and cattle fodder are also present. Other industries include shipbuilding, some household appliances, chemical plants, paper and textiles.

The Le Marche are noted for their musical instruments, especially accordions, and their *maiolicas* and other decorative tiles.

Some History

The region's ancient history is similar to Umbria's, except for the original inhabitants, who were Gauls to the north and *Piceni* to the south. It is interesting to note that the word *Marca* appears in the 10th century, signifying, in feudal language, that the region was faithful to one lord—a *marquis* or *marchese*—owing duty to the emperor. First there was the *marca di Camerino,* then the *marca di Fermo,* which upon enlarging included Ancona. Thus eventually the plural, *marches.*

During the course of history the feudal system gave way to the free *comuni,* and they in turn to the *signorie.* In the 13th century the Montefeltro family was in *Urbino,* the Varano in Camerino and the Malatesta in *Pesaro.*

[handwritten margin note: Signoria = feudal fief]

Then, again as in Umbria, the papacy claimed its ancient rights, and by treaty or by force the whole region was regained by the church. The unification of Italy (1860) was the last act of this region's history.

Some Thoughts on Art

There are significant Roman ruins in the Marches, some in good condition. The Arch of Augustus in *Fano* and the Arch of Trajan in *Ancona* are particularly worthy of notice.

The Romanesque period left a conspicuous number of structures. Even if the region never developed what may be called a style of its own, it occupies an important place in Italian art. From the 11th to 13th centuries the buildings in the region were done by artists who were influenced either by the Longobards or by the Byzantines. After the 13th century there was a strong turn to the Gothic, with some of the lovelier churches and palaces in Le Marche done in that style.

But the best in the region was done during the Renaissance, with *Urbino* with its splendid *Palazzo Ducale* in the forefront and *Iesi* and *Pesaro* close behind. Many of the famous architects, sculptors and painters of the era came to this region, and the local school of painting blended in with the one in Umbria, with Venetian influences as an added characteristic. The region's main contribution to the Renaissance bears two well-known names: *Raffaello* and *Bramante* were both *marchigiani.*

In the minor arts this area is known for its *maiolicas,* which are among the loveliest in Italy and the world.

Ancona

Ancona, an active city on the Adriatic Coast, is the capital of Marches. It was important at the height of the Roman Empire, as witnessed by the *arco di Traiano,* a monument to the 2nd-century emperor who achieved Roma's greatest territorial expansion. Note the church of *S. Ciriaco,* one of the most interesting medieval churches in Italy, built in Romanesque style with both Byzantine and Gothic influences. From Ancona, a short drive north-north-west will take you to *Pesaro* and then to *Urbino.* Urbino is one of the loveliest cities in Italy; it is birthplace of two great artists, Bramante and Raffaello, and a jewel of Renaissance art and panoramic beauty. Its *Palazzo Ducale* is the first princely residence of the Renaissance, embellished by Luciano Laurata in 1465 for Duke Federico di Montefeltro. Within the elegant palace is the *Galleria Nazionale delle Marche,* one of the best art galleries in Italy; visiting hours are in summer, 9 A.M.–1 P.M. and 3:30–6:30 P.M.; in winter, 9 A.M.–2 P.M.; holidays, 9 A.M.–1 P.M.

The most important city in the southern part of Marches is *Ascoli Piceno;* here the southern atmosphere can be felt approaching. This old capital of the *Piceni* fought Roma in the 1st century B.C., and a few ruins testify to the old city's greatness. It was a florid Middle Ages *comune* and has a pleasant *Piazza del Popolo.* Its *Palazzo dei Capitani del Popolo* and Gothic *S. Francesco* church are only some of the well-preserved buildings of that time. Note the warm color of the local travertine marble, used throughout the centuries giving the city its own special appearance.

Majolica tiles are famous world wide

** Arch of Trajan (A.D. 115)

** San Ciriaco Cathedral

*** Palazzo Ducale and its national Gallery

** Palazzo

LAZIO

Lazio is the region that contains Roma, but from a visitor's point of view it would be more accurate to say that Roma contains *Lazio*. Unless you come here for a specific purpose, such as for business in Latina or to visit a relative, you will probably see only the *Castelli Romani* or *Tivoli*. These are one-day excursions from Roma and worth seeing. But so is the rest of Lazio, one of the most characteristic regions of Italy.

The northern part of Lazio was inhabited by the Etruscans, and the large necropolis at *Cerveteri* is among the important ruins of that early nation. Going east from Rome, through the *Ciociaria*, is a charming experience, with Roman ruins and medieval towns following each other midst lovely hills. Or just going along the old *Appia* to *Terracina* and a visit to *Monte Circeo* is also interesting. This area is the playground of many rich Romans and a very fashionable seaside resort.

*[handwritten note in margin: *** Etruscan Cemetery]*

Lazio, a large agricultural region, is noted for good wines, cheeses and vegetables. This fertile land has been feeding Roma for many centuries, and if eating in Roma is a pleasure, much of it is because of the efforts of the industrious people in the hills that surround it.

As of the last 25 years, industry has been making its inroads. Cities around Roma and the province of Latina are slowly attracting large and small business establishments. But the greatest part of the population works either with or for the government, and another large portion makes its living from the tourist industry. Both of these are not recent phenomena. As far back as the days of Julius Caesar and through the centuries that followed, Rome and the area around it have been a seat of power and a magnet for visitors, and it will probably continue that way for many years to come.

Some History

Here again, it is difficult to distinguish between the history of Rome and that of the region. North of the Tiber River was Etruscan country, but the south (or left bank) was inhabited by several tribes that eventually merged and formed Rome. By the 4th century B.C. the area was Roman; and when Augustus made his famous division, southern Lazio (Latium) was included in the *I Regione* with *Campania,* while the north and northwest became part of the *VII Regione* with Toscana. After the fall of the Western Empire in 476 the area became a battlefield for Byzantines and Longobards. The papacy then made a bid for power, justified by the fact that the church owned property in the area and the population increasingly favored papal leadership. With the advent of the Franks, the church's claims gained substance, and Charlemagne donated his conquests to the pope.

The following years were characterized by the struggle of two powers: on the one hand, the church, on the other, the great families of the region (the Colonna, Orsini, Barberini, Caetani, and so on) who were the great feudal lords left over from the Longobard domination. With and without external influences and with alternating victories and defeats, these two forces represented the conflicts, interests and realities of Lazio until 1870 when Rome and its region were finally united with the rest of Italy under the Piedmontese Savoia.

Some Thoughts on Art

Much as with the history, the ancient art of Lazio is Etruscan to the north and northwest of the Tiber and pre-Roman and Roman to the south and southwest. There are important medieval structures, especially of religious nature, in several cities. The early ones are Romanesque with Longobard elements; the later ones are Gothic. With the 13th century the *Cistercensi* monks brought Burgundian–Gothic influences into their abbeys, while the city of *Viterbo* developed a Gothic style of its own.

The Renaissance, with its prosperity and increased travel opportunities, provided some unity between Roma and its region. Good examples of this are the *Palazzo Orsini* at *Bracciano* and the church of *S. Maria della Quercia* in Viterbo. But from every city there were local artists who went to Rome and brought the new trends back with them; evidence of Rome's influence on Lazio art is everywhere.

From Tivoli to Palestrina

The standard tour will take you to *Tivoli,* where the splendid *Villa d'Este* and its 100 fountains are a tourist's delight and *Hadrian's Villa* is one of the most remarkable sights of the power that was Rome. We suggest a slightly longer itinerary, still feasible in one day, and as rewarding as any in Italy.

Leave Rome by way of the *via Tiburtina,* through the crowded suburbs and traffic jams. Soon you'll be climbing the hills toward *Tivoli* and see the charming views below. The town of Tivoli is known for its waterfalls and *villas.*

At Tivoli visit the villa of Hadrian, one of Rome's greatest emperors. The villa, done in a style that reminded Hadrian of his eastern trips, was a favorite residence. Rome's *Castel Sant'Angelo* was also built by Hadrian as his mausoleum. Hadrian ruled at the time of Rome's greatest territorial extension, and his interest was maintaining prosperity and stability. It is largely a result of his efforts that the 2nd century A.D. was a time of peace.

Proceed to *Vicovaro,* which still has a part of its very ancient walls and a charming 15th-century octagonal temple. Leave Vicovaro for *Subiaco,* a drive that will take you through hills that are both barren and green and small, hill-hugging villages scattered among them. This small medieval town is famous for two Benedictine monasteries—*S. Scolastica* and *S. Benedetto or Sacro Speco.* Both can be visited by request; you must ring the bell and a monk will show you around; it is usual to make an offering. Visiting hours for both are 9 A.M.–12 noon and 3–7 P.M.

S. Scolastica is the last survivor of the 13 monasteries in this area. It was established during the 6th century by *S. Benedetto* before he went to Montecassino. It was quite active and well known for many years, especially in the 11th and 12th centuries. In 1464 two Germans, C. Sweynheym and A. Pannartz, installed the first printing press in Italy in this monastery. The Sacro Speco is remarkable because of a small church entirely carved into the rock with lovely 13th-century frescoes, including a picture of St. Francis done around 1228 soon after the saint visited Subiaco, covering the walls.

For those interested in winter sports, a fairly short and pleasant drive will take you to *Monte Livata,* a skiing resort. Otherwise, leave Subiaco and go

*** Tivoli's Villa d'Este and waterfalls

*** Hadrian's Villa

** Santa Scolastica

*** Sacro Speco or San Benedetto

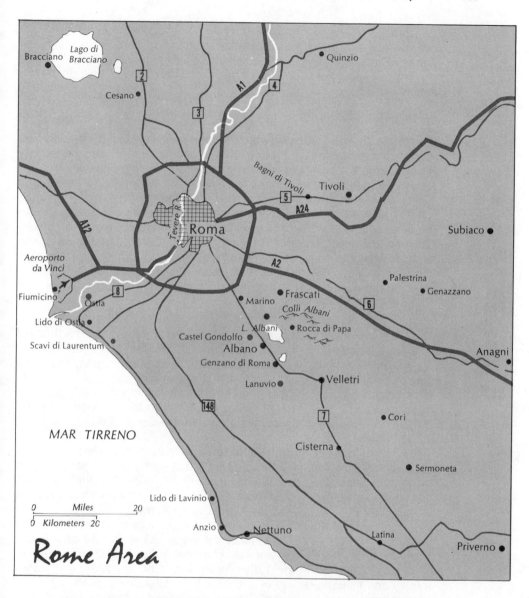

Bracciano

Lago di Bracciano

Quinzio

Cesano

2

A1

4

3

Bagni di Tivoli

Tivoli

5

A24

Subiaco

Tevere R.

Roma

Aeroporto da Vinci

A2

Palestrina

Fiumicino

8

Ostia

Marino

Frascati

Genazzano

Lido di Ostia

Colli Albani

6

Scavi di Laurentum

L. Albani

Rocca di Papa

Castel Gondolfo

Anagni

Albano

Genzano di Roma

Lanuvio

Velletri

148

Cori

MAR TIRRENO

7

Cisterna

Sermoneta

0   *Miles*   20

0   Kilometers   20

Lido di Lavinio

Anzio

Nettuno

Latina

Priverno

Rome Area

on to *Fiuggi,* a well-known and charming watering resort. From here we suggest you head back toward Rome by way of *Genazzano* and *Palestrina*. Visit Palestrina, an enchanting town famous for the musician, Pier Luigi di Palestrina, and for the ruins of a celebrated temple, the *Tempio della Fortuna Primigenia*. Palestrina was destroyed by consul Silla in 82 B.C., but he had the temple rebuilt and it was used until the 4th century when the medieval borough was built on its ruins. This little city was fought over by popes and feudal lords for many centuries, and it was again badly damaged in 1437. During World War II the bombings of this area were actually beneficial to Palestrina, for they brought to light a good portion of the old temple.

Temple ruin

Return to Rome on the old *via Prenestina.* About halfway there, on your right at Gabii, are the ruins of a temple to the goddess Juno. Before you reach Rome's *Raccordo Anulare,* the circular highway that goes around the city, you will pass an impressive Roman bridge, *Ponte di Nona,* built during the Republican period.

The Castelli Romani

*** Alban Hills tour of Roman castles*

A ride into the *Colli Albani,* which Roman and Italian, as well as foreign tourists, are happy to take on hot summer days in order to escape the city heat is the most popular and well-known itinerary. The *giro* includes *Frascati,* famous for its good white wine, *Grottaferrata, Marino, Albano Laziale* and *Castel Gandolfo,* where the pope has his summer residence.

We suggest that you take one of the guided tours since it is easy to take the wrong turn here or to miss restaurants that are not expensive, over-crowded and noisy. The area is full of lively vistas and charming villas with finely designed Italian gardens all over the countryside. There are clear lakes and woody hills, old churches and grand stone castles. This little tour is pleasant and relaxing; don't forget to drink some of the famous wine!

Ciociaria

** Walls of Alatri Acropolis*

* Santa Maria*

The charming drive to Ciociaria is a one-day excursion from Roma that will take you through modern plains and ancient hills. Take the *Autostrada* to *Frosinone,* an essentially modern city in the heart of the region, and make your stops on the way back. The first stop is at *Alatri,* a very old town with a medieval appearance. Note the *Acropoli* at the top of a hill, the best standing example of a fortified 4th-century B.C. citadel. The view is lovely, and the city's baroque cathedral and Romanesque–Gothic *S. Maria Maggiore* are also interesting.

A few miles away is another little town, *Ferentino.* It also has an *acropolis,* sustained by powerful pre-Roman walls that were partly remade by Silla, the famous Republican consul and general. Next to the old structure you'll find a simple Romanesque *Duomo* of the 11th century with a beautiful mosaic floor done by one of the Cosmati (see **Rome**).

** Ferentino Cathedral*

** Anagni Cathedral*

Another short drive will bring you to *Anagni,* a picturesque little center that sits on top of hill that dominates the valley below. Its cathedral is one of the most remarkable Romanesque churches in Lazio. Built from 1074 to 1105 and retouched in the 13th century with Gothic additions, it stands solitary and majestic on top of a small hill, looking down on the city. The interior is decorated by another Cosmati mosaic and contains a very interesting Easter candleholder and a crypt that alone is worth a trip here. There is also a chapel dedicated to St. Thomas à Becket. The 12th-century bell tower will remind you of similar towers in Toscana.

From here you can drive straight back to Roma or, if you haven't seen *Palestrina,* you can go there (see preceding itinerary).

Along Via Appia to Terracina and Gaeta

This itinerary could be a relaxing weekend, including a drive through the country that was once the playground of wealthy Romans. Take the *Appia* out of Roma and drive to *Velletri, Terracina* and *Gaeta.* At this last city, located at the foot of a promontory, take the ride up the *Monte Orlando* to admire the view and the tower. The tower is the mausoleum of *Lucio Munazio Planco,* a Roman who was the friend of Caesar, Cicero and Orazio and who founded the French city of Lyon. The city itself is now a fishing port and seaside resort. Other sights such as the *Duomo* and the *Santuario della Montagna Spaccata* are also worth admiring. If you come in the off-season months of March, April, May, June, September and October, it can be a good place to stop overnight. Avoid July and August; the city is overrun with tourists and there's not a room to be had.

Drive back to *Terracina* along the coast. Just before *Sperlonga* you'll find the *Grotta di Tiberio,* a large cave that belonged to a villa where the Emperor entertained his friends. It is decorated with interesting paintings depicting scenes from the Ulysses story. Proceed to *Terracina,* a modern city between the Appia and the sea with an old medieval center that clings to the side of a hill. The *Duomo,* built on top of a pagan temple and possibly dedicated to Apollo, can still be partially seen on one side. A few miles out of town, on top of Monte Sant'Angelo, up a lovely panoramic road, are the ruins of *Tempio di Giove Anxur.* The temple was built more than 2,000 years ago; not much is left except some columns, arches and a piece of portico, but the view is splendid and the ruin impressive.

From Terracina drive on to *S. Felice Circeo,* one of the elegant beaches near Rome and also noted for the many *grottoes.* Then drive to *Sabaudia* along a beautiful panoramic road between the sea and the lagoon behind. Behind the lagoon is the *Parco Nazionale del Circeo,* a large area established in 1934 for the protection of local fauna and flora.

You are now driving back to Roma, and if time allows we suggest you turn inland after *Sabaudia* and head for *Priverno* and the *Abbazia di Fossanova.* This abbey is one of the earliest Benedictine complexes, founded in the 9th century. It passed to the Cirstercian monks in the 12th century, and is one of the best examples of Gothic–Cistercian style in Italy. Visiting hours are in winter, 8 A.M.–12 noon and 3–5 P.M. in summer, 3–7:30 P.M. Do not overlook the lovely cloister. The small town of Priverno is picturesque; its central square is in Gothic medieval and the ruins of Roman *Privernum* are nearby.

Continue your drive back, passing the little town of *Sezze* and going on to the slightly larger town of *Sermoneta.* Here, you can visit the *Castello Caetani,* which is such a good example of this type of castle that many Middle Age adventure films have been made here.

Proceed to *Norma,* another charming medieval town located on the side of a hill. Not far from here, about 4 miles northwest, are the ruins of *Ninfa* surrounded by greenery. From here to Roma the road will take you past *Velletri,* a wine-producing town on the southern edge of the *colli Albani,* the soft hills that mean Roma is near. Here again the *piazza* is charming, there is a lovely tower and a church and the usual *caffè.* It is a nice place for a rest and a sip of the local wine. Roma is about 20 miles away.

Viterbo

The last itinerary out of Roma is a visit to *Viterbo,* a city in northern Lazio that is noted for its attractive medieval atmosphere and its lovely fountains.

[Handwritten marginal notes:]
** Orlando tower
* Duomo
* Grotto of Tiberius
** Terracina Cathedral
*** View from Temple of Jupiter
** Benedictine abbey
** Caetani Castle

The central part of the old town is triangular and closed in by towered walls that date back to the 11th–13th centuries with seven doors leading in and out.

The drive out of Rome is not very long, about 50 miles along the old *via Cassia,* another road that led to Rome—and away from it. *Piazza del Plebiscito* is the traditional center of town, closed in on the short sides by two 17th century palaces and on one long side by the *Palazzo Comunale.* On the other side is a small church, *S. Angelo,* which contains the sarcophagus of a 12th-century beauty, *la Bella Galiana.* Follow *via S. Lorenzo,* a picturesque and winding street that leads to a square of the same name and to the cathedral. About halfway there is a little square with a 17th-century fountain and a medieval tower, *Torre di Borgognone.* Further up is *Piazza della Morte* with a 13th-century fountain. Finally, there is *Piazza S. Lorenzo.* It is on the site of the old acropolis, dominated by the 12th-century cathedral. Its beautiful 14th-century bell tower and a Renaissance façade done in 1570. On the other side is the splendid *Palazzo Papale,* built between 1255 and 1267, done in local Gothic with an external stairway and an airy, charming *loggia* perched on a large vault that contains the lightest, most delicate intertwined arches on slender columns. It has been the residence of many popes.

Walk down *via S. Pellegrino,* the main street of the *Quartiere Medioevale,* perfect example of a 13th-century borough. It is almost entirely preserved, with its severe houses and towers. Turn left on *via delle Fabbriche* and you will come to the *Fontana Grande,* the largest and most beautiful of Viterbo's fountains. It was built in the 13th century; its tub is shaped like a Greek cross with two cups superimposed in the center.

Other monuments worth seeing are the two churches of *S. Maria della Verità* and *S. Francesco* and the *Museo Civico* in an exconvent of the church of S. Maria, with a charming Gothic cloister; the visiting hours are weekdays from May to September 8:30 A.M.–2:30 P.M., and from October to April 9 A.M.–4 P.M.; holidays, 9 A.M.–1 P.M., closed Mondays.

A few miles from Viterbo, on the road to *Bagnaia,* are two lovely Renaissance structures: *S. Maria della Quercia,* a small but exquisite church, and *villa Lante* at Bagnaia, with magnificent Italian gardens, fountains and waterworks and a building that represents the best in late Renaissance design.

* Palazzo Comunale

** Cathedral

** Papal Palace

*** San Pellegrino Quarter

** Santa Maria

** San Francesco

* Museo Civico (in S. Maria)

* Santa Maria della Quercia

** Villa Lante

Hotels

ANCONA, Le Marche

★★ **HOTEL JOLLY MIRAMARE**
Porta Pia, tel. 201171, 88 rooms with bath. Moderately expensive.

★★ **HOTEL PALACE**
Lungomare Vanuitelli, tel. 201813, 41 rooms with bath. Moderately expensive.

★★ **HOTEL PASSETTO**
Via Thaon de Revel, tel. 28932, 45 rooms with bath, view. Moderately expensive.

★ **HOTEL FORTUNA**
Piazza F.lli Rosselli 15, tel. 22035, 64 rooms, 44 with bath. Moderate.

AREZZO, Toscana

★ **HOTEL MINERVA**
Via Fiorentina 6, tel. 27891, 82 rooms with bath, garage. Moderately expensive. *Has ★★ restaurant*

ASSISI (PG), Umbria

★★ **HOTEL GIOTTO**
Seasonal, via Fontebella 41, tel. 812209, 72 rooms, 48 with bath, garage. Moderately expensive.

★ **HOTEL WINDSOR SAVOIA**
Porta San Francesco, tel. 812210, 32 rooms with bath. Moderate.

★ **HOTEL FONTEBELLA**
Seasonal, via Fontebella 25, tel. 812883, 32 rooms, 29 with bath, view. Moderate.

★ **HOTEL ROMA**
Piazza S. Chiara 15, tel. 812390, 29 rooms, 18 with bath. Inexpensive.

BOLOGNA, Emilia-Romagna

★★★★ **ROYAL CARLTON HOTEL**
Via Montebello 8, tel. 554141, 254 rooms with bath, conference rooms, garage. Expensive. *Has ★★★ restaurant*

209

★★★   HOTEL GARDEN
Via Lame 109, tel. 261861, 83 rooms with bath, garden, garage, building was
an old convent, interesting. Moderately expensive.

★★   HOTEL INTERNAZIONALE
Via dell'Indipendenza 60, tel. 262685, 144 rooms with bath, garage. Moderately expensive.

★★   HOTEL MILANO-EXCELSIOR
Via Pietramellara 51, in front of railroad station, tel. 239442, 82 rooms with
bath, garage, conference rooms. Moderately expensive.

★★   HOTEL JOLLY-DE LA GARE
Piazza XX Settembre 2, near railroad station, tel. 264405, 172 rooms with
bath, conference rooms. Moderately expensive.

★   HOTEL ROMA
Via d'Azeglio 9, in center of town, tel. 274400, 88 rooms, most with bath.
Moderate.

BUSSETO (PR), Emilia-Romagna

An agricultural city on the Emilia plain, Busseto was the birthplace of
Giuseppe Verdi. Approximate population: 7,600.

★   I DUE FOSCARI
Piazza Verdi, tel. 92337, 20 rooms with bath, terraces, garage, restaurant
(closed Mondays). Moderate.

CAMAIORE (LU), Toscana

Charming little town in a luminous valley, at the foot of the Apuan Alps.
Extends all the way to the sea, where Lido di Camaiore becomes a fashionable summer resort (about 13 km. from the center of the village). Approximate population: 30,000.

★★★★   HOTEL ARISTON
Seasonal, Viale Colombo 355, tel. 66333, 33 rooms with bath, park, tennis,
swimming pool, lovely 17th-century villa. Expensive.

★★   HOTEL CAESAR
Viale Colombo 365, on the seashore, tel. 64841, 36 rooms with bath, garden,
swimming pool, parking, restaurant closed in winter. Moderately expensive.

★   HOTEL PANORAMIC
Seasonal, Viale Colombo 397, on the seashore, tel. 64674, 66 rooms with
bath, garden, swimming pool, parking. Moderately expensive.

CAMALDOLI (AR), Toscana

Situated in a magnificent old forest of fir trees, this area is a popular summer resort and pilgrimage spot. The famous mother-house of the Camaldolesi monks is located here. It is composed of two distinct nuclei: *the monastery*, founded by S. Romualdo after 1012 and reconstructed in the 13th century; and *Eremo* (2.5 km. north of the monastery), located in a beautiful thick of the forest, the first seat of the Camaldolese order.

The order's most famous monastery overlooks Naples

★ IL RUSTICHELLO
Seasonal, 2 km. toward Poppi, tel. 5620, 30 rooms with bath, tennis, mini-golf, garden, located in an isolated spot. Moderate.

CARRARA (MS), Toscana

★ HOTEL MICHELANGELO
Corso F.lli Rosselli 3, tel. 70861, 36 rooms, most with bath. Moderate.

CASAMARI, ABBAZIA DI (FR), Lazio

Located in a solitary area along the Via Frosinone-Sora, this famous Abbey is a noted example of Gothic–Cistercian architecture. It was founded in 1095 by the Benedictine order and in 1151 was taken over by the Cistercian order. In 1204 it became one of the most thriving monastic centers of central Italy.

★ CIAO MARIO
On the Statale, tel. 36277, 10 rooms with bath. Inexpensive.

CASSINO (FR), Lazio

Cassino, is a modern city that was rebuilt after it was totally destroyed during World War II. It is situated on the Rapido River at the foot of the mountain on which the Montecassino Abbey (the most famous of the Benedictine abbeys) is located. It is an important agricultural, commercial and industrial center. Approximate population: 25,000.

British and Polish military cemeteries nearby

★ SILVIA PARK HOTEL
Via Ausonia (4 km.), tel. 21975, 52 rooms with bath, pool. Moderately expensive.

★ HOTEL ALBA
Via Di Biasio 71, tel. 21873, 26 rooms with bath. Moderate.

CATTOLICA (FO), Emilia-Romagna

This small city on the Adriatic Sea is a busy summer resort and fishing center. Approximate population: 16,000.

★★   HOTEL CARAVELLE
Seasonal, via Padova 6, tel. 962416, 45 rooms with bath, garage, pool, beach. Moderately expensive.

Own beach

★★   VICTORIA PALACE
Seasonal, viale Carducci 24, tel. 962921, 92 rooms with bath, beach, parking. Moderately expensive.

Own beach

★   HOTEL ALEXANDER
Seasonal, via Gran Bretagna 6, tel. 963241, 68 rooms with bath, pool, beach, parking. Moderate.

CERTALDO (FI), Toscana

★★   HOTEL IL CASTELLO
Via della Rena 6 (Certaldo Alto), tel. 65250, 15 rooms, 12 with bath, view, charming. Moderately expensive.

★   HOTEL LA STECCAIA
Beyond L'Elsa 1 km. toward San Gemignano, tel. 95929, 10 rooms with bath. Moderate.

CHIANCIANO TERME (SI), Toscana

One of the most important and modern spas in Italy, famous for waters that cure liver diseases. Many hotels. Approximate population: 7,000.

Hotel bus will meet you at station

★★★★   GRAND HOTEL
Seasonal, viale della Libertà 283, tel. 3333, 72 rooms with bath, pool, tennis, park, garage. Expensive.

★★★   EXCELSIOR HOTEL
Seasonal, viale S. Agnese 21, tel. 4351, 80 rooms with bath, garden. Expensive.

Ditto

★★★   HOTEL MICHELANGELO
Seasonal, via delle Piane 146, tel. 4004, 63 rooms with bath, tennis, garden, view. Expensive.

Ditto

★★   HOTEL BOSTON
Seasonal, Piazza Italia 5, tel. 3472, 97 rooms with bath, garage. Moderately expensive.

★★   HOTEL FORTUNA
Seasonal, via della Valle 76, tel. 4661, 87 rooms, 85 with bath, pool, tennis, garden, view. Moderately expensive.

★★   HOTEL TOURING
Seasonal, via delle Piane 35, tel. 3217, 72 rooms with bath, pool, garden, view. Moderately expensive.

★   HOTEL MACERINA
Seasonal, via Macerina 45, tel. 4241, 80 rooms with bath, garden. Moderate.

ELBA (ISOLA D') (LI), Toscana

Located approximately 10 km. from the continent, the island of Elba is the largest of the Archipelago Toscano. It is a famous vacation resort, with Portoferraio, the largest center, other well-equipped seaside villages of Marciana Marina, Porto Azzurro, Marina di Campo and Procchio. It has a coast that varies from high and rocky cliffs to bays with small sandy beaches. It is well known for its transparent blue water, serene skies and mild climate. It has a Mediterranean vegetation (cactus, aloe, prickly pear, palm and olive trees), and in the surrounding waters almost all the species present in the Mediterranean Sea can be found. The iron mineral that is extracted from its mountains has been for centuries the main source of income for the island. It was mined by the Etruscans. During the Roman era the island was used as a naval base; during the Middle Ages it was an object of dispute among the Spanish, French, English and Neapolitans. From May 3, 1814, until February 26, 1815, it was the residence of Napoleon when he was exiled for the first time.

a mass is said for Napoleon's soul on May 5th every year at Portoferraio's Misericordia church

At Portoferraio

★   HOTEL DARSENA
Tel. 92661, 45 rooms with bath, view of the port. Moderate.

★   HOTEL RESIDENCE
Calata Italia, tel. 93031, 57 rooms with bath, at the port. Moderate.

At Marina di Campo

★★   HOTEL ISELBA
Seasonal, in the city park, tel. 97096, 48 rooms with bath, private beach. Moderately expensive.

At Porto Azzurro

★   HOTEL CALA DI MOLA
Seasonal. On the road to Portoferraio, tel. 95225, 52 rooms with bath, swimming pool, tennis, view of the sea. Moderately expensive.

FAENZA (RA), Emilia-Romagna

★   HOTEL VITTORIA
Corso Garibaldi 23, tel. 21508, 39 rooms, 34 with bath, garage. Moderately expensive.

★   HOTEL CAVALLINO
Via Emilia Levante 10 (2 km. toward Forlì), tel. 30226, 34 rooms, 32 with bath, garage. Moderate.

FERRARA, Emilia-Romagna

★★   HOTEL DE LA VILLE
Piazza Stazione 11, tel. 53101, 85 rooms with bath. Moderately expensive.

FIESOLE (FI), Toscana

Located in an excellent spot on a hill overlooking the Florentine basin, Fiesole is the most popular village near Firenze. It is noted for its many monuments of the Etruscan, Roman and Medieval periods. Approximate population: 14,000.

★★★   VILLA SAN MICHELE
Seasonal, via di Doccia, tel. 59451, 31 rooms with bath, park, view, garage, located in an old convent. Moderately expensive.

Michelangelo helped design the convent

★   HOTEL AURORA
Piazza Mino da Fiesole 39, tel. 59100, 22 rooms, 15 with bath, garden, garage, view. Moderate.

FIRENZE (Florence), Toscana

★★★★★   HOTEL EXCELSIOR
Piazza Ognisanti 3, tel. 294301. 217 rooms with bath. Great location, fine, luxury hotel. Weather permitting, you are served very well-prepared meals on the panoramic terrace, service is excellent. Expensive.

Has ★★★ restaurant

★★★★★   HOTEL REGENCY
Piazza Massimo d'Azeglio, tel. 587655, 31 rooms with bath. This charming, small hotel which used to be an elegant villa, has well-decorated rooms and, while not far from the heart of town, allows as much privacy as is possible in Italy. Ideal for a romantic weekend. Expensive.

★★★★   HOTEL MINERVA
Piazza S. Maria Novella 16, tel. 284555, 108 rooms with bath. Central location, swimming pool and garage, adequate service. Moderately expensive.

★★★★   VILLA MEDICI
Via del Prato 42, tel. 261331, 104 rooms with bath, garden with swimming pool, a roof-top restaurant, large comfortable rooms. Service is somewhat less than it should be. Expensive.

★★★★   HOTEL SAVOY
Piazza della Repubblica 7, tel. 283313, 95 rooms with bath, very central location, very ancient tradition. Expensive.

Near Cathedral

★★★★   VILLA BELVEDERE
Via Benedetto Castelli 3, tel. 222501, 27 rooms with bath, closed from

December to March. A peaceful oasis of beauty, this villa belonged to the Medici and has been completely restored. The view is magnificent, there is a swimming pool and a tennis court, and the trip to town takes no more than 5 minutes by car. Some of the rooms are a bit dark and small, the service is average, and there is no restaurant. Moderately expensive.

★★★★   GRAND HOTEL VILLA CORA

Viale Macchiavelli 18, tel. 228451, 56 rooms with bath. Luxurious villa of the late 19th century surrounded by a lovely park, now a modern hotel in a quiet, panoramic setting. But the organized tours and small conferences create commotions. Moderately expensive.

★★★★   HOTEL KRAFT

Via Solferino 2, tel. 284273, 66 rooms with bath, traditional hotel, swimming pool allows you to swim while gazing at the cathedral or Fiesole. Moderately expensive.

★★★   HOTEL MAJESTIC

Via del Melarancio X 1, tel. 23961, 103 rooms with bath, central location, near railroad station and old center of town. Moderate prices.

★★★   HOTEL CROCE DI MALTA

Via della Scala 7, tel. 211740, 120 rooms with bath, central location, swimming pool. Moderately expensive.

★★   HOTEL PRINCIPE

Lungarno Vespucci 34, tel. 284848, 22 rooms with bath. Charming old building, rooms decorated with taste, all different from one another, some with a view of the river. Moderately expensive.

★★   PITTI PALACE HOTEL

Via Barbadori 2, on the corner of Ponte Vecchio, tel. 282257, 24 rooms, most with bath. In the heart of "touristy" Firenze. Sometimes a bit noisy. Moderate.

Near Ponte Vecchio; can be very noisy

★★   HOTEL CONTINENTAL

Lungarno Acciaioli 2, tel. 282392. 71 rooms, most with bath. Good location, some rooms have a view of the river. Moderate.

★★   TOURNABUONI BEACCI

Via Tornabuoni 3, tel. 268377. 30 rooms, some with bath. This famous boarding house has a glorious reputation. John Steinbeck and Frederic March were some of its illustrious guests, and its slightly decadent appeal still lin-gers and attracts those who like an old-fashioned "pensione." The prices include breakfast and one meal. But be sure to book in advance. Moderate.

FORTE DEI MARMI (LU), Toscana

This is a high-class seaside resort of the Versilia Riviera, located among pine forests. Many hotels. Approximate population: 10,000.

Some bunga-
lows and a
discotheque

★★★★   HOTEL AUGUSTUS
Seasonal, viale Morin 169, tel. 80202, 78 rooms with bath, park, beach.
Expensive.

★★★★   HOTEL AUGUSTUS LIDO
Seasonal, viale Morin 72, tel. 81442, 78 rooms with bath, park, beach.
Expensive.

★★★   HOTEL HERMITAGE
Seasonal, via C. Battisti, tel. 80022, 40 rooms with bath, park, pool, excellent
restaurant (Il Pozzetto). Moderately expensive.

★★★   HOTEL ATLANTICO
Seasonal, via Torino, along the seaside, tel. 81422, 46 rooms with bath.
Moderately expensive.

★★   HOTEL RAFFAELI-VILLA ANGELA
Seasonal, viale Mazzini 64, tel. 80652, 26 rooms with bath, garden. Moderately expensive.

★   HOTEL LA VERSILIA
Seasonal, via G. Pascoli 7, tel. 80941, 31 rooms with bath. Moderate.

FRASCATI (ROMA), Lazio

Best dessert
wine here is
Cannellino

The most famous of the "Castelli Romani," this agricultural and commercial
center is noted for its white wine and beautiful villas. Approximate population: 18,000.

★   HOTEL FLORA
Viale Vittorio Veneto 8, tel. 940198, 33 rooms with bath, garden. Moderately
expensive.

★   HOTEL BELLAVISTA
Piazza Roma 2, tel. 941068, 23 rooms, 10 with bath. Moderate.

At Monte Porzio Catone (5 km.)

★   HOTEL GIOVANNELLA
Piazza Trieste, tel. 944038, 43 rooms, 36 with bath, park, tennis, skating,
restaurant closed Wednesdays. Moderately expensive.

GIGLIO (ISOLA DEL) (GR), Toscana

This is the
place to get
away from
it all.

The second largest island of the Archipelago Toscano, it is completely hilly
with a steep coast and covered with vineyards that produce a quality wine.
Approximate population: 2,000.

★   CASTELLO MONTICELLO
Seasonal, tel. 809252, 31 rooms with bath, garden, pool, tennis. Moderately
expensive.

★ HOTEL DEL SARACENO
Seasonal, tel. 809234, 30 rooms with bath, view of the sea. Moderately expensive.

GROTTAMMARE (AP), Le Marche

This is a seaside resort of the Adriatic coast. Approximate population: 9,500.

★ HOTEL EUROPA
Seasonal, Lungomare, tel. 64226, 108 rooms with bath, view of the sea. Moderately expensive.

★ RESIDENCE TUTTOMARE
Seasonal, Lungomare, tel. 64450, 60 rooms with bath, view of the sea. Moderate.

★ HOTEL ROMA
Seasonal, Lungomare, tel. 64245, 60 rooms with bath, view of the sea. Moderate.

GUBBIO (PG), Umbria

★★ HOTEL CAPPUCCINI
Via Cappuccini (1 km. toward Umbértide), tel. 922241, 39 rooms with bath, garden, located in a former convent. Moderately expensive.

Quiet location

★ HOTEL SAN MARCO
Via Perugina 1, tel. 922516, 29 rooms, 24 with bath, garden, garage, restaurant closed Fridays. Moderate.

★ HOTEL TRE CERI
Via Benamati 6/8, tel. 922104, 15 rooms with bath. Moderate.

IMOLA (BO), Emilia-Romagna

Located along the Via Emilia, Imola is a good-size agricultural, commercial and industrial center. Approximate population: 60,000.

★ HOTEL MOLINO ROSSO
On the street leading to the Autostrada, tel. 26387, 41 rooms with bath, garden, parking, excellent restaurant closed Thursdays. Moderately expensive.

LIVORNO, Toscana

Livorno is a base for exploring other coastal towns

★★ HOTEL PALAZZO
Viale Italia 195, tel. 805371, 125 rooms, most with bath, garden, on the sea. Moderately expensive.

★   HOTEL ASTORIA
Via Ricasoli 96, tel. 22250, 130 rooms, fewer than half with bath, nice location. Moderately expensive.

LUCCA, Toscana

Note: Between the 17th and 19th centuries many attractive villas were built in the surrounding countryside, in the areas of Marlia, Segromigno, Camigliano and Pieve S. Stefano.

★★★★   VILLA PRINCIPESSA
Seasonal, Massa Pisana, tel. 379136, 44 rooms with bath, park, swimming pool, garage. Expensive.

★   UNIVERSO
Piazza Puccini 1, tel. 49046, 73 rooms, most with bath, facing theater, charming old building. Moderately expensive.

MASSA, Toscana

One of the smaller Tuscan provinces, Massa is an attractive town located at the foot of the Alpi Apuane. Here begins the famous Carrara marble country. The best hotels are at the waterfront, Marina di Massa. Approximate population: 63,000.

★★   HOTEL TIRRENO
Seasonal, via Manzoni 22, tel. 20016, 40 rooms, most with bath, view of the sea. Moderately expensive.

Own beach

★   HOTEL EXCELSIOR
Seasonal, via C. Battisti 1, on the sea, tel. 20141, 63 rooms with bath. Moderately expensive.

Pool

MODENA, Emiglia-Romagna

★★★   CANALGRANDE
Corso Canal Grande 6, tel. 217160, 78 rooms with bath, in 17th-century palace, garden, garage, good restaurant. Expensive.

★★   HOTEL FINI
Via Emilia Este 441, tel. 238091, 93 rooms with bath, garage, rooms for conferences, private station wagon to the chain's restaurant, which offers excellent regional cooking. Moderately expensive.

Very modern

MONTECATINI TERME (PT), Toscana

One of the best known Italian health resorts, this spa has excellent waters for intestinal problems. The city itself is attractive and modern, except for Montecatini Alta, which is a charming medieval town at the top of a hill. Approximate population: 20,000.

★★★★ GRAND HOTEL E LA PACE
Seasonal, via della Torretta 1/A, tel. 2451, 170 rooms with bath, swimming pool, garden, garage. One of the great turn-of-the-century hotels and still managed in that style. Large dining and sitting rooms, antique furniture. Expensive.

★★★ HOTEL CROCE DI MALTA
Seasonal, viale IV Novembre 18, tel. 3381, 118 rooms with bath, swimming pool, garden, garage. Moderately expensive.

★★ HOTEL NIZZA E SUISSE
Viale Verdi 72, tel. 3691, 109 rooms, 98 with bath or shower, garden, garage. Moderately expensive.

Closes in winter

★ HOTEL PANORAMIC
Seasonal, viale Bustichini 65, tel. 2381, 96 rooms with bath, garden, swimming pool, view. Moderate.

★ HOTEL S. MARCO
Seasonal, viale Rosselli 3, tel. 71221, 54 rooms with bath, swimming pool. Moderate.

ORVIETO (TR), Umbria

★ HOTEL ITALIA
Via di Piazza del Popolo 13, tel. 3045, 39 rooms, 37 with bath, garage. Moderately expensive.

No restaurant

★ HOTEL MAITANI
Via Maitani 5, tel. 3001, 34 rooms, 32 with bath, garage. Moderately expensive.

Out of town

★★★ RESIDENCE LA BADIA
In the abbey of Saints Severino and Martirio, 2.5 km. (1.6 mi.) east of Orvieto, tel. 90276, 15 rooms with bath, garden, pool, tennis, very good restaurant. Charming small hotel, modern comfort, atmosphere of an old *abbazia*. Moderately expensive.

PARMA, Emilia-Romagna

★★★ HOTEL PALACE MARIA LUIGIA
Viale Mentana 140, tel. 21032, 67 rooms with bath, garage, good restaurant. Expensive.

★★★ Restaurant

★★ PARK HOTEL STENDHAL
Via Bodoni 3, tel. 36653, 45 rooms with bath, restaurant. Moderately expensive.

★★   PARK HOTEL TOSCANINI
Viale Toscanini 4, tel. 23143, 48 rooms with bath, restaurant, garage. Moderately expensive.

PERUGIA, Umbria

★.★   LA ROSETTA
Piazza Italia 19, tel. 20841, 108 rooms, 78 with bath, garage, good restaurant. Moderately expensive.

★   DELLA POSTA
Corso Vannucci 97, tel. 61345, 56 rooms, 40 with bath, garage. Moderate.

Out of Town

★★   COLLE DELLA TRINITÀ
Seasonal, at Colle della Trinità (13 km. west), tel. 79548, 36 rooms with bath, park, tennis, view. Moderately expensive.

★   HOTEL GRIFONE
Via S. Pellico 1, (southern outskirts—access from Via dei Filosofi), tel. 31100, 50 rooms with bath. Moderately expensive.

PESARO, Le Marche

Capital of the province, this beautiful city is a busy seaside resort, as well as a commercial and industrial center. During the Renaissance it flourished under the Sforza and Della Rovere families. It is the birthplace of Rossini (1792–1858). Approximate population: 85,000.

★   HOTEL MARE
Viale Trieste 199, tel. 64430, 39 rooms with bath. Moderately expensive.

★   HOTEL AMBASSADOR
Open all year, viale Trieste 291, tel. 67481, 45 rooms with bath. Moderately expensive.

★   HOTEL CARAVELLE
Viale Trieste 269, tel. 64078, 65 rooms with bath, pool. Moderately expensive.

PIACENZA, Emilia-Romagna

★★   GRAND ALBERGO ROMA
Via Cittadella 14, tel. 23201, 96 rooms, 90 with bath, garage. Moderately expensive.

★   HOTEL CAPPELLO
Via Mentana 6/8, tel. 25721, 58 rooms, half with bath, garage. Moderate.

Old world charm

Very modern

Overlooks sea

★   HOTEL NAZIONALE
Via Genova 37, tel. 20387, 74 rooms, 70 with bath, garage. Moderate.

PISA, Toscana

★★   HOTEL DEI CAVALIERI
Piazza Stazione, near railroad station, tel. 43290, 102 rooms with bath, garage. Moderately expensive.

★★   HOTEL DUOMO
Via S. Maria 96, two steps from the leaning tower, tel. 27141, 95 rooms with bath, garage. Moderately expensive.

PISTOIA, Toscana

★   HOTEL LEON BIANCO
Via Panciatichi 2, tel. 26675, 30 rooms, 17 with bath. Moderate.

PORTO SANTO STEFANO (GR), Toscana

This maritime center and noted seaside resort is located in a picturesque site around the bay. Boats leave from here for the island of Giglio. Approximate population: 10,000.

★★★   HOTEL FILIPPO II
Seasonal, at Caluello (1 km. toward Orbetello), tel. 812640, 42 rooms with *Own beach* bath, garden, view, beach. Moderately expensive.

★   HOTEL VITTORIA
(Above the populated area), tel. 818580, 28 rooms with bath, view, good restaurant. Moderate.

Out of Town

★★★   HOTEL TORRE DI CALA PICCOLA
Seasonal, at Cala Piccola (8 km.), tel. 825133, 52 rooms with bath, garden, *Own beach, secluded* beach, pool, view of the sea. Moderately expensive.

PRATO (FI), Toscana

★★   HOTEL PALACE
Corner of via Pier della Francesca and viale della Repubblica, tel. 40841, 80 *Very modern* rooms with bath, pool, garage. Moderately expensive.

★   VILLA SANTA CRISTINA
At Santa Cristina, tel. 32398, 18 rooms with bath, located in an old villa with a park and pool. Moderately expensive.

★ HOTEL MILANO
Via Tiziano 15, tel. 23371, 75 rooms, 50 with bath, garage. Moderate.

RAVENNA, Emilia-Romagna

★★ HOTEL JOLLY MAMELI
Piazza Mameli 1, tel. 35762, 75 rooms with bath. Moderately expensive.

★ HOTEL BISANZIO
Via Salara 30, tel. 27111, 39 rooms, most with bath. Moderately expensive.

No restaurant

RIMINI (FO), Emilia-Romagna

Rimini Marina, together with Viserba, Viserbella and Torre Pedrera to the north and Rivazzurra and Miramare to the south, forms one of the largest seaside resort areas in Europe. It is also an important communications center. From 1417 to 1468 it was under thr rule of Sigismondo Malatesta, and many important monuments from the Roman and Renaissance periods still exist in its historical center. Approximate population: 126,000.

At Rimini Center

★ HOTEL NAPOLEON
Piazza C. Battisti 22, tel. 27501, 64 rooms, 52 with bath, parking. Moderate.

★ HOTEL DUOMO
Via G. Bruno 28, tel. 24215, 42 rooms, 40 with bath, garage. Moderate.

At Rimini Marina

★★★ GRAND HOTEL
Seasonal, Piazzale Indipendenza, tel. 24211, 130 rooms, most with bath, beach, garden, heated pool, tennis, parking. Expensive.

Own yacht club

★★ GOLDEN–IMPERIALE
Viale Vespucci 16, tel. 52255, 64 rooms with bath, garden, heated pool, sauna, parking. Moderately expensive.

Own beach

★★ AMBASCIATORI
Viale A. Vespucci 22, tel. 27642, 70 rooms with bath, garden, heated pool, sauna, parking. Moderately expensive.

Own beach

At Rivazzurra (3 km. toward Riccione)

★★ GRAND MEETING
Viale Regina Margherita 46, tel. 32123, 50 rooms with bath located on the sea, parking. Moderately expensive.

*Rivazzurra
is less fancy
than Rimini
Marina* [handwritten note]

★★   DE FRANCE
Viale Regina Margherita 48, 65 rooms with bath, pool, located on the beach, parking. Moderately expensive.

At Miramare (5 km. toward Riccione)

★★   TOURING
Viale Regina Margherita 82, tel. 33005, 74 rooms with bath, located on the beach, parking. Moderately expensive.

★   MULAZZANI
Viale Principe di Piemonte 1, tel. 32345, 66 rooms with bath, located on the beach, parking. Moderate.

At Viserba (4 km. toward Cesenatico)

Ditto [handwritten note]

★   BYRON
Via G. Dati 88, tel. 738161, 44 rooms with bath, view of the sea. Moderate.

At Viserbella (5 km. towards Cesenatico)

Ditto [handwritten note]

★   LIFE
Via Porto Palos 34, tel. 738370, 45 rooms with bath, pool, located on the beach. Moderately expensive.

★   SIRIO
Via Spina 3, tel. 734639, 37 rooms with bath, garden, tennis, view of the sea, parking. Moderate.

At Torre Pedrera (7 km. toward Cesenatico)

★   EL CID
Via Tocra 5, tel. 720185, 41 rooms with bath, parking. Moderately expensive.

★   DOGE
Via San Salvador 156, tel. 720170, 50 rooms with bath, view of the sea, parking. Moderate.

ROCCA DI PAPA (ROMA), Lazio

This picturesque village of the "Castelli Romani" is a favorite for vacations and day trips. Approximate population: 8,000.

★★   VILLA DELLE ORTENSIE
At the Madonna del Tufo (toward Nemi), tel. 949108, 49 rooms with bath, beautiful views. Moderately expensive.

★   HOTEL ANGELETTO
Via del Tufo 32, tel. 949020, 22 rooms with bath, beautiful views. Moderate.

SAN BENEDETTO DEL TRONTO (AP), Le Marche

This modern active city on the Adriatic coast is an important fishing center and an elegant seaside resort. Many hotels. Approximate population: 42,000.

★★   HOTEL ROXY
Lungomare B. Buozzi 6, tel. 4441, 77 rooms with bath, seafront location. Moderately expensive.

Charming garden

★   HOTEL GARDEN
Lungomare B. Buozzi 8, tel. 60246, 54 rooms with bath, seafront location. Moderately expensive.

★   HOTEL CONTINENTAL
Viale Europa, tel. 60046, 48 rooms with bath, seafront location. Moderately expensive.

SAN GIMIGNANO (SI), Toscana

★★   HOTEL LA CISTERNA
Piazza della Cisterna 23, tel. 95328, 47 rooms, 33 with bath, view, garage, good restaurant (*Le Terrazze,* closed Tuesdays). Moderately expensive.

Restaurant atop the hotel

★   HOTEL BEL SOGGIORNO
Via S. Giovanni 41, tel. 95375, 30 rooms, 11 with bath, view. Moderate.

SANTA MARINELLA (ROMA), Lazio

Located on the coast of northern Lazio along the Via Aurelia, Santa Marinella, along with Santa Severa, is a pleasant seaside resort. Approximate population: 8,000.

★   LE NAIADI
Lungomare Capo Linaro 23, on the sea, tel. 77019, 25 rooms with bath. Moderate.

At Santa Severa

★   LE FENICI
Via della Monacelle 35, tel. 78135, 42 rooms with bath. Moderately expensive.

SENIGALLIA (AN), Le Marche

The city is a modern, flourishing seaside resort. Approximate population: 38,000.

★★★   HOTEL CITY
Open year round, Lungomare D. Alighieri, tel. 63464, 60 rooms with bath, covered pool. Moderately expensive.

Restaurant on roof

★★   HOTEL RITZ
Lungomare D. Alighieri 142, tel. 63563, 150 rooms with bath, pool. Moderately expensive.

★   HOTEL BEAURIVAGE
Lungomare G. Marconi 28, tel. 61083, 42 rooms, 36 with bath, garden. Moderate.

Own beach

SIENA, Toscana

★★   VILLA SCACCIAPENSIERI
Seasonal, via di Scacciapensieri 24 (at the Osservanza), tel. 41442, 30 rooms, 29 with bath, garden, tennis, pool. Moderately expensive.

ask for a cottage in the garden

★   PALAZZO RAVIZZA
Seasonal, Piane dei Mantellini 34, tel. 280462, 28 rooms, 14 with bath, building of the 1600's, garden. Moderate.

Old World ambiance

★   HOTEL MINERVA
Via Garibaldi 72, tel. 284474, 49 rooms, 31 with bath. Moderate.

★   HOTEL MODERNO
Via Peruzzi 19, tel. 288453, 72 rooms, 44 with bath. Moderate.

Outside town walls

★   HOTEL CHIUSARELLI
Viale Curtatone 9, tel. 280562, 52 rooms, 18 with bath. Moderate.

SPOLETO (PG), Umbria

This medieval city located in a beautiful position on a hill at the foot of a wooded mountain is noted for its many Roman, medieval and Renaissance monuments. As of 1958 the important cultural festival, "Festival of Two Worlds," has been held in June–July; it includes theater, lyrics, dance and music. Approximate population: 36,000.

★★   HOTEL GATTAPONE
Via del Ponte 6, tel. 23125, 8 rooms with bath, terrace, view. Moderately expensive.

★   HOTEL DUCHI
Viale Matteotti 2, tel. 23105, 50 rooms with bath, garden. Moderately expensive.

nice view

★   HOTEL MANNI
Piazza Collicola 10, tel. 24135, 18 rooms with bath. Moderate.

Good location

★ **HOTEL CLARICI**
Piazza della Vittoria, tel. 24206, 18 rooms with bath. Inexpensive.

TARQUINIA (VT), Lazio

Located on the top of a hill with a view of the sea, this picturesque city of northern Lazio is rich in medieval monuments. It is known for its Necropolis, which testifies that it flourished from the 8th to the 4th centuries B.C., when it was one of the most powerful Etruscan cities. Approximate population: 12,500.

Excellent views

★ **HOTEL TARCONTE**
Via Tuscia, tel. 86002, 53 rooms with bath. Moderate.

At Marina di Tarquinia

★★ **HELLEN PARK HOTEL**
Viale Porto Clementino, tel. 88295, 81 rooms with bath, pool, garden. Moderately expensive.

★ **LA TORRACCIA**
Viale Porto Clementino, tel. 88000, 16 rooms with bath. Moderate.

TIVOLI (ROMA), Lazio

★★ **TORRE S. ANGELO**
Provinciale Marcellina (toward Quintiliolo), tel. 23292, 29 rooms with bath, pool, tennis, park. Moderately expensive.

★ **EUROPA E DEI CONGRESSI**
At Monte Ripoli (3 km. exit for viale Arnaldi), tel. 20208, 100 rooms with bath, beautiful views. Moderately expensive.

TODI (PG), Umbria

★ **HOTEL ZODIACO**
Via del Crocefisso, tel. 882625, 27 rooms, 22 with bath. Inexpensive.

Best in town

★ **HOTEL CAVOUR**
Via Cavour, tel. 882417, 21 rooms, 14 with bath. Inexpensive.

URBINO (PS), Marches

This Renaissance city, located on two hills between the valleys of Metauro and Foglia, is an important artistic and tourist center, as well as a large university town. It has many significant examples of the Renaissance period. It is the birthplace of two great artists—Donato Bramante (1444–1514) and Raffaello (1483–1520). Approximate population: 16,000.

★ **HOTEL PIERO DELLA FRANCESCA**
Via Comandino, tel. 4570, 88 rooms with bath. Moderate.

★   HOTEL ITALIA
Corso Garibaldi 32, tel. 2701, 41 rooms, 29 with bath. Inexpensive.

VIAREGGIO (LU), Toscana

★★★   PRINCIPE DI PIEMONTE
Seasonal, Piazza G. Puccini 1, tel. 50122, 123 rooms with bath, indoor pool, private beach. Expensive.

Splendid terrazza

★★   ASTOR E RESIDENCE
Open all year, viale G. Carducci 54, tel. 50301, 71 rooms with bath, seafront. Moderately expensive.

★   GRAND HOTEL E ROYAL
Open May to September, viale G. Carducci 44, tel. 45151, 125 rooms, most with bath, seafront. Moderately expensive.

Garden swimming pool

VOLTERRA (PI), Toscana

★   HOTEL NAZIONALE
Via dei Marchesi 2, tel. 86284, 40 rooms, most with bath. Moderate.

On main piazza

Restaurants

ANCONA, Marches

★★★   DA MISCIA
On the South Wharf 44 (Molo Sud), tel. 201376, closed Mondays and December 20th–January 6th. Reservations necessary, intimate atmosphere, good service, fish dishes only, very well prepared, excellent wine (made by the owners of the restaurant). Expensive.

★★   GIARDINO
Via F. Filzi 2, tel. 22998, closed Fridays (except during the summer). Small but pleasant restaurant with a garden. Very good genuine dishes, adequate wine list, good service. Moderate.

★   CARLONI
At Torrette, via Flaminia 247, tel. 888239, closed Mondays. Well-prepared traditional regional dishes, fair wine selection. Moderately expensive.

AREZZO, Toscana

Chianti is the best local wine, Montepulciano a sweeter one

★★   MINERVA
Via Fiorentina 2/6, closed August 1st–17th. On the roof of the hotel, this is one of the best restaurants in town. Excellent local, plus some international, food. Good wines. Moderate.

★   IL CANTUCCIO
Via Madonna del Prato 76, tel. 26830, closed Wednesdays. Nice modern place, good cooking, good wines. Moderate.

★   IL TORRINO
Superstrada dei due mari (about 13 km. out of town), tel. 357915, closed Tuesdays. Elegant and interesting place, worth a detour, good food. Moderate.

BOLOGNA, Emilia-Romagna

★★★★★   BACCO
Via M. E. Lepido 193 (Borgo Panigale), tel. 400218, closed Sundays and August. One of the best in town, both in traditional and modern cooking, excellent wine list. Moderately expensive. *Note:* Bacco raises his own snails.

★★★★★   DANTE
Via Belvedere 2/bis. tel. 224464, closed Mondays and August 7th–28th. Another superb restaurant in this city of gourmets. Order à la carte, excellent wine list, modern and refined surroundings. Expensive.

Ask for filetto di Tacchino (turkey) alla Bolognese

★★★★   FRANCO ROSSI
Via delle Donzelle 1a, tel. 279959, closed Thursdays and July. Three small rooms in a medieval building, very pleasant, plus very good food and very good wines. Moderately expensive.

★★★★   DA CARLO
Via Marchesana 6, tel. 233227, closed Tuesdays, January 1st–20th and August 21st–28th. Excellent traditional Bolognese food served in a charming *loggia* during the summer months, good wines. Moderate.

★★★★   GRASSILLI
Via Dal Luzzo 3, tel. 222961, closed Wednesdays, holiday evenings, January 2nd–12th, and from July 10th to beginning of August. One of the best "traditional" restaurants in town, everything carefully done and well planned, good wines. Moderately expensive.

★★★   ROYAL GRILL
Via Gramsci 5, tel. 557504, closed Sundays and August. Elegant restaurant of the equally elegant hotel, good food, some quite imaginative and modern, good wines. Expensive.

★★★   DIANA
Via dell'Indipendenza 24, tel. 231302, closed Mondays and August. Considered by some the most representative "temple" of local food, this simple restaurant offers excellent fare, good wines. Moderate.

★★★   IL BATTIBECCO
Via del Battibecco 4, tel. 275845, closed Sundays and July 25th–August 20th. Call ahead. In the center of town, this busy place offers imaginative cooking. Moderate.

★★   PALMIRANI
Via Calcavinazzi 2, tel. 236628, closed Sundays from June to September and and Thursdays from October to May. Conservative and serious, this restaurant is another old standby, good wines. Very moderate.

★★   LA CESOIA DA PIETRO
Via Massarenti 90. tel. 342854, closed Thursdays from July 20th–August 10th. The food is good, the atmosphere is cheerful, some good wines. Very moderate.

★★   SILVIO AI TORTELLINI
Via Valturino 4, tel. 233424, closed Tuesdays and June 20th–July 15th. Home cooking, specializing in the tortellini for which Bologna is famous, good wines. Very inexpensive.

BUSSETO (PR), Emilia-Romagna

★★★★★   CANTARELLI
Località Samboseto, tel. 90133, closed Sundays Mondays and July 15th–August 14th. Reservations necessary. Country *trattoria,* one of the finest in Italy, comfortable, pleasant atmosphere, excellent food, service and local wine, well-stocked cellar. Moderately expensive.

★★★   GUARESCHI
At Roncole Verdi di Busseto, via Processione 113, tel. 92495, closed Fridays, July and December 23rd–January 21st. Classical cooking, using fresh ingredients, excellent house wine, courteous service. Moderately expensive.

Ask for the involtini (veal stuffed with ham)

★   DELL'ALBERGO DEL SOLE
Piazza Matteotti 10, tel. 92243, closed Mondays and July 20th–August 18th. Well-prepared dishes, excellent regional wines and good service. Moderate.

CAMAIORE (LU), Toscana

★★   DA EMILIO E BONA
Candalla, tel. 68289, closed Mondays and three weeks in January. Attractive location in an old mill, good regional food, genuine wine. Moderately expensive.

★   LA RISACCA
Viale Colombo 604, tel. 64464, closed Mondays and winter months. The best and freshest fish in town, cooked with a gourmet approach. Few, but very well-chosen wines. Moderately expensive.

End the meal with bucellato, sweet Luccan pastries

CAMALDOLI (AR), Toscana

★   CAMALDOLI
At the monastery, tel. 5619, closed Tuesdays off-season. Moderate.

CARRARA (MS), Toscana

★   SOLDAINI
Via Mazzini 11, tel. 71459, closed Mondays. Regional well-prepared food. Moderate.

★   DA ROBERTO
Via Apuana 3, tel. 70634, closed Saturdays. Pleasant restaurant, mostly local clientele. Moderately expensive.

CASAMARI, ABBAZIA DI (FR), Lazio

★   ABBAZIA
Located at the Abbey, tel. 36038, closed Tuesdays. Moderate.

CASTEL GANDOLFO (ROMA), Lazio

In an excellent location on the western shore of Albano Lake, this city is the center of the Castelli Romani. It is a noted resort, as well as the summer residence of the Pontiffs. Approximate population: 5,000.

★   I CACCIATORI
Via Roma 1, tel. 930993, closed Tuesdays off-season, terrace on the lake. Moderately expensive.

CATTOLICA (FO), Emilia-Romagna

★★★   LA LAMPARA DA MARIO
Piazzale Darsena, tel. 963296, closed Tuesdays and from November to middle of December. The number one fish restaurant on the Romagna coast, is noted for its delicate preparation of fresh fish, its efficient, courteous service and excellent wine selection. Expensive.

ask for tonno (tuna) alla Bolognese

★   MORO-DA OSVALDO
Via Mazzini 91, tel. 922438, closed Thursdays. Fish. Moderately expensive.

★   AL DOLLARO
Via Verdi 33, tel. 962791, closed Mondays. Moderate.

ELBA (ISOLA D) (LI), Toscana

★★   DA GIANNI
At Marina di Campo, frazione La Pila, tel. 976965, closed Fridays (except in summer) and from November through February. This recently remodeled place is owned by a *pugliese*. The cooking reflects this fact, and is one of the interesting experiences on the island. Good wines. Moderately expensive.

Elba's own wine is Aleatico, best for dessert

★★   AL BRACIERE
At Portoferraio, via Carducci, tel. 93612, closed Fridays (except in summer).

An intimate place that serves good seafood and adequate wine. Moderately expensive.

★   DA SAURO
At Marciana Marina, viale Margherita (Porto), tel. 99027, closed Mondays (except in summer) and from October to March. A large, pleasant restaurant that serves good seafood and some well-prepared game, good local wines. Moderate.

★   RENDEZ VOUS DA MARCELLO
At Marciana Marina, Piazza della Vittoria, tel. 99251, closed Wednesdays (except in summer) and January. A quiet veranda right on the sea, good food (mostly fish), a well-stocked wine cellar. Moderate.

FAENZA (RA), Emilia-Romagna

★★★   IL GAROFANO
(At. S. Biagio Vecchio), via Salita Doriolo 13, tel. 42507, closed Mondays and 15 days in January. In a large park with a panoramic view of the sea, excellent food and service, large selection of fine national and regional wines. Expensive.

For a soft red wine, ask for Lambrusco

★   DA PIETRO
Viale Baccarini 23, tel. 21193, closed Saturdays. Specializes in grilled food. Moderately expensive.

FERRARA, Emilia-Romagna

★★   VECCHIA CHITARRA
Via Ravenna 11, tel. 62204, closed Tuesdays and July 10th–August 10th. Good regional cooking and wines. Moderate.

★   ITALIA DA GIOVANNI
Largo Castello 32, tel. 35775, closed Tuesdays and August 4th–25th. The most elegant restaurant in town, lovely location, good service. Adequate, if uninspired, food, good wines. Moderate.

Out of Town

★★★   TASSI
At Bondeno (about 32 km. on the road to Bologna), via della Repubblica 23, tel. 88030, closed Mondays, first 15 days in August and last 20 days of January. This very good restaurant is worth a detour, especially in the fall. Excellent truffles and game, good regional wines. Moderate.

FIESOLE (FI), Toscana

★   LE CAVE DI MAIANO
At Maiano, via delle Cave 16, tel. 59133, closed Thursdays, Sunday evenings

and August. Traditional Florentine dishes, courteous service, adequate wine list. Moderately expensive.

★   LE LANCE
Via Mantellini, tel. 599090, closed Mondays, garden. Moderate.

FIRENZE (Florence), Toscana

★★★★★   ENOTECA PINCHIORRI
Via Ghibellina 87, tel. 210193. Closed Sundays, Mondays, Tuesdays at noon and August. This wine-lover's paradise has everything. The building is a splendid 15th-century *palazzo,* the wines come from a cellar that contains 60,000 bottles of the best, the food is prepared with exquisite taste, know how, and imagination, the service is flawless. Be sure to call ahead; come in the evening if you can. Very expensive.

[handwritten: Try a robust red Brunello wine, perhaps]

★★★★   SABATINI
Via Panzani 9a, tel. 211559, closed Mondays and July 16th–31st. At one time *the* restaurant in Firenze, it still has a very good cuisine, a charming atmosphere, excellent service, well-stocked wine cellar. Expensive.

★★★   IL CESTELLO DELL'EXCELSIOR
Piazza Ognisanti 3, tel. 294301. The best hotel in town has a very good restaurant, which is open to the public. Well-known international dishes alternate with ingenious modern cooking. In summer the terrace offers one of the best views in Firenze. Expensive.

★★★   EXECUTIVE DEL MOTEL AGIP
Area de servizio Firenze-Nord, Autostrada del Sole, tel. 440081, closed Sundays. This slightly out-of-the-way place (not so if you're driving out of town and taking the Autostrada del Sole) is a surprise. A small comfortable room that seats no more than 30, it offers exceptional food, especially in summer. Excellent wine list, local wines such as Chianti, are best. Moderately expensive.

[handwritten: Chianti improves with age in the bottle; ask for at least 2 yrs. old]

★★★★   IL BARRINO
Via de' Biffi 2/r, tel. 215180, closed Sundays, Mondays and July 26th–September 2nd. Centrally located, this new place is meant for those "in the know." Elegant, refined atmosphere, very choice dishes, exquisite desserts, good wines, adequate service, famous for the regional *trattorie.* Expensive.

★★★   LA LOGGIA
Piazzale Michelangelo 1, tel. 287032, closed Wednesdays. Marvelous view, as well as most classical Florentine dishes, very good wine list. Moderate.

★★★   LE FONTICINE
Via Nazionale 79/r, tel. 282106, closed Saturdays and July. The best pasta in town; the owner is an *Emiliana* and has brought her art to Toscana. Local dishes are also good, good choice of Tuscan wines. Moderate.

★★★   COCO LEZZONE
Via del Parioncino 26/r, tel. 287178, closed Sundays, holidays and August. One of the old glories, this simple, noisy *trattoria* is a must. Chaotic, crowded, cheerful, it has been serving the same dishes for years, washed down with the same house wine, and we hope it will continue to do so for at least another century. Inexpensive.

★★★   LA MAREMMA DA GIULIANO
Via Verdi 16/r, tel. 218615, closed Tuesdays, Wednesdays and August. This family-run *trattoria* serves good, wholesome food, cooked the simplest way possible. Inexpensive.

★★   OMERO AD ARCETRI
Via Piane dei Giullari 11/r, tel. 220053, closed Tuesdays and August. In front of Galileo's house at Arcetri, this restaurant offers its own, special atmosphere and good, local fare. Go for lunch on a clear day, the view is lovely, mediocre wine. Moderate.

★★   HARRY'S BAR
Lungarno Vespucci 22/r, tel. 296700, closed Sundays and September 15th–January 15th. Offers well-prepared un-Italian dishes. You'll find many Americans and apple pie with cream, here. Moderately expensive.

★★   19 ROSSO
Via F. Corridoni 19/r, tel. 471183, closed Monday nights and Tuesdays. Interesting new place, good food prepared with imagination, pleasant atmosphere, attentive service, adequate wines. Moderate.

★★   SOSTANZA-IL TROIA
Via del Porcellana 25/r, tel. 212691, closed Sundays, holidays and August. The best known *trattoria* in Firenze, offers a few simple dishes, which you'll share with whomever happens to be seated at your table. If you avoid the steak (very good!), the price is very moderate.

★★   CANTINONE DEL GALLO NERO
Via S. Spirito 6/r, tel. 218898, closed Mondays and 20 days in August. This lovely 15th-century cellar is always crowded with the city's young people, who come here to enjoy the few simple dishes and a glass of Chianti Classico. Inexpensive.

FORTE DEI MARMI (LU), Toscana

★★★   LA BARCA
Viale Italico 3, tel. 89323, closed Monday evenings, Tuesdays and November. One of the finest restaurants in Versilia. Better make a reservation. Excellent food with new dishes and new wines being added continuously to the menu. Attentive, courteous service, excellent house wine. Moderately expensive.

Sit on the terrazza

★★ CERVO BIANCO
Via Risorgimento 9, tel. 89640, closed Wednesdays and October. Good location in the center of the city, selected clientele, good service and food. Expensive.

FRASCATI (ROMA), Lazio

★★★ D'ARTAGNAN
Strada Frascati—Colonna 4 km. (autostrada exit for Montecompatri), tel. 9485293, closed Mondays and January. Regional (Umbria-Lazio), as well as local traditional dishes. Excellent local wine (one of the best of the zone), as well as a well-stocked cantina, excellent service. Moderately expensive.

★★ SPARTACO
Viale Letizia Bonaparte, tel. 9420431, closed Tuesdays. Genuine home-style cooking, good local wine, good service, excellent view of the *Castelli Romani* from the terrace. Moderate.

GIGLIO (ISOLA DEL) (GR), Toscana

★ TRATTORIA DA DONNA ROSA
At Giglio Castello, via Roma, tel. 809291. Moderate.

GROTTAMMARE (AP), Le Marche

★ GROTTINO SISTO
Via Palmaroli 10, tel. 64359, closed Tuesdays. Moderate.

★ SAN FRANCISCO
On the highway toward Ancona, tel. 60415, closed Tuesdays off-season. Moderately expensive.

GUBBIO (PG), Umbria

★★★ PORTA TESSENECA
Via Baldassini 26/A, tel. 924365, closed Wednesdays, open holidays. Excellent location in the heart of the city. Varied menu, for fish dishes it is necessary to make reservations on Tuesday for Friday. Excellent selection of Italian and French wines. Moderate.

★★ TAVERNA DEL LUPO
Via G. Ansidei 21, tel. 922968, closed Mondays (except during the summer), open holidays. Excellent local traditional cooking, good local wines, good selection of Italian wines. Moderate.

Near main piazza

★ DEI CONSOLI
Via dei Consoli 59, tel. 922135, closed Wednesdays (except during the summer). Courteous service, local and regional specialties, most ingredients are locally grown, good wine. Moderate.

IMOLA (BO), Emilia-Romagna

★★★★★ SAN DOMENICO
Via Sacchi 1, tel. 29000, closed Wednesdays. One of the finest restaurants
of the region in all respects: refined and elegant atmosphere, food of the best
quality, prepared by excellent chefs, attentive and courteous service, excellent choice of wines. Reservations necessary. Expensive.

★ NALDI
Via Santerno 13, tel. 29581, closed Mondays and July 10th–30th. Relaxing
atmosphere, regional cooking, good service and wine. Moderate.

LIVORNO, Toscana

★★ DA CAPPA LA BANDERUOLA
At Ardenza, via Diego Angioletti 3, tel. 501246, closed Sundays and first 15
days in August. Slightly out of town. The fresh fish is cooked to perfection,
the wines are well matched to the fish (no easy feat). Moderately expensive.

★ LA BARCAROLA
Viale Carducci, 63, near the railroad station, tel. 402367, closed Mondays
and first 15 days in August. Unassuming, serves excellent food, sometimes
a little chaotic. Moderate.

★ ANTICO MORO
Via di Franco 59, tel. 34659, closed Wednesdays and August. In the heart
of town, but not easy to find, this small *bistrot* is an old, traditional fish eatery
worth trying. Moderate.

ask for baccalà alla Livornese (stewed cod)

LUCCA, Toscana

★★★★ SOLFERINO
At S. Macario in Piano, about 6 km. (3.7 mi.) toward Viareggio, tel. 59118,
closed Tuesday evenings and Wednesdays and last three weeks in August.
Excellent food, combining the local tradition with a new approach, good wine
list and service, worth a detour. Moderately expensive.

★★ BUCA DI S. ANTONIO
Via della Cervia 5, tel. 55881, closed Sundays, Mondays and August. In the
heart of town, attractively decorated, serves good food. Moderately expensive.

★ ANTICO CAFFÈ DELLE MURA
Piazza Vittorio Emanuele 4, tel. 47962, closed Fridays. Lovely location, on
one of the ramparts of the old walls, this is where the city's prominent
citizens meet. The food is adequate, the service courteous. Moderately
expensive.

MODENA, Emilia-Romagna

★★ FINI
Largo San Francesco, tel. 223314, closed Thursdays and August 1st–16th.

The tortellini here is outstanding

Excellent regional food, famous in Italy and abroad, good wine list. Moderately expensive.

★   DA ENZO
Via Coltellini 17, tel. 225177, closed Fridays and August 1st–25th. Good, simple fare, with the rich Emilian touch. Moderate.

MONTECATINI TERME (PT), Toscana

★★   LE PANTERAIE
Via Panteraie, tel. 2528, closed Tuesdays. This is not only a restaurant, but a charming garden with music for the enjoyment of those who spend the morning taking the Montecatini waters. Expensive.

★   DA GIOVANNI
Corso Roma 11, tel. 71695, closed Mondays and several weeks during the year. Call ahead. Small and pleasant, this is also a wine-tasting place. The food is well prepared and fresh. Moderate.

ORVIETO (TR), Umbria

Try anything with truffles here

★★   MORINO
Via Garibaldi 37, tel. 35152, closed Wednesdays and January 15th–25th. Well-established restaurant, high-quality local dishes, excellent local wine. Moderately expensive.

★   DELL'AURORA
Via di Piazza del Popolo 7/11, tel. 35446, closed Fridays, open holidays. Excellent location in the heart of the city, traditional local cooking, good house wine. Moderately expensive.

★   DEL PINO DA CECCO
Via di Piazza del Popolo 15/21, tel. 35381, closed Tuesdays. Good local cuisine and local wine (product of the restaurant). Moderately expensive.

OSTIA ANTICA (ROMA), Lazio

Once the port of Roma, this agricultural hamlet is located at the mouth of the Tevere River on the border of the Roman Ostia. Its excavation sites are one of the best known archaeological zones of Italy. Approximate population: 3,000.

★★   FERRANTELLI
Via Claudio 7, tel. 5625751, closed Mondays, open holidays. Fish restaurant, abundant portions, attentive service, good selection of wine. Moderately expensive.

★   AL MONUMENTO
Piazza Umberto 8, tel. 6650021, closed Mondays. Specialty is fish. Moderately expensive.

PARMA, Emilia-Romagna

★★★   MAXIM'S
Del Palace Hotel Maria Luigia, viale Mentana 140, tel. 21032, closed Sundays. Excellent hams and cold cuts (in this city of hams!). This restaurant would make a good showing anywhere. Only the wine list is mediocre. Moderate.

★★★   STENDHAL DA BRUNO
A Sacca di Colorno, tel. 81393. Closed Tuesdays and January 15th–31st. About 24 km. (15 mi.) outside Parma, at Colorno, this rambling country place houses a restaurant that offers the best in *Parmense* cooking. Decidedly worth a detour. Moderate.

★★   PARIZZI
Strada della Repubblica 71, tel. 25952, closed Mondays and July. The best traditional, regional cooking in town. Exceptional choice of roasts, desserts, good wines. Moderate.

★★   IL BAULE
Località Cavalli, tel. 804110, closed Mondays from March to October and Sundays from November to March. About 8 km. out of town, this old country house contains an interesting restaurant worth visiting. Interesting treatment of local food, good wines. Moderate.

★   LA GREPPIA
Strada Garibaldi 39, tel. 33686, closed Thursdays June 15th–July 15th, mid-August and Christmas. Good food, elegant service. Moderate.

PERUGIA, Umbria

★★   FALCHETTO
Via Bartolo 20, tel. 61875, closed Mondays and July 1st–15th. Well-prepared traditional dishes, excellent regional wine. Moderately expensive.

Falchetti is spinach with cheese dumplings

★★   DEL SOLE
Via Oberdan 28, tel. 65031, closed Saturdays and December 23rd–January 7th. Large terrace with a beautiful view of the surrounding countryside; well-prepared regional dishes, good selection of regional wines. Moderately expensive.

★   LA LANTERNA
Via Rocchi 6, tel. 66064, closed Fridays, some days in July. Moderate.

PESARO, Le Marche

★★★   DA CARLO AL MARE
Viale Trieste 265, tel. 31453, open May 1st–September 30th. The best restaurant in the area. Excellent, well-prepared dishes, courteous service, well-stocked wine cellar, excellent local wine. Moderately expensive.

Known for its game, too

★★   DELLA POSTA

Via Giordano Bruno, tel. 33292, closed Tuesdays and June 15th–30th. Excellent location in the middle of the historical center. Traditional well-prepared dishes, courteous efficient service. Moderately expensive.

★   LO SCUDIERO

Via Baldassini 2, tel. 64107, closed Thursdays and July. Well-prepared dishes, well-stocked wine cellar, attentive service. Moderate.

PLIACENZA, Emilia-Romegna

★★★★   ANTICA OSTERIA TEATRO

Via Verdi 16, tel. 23777, closed Sundays and August. Located in a restored 15th-century palazzo and run by a Frenchman who has made Italy his home. You can choose between regional Emilia cooking or classical French cooking. The menu varies depending on the fresh products of the day. An excellent selection of wine from the old cellars of the palazzo. Expensive.

★★   BERTÈ

At the Quarto di Piacenza, tel. 560105, closed Mondays and from the end of July to August 20th. Clean, comfortable atmosphere, regional cooking using locally grown food, excellent wine made by the owner, good service. Moderately expensive.

PISA, Toscana

★★   SERGIO

Lungarno Pacinotti 1, tel. 48245, closed Sundays, Mondays at noon, July 15th–31st and January 1st–15th. The best restaurant in town, features both regional and international dishes, good wine list. Moderately expensive.

★   UGO

Via Aurelia km. 342, tel. 811055, closed Mondays, Tuesday evenings. Once a truck-driver's restaurant, it still offers good, genuine food. About 13 km. out of town. Moderate.

PISTOIA, Toscana

★   RAFANELLI

Via S. Agostino 47, tel. 23046, closed Mondays and August 1st–15th. In the country but close to the city, traditional Pistoiese cooking, adequate wine list. Moderately expensive.

★   CUCCIOLO DELLA MONTAGNA

Via Panciatichi 4, tel. 29733, closed Mondays. Moderate.

PORTO SANTO STEFANO (GR), Toscana

★★   ALL'ARGENTARIO
Corso Umberto 100/102, tel. 812538, closed Mondays and December. Restaurant divided in two—on one side of the street is the kitchen and on the other side is a comfortable terrace for the clientele. Excellent food and service, good wine list. Moderately expensive.

★   LA BUSSOLA
Piazza del Valle 10, tel. 814225, closed Wednesdays. Moderate.

★   ARMANDO
Via Marconi 2/6 (on the harbor), tel. 812568, closed Wednesdays off-season. Moderate.

PRATO (FI), Toscana

★★   IL PIRAÑA
Via Valentini 110, tel. 25746, closed Saturdays and August. Modern restaurant with an intimate atmosphere, one of the best fish restaurants in Toscana; attentive service, good wine list. Moderately expensive.

★★   CEPPO VECCHIO
Via dei Sei 5, tel. 38811, closed Thursdays and June 12th–July 3rd. Located in the center of the city in a '400 palazzo. Good home-style cooking, adequate wine list. Moderately expensive.

★   LIVIO
Via C. Guasti 62/66, tel. 23709, closed Saturdays and August 5th–20th. Modest *trattoria,* simple, well-prepared dishes, good service. Moderate.

Cod is well-loved by Tuscans, "the Bostonians of Italy"

RAVENNA, Emilia-Romagna

★   TRE SPADE
Via G. Rasponi 35, tel. 32382, closed Mondays in winter and Sundays in summer. Near the cathedral, this somber, elegant place offers good food and wine. Moderately expensive.

★   BELLA VENEZIANA
Via IV Novembre 16, tel. 22746, closed Sundays. Good regional food. Moderate.

★   ALLA TORRE
Via Costa 3, tel. 22098, closed Tuesdays. Grilled fish and meat in a classical restaurant. Moderate.

ROCCA DI PAPA (Roma), Lazio

★　LA FORESTA
On the Via dei Laghi at the crossroad of Ariccia (3 km.), tel. 949167, closed Tuesdays. Moderately expensive.

★　MONTE CAVO
At Monte Cavo (63 km.), tel. 949016, closed Fridays during the winter. Moderate.

SAN BENEDETTO DEL TRONTO (AP), Marches

★　ANGELICI
Via Mazzocchi 34, tel. 3597, closed Mondays and January 15th–March 1st. Excellent food and wine, best to eat here on weekdays when it's not overcrowded. Moderately expensive.

★　LA STALLA
Via Marinuccia 21, tel. 4933, closed Mondays during the winter. Characteristic atmosphere. Moderate.

SAN GIMIGNANO (SI), Toscana

★★　BEL SOGGIORNO
Via San Giovanni 89, tel. 940375, closed Mondays. Genuine home-style cooking using products grown and produced by the owners of the restaurant (from the wine and oil to the vegetables and fruit). Abundant portions and good service; excellent Vernaccia (dry for the meal and liqueur for desert). Moderate.

★　LE TERRAZZE
Piazza della Cisterna, tel. 940328, closed Tuesdays and January. Excellent local dishes and wine. Moderately expensive.

SENIGALLIA (AN), Le Marche

★★　IL BOSCHETTO
At Filetto, tel. 66404, closed Mondays and November. Beautiful country location, traditional Marches dishes. Moderate.

★　DA LORÈ
Via Nazionale, tel. 90132, always open. Well-prepared yet simple dishes, good regional wine. Moderate.

★　DA BICE
Via Leopardi 105, tel. 62951, closed Saturdays (except during the summer). Calm, comfortable atmosphere, well-prepared food, good wine (produced on the premises). Moderate.

Loved for its pasta

RIMINI (FO), Emilia-Romagna

★★   VECCHIA RIMINI
Via Cattaneo 7, tel. 26610, closed Mondays and some holidays. The finest restaurant of Rimini. Refined atmosphere, as well as food, punctual service, excellent wines. Moderately expensive.

★★   DA MARIO CUCINA 2000
Via Marechiese 56, tel. 772235, closed Mondays and some holidays. Excellent food prepared from carefully selected ingredients and served with much care and attention, good wines. Moderately expensive.

★   TONINO
Via Rotaggi 7, tel. 24834, closed Tuesdays and September 15th–October 15th. Quiet atmosphere during low season, crowded with tourists during the summer, traditional Romagna dishes. Moderately expensive.

SIENA, Toscana

★★   TULLIO AI TRE CRISTI
Vicolo Provenzano 1, tel. 280608, closed Mondays and July 3rd–24th. Pleasant atmosphere, good food, excellent house wine. Moderately expensive.

★   DA GUIDO
Vicolo Pier Pettinaio 7, tel. 280042, closed Mondays and July 1st–25th. Located in a building from the 500s. Noted for its courteous and attentive service, ordinary menu. Moderately expensive.

also noted for its pasta

★   MEDIOEVO
Via dei Rossi 40, tel. 280315, closed Thursdays and January. Pleasant atmosphere, varied menu with many traditional local dishes, good house wine. Moderately expensive.

★   NELLO LA TAVERNA
Via del Porrione 28, tel. 289043, closed Mondays and July 1st–15th. Comfortable atmosphere, excellent location near Piazza del Campo, ordinary menu, good house wine. Moderately expensive.

SPOLETO (PG), Umbria

★★   IL TARTUFO
Piazza Garibaldi 24, tel. 25136, closed Wednesdays and the second half of July. The best restaurant within the walls of Spoleto. Best to make reservation. Excellent food and a good wine list. Moderately expensive.

★★   FONTECUPA
Piazza Collicola, tel. 21220, closed Tuesdays. Very good local food, open fire grill, special brook trout. Moderate.

★★ TRIC TRAC

Piazza del Duomo, one of the "musts" in town. Elegant restaurant, serves good food and wine, has a splendid location. If you can't have a meal here, at least enjoy a drink, preferably at sunset. Expensive.

★ MADRIGALE

State highway Flaminia, 112 km., tel. 54144, closed Tuesdays and from November to March. Traditional Umbrian dishes, menu varies according to foods in season, limited selection of wine. Moderately expensive.

TARQUINIA (VT), Lazio

★ VELCAMARE

Via degli Argonauti 1, tel. 88024, closed Tuesdays except during the summer. A variety of traditional Italian dishes, specialty is fish, good local wine. Moderately expensive.

★ IL BERSAGLIERE

Viale della Stazione, tel. 86047, closed Tuesdays. Moderate.

TIVOLI (ROMA), Lazio

★ CINQUE STATUE

Via Quintilio Varo 1, tel. 20366, closed Fridays, Sunday evenings and August 18th–30th. Comfortable atmosphere, excellent food and wine. Moderately expensive.

★ VILLA GREGORIANA

Via Ponte Gregoriano 33, tel. 20026, closed Mondays. Moderately expensive.

TODI (PG), Umbria

★★ UMBRIA

Via S. Bonaventura 13, tel. 882390, closed Tuesdays and December 18th–January 3rd. Small dining room, terrace with a beautiful view of the surrounding country, excellent regional dishes and local wine. Moderate.

★ JACOPO DA PEPPINO

Piazza Jacopone 5, tel. 882366, closed Mondays and July 1st–15th. Simple traditional cooking, excellent local wines. Inexpensive.

URBINO (PS), Le Marche

★ SAN GIOVANNI

Via Barocci 13, tel. 3486, closed Wednesdays. Excellent location near the central piazza, tranquil atmosphere, well-prepared regional dishes, good wine, courteous service. Moderate.

Try pasta specialties or pork

★   IL CORTEGIANO
In front of the duomo, tel. 4539, closed Mondays. Moderate.

VIAREGGIO (LU), Toscana

★★   ROMANO
Via Mazzini 122, tel. 31382, closed Mondays and November 15th–December 15th. Excellent modern restaurant, specializes in fish, which is always fresh, good wine list. Moderately expensive.

★★   MONTECATINI
Viale Manin 8, tel. 42129, closed Mondays. One of the oldest in town, this is probably the most international restaurant in the area, catering to locals as well as to travelers. Moderately expensive.

★★   IL PATRIARCA
Viale Carducci 79, tel. 53126, closed Wednesdays. Fancy and exclusive (Frank Sinatra ate here), this place offers more atmosphere than any other in the area, but the food is uneven. Expensive.

★   MARGHERITA
Viale Margherita 30, tel. 42553, closed Wednesdays. Spacious, near the beach, offers an honest meal. Moderately expensive.

VOLTERRA (PI), Toscana

★   ETRURIA
Piazza dei Priori 8, tel. 86064, closed Saturdays. Good local dishes, game when in season. Moderate.

Entertainment

Opera

The greatest entertainment of all in this region is the Festival of the Two Worlds in Spoleto in June and July, run by Gian Carlo Menotti. Opera can be seen in Bologna and Piacenza from February to May, in Firenze from December. Summer opera in Firenze is inside at the Teatro Communale, starting in July.

Music

Music festivals take place in Firenze in May and June; in Ravenna from June through August; in Bologna in June; in Perugia in September.

Nightlife

Nightlife may be experienced in the local sidewalk cafes with fellow tourists and the natives. There is a Harry's Bar in Firenze. If you must dance, try the roof of the Hotel Balglioni, Piazza dell'Unita. There is a floor show at the

(a local dry white wine is Ugolino (or Biserno))

(and don't forget Parma's famous opera house)

Pozzo di Beatrice, Piazza Santa Trinita, and you can dance in a garden at Oliviero's, Viale Michaelangelo.

Festivals and Fairs

These festivals and fairs should provide plenty of pleasure for you. Here are a few major events.

February.   Carnival festivities in Viareggio, with a marvelous procession of grotesque giant figures.

Holy Week and Easter.   Maundy Thursday religious rites in Assisi. On Easter Sunday, the Scoppio del Carro festival takes place in Firenze's Piazza del Duomo.

May.   Strolling minstrels in Renaissance costumes play on the streets of Assisi in early May. On the May 30th, the Palio Belstrieri contest of medieval arms takes place in Gubbio. On May's first Sunday, see the Renaissance football game, the Gioco del Calcio, at Firenze's Boboli Gardens.

June.   On June 5th in Pisa see ancient games on the bridge, on June 16th see lighted boats in procession on the feast day of Pisa's patron, San Ranieri. On June 24th there is another game of Gioco del Calcio (see May) in Firenze's Boboli Gardens, with a similar performance in the Piazza Santa Croce on the following day.

July.   On July 2nd see the exciting Palio festivities begin in Siena, though the race itself is not run until August 16th, Castel Gondolfo, summer residence of the pope, has its peach festival this month.

August.   In Siena on August 14th is the biggest procession of Palio participants; the race itself is on August 16th. Assisi has three festivals in a row from August 10th through 12th.

September.   Foligno presents the Giostra della Quintana, a Renaissance jousting event with several hundred knights in armor, on the second Sunday (procession previous evening). Another military event is Arezzo's recreation of the 13th-century Battle of the Saracens, on the first Sunday of the month.

September–October.   International Antiques Fair in Firenze.

Museums and Galleries

BOLOGNA, Emilia Romagna

★★★   MUSEO CIVICO ARCHEOLOGICO
Via Musei 8, tel. 221896. Several collections were united in 1881, then transported to this present location. There's an important Iron Age section and a Roman section of the first century A.D. This museum is one of the largest of its kind in Italy.

★★★   PINACOTECA NAZIONALE
Via Belle Arti 56, tel. 223774. Contains excellent paintings from the 13th to 18th centuries; some are masterpieces.

★   MUSEO D'ARTE INDUSTRIALE E GALLERIA DAVIA BARGELLINI
Strada Maggiore 44, tel. 236708. This museum consists of several sections; the largest is the collection of local crafts from the 17th and 18th centuries. It also has an interesting section of model doll houses and of marionettes depicting biblical characters.

MUSEO STORICO DIDATTICO DELLA TAPPEZZERIA
Via Barbera 13, tel. 331154. With only a selection of its 6,000 pieces in view, this museum exhbits fine examples of Italian, European and Oriental tapestries from the 14th to 19th centuries.

CARRARA (MS), Toscana

MOSTRA NAZIONALE DEL MARMO
Via XX Settembre, Stadio, tel. 72360. This is an exhibition of all types of marble and travertine found in Italy. There are several finished articles plus tools.

CHIUSI (SI), Toscana

★★   MUSEO ARCHEOLOGICO NAZIONALE
Via Porsenna, tel. 20177. One of the most interesting museums of the Etruscan region with Etruscan, Greek and Roman sections.

FAENZA (RA), Emilia-Romagna

★★   MUSEO INTERNAZIONALE DELLE CERAMICHE
Via Campidori 2, tel. 21240. Founded in 1908, this museum houses a rich collection of ceramics from the Renaissance to present times. There are examples of Pre-Columbian, Middle Eastern ceramics as well. It has a noted collection of contemporary ceramics by such artists as Chagall, Matisse and Picasso.

FERRARA, Emilia-Romagna

★★   CIVICO MUSEO DI SCHIFANOIA
Via Scandiana 23, tel. 37326. This museum contains many collections; the most important are the frescoes by the 15th-century Ferrara artists and the bronzes and vases of the Etruscan, Roman and Renaissance periods.

★   PINACOTECA NAZIONALE DI PALAZZO DEI DIAMANTI
Corso Ercole I d'Este 21, tel. 21831. This collection of Ferrarese paintings (1300–1600), is housed in the *Palazzo Diamanti,* one of the most important examples of 15th-century architecture in Italy.

FIESOLE (FI), Toscana

★   MUSEO ARCHEOLOGICO
Via Marini 1, tel. 59477. A collection of archaeological materials found during excavations in the surrounding area, as well as Roman and Etruscan bronzes, sculptures and portraits.

FIRENZE, Toscana

★★★★★   GALLERIA DEGLI UFFIZI
Piazzale degli Uffizi 6, tel. 218341. One of the most famous art galleries in the world, it contains a collection by the best-known painters from the 8th to the 18th centuries, as well as a collection of classical sculptures, tapestries and furniture. There are approximately 1,700 works of art exhibited here. Also included in this museum is the *Corridoio Vasariano,* a covered passageway containing 715 works of art, which connects the Uffizi with the Palazzo Pitti via the Ponte Vecchio.

★★★★   MUSEO NAZIONALE DEL BARGELLO
Via del Proconsolo 4, tel. 210801. The most important museum in Italy for medieval and Renaissance sculpture. Also has important collection of minor arts—medals, ceramics, seals, small bronzes.

★★★★   MUSEO DELLE CAPPELLE MEDICEE
Piazza Madonna degli Aldobrandini, tel. 23206. This museum is most noted for Michelangelo's *New Sacristy,* which contains his sculptures: *Dawn and Dusk, Night and Day.* Drawings on the walls of a recently discovered room underneath the *New Sacristy* have been attributed to Michelangelo (it is necessary to ask at the ticket office for a special ticket to see these drawings). Also housed in this building is the *Chapel of the Princes* and the mausoleum of the last of the Medici.

★★★   MUSEO ARCHEOLOGICO
Via della Colonna 36, tel. 215270. The second most important archaeological museum in Italy, noted for its excellent Etruscan collections. It also has important Greek, Roman and Egyptian sections.

★   GALLERIA D'ARTE MODERNA
Palazzo Pitti, tel. 287096. This gallery has a collection of Italian paintings and sculptures from the 19th century to modern times.

★★   MUSEO DELL'OPERA DI S. MARIA DEL FIORE
Piazza Duomo 8. This small but elegant museum houses many special works of art, the *Pietà* by Michelangelo, *Mary Magdalen* by Donatello, the famous choir lofts by Luca della Robbia and Donatello, as well as the original statues and panels from Giotto's Bell Tower.

★★   MUSEO DI SAN MARCO E DELL'ANGELICO
Piazza di San Marco 1, tel. 210741. Located in the same complex as the convent of San Marco, the museum exhibits the works of famous Dominican painters. The most important is Fra Angelico.

★★   BIBLIOTECA MEDICEO-LAURENZIANA
Piazza San Lorenzo 9, tel. 210760. Founded by the Medici family, in a building designed by Michelangelo, it houses one of the best collections of illuminated manuscripts and documents.

★★★   GALLERIA DELL'ACCADEMIA
Via Ricasoli 60, tel. 214375. This museum is known for Michelangelo's *David* and *Captives.* It also has one of the richest picture galleries in Firenze, with paintings of the Florentine school from the 13th to 16th centuries.

CASA E MUSEO DI DANTE
Via S. Margherita 1, tel. 283343. Exhibited here are graphics and documents relating to Dante's life.

FORTE DI BELVEDERE O DI SAN GIORGIO
Via di San Leonardo, tel. 219263. Founded at the end of the 16th century, this is one of the most impressive military complexes of its time in Italy. Beautiful view of Firenze. Many important art exhibitions are held here throughout the year.

MUSEO DI CASA BUONARROTI
Via Ghibellina 80, tel. 287630. In this house (which Michelangelo bought for his nephew) are exhibited the first two marble reliefs done by the artist: *The Battle of the Centaurs and Iapites* and the *Madonna of the Stairs,* as well as other sculptures, drawings, and family belongings.

MUSEO DI FIRENZE COM'ERA
Via dell'Oriolo 24, tel. 217305. Located in an exconvent, this museum exhibits graphic and iconographic materials and documents relating to the history of Firenze from the 15th to the 20th centuries.

LUCCA, Toscana

★   MUSEO NAZIONALE DI VILLE GUINIGI
Via della Quarguonia, tel. 46033. Located in a 15th-century country villa, this museum has an archaeological section with Etruscan, Roman and Ligurian works, an important medieval and Renaissance sculpture section and a painting section representing the Lucchese school from the 13th to the 18th centuries.

MODENA, Emilia Romagna

★★   GALLERIA ESTENSE
Piazza S. Agostino 309, tel. 222145. An excellent collection of primitive *Bolognesi* and *Emiliani* works of art, as well as an important collection of paintings from the 14th to the 18th centuries.

PERUGIA, Umbria

★★   GALLERIA NAZIONALE DELL'UMBRIA
Palazzo dei Priori-Corso Vannucci, tel. 23385. This museum houses a series of collections, including paintings on wood and cloth, frescoes and sculptures on wood and stone. It also has a laboratory of restoration and a library.

★   MUSEO ARCHEOLOGICO NAZIONALE DELL'UMBRIA
This museum is the former convent of San Domenico, Piazza Giordano Bruno, tel. 21398. The museum is composed of two sections—the prehistoric and the Etruscan and Roman, both have important collections.

PISA, Toscana

★   MUSEO NAZIONALE DI SAN MATTEO
Lungarno Mediceo, Tel. 23750. Located in the old Benedictine monastery of San Matteo, this museum has a rich sculpture collection (primarily of the Pisan school). It also has many fine examples of Tuscan paintings from the 14th to 18th centuries.

SETTIGNANO (FI), Toscana

PINACOTECA DELLA FONDAZIONE BERENSON
San Martino a Mensola, tel. 603251. After Bernard Berenson's death in 1959, his villa, *I Tatti,* became the property of Harvard University and is now a foundation for Italian Renaissance studies. His library and art collection, left as they were, can be visited by appointment.

SIENA, Toscana

★★   MUSEO DELL'OPERA DEL DUOMO
Piazza Duomo, tel. 283048. Contains objects related to the history of the Duomo as well as a series of Sienese masterpieces from the 13th to 16th centuries.

MUSEO DELLE TAVOLETTE DI BICCHERNA
Archivio di Stato, via Banchi di Sotto 52, tel. 51271. This small but interesting museum contains a collection of painted tablets (124 pieces) used as book covers at the time of the Sienese Republic.

★★   PINACOTECA NAZIONALE
Via San Pietro 29, tel. 281161. This museum houses the largest collection of Sienese art from its origin to the 17th century.

TARQUINIA (VT), Lazio

★★   MUSEO NAZIONALE ETRUSCO TARQUINESE
Palazzo Vitelleschi, tel. 856036. This museum contains many objects from excavations in this noted archaeological zone.

VIAREGGIO (LU), Toscana

★ MUSEO PUCCINIANO
Torre del Lago, Villa Puccini, tel. 341445. This villa, where Giacomo Puccini lived from 1891 until 1921, is where he composed most of his great operas. Exhibited are many of the composer's personal articles, including his piano.

VINCI (FI), Toscana

MUSEO VINCIANO
Via Castello Conti Guidi, tel. 56055. Located in the old castle of Vinci, this museum houses models of machinery and tools invented by Leonardo da Vinci.

VOLTERRA (PI) Toscana

★★ MUSEO ETRUSCO GUARNACCI
Via Don Minzoni 1, tel. 86347. Noted for its important Etruscan collection, which contains more than 600 pieces.

Shopping

Though Firenze (Florence) (especially for leather goods) and Venezia (Venice) (for lace and glass) are generally acknowledged as Italy's best cities for shopping, there is a dazzling array of traditional arts and crafts—from exquisite silver jewelry to fine woolens to superb woodwork—to be found throughout the country.

The center of Italian handicraft and fine craftsmanship, Firenze can be a shopper's paradise. Rather than specifying special shops, we prefer to describe streets where you may browse, using your own good judgment about what to buy. For silver and gold jewelry and for history, go to the Ponte Vecchio. For fashions and beautifully designed accessories, stroll down the Via Tornabuoni or the Via della Vigna Nuova. For fine cameos, try the Borgognissanti, which is also good for antiques. Outdoor markets include a small one near the Ponte Vecchio, and a bigger, more famous one, the so-called Straw Market in the Loggia del Mercato Nuovo, in Piazza San Lorenzo, right in the heart of Firenze. At its entrance you'll recognize the famed and much copied reclining pig, Il Porcellino.

There are some chain stores, such as La Rinascente, Upim, or Standa, but in general the idea of the department store as it is known in the USA has not flourished. On the other hand, the outdoor flea market has, and you will find vendors spreading their colorful wares on certain days each week in numerous cities and towns.

Tours

Tours of Firenze and its environs are available from many agencies. Details are provided by EPT, the local tourist office, at 16 Via Manzoni. There are tours of the wine country and of villas (including I Tatti, Bernard Berenson's place which he bequeathed to Harvard). Another good touring center in central Italy is Bologna and, of course, Rome.

Sports

Horse racing can be seen in Firenze nearly all year (not in August), with legal betting, of course. Here and in Bologna you can watch soccer except in summer. Firenze's 18-hole golf course, L'Ugolino, is available for nonmembers through your hotel concierge, as is access to tennis courts, though with some amount of difficulty.

Getting Around

Use the trains whenever you can in central Italy, or else use private car. Bus service requires some knowledge of Italian or a brave soul. If you drive, avoid the Autostrata.

Directory

Consulates

Consulates are few and far between. American: Lungarno Vespucci, Firenze; British: Lungarno Corsini, Firenze.

Churches and Synagogue

English-speaking religious services in Firenze: Protestant services at Episcopal Church, 15 Via Ruccelai or Church of England, 18 Via Maggio. Catholic masses and confessions in English, at Firenze cathedral, the Basilica S. Maria dei Fiore, Piazza Duomo. Synagogue at 4 Via Farini.

Firenze—Hairdressers

DANTE
Lungarno Corsini 36r, tel. 294893. A great favorite with the Anglo-Saxon colony; competent. Expensive.

MARIO
Via Vigna Nuova 22r, tel. 294813. One of the best in town, efficient organization, every beauty care imaginable. Expensive.

Southern or Mediterrean Italy

The regions of southern Italy are as varied as they are fascinating: Campania, with Napoli (Naples), the Vesuvius, Capri, Pompei; Sicilia, the mysterious island of mellow wines and silent men; Calabria, poor and proud; Puglia (Apulia), the Middle East and Greece with an Italian accent; Sardegna, a splendid setting for both international romping and primitive life; plus the smaller regions of Basilicata, Abruzzi and Molise.

The South is a different Italy, and yet it *is* Italy. It's the toughest part of the country, the most beautifully endowed by nature, the most romantic and emotional, the most abandoned and, for the central government, the most problematic.

Here, nature has been unkind, with earthquakes, volcanic eruptions and few natural resources. The racial mixture is unique; this part of the country has been Etruscan, Greek, Roman, Byzantine, Goth, Lombard, Norman, Arab and Spanish. With few exceptions, most of these peoples have come by sea, have settled on the coast, have been attacked from the sea, have been fed by the sea and often have died at sea.

Southern Italy includes the two large islands, Sicilia (Sicily) and Sardegna (Sardinia), which alone, would explain the additional adjective Mediterranean. But there are other reasons. The sea, present in almost every Italian region, is more important in the South. The sea provides its most spectacular scenery, it influences the food, it has brought friendly and unfriendly invaders, it accounts for a major portion of the local economy, it inspires poets and it attracts travelers.

The distance that separates the southern coasts of both Sicilia and Sardegna from Africa is smaller than the distance that separates each from Milano (Milan). Therefore, African and Arab influences have been, and continue to be, of major importance. Sicilian churches have a distinct Islamic style. The dialect of Calabria is closer to Arabic than to Italian. The pottery of Amalfi (Campania) is decorated with geometric patterns reminiscent of some Oriental art. And the sweet concoctions of Sicilian bakers are definitely more Arabic than European.

Modern life is beginning to change these aspects of southern Italy. Mass-distributed magazines, national television, widely available goods and in-

Typically Arabic is Trapani's Scursumera, water ice flavored with jasmine

251

creasingly easy travel are changing life everywhere, including the extreme southern part of the Italian peninsula. But our guess is that the ancient culture will not be completely eradicated and that Southern Italy will always remain closer to the Mediterranean and Africa than to the rest of Europe.

CAMPANIA

Campania is one of the geographically smaller regions of the South, but it is the the most densely populated, the most fascinating, and one of the most important areas in Italy, especially from the tourist's point of view. Who hasn't heard of Napoli, Capri, Pompei? How many have dreamed of Amalfi and Sorrento? As far back as 2,000 years ago the rich Roman merchants, and even the emperors, were attracted by the charm of Campania with its mild climate and enchanting panoramas, so much so that they had their country homes built there. In fact, *campania* means "country" in old Latin.

The region, which covers only 13,594 sq.km., has a population of more than 5 million inhabitants. It borders on Lazio, Molise, Puglia and Basilicata. Its coastline is 430 km., going from the Garignano River to the Bay of Sapri (which is within the Gulf of Policastro), and the coast is justly famous for the bays of Napoli and Salerno and, within the former, the enchanting islands of Capri, Ischia and Procida.

Deeply damaged by the 1980 earthquake, today's Campania has a problematic economy, which is slowly recuperating in spite of the many social, economic, and political problems.

Campania is a romantic region, with a people that has always fought in order to survive. They have done it with courage and imagination and without losing the shrewdness and sly humor that have made their region famous.

Some History

Campania is a land of ancient settlements where paleolithic and neolithic traces, as well as innumerable objects left from the Iron Age, have been found.

Later, it was inhabited by tribes of Ausoni and Opici, and around the 8th century B.C., it was colonized by the Greeks, who founded the city of Cuma on the coast. Around the 6th century B.C. the Etruscans arrived and occupied the inland area of southern Italy. They founded one of their 12 city leagues, headed by Capua which, in the year 330 B.C., joined Roma against the Sannites. This began a Romanization process that was so successful that Emperor Augustus assigned the area, together with Latium—the present-day Lazio, to his First Region.

With Diocletian, Campania became a province and was able to maintain its unity under both the Ostrogoths and Byzantines. Only the Longobard occupation of Benevento in A.D. 570 broke this territorial unity. Benevento first became a duchy and, then two centuries later (758) the Kingdom of Benevento, incorporating the cities of Capua and Salerno, which had been small independent Longobard kingdoms in their own right.

In the rest of the Campania territory, the Byzantine presence was still felt, but by the 8th century A.D. Napoli was beginning to break away from that

Diocletian was the last (and worst) persecutor of the Christians

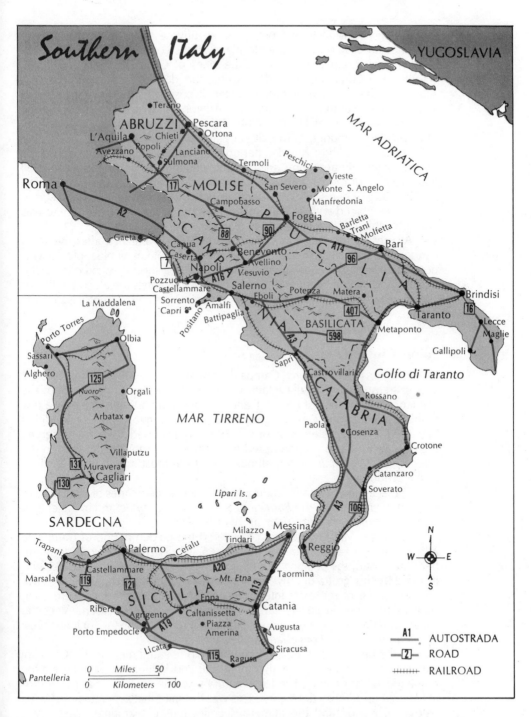

Southern Italy

YUGOSLAVIA

MAR ADRIATICA

Terano
ABRUZZI   Pescara
L'Aquila   Chieti   Ortona
Avezzano   Popoli   Lanciano
Sulmona   Termoli   Peschici
17   MOLISE   Vieste
Roma   San Severo   Monte S. Angelo
Campobasso   Manfredonia
A2   Foggia
88   90   Barletta
Gaeta   Trani
Capua   A14   Molfetta
Caserta   Benevento   Bari
Napoli   Avellino   96
Pozzuoli   A16   Vesuvio
Castellammare   Salerno   Brindisi
Sorrento   Eboli   Potenza   Matera   16
Capri   Amalfi   407   Taranto
Positano   Battipaglia   Lecce
598   Metaponto   Maglie
Sapri   Gallipoli
Castrovillari   Golfo di Taranto
Rossano
MAR TIRRENO   Paola   Cosenza
Catanzaro   Soverato
Lipari Is.   106
A3
Milazzo   Messina
Tindari   Reggio
Trapani   Palermo   Cefalu
Castellammare   A20
Marsala   119   121   Mt. Etna   A13   Taormina
SICILIA   Enna
Ribera   Caltanissetta   Catania
Agrigento   A19   Piazza   Augusta
Porto Empedocle   Amerina
Licata   115   Siracusa
Pantelleria   Ragusa

La Maddalena
Porto Torres   Olbia
Sassari
Alghero   125   Orgali
Nuoro
Arbatax
Villaputzu
131   Muravera
130   Cagliari
SARDEGNA

N
W   E
S

A1   AUTOSTRADA
2   ROAD
+++++++   RAILROAD

Miles   50
Kilometers   100

distant empire. Meanwhile Amalfi, prosperous because of its maritime traffic, also became an independent duchy, free from both Longobards and Byzantines.

But this division turned out to be an unwise thing, for it made these territories an easy prey for the Normans who swooped down in 1030, expanding their conquests by taking the cities of Capua, Salerno and finally Napoli. Thus Campania was added to the Kingdom of Sicilia and became a subject of the Norman monarchs. Later, it passed to the French house of Anjou and then to the Spanish house of Aragona, in whose hands it remained for over two centuries (1503–1734). This was the domination that left the most profound imprint, both culturally and politically.

There was a short Austrian period, but with Charles VII of Borbone the region regained its autonomy and became identified as the Kingdom of Napoli and Sicilia, later the Partenopean Republic and Kingdom of the Two Sicilies.

In 1860, when Campania became part of unified Italy, and especially Napoli were faced with serious political and economic problems, there was also a terrible cholera epidemic in 1884.

At present the region is struggling to regain its balance after the 1980 earthquake, as well as trying to cope with the problems of Neapolitan overpopulation, which breeds unemployment, housing shortages and criminality.

But the natural beauties are as lovely as ever, songs are always in the air and tourists flock to see Vesuvius and Pompei, Capri and Sorrento, Ischia and Amalfi.

Some Thoughts on Art

Unlike other Italian regions, Campania can still display many of its ancient artistic treasures practically intact. Cuma, Pompei, Paestum, Ercolano, the Roman amphitheaters of Pozzuoli and S. Maria Capua Vetere are only a few of these splendid offerings, and they have remained in their present condition because the Vesuvius eruption of A.D. 79 not only buried them but preserved them as well. If you are interested in persuing the subject, the *Museo Archeologico Nazionale* at Napoli has one of the most important collections in the world.

There are fewer artistic landmarks from the first centuries of the Christian era, but the mosaics in the *Basilica of San Felice a Cimitile* and in the chapel of *Santa Matrona a San Prisco* are worth seeing.

The latter Middle Ages are considered the golden period of Campania art. Very good examples are the murals at *S. Vincenzo al Volturno*. Remember that most of the painting done between the 11th and 13th centuries was inspired by the 'grotta di Calvi' cycle. At the end of this era, during the 13th century, some of the most interesting churches and cathedrals were built, such as the ones in Sessa, Capua, S. Angelo in Formis, Caserta Vecchia, Amalfi and Ravello. In them, you will find an interesting mixture of influences: classical, Byzantine, Longobard and Arab–Norman.

At the beginning of the 14th century two talented men, Pietro Cavallini and Simone Martini, were active in Napoli and influenced painting for the remainder of the century. The 15th century saw a new rebirth of artistic fervor at the court of Alfonso d'Aragona. This was the spirit that generated the Castel Nuovo di Napoli and the numerous collections of paintings, *arazzi* and miniatures.

The 17th century was dominated by Caravaggio, and the 18th witnessed the blossoming of the Capodimonte porcelains, a factory of charming miniatures that was built by Charles II of Borbone and still is one of the big attractions of the region. But the most impressive accomplishment of that period was made in the province of Caserta, the splendid *Reggia* by Vanvitelli.

The main 19th-century artistic attraction left in Campania is the *Scuola di Posillipo.* It tends to accentuate the lyrical aspects in a scene, as well as the ways and habits of country folk.

From Bacoli to Pompei (through Napoli)

This first suggested itinerary is both long and interesting and can be done whole or in part, depending on your time and interest. We propose it this way because we love it all.

Start from *Cuma,* near Bacoli and Pozzuoli, at the very end of the *Campi Flegei.* This city was founded by the Greeks and was destroyed during the Middle Ages. Its primary claim to fame is the *grotta,* that once held the oracle of the Sibilla Cumana, near the temples of Jupiter and Apollo.

The gloomy appeal of the oracle still exists after 2000 years. This is the spot Virgil chose for his hero, Enea, when he had to seek advise and solace for himself and his men. Enea asked if they were ever going to find a new land and promised the Sybilla that when they did the city founded by them would worship her forever. She then offered them a collection of prophecies, called the "sybilline books," which were kept in the temple of Giove Capitolino. Their importance to Roma was so great that after the fire of 83 B.C. a new collection was put together. Through the years of Roman power the emperors consulted them, and it seems that the last one to do so was Giuliano l'Apostata, in A.D. 364. One last word on the grotta—for the Romans this was the place where Hades began.

Once out of the Cuma ruins, proceed toward *Baia,* an old seaside resort, then onto *Capo Miseno* and *Pozzuoli,* where the panorama of the lively city beneath and on top of a hill that dominates the splendid gulf is breathtaking. In the lower part of the city, *Serapeo* is covered by the sea. In the higher part, the *Flavian Amphitheater* is worth a visit. It is one of the largest of its kind built during the 1st century A.D. by Vespasiano, that is in good condition.

A few years ago it was feared that the charming city was to be claimed by the sea. Pozzuoli and the surrounding area are on land that is forever moving; they are on top of a fully active underground volcano that has never erupted. Fortunately, the movement that was threatening the town stopped, and the population is tranquil again and pursuing its daily activities.

Next, you can coast along the gulf again, on a scenic road that rises on the promontory, above the small center of *Marechiaro* and *Posillipo.* You then reach Napoli.

Napoli

Napoli (Naples) is definitely the big metropolis of southern Italy. Its port is one of the main ports of the Mediterranean. It nestles around one of the most famous bays of the world, at the foot of a volcano that is known to everyone —the Vesuvius. According to an old saying you haven't lived until you've seen Napoli.

*[handwritten margin note: ** Cumae is the oldest Greek settlement in Italy (8th c. B.C.)]*

*[handwritten margin note: ** Amphitheater is Italy's 3rd largest]*

It is easy to reach, from the north or south, by highway. From Rome, the *Autostrada del Sole* is the fastest approach. There is also an airport for national flights and boats called *canguro* (kangaroo), that take cars, going to Cagliari, Palermo, Messina, Catania, and the Eolian Islands. Smaller boats and ferries take you to Capri, Ischia and Procida, as well as to Sorrento, Amalfi and Positano.

The origin of Napoli dates back to the 5th century B.C. It was founded by the Greeks, but there are hardly any ruins of that period left. The Roman period is represented by the remnants of the amphitheater, the *Temple of the Dioscuri,* the *Odeon* and some thermal ruins.

The history of Napoli is much as the history of the whole region during the Middle Ages. At first it was a duchy, dependent on Byzantium. Later it was conquered by the Normans, then by the French, who made it their capital. It continued to grow, both as port and as a city. At the beginning of the 16th century it contained more than 110,000 inhabitants. By then the rulers were no longer the Anjou but the Aragonese, who loved the city and continued to improve it and to add monuments and buildings.

But at this point Napoli fell into Spanish hands, and the city's complexion changed. Don Pedro de Toledo, the viceroy, brought in whole families of Spanish nobility, and many palaces were built on the western side between the city walls and the hills. Later this area became known as the *Vomero.*

By 1656 Napoli was the most populated city in Europe, with about 360,000 inhabitants. Unfortunately, a pestilence reduced that population to less than half its size. But the reigning house of Borbone made Napoli its capital in 1734, and it remained a capital until 1860 (except for the Napoleonic years, 1806–1815), when all Italy became a unified country.

Napoli has a very special character, largely because of the contrast between the rich palaces of the wealthy, quiet and aristocratic, and the teeming life of the *vicolo,* where the everyday business of living goes on noisily. The Spacca section, otherwise known as *spaccanapoli,* is full of overcrowded narrow streets, filled with the sounds and sights of men, women and children leading their simple, precarious lives and letting everyone know it. After the 1980 earthquake even the houses are no longer stable, and the brave people of Napoli have to face further housing shortage, unemployment and the many hardships that go with general uncertainty.

But the popular spirit finds expression in many ways. The religious festivals of Napoli are outstanding, often taking on the appearance of a "happening." There are the song festivals, celebrating the unforgetable and undying Neapolitan song. Of these, the most important is at *Piedigrotta* during September. Among the religious festivals the most intense is the *Feast for S. Gennaro,* in May and again in September. On July 16th there is *Feast for the Madonna del Carmine.* And the Christmas and Easter holidays are deeply felt. The racetrack of *Agnano* is a meeting place for racing fans, and the large commercial fair, *Mostra d'Oltremare,* is another major attraction.

A visit of the city can be, as with any big city, as detailed and lengthy or as superficial and quick as your time and inclination allow. We give you four itineraries that will take you across the city, highlighting the most important aspects on your path. If you have a very limited amount of time, the local tourist agencies offer short, organized tours. Itinerary 2 is the most interesting for art and local color; don't miss a walk through the little streets of spac-

The Italian Bourbons descended from the French Bourbons through their Spanish line

canapoli. Itinerary 1 provides some important buildings and an important museum; itinerary 3 shows you some excellent art and porcelain; itinerary 4 is for nature lovers and children.

Napoli: Itinerary 1:

Start out on the *Piazza del Plebiscito,* the large and harmonious square at the foot of a hill, enclosed on its eastern side by the *Palazzo Reale,* built during the Spanish period (1600–1602) and renewed twice, once by Murat and once by Carolina Bonaparte. It can be visited on weekdays from 9 A.M. to 2 P.M., on holidays from 9:30 A.M. to 1 P.M.; closed Mondays; Sundays free admission, ticket L.1,000.

✱✱ Palazzo Reale

Across from the palace is a neoclassical church, *S. Francesco di Paola,* built from 1817 to 1846 by Ferdinand I in order to celebrate the ending of Napoleon's intrusion. Then proceed toward Via S. Carlo, passing the smaller square *Piazza Trieste e Trento,* and you will come upon the famous *S. Carlo Theater,* one of the largest and loveliest in Italy. You will soon reach *Piazza del Municipio,* spacious and green, with a view of the port and, on its south side, the Castel Nuovo, a massive medieval structure started by the Anjou in 1279 and redone by Alfonso I d'Aragona in the 15th century, with the help of Spanish and Tuscan artists. After a look at this impressive castle continue down Via Medina and Via Monteoliveto until you reach *S. Anna dei Lombardi,* a church that is almost a small museum of Renaissance sculpture. On leaving the church go further inland, reach Via Roma, pass Piazza Dante, go up Via Enrico Pessina, and you will reach the *Museo Archeologico Nazionale.* This museum is one of the most important of its kind, with large collections of paintings, mosaics, sculpture and objects representing the Greco–Roman civilizations that thrived in this area for several centuries. Open Weekdays from 9 A.M. to 2 P.M.; holidays from 9 A.M. to 1 P.M.; closed Mondays; ticket L.1,000.

✱ San Francesco copies Rome's Pantheon

✱✱ San Carlo

✱✱✱ Castel Nuovo

✱ Sant'Anna

✱✱✱ National Archeological Museum

Napoli: Itinerary 2:

Itinerary 2 for Napoli begins at *Piazza del Gesu Nuovo,* one of the most characteristic squares of old Napoli, located on the path of the long and narrow *spaccanapoli,* the famous street that literally bisects the city—*spacca* means "crack" or "break." At the center of the piazza is a monument, *Guglia dell' Immacolata,* laden with ornaments, which is a typical example of Neapolitan baroque. On the southern side of the square is the *Monastero di S. Chiara,* one of the most important medieval churches in town (1310–1328); it has a charming cloister and is celebrated by a famous song. From there, take Via S. Croce, which continues as Via S. Biagio and Via dei Librai, then make a right onto Via Duomo and you will reach *Palazzo Cuomo,* a lovely Renaissance building erected between 1464 and 1490 and now housing a museum. Returning back up Via Duomo, you'll reach the cathedral, built in the 13th century over the ruins of an old 5th-century basilica and restored several times. Once inside be sure to look for the third chapel on the right, for it is dedicated to the city's patron saint, S. Gennaro. After leaving the cathedral go back a few steps to Via dei Tribunali and you'll come upon a splendid medieval church, *S. Lorenzo Maggiore.* Not only is this one of the

✱✱ Santa Chiara

✱✱ Palazzo Cuomo and its museum

✱✱ Cathedral

✱✱✱ San Lorenzo

best examples of medieval architecture in town—begun by French architects toward the end of the 13th century, on commission of the Franciscan order, and finished by local architects a few years later—but in it Boccaccio saw his Fiammetta in 1334 and fell in love with her. This is still a Francescan church, and from the cloister there is an access to an archaeological area where digging is still going on.

Napoli: Itinerary 3:

Near the railroad station, start out from the large, rectangular *Piazza Garibaldi* and, bearing inland, go to the picturesque and lively *Piazza di Porta Capuana,* surrounded by lovely buildings, including the grey *Castello Capuano,* built by the Norman rulers in the 12th century and now used as a court house. Its front is on the other side of the piazza, and its inside *cortile* is usually filled with people and noise, especially in the morning. On another side of the piazza is a Renaissance church, *S. Caterina a Formiello.* But the real attraction is *Porta Capuana,* which opens up between two powerful towers of the Aragonese walls. The door itself was built in 1484 by Giuliano da Maiano, and because of its elegant proportions and lovely marble decorations, it is considered one of the most outstanding doors of the Italian Renaissance. After admiring this lovely piece of art, continue up Via Carbonara until you reach *S. Giovanni a Carbonara,* a medieval church noted for its sculptures. Proceed through *Piazza Cavour* and on to Capodimonte Hill, where you'll find yourself at the *Museo e Gallerie di Capodimonte,* which is open weekdays from 9:30 A.M. to 3 P.M.; holidays from 9:30 A.M. to 1 P.M.; closed Mondays; admission L.1,000. The museum is in the royal palace of Capodimonte, a structure begun in 1738 for King Carlo di Borbone and finished almost 100 years later. There are two galleries and a museum containing several collections of paintings and porcelain. The *Galleria dell'800,* provides an excellent overall panorama of Neapolitan and southern Italian paintings of the 18th century, plus important items of national and international paintings of that century. In the museum be sure to see the *Collezione De Ciccio,* an excellent collection of oriental, Spanish, Italian, French, German and so on, majolicas and porcelains, which has more than 1300 pieces, some dating as far back as the 14th century. After this visit, if you feel like more of the same, continue toward the *Certosa di S. Martino,* which is on the top of the large hill called *Vomero* and has a splendid view. It now houses an interesting museum, the *Museo Nazionale di S. Martino.* It is open weekdays from 9:30 A.M. to 3 P.M., holidays from 9:30 A.M. to 1 P.M.; closed Mondays; ticket, L.1,000. There are several interesting sections, and portions of the museum are being redone at this writing.

Napoli: Itinerary 4:

Napoli is a city that makes you think of the sea, and itinerary 4 emphasizes that feeling. Begin at the *Via Caracciolo,* a lovely stretch of road that goes along the sea coast in an arch that has the city as a backdrop. Note the *Villa Comunale,* the green public garden, the fountains, statues and kiosks, the Napoli Tennis Club. At the center of the villa is the *Stazione Zoologica* and within it, the famous *Acquario.* This is open weekdays from 9 A.M. to 5 P.M.;

handwritten margin notes:
* Castello Capuano
* Santa Caterina
** Porta Capuano
** San Giovanni
*** Capodimonte Museum and Palace
*** View from
** San Martino Carthusian monastery

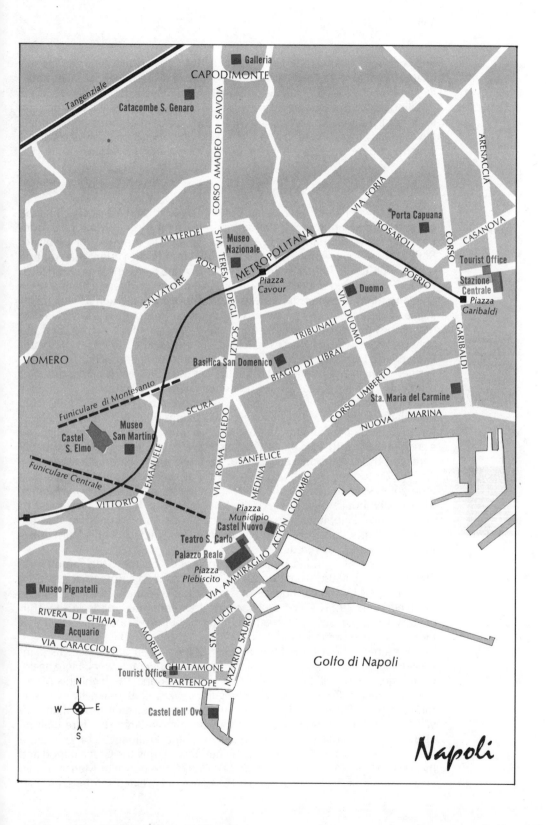

holidays from 9 A.M. to 1 P.M.; ticket, L.1,000, as of this writing. The acquarium contains 29 tubs with about 200 species of animals and vegetable life, all from the Gulf of Napoli. After that, if you have a car, proceed toward Posillipo, going through the *Mergellina,* a charming place that has to be seen to be appreciated. The whole trip is so panoramic that innumerable poets have sung its beauties. At the end you will find yourself back at Marechiaro, which is where the main itinerary stopped for a visit to Napoli.

Pompei and Herculaneum

We can now proceed to Ercolano (Herculaneum) and Pompei, either by going through Napoli or by avoiding it and taking the road that goes from Pozzuoli to Avellino and, at S. Anastasia, change to the road for Ercolano. Both of these cities—Pompei and Ercolano, were destroyed by the eruption of Vesuvius in A.D. 79. While Ercolano was covered by rivers of mud and lava, Pompei was buried under a descent of incandescent cinders. That is why in Ercolano many wooden structures and details of houses, such as wall paintings and decorations, were preserved, while in Pompei the roofs caved in (under the accumulated weight of the cinders), many things were burned and only the outer walls of houses remained. In fact, while Pompei is the better known city, Ercolano is probably the more interesting and better preserved. Further damage was done to both cities by the 1980 earthquake, but after a security check, the authorities reopened both to the public.

According to legend, Ercolano was founded by Hercules. In its early period, it was influenced by the Greek civilizations of Napoli and Cuma. Next it was taken by the Sannites, but by 89 B.C. it was a Roman municipality and a great favorite with Romans as a vacation spot. In A.D. 62 Ercolano was badly damaged by an earthquake, a prelude to the the terrible eruption of 79.

****
Herculaneum

A visit to the excavation sites will take at least two to three hours. The more interesting houses are the following: the one with the *Atrio a Mosaico,* the wooden house of *Tramezzo,* the Sannite house, the Baths, the house of Neptune and Anphitrite, the Bicentenary house, the Gymnasium and the Suburban Baths. Local guides are a good idea since they know the latest things that have been uncovered.

*****
Pompei

Pompei was founded by the Osci tribe and became Greek around the 6th century B.C. It also went through a Sannite and then a Roman occupation, was damaged by the earthquake of A.D. 62 and was then submerged under the cinders in 79. The first archaeological explorations, made in the 18th century were pursued with great enthusiasm, but it was not until 1860 that they become systematic and rational.

Presently, about three-fifths of the city have been uncovered. Its plant was eliptical, with walls that had eight doors and several towers. Here again, even a quick visit will take at least two or three hours. The highlights of this old city are the Forum, a vast rectangular *piazza* that originally was surrounded by columns on three sides; Jupiter's temple, built more than 200 years before the earthquake; Eumachia's building, a large structure built by High Priestess Eumachia for headquarters of the "fullones" corporation, a union of washers and dyers; the big theater, built during the Greek period and the smaller one nearby, built around 80–75 B.C.; the house of Menandro, an elegant home of the Imperial period; the house of Loreius Tiburtinus, another

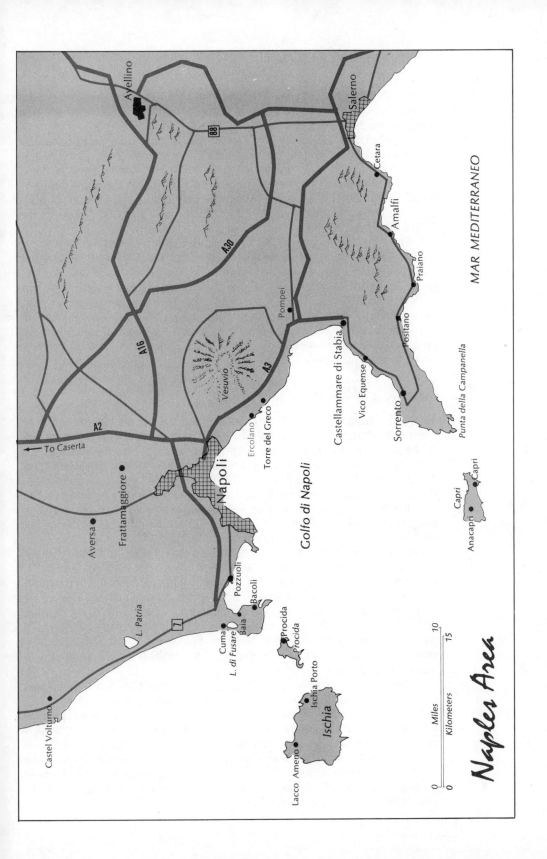

Naples Area

rich man's villa (the name itself tells he was a Roman: Tiburtinus is from the Tiber river); and the amphitheater of Pompei, built about 80 B.C., the oldest one known.

Another itinerary will take you to the Stabian Baths, the largest and best preserved baths in Pompei; the house of Vetti, with interesting *affreschi;* the house of the Golden Cupids; the house of the *fauno,* one of the nobler and larger private homes; and the *Villa dei Misteri,* probably the most important house in Pompei, for its structure and the decorations—it contains, among others, a mural by a local painter of the 1st century B.C. that represents the initiation of young wives into the Dionysian mysteries.

These two cities have made a great contribution toward our knowledge of the Roman world. Here, archaeology becomes a science, not merely conjecture. We even know what flowers the Pompeians preferred. We also know that this favorite piece of the Italian coast was considered a true paradise. The verses of Horace and Martial bear witness to this opinion. The most powerful men in Rome lived here at one time or another: Caesar, Pompei, Cicero and even mad emperor Caligula—in fact, the latter liked the area so well that he ordered a bridge of boats built from Baia to Pozzuoli in order to get to the area faster.

Itinerary 1: From Vietri to Sorrento

This fairly short trip is not only charming and lovely, enchanting you with constantly changing sights, but it also (at least in part) will take you on one of the most famous roads in the world. Start at *Vietri,* on the coast, a little beyond Salerno, and go north. Always coasting the sea, you pass *Maiori* and *Minori* and reach *Castiglione.* At this point turn inland for an interesting detour; climb 350 meters, and you'll arrive at *Ravello,* a quiet and beautiful little town that holds a Wagnerian festival in the villa Rufolo. This city flourished from the 11th to the 13th centuries due to commerce with Sicilia and the Orient, and its churches and palaces reflect this influence. Go back to the coast and head for *Amalfi,* the most ancient sea republic and with a past so glorious, that it rivals those of Pisa and Genova (Genoa). It was at its height of power during the 10th and 11th centuries, which is reflected in the architecture of the Duomo, which is along Arab–Norman lines. The city is squeezed into a narrow space, twixt mountains and sea, with its streets often covered, like corridors in a convent. The Duomo is particularly lovely, dominating the small central square from the top of a steep stairway. Note the small craft shops that are all over this city. The Amalfi-designed ceramics are especially attractive.

✱✱ Amalfi Cathedral

After Amalfi, and always following that magnificent road that will give you thrills and surprises at every turn, you'll reach ˏ*Positano,* famous as a resort that attracts tourists even in winter due to its mild climate and pleasant atmosphere. The houses are built on terraces of land—a cone-shaped hill of pure rock. The architecture is unusual, with roofs that resemble pavillions, sometimes with verandas. The whole picture seems somewhat oriental. Recently, some more modern concrete and cement houses have been built, damaging the beauty of the countryside. This is the price Italy pays for popularity and overpopulation.

From Positano you will quickly reach *Sorrento,* the last stop of this tour of the fabulous *Costa Amalfitana.* This is the most modern and well-equipped city of the small peninsula you've just seen. Like so many cities in the area, it was first a Greek colony, then a Roman resort—the favorite of emperors Augustus and Marcus Aurelius. Sorrento produces oranges and lemons and the best walnuts in Italy. From here you can take a boat to Capri, a 45-minute trip that few people miss. But that is another itinerary, which we will cover later in this section.

Itinerary 2: From Caserta to Teano

This itinerary is a short and interesting trip into the inland area of Campania that will take you from Caserta to Teano. The most important thing to see at Caserta is the Royal Palace, *la Reggia di Caserta,* and it's worth the trip. This grandiose building of 1200 rooms was built by Carlo di Borbone in order to rival the French court at Versailles. Architect Luigi Vanvitelli outdid himself, and the result is a neoclassical structure of imposing beauty. It can be visited weekdays from 9 A.M. to 2 P.M., by paying L.500; holidays from 9 A.M. to 1 P.M., for free. The building was finished in 1774, but because of its size the interior was completed almost a century later. It was the splendid residence of the last three kings of Napoli. Later, it housed Garibaldi when he returned from his Sicilian expedition and, finally, on April 29th, 1945, it saw the surrender of the German troops in Italy to the Allied Forces.

The gardens, the waterfalls, the lovely statues and the harmony of the whole delights every visitor. From Caserta, going across the *autostrada* in the direction of the sea, you will arrive at *S. Maria Capua Vetere,* that modern and industrial town that was once Roman and still has the ruins of a large amphitheater built in the 1st century and later restored by Hadrian and Antoninus. Again, cross the autostrada to reach *S. Angelo in Formis* in order to see one of the most important medieval *basilicas* in Campania. It dates back to 1073, at present it belongs to the monks of Montecassino and its frescoes are of the 11th, 12th and 13th centuries. Its position is also interesting, for it dominates the area from high above.

From S. Angelo, you may double back to Capua for a visit to its *Museo Campano* and its cathedral, which also goes back to the 11th century; it was rebuilt after World War II.

At this point in the itinerary you have several choices. A slightly longer ride will take you to *Sessa Aurunca*—which also has a Duomo done in Romantic lines—then up the sides of an errupted volcano to *Roccamonfina* to enjoy the view. Next, go down the hill to *Teano,* another center of old Roman life that has both old ruins and a 12th-century church. From here, you can take the autostrada either north toward Rome or south toward Napoli.

CAPRI

The famous island of Capri is one large trapezoid-shaped block of calcareous rock about 6 km. long and 2.75 km. at its widest point. Its natural beauties, pleasant climate, rich vegetation and short distance from Sorrento have made

*** Best view along Positano - Sorrento road is from Chapel of Sant'Angelo, near Positano

*** Caserta's Royal Palace was Allied HQ in World War II

** Amphitheater

*** Sant'Angelo basilica stands on an ancient Temple of Diana

** Museo Campano in Capua

* Ruins at Roccamonfina

it a favorite vacation spot for centuries. It can be reached by hydrofoil from Napoli (40 minutes) or Sorrento (20 minutes) or by ferryboat from Napoli, Amalfi, Positano and Marina del Cantone. Service which is always daily, is more frequent during the summer. A new helicopter service is also available from Napoli Capodichino to Anacapri.

The most famous single excursion is the *Grotta Azzurra* (Blue Grotto), which is best on sunny days when the light plays wonderful tricks on the walls and roof of the low cave and the water takes on strange-looking depths and shadings. The special little boats will be waiting to take you out from 9 A.M. to one hour before sunset; the trip itself is charming and can last from one to two hours, depending on whether you take a rowboat or motorboat. The fees vary, but the experience is always worth the expense, specially if done by people with romantic inclinations. But remember that the cave opening is 1 meter (little more than 3 feet), so you must enter in a prone position. Once inside, the grotta is over 45 meters (150 feet) long, about 27 meters (90 feet) high, 14 meters (45 feet) wide and the water is from 12 to 20 meters (42 to 66 feet) deep.

*** Blue Grotto's best time is between 11 am. and 1 p.m.

Another excursion circumnavigates the island. It takes about two hours, with boats leaving every morning at about 9:15 A.M. The views you'll see are fantastic, as well as beautiful. The passage between the *Faraglioni* is particularly exciting.

The Faraglioni are 3 stacks of rocks

The boats arrive at *Marina Grande.* From here, you can take the short bus ride to *Capri* and *Anacapri,* the two small cities with most of the island's hotels, restaurants and shops. While we cannot omit mentioning such well-known structures as the grand *Villa Imperiale Romana* of Anacapri, or the *Torre Damecuta* built during the 12th century as a watch point against pirates, or the *Certosa di S. Giacomo* and church of *S. Stefano of Capri* (an interesting Oriental-like baroque), it is our feeling that this is not a place for looking at ruins and other buildings but a place to relax and enjoy nature. Few places have been so blessed with beauty and charm, few places offer such a sense of luxury and elegance. When you come to Capri, come prepared to enjoy and relax, to wallow in the pleasures and comforts you'll find here, to leave schedules and pressures behind. It will be a lovely experience to remember.

ISCHIA

Ischia is the largest island in the Bay of Napoli and, unlike Capri, is of volcanic origin. *Monte Epomeo,* the highest peak on Ischia (788 meters), is an extinct volcano, and the many hot water springs scattered everywhere are reminders of the underlying endogenous activities.

Ischia can be reached from Napoli in one hour by motorboat or in one and one-half hours by ferry; or in one hour from Pozzuoli, with a short stop in *Procida.* There are several trips per day, especially during the summer. Hydrofoils go from Napoli Mergellina to Porto Ischia in 40 minutes, with several runs everyday in summer. A daily boat to Capri is also available in the summer, and a new helicopter run has been established from *Napoli Stazione Marittima* to Casamicciola and Lacco Ameno.

Ischia is not only beautiful, it's a very well-established health resort. Its radioactive waters cure innumerable ills, including arthritis, rheumatism, gynecological problems, skin problems and circulatory diseases.

The island has become extremely popular in the last 25 years and now offers some of the best hotel accommodations in this part of Italy. The lovely scenery, the good wine made from grapes grown on the slopes of M. Epomeo, and the infinite therapeutic virtues of the many hot water springs are enjoyed by a growing number of visitors.

Again, unlike Capri, Ischia is made up of several small towns, each with a somewhat different character. The most important center on the island is Ischia, which subdivides into *Ischia Porto* and *Ischia Ponte.* The port is also an elegant resort, with several good hotels and all the other things that make up a resort town. Ischia Ponte, a charming fishing village, is connected by *Ponte Aragonese* to a little island where an old 15th-century castle can be seen.

Ischia's hot springs are quite radioactive

The next two cities, *Casamicciola Terme* and *Lacco Ameno,* both on the northern shore of the island, are the most fashionable resorts there. The most luxurious hotel on the island is in Lacco Ameno; it's open from March to October. Here the temperature of the water is quite high and the cure is the most intense.

Other centers are *Forio, Barano d'Ischia* and *Sant'Angelo,* all at the extreme southern tip. They each have hot water springs; the Sant'Angelo ones are close to boiling. Anyone wishing to come to Ischia for a series of baths should consult a doctor who is familiar with the island's waters.

If you're interested in sightseeing, do not overlook the *Fungo,* an unusual rock that juts out of the water near Lacco Ameno. Not far from here is the lovely *Lido di S. Montano,* and on the main square is the *Santuario di S. Restituta,* which is made up of two churches: one a 19th-century building, the other an 11th-century one. After admiring the castle at Ischia Ponte, you can admire the view from *Belvedere di Cartaromana.*

But the most interesting part of this trip is simply a boat or helicopter voyage around the island. Note the southern shore, where at one point there is a stretch of lava from the 1301–1302 eruption.

LA PUGLIA

Set on the heel of the Italian boot, La Puglia region is not very familiar to most tourists. The reason for this oversight is simple. Puglia is toward southeastern Europe, and most tourists who come to Italy land in Roma and go north or to Napoli and Sicilia. The few that do head toward La Puglia do so with the intention of taking the short boat ride from Bari to Greece and miss the mystery of this enchanting land. But this is one region of Italy that should not be overlooked. It's full of interesting art, has had a fascinating history, has natural beauties that are unique, and has food and wine that are most characteristic of the region.

Known as Apulia in English

The large territory of Puglia goes from the Adriatic Sea to the Ionian Sea, and much of it is a fertile plain. This accounts for the region's intense agriculture. It is the greatest producer of oil and wine in Italy, as well as an important producer of cereals—including durum wheat—tobacco and vegetables.

There is little cattle raised due to the lack of grazing land, but there is much fishing.

Industry is also finding its way to this area, and some of its larger cities, such as Bari, Brindisi and Taranto, are busy ports.

The *Gargano,* the promontory that is the spur on the boot, rises more than 1,000 meters above sea level at some points and has some of Italy's most untouched, natural landscapes. At the very tip of the protuberance is the city of *Vieste,* which boasts lovely white cliffs and a castle built by the original Swabian monarch, Frederico II.

The importance of contacts with the Middle East is deeply felt here. *Bari,* the capital of the region, holds a yearly fair, called *Fiera del Levante,* in an attempt to become a connecting bridge between East and West. The products of many Mediterranean and Asiatic countries are shown here, and business-people from all Europe come to admire and buy.

Some History

Recent archaeological finds tell us that Puglia was visited by ships from the Orient as far back as the 4th century B.C. and that the pioneers on these ships, along with the natives, developed a high level of civilization. This takes Italian history into a period that has usually been the domain of Egypt, Babylon and the land of Canaan—an exciting prospect for all those interested in the peninsula. It also means that Puglia was probably one of the first civilized areas of Europe.

The traditional history books tell us that the first ones to colonize this region were the Greeks, around the 8th century B.C. They were followed by the Romans, who incorporated the area into the Second Region when Augustus made his well known division of the empire. A period of prosperity followed, but it receded as the empire deteriorated. At this point the fertile plain was open to all invaders, and Byzantines, Longobards, Franks and even Saracen pirates attacked with various degrees of success.

The Byzantines were the ones that held Puglia, and their domination during the 9th century A.D., brought about a depressed period. But the contacts with Eastern ports during the Crusades and with the flourishing sea–state of Amalfi brought about an improvement, and the economic life of the region was better by the 11th century and even more developed when the Norman dynasty settled in.

Puglia's golden age in art, trade and agriculture was during the Swabian domination, reaching its peak under Frederico II (1220–1250). After his downfall and the advent of the Anjous and the Aragonese, the region went into another decline. Not only was the central power uninterested in the area, but frequent bouts with pestilence and the threat of Turkish pirates did much damage to the population, which either died or emigrated.

The rest is modern history, which includes further attempts on the part of the local population and the central government to raise the standard of living in the area and bring the modern world to this ancient land.

Some Thoughts on Art

Few Italian regions contain prehistoric monuments, and the Puglia is one of them. Ancient tombs, called *dolmen* and *menhir* are present in several places; the more interesting ones are in *Biscaglie,* near the town of Chianca, and at Giundignano, province of Lecce.

Remnants of the Greek colonization can be found in the museums in the main cities of Foggia, Bari, Lecce and Taranto, as well as in some minor museums in the region.

An important archaeological zone in Barletta, province of Bari, reminds us of the battle of Canne, fought between the Romans and the Carthaginians in 216 B.C. and won by Hannibal. The huge battle engaged more than 50,000 men, and calcified bones are scattered over a large area.

Interesting Roman monuments, such as the amphitheaters in Lecce and Lucera and the columns of Brindisi, can be seen in several places. The columns, which are different from one another, are on top of a series of steps near the port, and they are said to symbolize the end of the Appian Way. One is Byzantine; the other, from a somewhat later period, unfortunately fell in 1528 and now there is only a base.

Since art is so closely connected with history, it is no surprise that the splendid period of art in Puglia begins with the 11th century and continues until the 13th. Great Romanesque cathedrals, some of the best medieval architecture in Italy, were built then. Some show a decidedly Western influence, such as the two most important churches in Bari, the *Cathedral* and the *Basilica di S. Nicola.* The same can be said for the cathedrals of *Trani,* *Barletta* and others. Others were more influenced by Eastern design, such as the cathedrals of *Troia* and *Foggia* and the churches of *S. Maria* and *S. Leonardo at Manfredonia,* the latter 10 km. out of the city in the direction of Foggia. The sculptures within these churches are all of mixed influences: Byzantine, classical, Arabic.

Much of the castles built in the medieval style are a result of the Crusades, influenced by knights who came from the North, mainly France, and returned, after they had been exposed to Eastern concepts.

After the 14th century the region lost its autonomous character, for its sea commerce passed to the Venetians. The Renaissance did not reach this land, except for an occasional painting imported from Venezia (Venice).

After several centuries of inertia, the city of Lecce brought forth a vigorous style, known as *barocco Leccese.* Its decorative exuberance combined elegance and harmony of line so well that connosseurs from everywhere are attracted here, intent on admiring the charming baroque style. Later art has been influenced by Napoli, with serious attempts at inserting local themes.

The five provinces of Puglia are Bari, Foggia, Brindisi, Lecce and Taranto.

Itinerary 1: Gargano

The most interesting weekend trip in this area is a tour of the *Gargano,* with much to admire and enjoy. You will discover an Italy so different from the rest it will surprise you.

Start out from Foggia, the most modern city of Puglia, at the center of the *Tavoliere,* the vast plain that produces much of the region's agricultural goods. A good road takes you toward the sea, with a first stop at *Manfredonia,* the city named for Manfredi the last of the Swabian kings and natural son of Frederico II who was encountered by Dante in purgatory. Do not miss the Romanesque churches of *S. Leonardo and S. Maria di Siponto;* the latter is 3 km. before town, on the road from Foggia. Its flat roof and small cupola show the Oriental influence. At Manfredonia note the *castle* at the port. From here take the road that follows the coast for the most interesting scenic ride. Go past the small town of *Mattinata,* the more modern center of *Pugnochiuso,* on toward *Vieste.* This portion of road is one of the most varied, exciting and scenic in all Italy, and the little village with its narrow streets and steps will enchant you. Its history is full of accidents and incidents, for it was often a prey of Turkish pirates, and in 1646 an earthquake practically destroyed it. If time allows, visit the *Grotta Campana,* a marine cavity that has unusual light effects during the early morning hours, when the sun is shining, of course.

(margin note: ✷✷ Coast road to Vieste)

As you leave Vieste you'll be pointing west—you can't help it since this is the farthest east you can go in Italy. There is more scenic beauty as you ride through Manacore, Peschici and Rodi Garganico. From Rodi Garganico, if you have the time, you can visit the *Isole Tremiti,* a group of four small islands and some rocks 12 km. from the shore. Proceed inland from Rodi, through the *Foresta Umbra,* until you reach *Monte Sant'Angelo.* The little town itself is worth seeing, as well as an interesting sanctuary built for Gabriel, the Archangel. Legend has it that he appeared to the Bishop of Manfredonia in the year A.D. 490 and left a footprint to indicate that this was his residence. The apparition came again in 491 and again in 493, and when a spring of miraculous water gushed forth, the location gained fame. The bronze doors of the sanctuary were made in 1076 in Constantinople, and tradition says you must knock on them with the heavy ring handles in order to be heard by the divinity.

(margin note: ✷✷ Monte Sant'Angelo)

Continuing on the road back to Foggia, you will pass *S. Giovanni Rotondo.* Visiting here is the goal of many latter-day pilgrim's, since it was the residence of *Padre Pio,* a priest (he died only a few years ago) who had the *stigmata* and performed many miraculous cures.

Then on to *S. Marco* in Lamis, *Rignano Garganico* and finally *Lucera.* This little city was built by the same Frederico II who is reponsible for so many of the great monuments of this region. The castle is one of his better known structures; the (early 14th-century) Gothic cathedral is a result of the Anjou domination. Note the Roman amphitheater and the *Museo Civico,* with its unusually good collection of old coins.

(margin note: ✷ Castle and Cathedral)

On the road back to Foggia, you can visit a small town, *Troia.* It has one of the best examples of Puglia Romanesque architecture: the cathedral. Nearby is a charming pre-Romanesque church, *S. Basilio.* Then from here you can return to Foggia, and the tour of the Gargano is completed.

(margin note: ✷✷ Troia Cathedral)

Itinerary 2: Bari

The second itinerary is primarily a visit to Bari, capital of the Puglia, Italy's doorway to the Orient. At the end, for those with more time, there are two other excursions, one going north and the other south.

The ideal time for a visit here is October, not only because of the mild climate, but because during that month the *Fiera del Levante* takes place. It's one of the largest annual fairs held in Europe; it's the largest one in southern Italy; and its purpose is to encourage exchange between east and west.

The most interesting part of the city is the *Citta Vecchia,* the old city that retains the imprint of its Byzantine origins. During the 11th and 12th centuries this was the main meeting and departure point for the Crusaders on their way to the Holy Land. As a natural consequence, many monuments were built here, such as the *Basilica of S. Nicola* and the cathedral. There is a *Castle,* which antedates Frederico II, who later (between 1233 and 1240) ordered changes made on it. It was "modernized" in the 16th century in order to receive Isabella of Aragon and her daughter Bona. The cathedral, S. Nicola and the castle are all within walking distance from each other.

The Cathedral. The cathedral was built during the first half of the 11th century and was reconstructed at the end of the 12th, after the city had been destroyed by Guglielmo il Malo (William, the Bad) in 1156. It's considered one of the most majestic structures in the Romanesque–Pugliese style, its exterior simple with three 11th-century portals and its interior remarkable for its harmony and solemnity. Much was retouched in the 18th century, but there are still traces of 13th-century frescoes.

S. Nicola. S. Nicola was built between 1087 and 1197 to safeguard the body of the saint. It was brought back from Mira in Turkey, by 62 sailors. The church is a prototype of Romanesque–Pugliese style, its simple, imposing front flanked by two short bell towers. The central portal is ornate; the left one is called *la porta dei Leoni.* Note the asymmetrical details of the middle nave; they were added in the 15th century. Don't miss a visit to the treasures (Tuesdays, Fridays and Saturdays, 10–12 A.M.)

The Castle. The third important Bari monument is *the Castle.*
The *Museo Archeologico* has the most complete collection of local material, especially on the *apula* civilization, with pieces dating from the 7th to the 3rd centuries B.C.
On the other side of the port, the *Fiera del Levante* area can be visited. In order to reach it you must pass a very different Bari, one that is modern and spacious.
At this point, if you wish to head south for Brindisi, you will see the best known Pugliese sights—the *trulli.* While these circular one-room dwellings made of stone are not unique to this region, their largest concentration is here.

Southern Detour

You can leave Bari by the road that follows the coast and continue south through *Mola de Bari* to *Polignano a Mare.* Here begins the detour that goes to *Alberobello,* and on the way you will pass *Grotte di Castellana.* These subterranean caves were discovered by accident, and they are some of the most interesting spectacles nature has provided for us. Guides and other technical help are provided if you wish to visit this fascinating underground world. We advise you to allow several hours for the trip because the shorter hike is 1 km. and the longer is 3 km., with much stopping on the way.
If your main interest is Alberobello, proceed onward, and the dazzling white trulli with their dark conical roofs will soon start appearing even before you reach the town.
But do not stop at the spectacle of these ancient dwellings. We suggest you continue driving inland for just a bit longer through the *valle d'Itria,* past

** Cathedral

*** Church of San Nicola

* Castle

*** Europe's best stalactite caves

Locorotondo, to *Martina Franca,* a characteristic little town with interesting buildings in baroque and even rococo (one of the rare examples of this style in Italy) styles.

After this detour within the detour, back to the coastal road and south to *Brindisi.* This is where the two columns that mark the end of *Via Appia* can be seen, and it's also where ships for Greece and points east can be taken. If you would like to see another Swabian castle, the one in Brindisi is picturesque. The *Piazza del Duomo* is also interesting; the cathedral itself was built in the 12th century and redone in the 18th.

Here the southern detour ends, but two important points must be made. First, the trulli of Alberobello are not as old as they seem; most of them were built during the Middle Ages. There were tax privileges and other advantages given if a citizen did his home in that style, which accounts for the large number of trulli in the area. Some may be older, but dwellings of this type are so ancient that it is unlikely any of the ones found here belong to the era when trulli were the only type of houses built.

Second, S. Nicola di Bari, whose bones lie in the basilica of the same name, is the saint whose feast is on December 6th, in other words, Santa Claus. He lived during the 4th century, was Bishop of Myra in Licia (now Turkey) and was known for his love of children. His most noted miracle is connected with a murdered boy. The kind bishop brought him back to life and was canonized as a result of the miracle.

Northern Detour

If you had decided to go north from Bari, again always hugging the sea coast, a different world would have met your eyes. Here is a florid area of the Puglia, with prosperous little towns and well-known art centers strung out along the coast. At *Molfetta* note the *Duomo Vecchio,* the old cathedral near the port, and then admire the newer one, done in baroque. Then onward to *Bisceglie,* with its medieval center, the remnants of a castle and some lovely old churches. Take a short drive inland where you can admire large, old dolmen. A few kilometers away you'll find *Trani,* with an old Benedictine abbey and a cathedral that is one of the gems of Romanesque–Pugliese style. The old center near the port is worthy of a visit. The next little town is *Barletta,* with the Gothic church of S. Sepolcro at its center and next to it the *colosso,* a gigantic bronze statue more than 5 meters, (15 feet) in height. It was originally from Constantinople, dates back to the 4th century and is thought to represent an emperor, perhaps Valentiniano I. This city was the scene of a singular episode, the *Disfida di Barletta,* when 13 Italian champions challenged an equal number of Frenchmen and won the day—February 13, 1503. The *Piazza della Sfida* is now a peaceful square in the heart of town, not far from the cathedral and castle.

The last stage of this itinerary takes you inland for a visit to the archaeological site of Canne and the *Museo della Battaglia.* From here you can go to *Canosa,* which has a Cathedral endowed with lovely Romanesque statues and a single medieval tomb, that of Boemondo. At this point we suggest you return to Bari. If you do so by following the inland road the landscape will be different from the one just passed. The *Murge* is semidesert country, with some scattered vines and olive trees, thinly planted wood trees and some

(handwritten margin notes)

The Castello Svevo is not open to the public

*** Trani Cathedral

** Bronze Statue of Barletta

* Cathedral and Castle

** Canosa Cathedral

white calcarean rocks. Admire the large *Castel del Monte,* built by Federico II between 1240 and 1250, one of the purest Gothic structures in Italy. It has an unusual octagonal shape, with eight towers that are also octagonal at the corners. The castle, which is on a hill, dominates an extensive panorama. Finally, go to Bari, passing *Bitonto,* which also has one of the loveliest Romanesque cathedrals in this region.

*** Castel del Monte

** Bitonto Cathedral

Itinerary 3: Coast of Salentine Peninsula

The last itinerary we suggest in this area is along the coast of the Salentine Peninsula, the heel of the Italian boot. Here the Mediterranean light will blind you, the fluid sea and colorful vegetation will enchant you, the little seaside resorts will amuse you. It's a fairly long drive from Lecce—where there are unique baroque churches—to Taranto—an old Greek port and a modern NATO base.

The city of *Lecce* is the most important city on the heel, and as you arrive you'll note the difference in pace from the rest of Italy, and even from the rest of the south. Here life moves slowly; the speed reflects Lecce's Byzantine heritage. But the most singular thing about this town is the presence, almost everywhere, of a unique artistic expression, the *barocco leccese.* Both religious and secular buildings are adorned with sculptures made from the soft local stone, depicting the most varied subjects, sometimes exuberant, sometimes more controlled, always original. Twisting columns, flowered window frames, building fronts covered with curves, curls and curlicues, vases of fruit and ribbons covered with masks, *putti* and *cariatidi* are all bursting with inexhaustible imagination and fantasy.

Cupids and caryatids just go together here!

Lecce, an old Roman town, was a Byzantine stronghold, but its artistic achievements were accomplished between the end of the 16th and the 18th centuries. Enjoy a walk through this city, once called the Firenze of the Puglia because of its many cultural activities and its famous academies of the 15th century.

* Roman amphitheater

The most important places to visit here are the Roman amphitheater in *Piazza S. Oronzo* and the *Basilica di S. Croce,* built between 1548 and 1646, which is an extraordinary symbol of Lecce baroque, with the *Palazzo del Governo* almost annexed to it, and behind that the public gardens. Also interesting, is the little church of *S. Nicolo e Cataldo.*

** Basilica

*** Santi Nicolò e Cataldo

Once you leave Lecce—albeit unwillingly—head east once more, toward the shore and the little town of *San Cataldo.* Continue down the coast (you are now on the Otranto Strait), where on a good day the white hills of Albania can be seen. The next interesting stop is *S. Cesarea Terme,* a small spa; but the main attraction is the whole coast, with its ins and outs, its sands and rocks, its vegetation and light.

At this point you will reach the extreme south of Italy, *S. Maria di Leuca,* with a lighthouse that illuminates the nights for sailors and travelers and marks the southern tip of Italy. According to tradition, the city was built on a site that had been dedicated to the pagan goddess Minerva.

A Note for Spelunkers

For those who are interested in visiting caves, the whole area between Otranto and S. Maria di Leuca is filled with *grotte,* mostly of the marine variety but all very worthwhile and some quite unique. Note the complex of neolithic caves found recently at Porto Badisco, about 10 km. south of Otranto, and the Grotta Zinzulusa, between S. Cesarea Terme and Castro, and the most remarkable marine *grotta,* both for its paleolithic and neolithic items, as well as for its minute crustacean inhabitants.

Now, continue your voyage on the road bearing north to the instep of the boot. A very short detour inland brings you to *Patu,* which has an interesting megalithic structure, the *Centopietre.* Then back to the coast, at this point a bit flat and monotonous, until you reach the promontory of Gallipoli, with its Island of *S. Andrea.* Here you've entered the Gulf of Taranto, and the sea is changed. The little town of Gallipoli has a medieval section, with a remarkable castle and an interesting Greco–Roman fountain. From Gallipoli to Taranto you can either take the road along the coast or you can make a small inland turn to Manduria for a visit to the 16th century cathedral, the *Palazzo Imperiali,* a baroque building set on a triangular *piazza,* and the old walls.

Finally, you will reach Taranto, one of the busier southern ports, a city placed in an enviable location with a 19th- and- 20th-century appearance. What is left of the older city—one of the important towns of Magna Grecia —can be found in the *Museo Nazionale,* which has a good classical section. Visit the *Citta Vecchia,* set on a little island and, in particular, the *Duomo,* originally built in the 10th century but with a baroque façade dated 1713 and an interesting cupola that tells of the Byzantine influence. If you have time, visit the *Castle* with its rotating bridge, the *church of S. Domenico Maggiore* and the *Villa Peripato,* with its lovely public gardens. For a more modern Taranto, the walk along *Lungomare Vittorio Emanuele III* is very attractive.

Before you finish our visit to the heel of Italy, please note that Taranto hosts an annual International Conference for Magna Grecia Studies and a biannual Conference for Wood and Metal Carving.

SICILY

The drama of Sicily is ageless. From its role as the center of Mediterranean culture in a time when the Mediterranean basin was the entire Western world, to 1860 when Garibaldi began his drive to create a unified Italy by landing in Sicily, this rugged island has experienced countless tragedies and a few triumphs.

A visit to Sicily with a sense of history reminds you of the forces that shaped the island through its people, its architecture, and its customs. You'll see plenty of blond-haired, blue-eyed children—a legacy from the Norman period (11th century on). There are churches made from abandoned mosques that reflect an Islamic influence (9th–11th century). Greek ruins (7th–3rd centuries, B.C.), among the best in the world, remind us that once Plato lived and taught here. Gothic churches evoke the spanish period (thirteenth to nineteenth centuries), and Germanic facades the era of the German princes (12th century). If North America is now the melting pot of the world, Sicily was its predecessor in ancient times.

Today, the theater of Sicilian life continues to play itself out in assassination, blackmail and kidnapings. We should hasten to add that foreigners are rarely involved in any of these incidents, if ever. Under a determined, but

** National museum

** Cathedral

ineffective central government, the real life of Sicily continues today to be regimented by the murderous etiquette of the *Mafia,* bound and determined to keep Sicily "for the Sicilians."

For visitors to Italy with limited time, we would suggest that Sicily be third in your order of priorities, after central Italy (of Florentine fame) and northern Italy (Where Venice rules). But Sicily should come before southern Italy in your planning, because it encompasses so much in such a small space.

Palermo could be a first stop, reachable not only by plane from Rome but by ferry from Naples, or overland from Messina where the ferry from the mainland will leave you.

The highlight of a Palermo visit is the view of the town itself, stretched along the bay in golden majesty, as colorful and alive as any Mediterranean city of comparable size. Capital of the island and headquarters of its commerce and culture, one is sure to find Palermo a place of warmth and laughter in an otherwise dull European winter. (But even here, we can't guarantee sunshine in winter.)

Tops on your sightseeing list here is the *Palazzo di Normanni,* built originally by the Arabs, modified by the Normans, then transformed explosively by the Germans into a truly royal dwelling. The Palatine Chapel here is a bold montage of Byzantine, Norman and Islamic mosaics, all color and light. In a brilliant room upstairs, where more mosaics dominate, the Sicilian Parliament meets.

*** Palazzo di Normani

Adjacent to the charming *Piazza Bellini,* named for the composer, La Martorana Church and San Cataldo are both well worth a visit. *La Martorana,* like the Palatine Chapel is a perfect example of the architectural style called Arab-Norman. Next door is *San Cataldo,* another hybrid, with more curious domes.

** La Martorana

The *Cathedral of Palermo* was first a church, then a mosque, then a cathedral, again, its long history attesting to the blend of cultures which gives Sicily its exotic air.

** Cathedral

San Giovanni degli Eremiti is a prime example of Arab-Norman artistry, its pink towers and peaceful cloisters combining to form a perfectly harmonious picture, born nonetheless from incongruity.

** San Giovanni

Lovers of the grotesque may wish to visit the Capuchin Catacombs, at the edge of town. There are more than 1,000 mummies here, mostly from centuries past; though burials were permitted here until just over 60 years ago.

* Catacombs

Farther from town, but well worth the trip, is the *Cathedral of Monreale,* perhaps the best medieval cathedral in all Italy. Here, lovers of mosaics will find sheer delight. Almost every inch of the church's interior is covered with pictures of biblical scenes, all in strong colors despite the years. The events of the life of Christ are recorded here, as in the Sistine Chapel, but in perhaps a more permanent medium.

**** Monreale Cathedral

Beachlovers will like *Mondello* beach, one of Sicily's finest, also at the edge of Palermo. Not far from town (20 miles) is the *Villa Palagonia,* which boasts a garden full of grotesque statues. We would recommend this only if you've spent two weeks in Sicily seeing all the worthwhile sights first.

Your most important destination in Sicily should be Agrigento, with its spectacular Valley of the Temples—among the best examples of ancient Greek architecture to be found anywhere. Strewn like dragon's teeth along

**** Agrigento

the slopes of a valley below the new town of the same name, Agrigento's temples are especially beautiful in the spring, when pink and white almond trees blossom and give the scene a heavenly air.

Foremost among the temples is that of Concord, perhaps the best-preserved Greek temple anywhere outside Athens. Its 28 columns stand in golden splendor as a monument to the temple's 5th century B.C. builders. Historians credit the temple's good state of preservation to its conversion into a Christian church centuries ago. Thus it was spared the cunning hands of looters and zealots down through the ages. Other temples of note are those dedicated to Demeter (sometimes thought to be dedicated to Castor and Pollux), to Juno, to Hercules and Jupiter.

In Syracuse, you should visit the cathedral built on the site of a temple to Minerva. Then tour both the Greek theater and the Roman amphitheater. Imagine yourself watching a play in the former with Plato, who lived and taught here. While you amble in the narrow streets give a thought to Archimedes who lived and died here, killed by invading Roman soldiers.

If you have time, visit these other cities of Sicily and enjoy their highlights:

Cefalù boasts a fine Norman cathedral (12th century) with a glorious Christ mosaic behind the altar.

Enna, high in the mountains, was a seat of Frederick II. It offers glorious views over the island from Frederick's ruined castle.

Erice is a real find, a small village where nothing ever happens, where nothing ever did happen, and we hope, nothing ever will happen. If you like tiny towns, all whitewashed and flower-strewn, you'll love Erice.

Marsala is not only home to the sweet dessert wine to which it gave its name, but is celebrated in Italian history because it was here that Garibaldi landed in 1860 to begin his campaign that united Italy under one flag.

Segetsa, about 40 miles southwest of Palermo, is noted for its fine Greek temple and its theater (5th and 3rd centuries B.C. respectively).

Selinunte, halfway between Palermo and Agrigento, known for its Temple of Apollo. With the other temples here, this place has one of the largest collections of Greek temples outside Greece.

Trapani is known best for its craftsman, who turn coral into beautiful works of art.

The best town in which to base your Sicilian adventure is Taormina, known primarily as a resort. Here you will find the island's best hotels and restaurants, and even a fabulous ancient Greek theater, that was later converted by the Romans.

Offshore lie the Lipari Islands, including famous Stromboli. Lipari Island, the largest of the group, is a fantastic place for water sports, including scuba diving, because this is one of the least polluted spots in all the Mediterranean.

SARDINIA

Recommended only for those wanting to get away from anything remotely resembling civilization, Sardinia nearly misses being part of Italy. The ambience is Arab, the mood medieval, the people suspicious and inhospitable. If you must see this island, you should be prepared to come either as a hedonist or an adventurer.

** Syracuse Cathedral and Greek theater

** Cefalù Cathedral

*** View from castle

*** Erice is just outside of Trapani

** Segesta temple

*** Selinunte ruins

** Greek theater

Hedonists will make their base at the Aga Khan's *Costa Smeralda,* a watering hole devised for Europe's smart set, but now peopled by gentle representatives of the middle class on the make, continental style. Along the 50-mile stretch that constitutes the Emerald Coast, you can bathe in the blue-green, crystal clear water, ogle occasional minor royalty and the ever-present yachts of millionaires, and dine very well. This is an international playground, where North Americans are scarce (as are the British), so it helps to speak French, Italian or German.

Adventurers will want to avoid the Costa Smeralda, and take to the hills of Sardinia, replete with legend, a few bandits (still), and dusty villages sleeping in the diffused sunlight of late afternoon. In addition to the one or two historic sites of the island, mentioned below, there are gorgeous, nearly deserted beaches everywhere, even near the main cities (those near Alghero are especially attractive.)

Never completely colonized (even by modern Italy), Sardinia has seen invaders come and go, from Phoenicians to Vandals, Carthaginians to English, but it was the Arab influence that seems to have stuck most profoundly to the Sard people. From dress to temperament, the Sardinians exude a nearly Islamic air, fatalism and a secondary role for womenfolk sitting heavily on the Roman Catholic formal religion.

In Cagliari, the capital, you should climb up to the fortress for a splendid view of the city and harbor. Among sightseeing highlights are two towers, the Torrione de San Pancrazio, and the Torre dell'Elefante, both built when Pisa occupied the island. The museum specializes in Sardinian antiquities, of course, with a few objects from the unknown Nuraghic civilization. See also the 15th-century cathedral and the Roman amphitheater.

Sassari, the island's second city, is of little interest, but between it and Cagliari, in the center of the island's mountain range, lies La Barbagia, land of the barbarians. This is the area where the *Maquis* (wild undergrowth) hides bandits, kidnapers and crazed men pursuing private vendettas. It is no coincidence that the French resistance fighters in World War II referred to their secret army as the *Maquis* and themselves as *maquisards.* You can travel safely here by day, but we don't advise stopping to chat with the townspeople about anything other than breakfast, lunch or dinner, or possibly a few liters of gasoline for your car.

The sections on Sardinia and Sicily, above, were contributed by the editor.

Hotels

AGRIGENTO, Sicilia (Sicily)

Capital of the province, this old city on the southern coast of Sicilia overlooks the Valley of the Temples and the sea. An important tourist center because of its archaeological material. Approximate population: 50,000.

★★   VILLA ATHENA
Valle dei Templi, tel. 23833, 31 rooms with bath, garden. Moderately expensive.

Pool

★   HOTEL JOLLY
Piazza Roma 1, tel. 29190, 52 rooms, 40 with bath. Moderate.

★   HOTEL DELLA VALLE
Via dei Templi, tel. 26966, 88 rooms with bath. Moderate.

★   HOTEL AKRAGAS
Strada di S. Leone, tel. 44082, 15 rooms, 11 with bath. Inexpensive.

ALBEROBELLO (BA), Puglia

★   HOTEL ASTORIA
Exit for Putignano, tel. 721190, 47 rooms with bath. Moderate.

Cottages shaped like trulli

★   CUCINA DEI TRULLI
Piazza Ferdinando IV, tel. 721179, 12 rooms, 8 with bath. Moderate.

ALGHERO (SS), Sardegna (Sardinia)

Located on a promontory of the western coast, this attractive city was a Spanish colony in the 14th century and now is a popular beach resort. There is a small tourist port, a sailing school and a water-skiing school. Approximate population: 32,000.

★★   VILLA LAS TRONAS
Lungomare Valencia, tel. 975390, 31 rooms with bath, swimming pool, on the sea. Moderately expensive.

a renovated mansion

★★   CALABONA HOTEL
On the way to Bona, tel. 975728, 113 rooms with bath, swimming pool, beach. Moderately expensive.

★★   SOLEMAR E 4 MORI HOTEL
Lungomare Valencia, tel. 976696, 110 rooms with bath, swimming pool, tennis. Moderately expensive.

276

★ HOTEL RIVIERA
Seasonal, traversa via Lido, tel. 979784, 42 rooms with bath, swimming pool.
Moderate.

★ HOTEL CONTINENTAL
Seasonal, via Kennedy 66, tel. 975250, 32 rooms with bath. Moderate.

At Porto Conte, about 21 km.

★★★ HOTEL EL FARO
Tel. 94009, 92 rooms with bath, beach, swimming pool, nice location. Moderately expensive.

AMALFI (SA), Campania

★★★ HOTEL S. CATERINA
On the road to Positano, tel. 871012, 53 rooms with bath, swimming pool, terraces, elevator to the beach, view. Moderately expensive.

★★★ HOTEL CAPPUCCINI-CONVENTO
On the road to Positano, tel. 871008, 49 rooms, 31 with bath, located in an old, 13th-century convent, garden, lovely view. Moderately expensive.

Hotel has own bus

★★ HOTEL MIRAMALFI
On the road to Positano, tel. 871427, 44 rooms, most with bath, swimming pool, view, elevator to the beach. Moderately expensive.

★ HOTEL LA BUSSOLA
Lungomare dei Cavalieri 14, near the port, tel. 871131, 52 rooms, most with bath. Moderate.

BARI, Puglia

★★★ HOTEL PALACE
Via Lombardi 13, tel. 216551, 153 rooms with bath. Moderately expensive.

Good location

★★ HOTEL JOLLY
Via G.Petroni 15, tel. 364366, 164 rooms with bath. Moderately expensive.

Near rail station

★★ HOTEL LEON D'ORO
Piazza Roma 4, tel. 235040, 116 rooms with bath. Moderate.

★ HOTEL MODERNO
Via Crisanzio 60, tel. 213313, 51 rooms, 21 with bath. Moderate.

BRINDISI, Puglia

★★   HOTEL INTERNAZIONALE
Viale Regina Margherita 26, on the harbor, tel. 23905, 87 rooms with bath. Moderately expensive.

★★   HOTEL JOLLY
Corso Umberto I 151, tel. 22809, 77 rooms, 58 with bath. Moderately expensive.

★   HOTEL MEDITERRANEO
Viale Liguria 70, tel. 82811, 69 rooms with bath. Moderate.

CAGLIARI, Sardegna

Capital of the island, this modern city is Sardegna's most important port. Located at the southern end of this large island, Cagliari is one of the warmest cities in Italy since it gets many of its breezes straight from the Sahara. Approximate population: 220,000.

★★   HOTEL MEDITERRANEO
Lungomare Colombo 46, a little distance from the center of town, tel. 301271, 140 rooms with bath, quiet location. Moderately expensive.

[handwritten: ask for room with balcony]

★★   JOLLY REGINA MARGHERITA HOTEL
Viale Regina Margherita 44, central location, tel. 651971, 130 rooms, most with bath, swimming pool. Moderately expensive.

★   HOTEL ENALC
Piazza Giovanni XXIII, on the edge of town, tel. 46671, 57 rooms with bath. Moderately expensive.

CAPRI (NA), Campania

★★★★★   QUISISANA E GRAND HOTEL
Via Camerelle 2, Capri, tel. 8370788, 130 rooms with bath, park, swimming pool, tennis, view. Expensive.

★★★   HOTEL LA PALMA
Via Vittorio Emanuele 39, Capri, tel. 8370133, 80 rooms with bath, roof garden. Moderately expensive.

★★★   EUROPA PALACE HOTEL
Via Capodimonte, Anacapri, tel. 8370955, 85 rooms with bath, swimming pool, tennis. Moderately expensive.

★★★   TIBERIO PALACE HOTEL
Via Croce 13, Capri, tel. 8370380, 95 rooms with bath, terraces, view. Moderately expensive.

★★   HOTEL GATTO BIANCO
Via Vittorio Emanuele 32, Capri, tel. 8370446, 42 rooms with bath. Moderately expensive.

Quiet, yet central (handwritten)

★★   HOTEL S. MICHELE DI ANACAPRI
On the road to Capri, tel. 8371427, 37 rooms with bath, lovely location. Moderately expensive.

CASERTA, Campania

★★   HOTEL JOLLY
Viale Vittorio Veneto 9, tel. 25222, 92 rooms with bath. Moderately expensive.

★   HOTEL EUROPA
Via Roma 29, tel. 25400, 64 rooms with bath. Moderate.

Near palace (handwritten)

CATANIA, Sicilia

Capital of the province, this characteristically baroque city on the eastern coast of Sicilia is located in a fertile plain at the foothills of Etna. It is an important commercial and industrial center and has an active port. It was founded by the Greeks in the 8th century B.C. and came under Roman rule. in 263 B.C. In 1693 it was destroyed by an earthquake and had to be completely rebuilt. Approximate population: 400,000.

★★★   HOTEL EXCELSIOR
Piazza Verga, tel. 224706, 151 rooms with bath. Expensive.

★★   HOTEL CENTRAL PALACE
Via Etnea 218, tel. 224880, 104 rooms with bath. Moderately expensive.

Good location (handwritten)

★★   HOTEL JOLLY TRINACRIA
Piazza Trento 13, tel. 228960, 159 rooms with bath. Moderately expensive.

COSENZA, Calabria

Capital of its province and one of the active centers of the south, Cosenza is near the Sila, a green plateau that covers a good portion of Calabria. The city flourished during the Middle Ages; during the 16th century it was a center of a cultural revival. Approximate population: 102,000.

★★   JOLLY HOTEL
Lungo Crati de Seta 2, tel. 24489, 64 rooms, most with bath. Moderately expensive.

★★   HOTEL IMPERIALE
Viale Trieste 50, tel. 27000, 68 rooms, most with bath. Moderate.

ENNA, Sicilia

Capital of the province, this ancient city is located in the heart of Sicilia on a high ledge overlooking a valley. This excellent position offers a magnificent view, and the city has been nicknamed "Belvedere della Sicilia." It is also a well-known agricultural center and a summer resort. Approximate population: 28,000.

★   HOTEL SICILIA
Piazza Colaianni, tel. 21127, 60 rooms with bath. Moderate.

★   HOTEL BELVEDERE
Piazza F. Crispi 5, tel. 21020, 62 rooms, 32 with bath. Inexpensive.

Good location, good view

FOGGIA, Puglia

Capital of the province, this active and modern city is an important communication junction. One of the most important agricultural fairs in Italy is held every year at the end of April. Approximate population: 142,000.

★★   PALACE H. SARTI
Viale 24 Maggio 48, tel. 23321, 79 rooms, most with bath. Moderately expensive.

★   HOTEL CICOLELLA
Viale 24 Maggio 60, tel. 21741, 168 rooms, 157 with bath. Moderate.

★   HOTEL PRESIDENT
Via Ascoli Satriano (1.2 km.), tel. 79648, 60 rooms, 56 with bath, indoor pool, tennis. Moderate.

ISCHIA (NA), Campania

★★★★★   REGINA ISABELLA E ROYAL SPORTING HOTEL
Seasonal, Lacco Ameno, piazza Umberto I, tel. 994322, 133 rooms with bath, beach, thermal spa, swimming pool, tennis. Expensive.

★★★★   EXCELSIOR BELVEDERE HOTEL
Seasonal, Ischia, via E. Gianturco 3, tel. 991522, 67 rooms with bath, garden, swimming pool, view. Expensive.

★★★★   HOTEL PUNTA MOLINO
Seasonal, Ischia, Lungomare C. Colombo, tel. 991544, 88 rooms with bath, garden, swimming pool, incorporated thermal care, beach. Expensive.

★★★★   JOLLY HOTEL
Ischia, via del Duca 42, tel. 991744, 220 rooms with bath, thermal spa, garden, swimming pool. Expensive.

★★★★   HOTEL SAN MONTANO
Seasonal, Lacco Ameno, a Monte Vico, tel. 994033, 65 rooms with bath, thermal spa, swimming pool, tennis, view. Expensive.

★★   HOTEL AMBASCIATORI
Seasonal, Ischia, via R. Gianturco 20, tel. 991139, 41 rooms with bath, swimming pool, view. Moderately expensive.

★★   HOTEL MANZI
Seasonal, Casamicciola Terme, piazza Bagni 1, tel. 994722, 62 rooms with bath, thermal spa, garden, swimming pool. Moderately expensive.

★★   HOTEL CRISTALLO PALACE
Seasonal, Casamicciola Terme, via Eddomade 1, tel. 994362, 77 rooms, most with bath, garden, swimming pool, view. Moderately expensive.

★★   HOTEL AUGUSTO
Seasonal, Lacco Ameno, viale Campo, tel. 994809, 94 rooms with bath, thermal spa, terraces, swimming pool. Moderately expensive.
Note: The island has more than 50 hotels of different caliber. The above are only our favorite; most others are adequate. For information write the tourist office: Azienda Autonoma del Turismo, Piazzale Trieste, 80077, Ischia Porto, or phone (081) 991146.

L'AQUILA, Abruzzo

Capital of the province and region, L'Aquila is the principal city of Abruzzo for art and history. It is a well-preserved medieval city situated on the slope of a hill in a large basin surrounded by high mountains. It is an important agricultural and commercial city. Approximate population: 60,000.

Restaurant on roof

★★   DUCA DEGLI ABRUZZI
Via Duca degli Abruzzi 10, tel. 28341, 85 rooms with bath, garage. Moderately expensive.

★★   GRAND HOTEL E DEL PARCO
Corso Federico II 74, tel. 20249, 99 rooms, 83 with bath, garden, garage. Moderate.

★   HOTEL LE CANNELLE
Via S. Maria del Ponte, tel. 27847, 84 rooms with bath, pool, tennis, garden. Moderate.

★   HOTEL CASTELLO
Piazza Battaglione Alpini, tel. 29147, 44 rooms with bath.

LECCE, Puglia

★★   HOTEL PRESIDENT
Via Salandra 6, tel. 51881, 153 rooms with bath. Moderate.

★★ Restaurant

★ HOTEL JOLLY
Via 140 Fanteria 69, tel. 26911, 66 rooms, 57 with bath. Moderate.

★ HOTEL DELLE PALME
Via Leuca 90, tel. 25551, 96 rooms with bath. Moderate.

LUCERA (FG), Puglia

★ HOTEL STELLA DAUNIA
Viale Ferrovia 15, tel. 941825, 36 rooms, 29 with bath. Moderate.

★ HOTEL AL PASSETTO
Piazza del Popolo 28, tel. 941124, 20 rooms, 13 with bath. Moderate.

MARSALA (TP), Sicilia

An active, wine-producing center on the western coast of Sicilia, this city was originally Carthaginian, then Roman, then Arabic. Its name, in fact, comes from the Arabic "Marsa Ali," which means Ali's Port. On May 11, 1860, Garibaldi landed here. boats for the island of Pantelleria leave from here daily. Appproximate population: 80,000.

★ STELLA D'ITALIA
Via M. Rapisardi 7, tel. 953003, 35 rooms, 26 with bath. Inexpensive.

★ MOTELAGIP
On the road to Mazara del Vallo, tel. 951611, 32 rooms with bath. Moderate.

MATERA, Basilicata

One of the more interesting cities in Italy, it is part old and part new. Of special interest are the houses dug into the hill, scattered at different levels in fascinating chaos (i Sassi). Approximate population: 45,000.

Pool

★ HOTEL PRESIDENT
Via Roma 13, tel. 24075, 76 rooms with bath, restaurant. Moderate.

NAPOLI, Campania

*★★★★
Grill*

★★★★ HOTEL EXCELSIOR
Via Partenope 48, tel. 417111, 160 rooms, most with bath, lovely view. Expensive.

★★★ HOTEL VESUVIO
Via Partenope 45, tel. 417044, 179 rooms, most with bath, lovely view. Expensive.

★★★ HOTEL MAJESTIC
Largo Vasto a Chiaia 68, tel. 416500, 123 rooms with bath, good restaurant, roof garden, view of gulf. Moderately expensive.

★★★ HOTEL S. GERMANO
Via Domiziana, slightly out of town, on the way to Agnano, tel. 7605422, 110 rooms with bath, garden, swimming pool, sauna, tennis. Moderately expensive.

★★★ HOTEL AMBASSADOR
Via Medina 70, central location, tel. 312031, 278 rooms, 143 with bath or shower. Moderately expensive.

★★★ HOTEL ROYAL
Via Partenope 38, tel. 400244, 316 rooms with bath, terrace with swimming pool, lovely view. Moderately expensive.

★★ HOTEL MEDITERRANEO
Via Nuova Ponte di Tappia 25, central location, tel. 312240, 223 rooms with bath. Moderately expensive.

nice garden on roof

★★ PARKER'S HOTEL
Corso Vittorio Emanuele 135, tel. 684320, 87 rooms, most with bath. Moderately expensive.

Near Vomero

PALERMO, Sicilia

Capital of the region, this beautiful city has a baroque appearance, especially in its historical center. The largest city of Sicilia, it is an important commercial and industrial center with an active port. It is one of the main tourist centers of Italy, known for its warm climate, its many gardens and its beautiful monuments. Approximate population: 643,000.

★★★★★ VILLA IGIEA
Salita Belmonte 1, tel. 543744, 92 rooms with bath, park, pool, beach. Expensive.

Tennis and gardens on the sea

★★★ GRAND ALBERGO E DELLE PALME
Via Roma 398, tel. 215570, 178 rooms, 162 with bath. Moderately expensive.

★★★ HOTEL JOLLY FORO ITALICO
Foro Italico 22, tel. 235685, 304 rooms with bath, pool. Moderately expensive.

★★ HOTEL PONTE
Via F. Crispi 99, on the harbor, tel. 243621, 90 rooms with bath. Moderate.

POSITANO (SA), Campania

★★★★   HOTEL SAN PIETRO
On the road to Amalfi, tel. 875454, 46 rooms with bath, swimming pool, tennis, elevator to the beach. Expensive.

★★★   HOTEL LE SIRENUSE
Via C. Colombo 22, tel. 875066, 62 rooms with bath, swimming pool, terraces. Expensive.

★★★   HOTEL MIRAMARE
Via Trara Genoino 31, tel. 875002, 14 rooms with bath, view, noted for a *glass bathtub* located on a terrace midst blooming flowers. Expensive.

★★   HOTEL SAVOIA
Via C. Colombo 33, tel. 875003, 44 rooms with bath, view. Moderately expensive.

★   HOTEL VILLA FRANCA
Viale Pasitea 118, tel. 875035, 25 rooms with bath, view. Moderate.

Magnificent views over sea [handwritten margin note]

RAVELLO (SA), Campania

★★★   HOTEL PALUMBO
Via Toro 34, tel. 871541, 32 rooms, most with bath, lovely garden, view. Moderately expensive.

★★   HOTEL VILLA CIMBRONE
At the villa, tel. 871505, 19 rooms, 8 with bath, lovely furniture, park, view. Moderately expensive.

★★   HOTEL CARUSO BELVEDERE
Via Toro, tel. 871527, 26 rooms, most with bath, garden, view. Moderately expensive.

Old fashioned ambience [handwritten margin note]

Good restaurant [handwritten margin note]

SALERNO, Campania

This lively and attractive city that stretches between hills and sea has a picturesque medieval section—once famous for its Medical School—and a modern industrial section, which includes an active port. Approximate population: 156,000.

★★★   LLOYD'S BAIA HOTEL
On Statale No. 18, exit for Vietri, tel. 210145, 135 rooms, most with bath, swimming pool, elevator to beach. Moderately expensive.

★★   JOLLY DELLE PALME
Lungomare Trieste 1, tel. 225222, 106 rooms, most with bath. Moderately expensive.

★ HOTEL MONTESTELLA
Corso Vittorio Emanuele 156, tel. 225122, 51 rooms with bath. Moderate.

SASSARI, Sardegna

This second city of the island is located on a calcarean slab, about 198 meters above sea level. Sassari was already of some importance during the Middle Ages; later it was a free commune; now it's a modern and lively city that contains many industries and a good university. Approximate population: 107,000.

★★ HOTEL JOLLY GRAZIA DELEDDA
Viale Dante 47, tel. 271235, 140 rooms with bath, swimming pool. Moderately expensive.

★★ HOTEL JOLLY SANDARD
Viale Mancini 2, tel. 35001, 49 rooms with bath. Moderate.

no dining room

SIRACUSA (Syracuse), Sicilia

Capital of the province, this famous city on the eastern coast of Sicilia is divided into two sections—the new on the mainland and the old on the small island of Ortigia. It is one of the major archaeological centers of the ancient Greek civilization. Approximate population: 109,000.

★★ VILLA POLITI
Via M. Laudien 2, tel. 32100, 98 rooms with bath, park, pool, tennis. Moderately expensive.

★★ HOTEL JOLLY
Corso Gelone 45, tel. 64744, 102 rooms with bath. Moderately expensive.

★ MOTELAGIP
Viale Teracati 30, tel. 24610, 76 rooms with bath. Moderately expensive.

near archeological digs

★ PARK HOTEL
Via Filisto 22, tel. 32644, 104 rooms with bath, garden. Moderate.

SORRENTO (NA), Campania

★★★ HOTEL PARCO DEI PRINCIPI
Via Rota 1, a bit from the center of town, tel. 8782101, 200 rooms, 185 with bath, garden, swimming pool, tennis court, view, elevator to the beach. Moderately expensive.

Renovated villa and modern annex

★★★ HOTEL EXCELSIOR VITTORIA
Piazza T. Tasso 34, close to the port, tel. 8781900, 115 rooms with bath, garden, swimming pool. Moderately expensive.

★★   HOTEL IMPERIAL TRAMONTANO
Via Vittorio Veneto 1, central location, tel. 8781940, 111 rooms with bath, park, elevator to the beach. Moderately expensive.

★★   HOTEL BEL AIR
Via Capo 29, tel. 8782964, 39 rooms with bath, swimming pool, view. Moderately expensive.

★   HOTEL BRISTOL
Via Capo 22, tel. 8781436, 87 rooms with bath, terrace, heated swimming pool. Moderate.

TAORMINA (ME), Sicilia

This fashionable resort sits on a lovely terrace of the eastern Sicilian coast, amongst rocks and sea, with the Etna behind. Colorful and lively, it offers the longest sea-bathing season in Italy and lots to see, from old structures to fashionable shopping.

★★★★★   S. DOMENICO PALACE
Piazza S. Domenico 5, tel. 23701, 100 rooms with bath, in a 16th-century convent, garden, swimming pool, view. Expensive.

Cloistered elegance

Huge grounds

★★★★   JOLLY DIODORO
Via Bagnoli Croce 75, tel. 23312, 103 rooms with bath, garden, swimming pool, view. Moderately expensive.

★★★★   MAZZARO SEA PALACE
About 6.5 km. from town, Lido di Mazzarò, tel. 24004, 77 rooms with bath, swimming pool, beach. Expensive.

★★★   CAPO TAORMINA
About 5 km. from town, at Capo Taormina, tel. 24000, 209 rooms with bath, swimming pool, beach. Moderately expensive.

★★   MONTE TAURO
Via M. Delle Grazie, tel. 24402, 67 rooms with bath, swimming pool, view. Moderately expensive.

TARANTO, Puglia

★★   HOTEL DELFINO
Viale Virgilio 66, on the sea, tel. 39981, 217 rooms with bath, pool. Moderately expensive.

★★   HOTEL JOLLY MAR GRANDE
Viale Virgilio 90, on the sea, tel. 30861, 97 rooms, 85 with bath, pool. Moderately expensive.

★ Restaurant

★   HOTEL LA SPEZIA
Via La Spezia 23, tel. 37950, 28 rooms with bath. Moderate.

TRANI (BA), Puglia

★ HOTEL MIRAMAR
Via Bisceglie III, tel. 42012, 26 rooms with bath, pool. Moderate.

★ HOTEL TRANI
Corso Imbriani 137, tel. 42315, 51 rooms with bath. Moderate.

TROPEA (CZ), Calabria

Picturesque old village on the Calabrian coast, at the edge of a promontory that juts out between two small gulfs. Approximate population: 7,000.

★ HOTEL ROCCA NETTUNO
Uscita per Nicotera, tel. 61526, 283 rooms with bath, in several buildings located in a flowered garden, with tennis, swimming pool, private beach. Moderate.

VIBO VALENTIA (CZ), Calabria

Was a Greek colony (Hipponion) and a flourishing medieval center. Now a beautiful little town with many activities—commercial, industrial and agricultural. Approximate population: 31,000.

★★ 501 HOTEL
Uscita per Pizzo, tel. 43400, 124 rooms with bath, tennis, swimming pool. Moderate.

★★ Restaurant

Restaurants

AGRIGENTO, Sicilia

★★ TAVERNA MOSÈ
2 km. from Agrigento—in Contrata Mosè, tel. 26768, closed Mondays and August 20th–30th. Traditional local dishes. Sundays and days when there are wedding parties should be avoided; otherwise it's a delightful place to dine. Moderate.

★ TRATTORIA DEL VIGNETO
Via Magazzeni Cavaleri, tel. 44319, closed Tuesdays and October. Family-style restaurant, good food, local wine; excellent location near the Valley of the Temples. Moderate.

ALBEROBELLO (BA), Puglia

★ CUCINA DEI TRULLI
Piazza Ferdinando IV, tel. 721051, closed Mondays except during the summer. Traditional local dishes. Moderate.

ALGHERO (SS), Sardegna

★★★   LA LEPANTO
Via Carlo, Alberto 135, tel. 979159, closed Tuesdays in winter. This small hotel makes very good food. In a town that cooks lobster often and well, here you can eat the best. Moderate.

★★   AI TUGURI
Via Maiorca 54, tel. 979822, closed Wednesdays and October 15th–November 15th. Good meat dishes, which is rare in this city of seafood. Also good wines. Moderate.

★★   DIECI METRI
Vicolo Adami (corner of via Roma), tel. 979023, closed Mondays and November. A city institution, this small place makes an excellent grilled fish, has good wines; call ahead. Moderate.

AMALFI (SA), Campania

★★   LA CARAVELLA
Via Nazionale 36, tel. 871029, closed Tuesdays in winter and from November 10th–30th. This centrally located restaurant has the best seafood in town and good local wine. Moderate.

★★   DA CICCIO, CIELO, MARE, TERRA
Località Vettica, tel. 871030, closed Tuesdays in winter and February. The location is so lovely you won't believe it's real. The food is good, some very good, wine is adequate. Moderate.

★   DELL'HOTEL LUNA CONVENTO
Tel. 871084, closed from October to March. A terrace on top of a Saracen tower, need we say more? The food is adequate. Moderately expensive.

★   LA TAVERNA DEL DOGE
Via Supportico 1, tel. 872303, closed Mondays except in summer and November. Good seafood cooked before your very eyes, house wine. Moderate.

BARI, Puglia

★★★   LA PIGNATA
Via Melo 9, tel. 232481, closed Wednesdays and August. The best restaurant in town. Impeccable service, excellent regional dishes and wine. Moderately expensive.

ask for cozze alla marinara (mussel stew)

★★   LA PANCA DA NANNUCCIO
Piazza Massari 12, tel. 216096, closed Wednesdays. Excellent traditional dishes and selection of wine. Moderately expensive.

★   MARC'AURELIO
Via Fiume 1, tel. 212820, closed Tuesdays. Good local dishes and good selection of local wine. Courteous service. Moderate.

BRINDISI, Puglia

★★   LA LANTERNA
Piazza della Vittoria 6, tel. 24950, closed Mondays and the middle of August. Good food and wine. Moderate.

★   G. GIUBILO
Via del Mare 56, tel. 29688, closed Sundays. Excellent traditional dishes, fine wines. Moderate.

★   IL PESCATORE DI JACCATO
Lennio Flacco 32, tel. 24084, closed Tuesdays and November. Good local dishes and wine. Moderate.

CAGLIARI, Sardegna

★★★   DAL CORSARO
Viale Regina Margherita 28, tel. 664310, closed Tuesdays and November. This fine restaurant is the best in town, makes regional food with excellent, fresh ingredients and a sure hand. Adequate choice of local wines. Moderately expensive.

ask for acciughe ripiene (stuffed anchovies)

★★   LA BUCA
Via Torino 16, tel. 668436, closed Mondays. A new place that offers good food that is not entirely regional, but allows room for imagination. Very good choice of wines. Moderate prices.

★   DA LILLICU
Via Sardegna 78, tel. 652970, closed Sundays and last 15 days in August. Of the several *trattorie* along this street our choice is this one, with its warm, simple atmosphere and fresh, well-prepared dishes. Excellent choice of wines. Moderate.

CAPRI (NA), Campania

★★★   I FARAGLIONI
Via Camerelle 75, Capri, tel. 8370320, closed from October to Easter. Everyone comes here—to eat, see, to be seen. Unexpectedly the food is good, the wines well selected. Reasonable.

ask for fritto misto al mare (mixed seafood, fried)

★★★   AURORA
Via Fourlovado 18, Capri, tel. 8370181, closed from November to March. Excellent regional food in a *trattoria* that forgets its location. Moderate prices.

★★★ LA CANZONE DEL MARE
Via di Marina Piccola, tel. 8370104, closed from October to Easter and evenings. Splendidly located in the villa that belonged to Gracie Fields, this place is a tradition with Capri *habituès*. The food is good, the service excellent, the cellar well stocked. Expensive.

★★ LA CAPANNINA
Via delle Botteghe 14, Capri, tel. 8370732, closed from November to Easter. Lovely garden, charming atmosphere, good food and even an occasional celebrity. A place to remember. Moderately expensive.

★★ LA PIGNA
Via Lo Palazzo 30, Capri, tel. 8370280, closed Wednesdays in winter. Charming place that serves imaginative food and good white wine. Moderately expensive.

★★ DA LUIGI
Strada dei Faraglioni, tel. 8370591, closed from October to Easter. Fabulous location plus good food. Moderate.

★★ DA GEMMA
Via Madre Serafina 6, Capri, tel. 8370461, closed Mondays, November and Christmas Day. This centrally located *cantina* is a local tradition. Very good fish and wonderful desserts. Moderate.

CASERTA, Campania

Try bisteca alla pizzaiola (steak with garlic)

★★ LA CASTELLANA
Via Torre 4, tel. 320030, closed Mondays during the winter. In the medieval part of town, this place offers excellent home-made local food, good choice of wines. Moderate prices.

★ LA TEGOLA
Viale Carlo III 1, tel. 442689, closed Wednesdays and Sunday evenings. Fairly new, this place is rapidly acquiring a reputation for good food and excellent fish, very good wines. Moderately expensive.

CATANIA, Sicilia

★★ LA SICILIANA
Via Marco Polo 52, tel. 376400, closed Wednesdays. During the summer there is service in the garden and on the veranda. Family-style restaurant, excellent traditional Sicilian dishes and house wine, courteous service. Moderately expensive.

★★ PAGANO
Via De Roberto 37, tel. 322720, closed Mondays and in August. Excellent dishes made with fresh ingredients, good wine selection, courteous service. Moderately expensive.

★   DA RINALDO

Via Simili 59, tel. 249335, closed Tuesdays and 15 days in August. Pleasant atmosphere, well-presented traditional dishes, excellent selection of Sicilian and Italian wines. Moderately expensive.

COSENZA, Calabria

★   ELEFANTE ROSSO

Via Don Minzoni 102, tel. 838179, closed Tuesdays and mid-August. Good cooking, especially the regional dishes, adequate wine. Moderate.

ask for lasagne alla Calabrese (meat, tomato, cheese)

Out of Town

about 65 km. toward Catanzaro, at Castrovillari.

★★★   ALIA

Via Roma 116, tel. 21715, closed Sundays. One of the best restaurants in the South, worthy of a detour. Small family-run place, it offers a splendid combination of regional cooking and modern point-of-view, excellent wines. Moderate prices.

a good local dry red is Savuto

ENNA, Sicilia

★★   ARISTON

Via Roma 365, tel. 26038, closed Sundays and the second half of August. Excellent traditional dishes and a good selection of regional and national wines. Moderate.

★   CENTRALE

Via 6 Dicembre 9, tel. 21025, closed Saturdays and from mid-September to October. Good local dishes. Moderate.

FOGGIA, Puglia

★★   CICOLELLA IN FIERA AL SIGILLO DI FEDERICO II

Viale Fortore, tel. 32166, closed Tuesdays. Excellent traditional as well as international dishes, well-stocked cellar, excellent house wine. Moderately expensive.

★   NUOVA BELLA NAPOLI

Via Callisto Azzarita 26/28, in the center of the old town, tel. 26188, closed Saturdays and August. Pleasant restaurant with a warm atmosphere. Better make a reservation. Well-prepared dishes and a good regional wine. Moderate.

a good local wine is Castel del monte (red, white, rose)

ISCHIA (NA), Campania

★★★   DA UGO, GIARDINI EDEN

Ischia Ponte, via Nuova Casta romana 40, tel. 993909, closed evenings and from October to April. Charming location and very good food. Everything fragrant, including the wine. Moderately expensive.

★★★   DA LEOPOLDO
Panza d'Ischia, tel. 907086, closed noon and from October to April. The best nonfish kitchen on the island, strong and zesty mountain flavors, a pleasant experience. Moderate.

[handwritten margin note: ask for alici alla Ischiana (deep fried anchovies)]

★★   LA MERIDIANA
Forio, spiaggia di S. Francesco, tel. 998464, closed October 20th–April 30th. Most romantic place on the island, good seafood, good local wines. Moderate.

★★   NEGOMBO
Forio, spiaggia di S. Montano, tel. 986152, closed October 20th–April 20th. Not only a restaurant but a whole beach establishment, the food is adequate. Moderate.

★   GENNARO
Ischia Porto, via Porto 66, tel. 992917, closed from November to March. An old-fashioned *trattoria* that serves simple, tasty food. Moderate.

★   ANNA DI MASSA
ISchia Ponte, via Seminario 29, tel. 991402, closed Tuesdays in winter. A good pizzeria near the sea. Inexpensive.

L'AQUILA, Abruzzo

★★   TRE MARIE
Via Tre Marie 5, tel. 20191, closed Mondays. Abruzzese cuisine. Moderate.

★   AQUILA, DA REMO
Via S. Flaviano 9, tel. 22010, closed Sundays. Moderate.

★   MAKALLÈ
Via Tre Marie 22, tel. 24458, closed Saturdays. Moderate.

LECCE, Puglia

★★   DELL'HOTEL PRESIDENT
Via Salandra 6, tel. 51881, always open. Excellent traditional and international dishes, prompt service, good selection of local wines. Moderately expensive.

[handwritten margin note: ask for ear-shaped pasta, recchietelle]

★★   PLAZA
Via 140° Fanteria 14, tel. 25093, closed Sundays and August. Well-prepared traditional dishes, excellent house wine. Moderate.

MARSALA (TP), Sicilia

★★★ VILLA FAVORITA
Via Favorita, tel. 956377. In a superb villa with garden and horse back riding
facilities, this restaurant offers very good food and serves good wines, including a Sicilian sherry called "Spagnolito" that deserves a try. Moderately
expensive.

a good dry Sicilian white wine is Corvo

MATERA, Basilicata

★ DA BELISARIO, TAVERNA DEI SASSI
Vico Don Minzoni 4, near the railroad station, in the modern part of town,
tel. 24557, closed Wednesdays and end of July. The best eatery here, fresh
fish and good wine. Inexpensive.

NAPOLI, Campania

★★★★ LA SAGRESTIA
Via Orazio 116, tel. 664186. Closed Wednesdays. The best in town, this large
place serves excellent food in season—seafood in summer, meat and hearty
vegetables in winter—and has a cellar that keeps the best local wines. Moderately expensive.

★★★★ LA FAZENDA
Calata Marechiaro 58, near Posillipo, tel. 7697420. Closed Sundays and 15
days in August. A country place made into a restaurant, charming and simple.
The food very good, as are local wines. Moderate.

★★★★ CASANOVA GRILL DELL'HOTEL EXCELSIOR
Via Partenope 48, tel. 417111, always open. Even if you don't stay at the
hotel, this restaurant is worth a try. Truly Neopolitan food, the "rich" and
"poor" prepared by a cooking staff that knows its business. Very good wine
list. Expensive.

★★★ VINI E CUCINA
Corso Vittorio Emanuele, in front of the Mergellina Station, no telephone,
closed Sundays. In a very good location, this small restaurant serves very
good food, inspired by a tradition of "poor" ingredients. An interesting experience. Inexpensive.

Zuppa di pesce (fish stew) is a Naples favorite

★★★ CIRO A SANTA BRIGIDA
Via S. Brigida 71-74, tel. 324072, closed Sundays. One of the city's old
glories, this active place has a mixed clientele and reliable good food and
wine. Moderate.

★★★ AL 53
Piazza Dante 53, tel. 341124. Closed Sundays and August. One of the city's

best *trattorie,* located in a very busy section that is quieter at night, here the simple Neapolitan dishes are served with the pride of those who know their business. Moderate.

★★★   IL GALLO NERO
Via Tasso 466, tel. 643012, closed Mondays. In a slightly decadent villa, this new restaurant proposes something new for Napoli and is a refreshing change. Moderately expensive.

★★   DORA
Via Ferdinando Palasciano 30, tel. 684149, closed Sundays and August. The best seafood in town, even if the surroundings are far from perfect. Moderately expensive.

★★   AMICI MIEI
Via Monte di Dio 78, tel. 405727, closed Mondays. The service and atmosphere are charming, a little dated and unique. The food is good, as are the desserts and wines. Moderate.

★★   DA GIOVANNI
Via Morelli 14, tel. 416849, closed Sundays. Elegant and formal, suitable for a business lunch. The location is fashionable, the food, authentic and refined, good choice of local wines. Moderately expensive.

A good local wine is Lacrima Christi del. Christi (red Vesuvio (red is best)

★   SBRESCIA
Rampe S. Antonio 109, tel. 669140, closed Mondays. One of the city's beloved restaurants, where the Neapolitans bring the whole family on Sunday, thus noisy. The fish is good. Moderate.

PALERMO, *Sicilia*

Good Sicilian wine is Capo, both red and white, from messina

★★★★   CHARLESTON
Piazzale Ungheria 30, tel. 321366, closed Sundays. During the summer it is transfered to Mondello (Charleston Le Terrazze). Elegant and comfortable restaurant, one of the most renowned kitchens in the world for Sicilian dishes. Excellent *cantina* stocked with good quality Sicilian wines. First-class courteous service. Moderately expensive.

★★★★   LE GOURMAND'S
Via della Libertà 37e, tel. 323431, closed Sundays and in August. Modern restaurant with a cosmopolitan atmosphere. Very well-prepared dishes by one of the most famous Sicilian chefs. Adequate wine list, excellent service. Moderately expensive.

★★   LO SCUDIERO
Via F. Turati 7, tel. 581628, closed Sundays and August. Central location, family-style restaurant with well-prepared dishes. Excellent wine selection. Moderate.

POSITANO (SA), Campania

★★   LA BUCA DI BACCO
On the beach, tel. 875004, closed from November to March. In the very heart of this small city, you can have a coffee, an *aperitivo* or a good meal. Good local wine. Moderately expensive.

★★   CHEZ BLACK
Via del Brigantino, tel. 875036, closed from November to January 2nd. Lovely location and very good local food. Good ice cream and sweets. Moderately expensive.

RAVELLO (SA), Campania

★★★★   CARUSO AL BELVEDERE
Via Toro 50, tel. 857111, closed Tuesdays and October 31st–May 31st. Not often is one blessed with a splendid view plus an excellent meal. The wine is equal to the task. Moderate.

★★   DA PALUMBO AL CONFALONE
Via Toro 28, tel. 857244, closed Wednesdays in winter. Regional cooking with a touch of international flavor as befits a place that has housed many famous personalities, such as Ingrid Bergman Rossellini and John Houston. The wine, which is produced by the owner, is good. Moderately expensive.

SALERNO, Campania

★★★   ANTICA PIZZERIA DEL VICOLO DELLE NEVE
Vicolo della Neve 24, tel. 225705, closed Wednesdays and Christmas week. Considered a temple of genuine Neapolitan food, this *fin de siècle* place is worth an extra day in town. Inexpensive.

★★   LA BRACE
Viale Trieste 13, tel. 225159, closed Thursdays. Excellent fish, very good cheeses, marvelous vegetables and wine. Moderate.

★   NICOLA DEI PRINCIPATI
Corso Garibaldi 201, tel. 225435, closed Thursdays and Sunday evenings. Once more, fish, fish, fish. Good desserts and wine. Moderate.

SASSARI, Sardegna

★★   DAL TOMMASO
Via Ospizio dei Cappuccini 1/B, tel. 235041, closed Sundays and July 12th–August 15th. In the oldest part of town, this "grotto" serves excellent wine. Inexpensive.

Try coniglio alla Sarda (wild rabbit casserole)

★★   TRE STELLE
Via Porcellana 6, tel. 232431, closed Sundays. A truly nice restaurant that

serves good food, regional and otherwise. Good house wine, good choice of local wines. Moderate.

SIRACUSA (Syracuse), Sicilia

★★★   JONICO A RUTTA 'E CIAULI
Riviera Dionisio il Grande 194, tel. 65540, closed Tuesdays and October. Traditional Sicilian cooking with a new touch; an excellent selection of wine, courteous service. During the summer dinner can be served on a terrace with a view of the sea. Moderate.

★★   DA PIPPO
Via XX Settembre 13, tel. 65945, closed Mondays and October. Good family-style restaurant; their specialty is seafood, excellent regional wine. Moderate.

★   ARLECCHINO
Largo Empedocle 8, tel. 66386, closed Mondays and August. Traditional local dishes, good selection of regional wines. Moderate.

SORRENTO (NA), Campania

★★★   LA FAVORITA O' PARRUCCHIANO
Corso Italia 71–73, tel. 8781321, closed Wednesdays from January to June, always open in season. Once a temple of the great Neapolitan cuisine, this elegant place with its unusual terraced gardens has maintained most of its reputation. An interesting experience! Moderate.

★★   LA MINERVETTA
Via Capo 25, tel. 8781098, closed Tuesdays. Lovely place with a view, good food. Moderate.

TAORMINA (ME), Sicilia

★★★   DELL' HOTEL TIMEO
Via Teatro Greco 59, tel. 23801, closed November–December 19th. The best Sicilian cooking can be savored here, as well as a lovely view of the Etna. The wines are equivalent to the food. Expensive, within reason.

★★   IL PESCATORE
At Mazzarò, tel. 23460, closed Mondays and from November to February. A limited menu, but every dish done to perfection. Try the grilled fish, it's a feast! Very good Sicilian wines. Moderately expensive.

★★   CHEZ ANGELO
Corso Umberto 38, tel. 24441, closed Mondays and January. The oldest restaurant in town, good food for a sophisticated clientele, good local white wine. Moderate.

Insalata Siciliana is a salad with beans, octopus, olives, etc.

TARANTO, Puglia

★   L' APPRODO
Via Matteotti 4, tel. 23324, closed Fridays and the first week of July. Good local dishes. Moderate.

★   PIZZERIA MARCAURELIO
Via Cavour 17, closed Tuesdays. Good local dishes, excellent house wine. Moderate.

Cozze fritte (fried mussels) are a local favorite

★   DEL GRAND HOTEL DELFINO
Viale Virgilio 66, tel. 339981, closed Fridays. Well-prepared dishes, excellent local wines, courteous service. Expensive.

TRANI (BA), Puglia

★   CRISTOFORO COLOMBO
Lungomare C. Colombo 21, tel. 41146, closed Tuesdays and November. The specialty is fish, good local wines. Moderately expensive.

VIBO VALENTIA (CZ), Calabria

★★   501
Via Madonella, tel. 43400. Belongs to the hotel above. Decent food, especially if you eat the local specialties, fresh fish and average wines. Moderately expensive.

★★   VECCHIA VIBO
Via G. Murat, tel. 45337, closed Sundays and 15 days in December. Elegant, serves very good food. Moderate prices.

Shopping

The south of Italy is not famous for its shopping opportunities, unless you like rustic ceramics and straw pieces. One outstanding craft, the tortoise shell work, is declining. It can still be seen in Torre del Greco, just south of Napoli, where coral is carved into fine shapes, often before the eyes of tour group members.

Entertainment

Napoli's San Carlo Opera House begins its season in December and ends it in May.
   Nightlife is best confined to your hotel or the sidewalk cafes.
   Special events, such as festivals, should provide plenty of amusement. Here are just a few.

Holy Week.   Bari has a very significant procession on Good Friday.

July.   On July 2nd, the Bruna Festival takes place in Matera, home of the rock dwellers.

September.   Napoli celebrates the Piedigrotta during the first ten days of the month with fireworks, floats, parades and general levity.

Museums

★★★   MUSEO NAZIONALE
Piazza del Museo, Napoli. Huge and somewhat disorganized, but filled with treasures from Pompeii, Herculaneum and all of southern Italy. Excellent, old copies of famous Greek sculptures.

★★   CERTOSA DI SAN MARTINO
Vomero, Napoli. Carthusian monastery that is now a museum, filled with fine paintings and treasures of the old Kingdom of Napoli.

★   VILLA FLORIDIANA
Vomero, Napoli. National Museum of Ceramics, with fine collection of majolica.

★   PALAZZO CAPODIMONTE
Tondo di Capodimonte, Napoli. Armor is the thing to see here, as well as 18th-century Neapolitan paintings and some porcelain.

Tours

Tours of Napoli and environs, as well as those covering all of southern Italy, can be arranged through CIT offices in North America and England or upon arrival. You'll find American Express in Napoli on the Via San Carlo and Thomas Cook's at Via Depretis. Day excursions from Napoli to Pompeii, Herculaneum, Capri and Ischia are available through your hotel concierge or you can ask EPT, the local tourist authority, at the airport, at the rail station or on Via Partenope.

Sports

One warning about swimming: don't try it anywhere near Napoli. The rest of southern Italy has miles upon miles of beautiful, often untouched, beaches, those of the Gulf of Taranto are among the best. Capri and Ischia are of course safe for bathing. Golf and tennis are hard to find, but your hotel concierge is the man to do it.

Getting Around

The rail network in southern Italy is less important than the bus routes, and we don't recommend the bus for pleasant traveling. First, you should rely on whatever train service there is, then on your own car, obtainable through the usual Avis and Hertz centers, particularly in Napoli.

Directory

American Consulate: Piazza della Repubblica, Napoli.

A Bit of Background

Inside Today's Italy

With all due respect to the USA, one of the best definitions of Italy today is that it is a melting pot. Not so much of different ethnic groups and cultures, of languages and religions, but a melting pot of entire civilizations. If we are to agree with the theory that the difficulties of the world in the eighties are a reflection of the fact that we are entering a new stage of civilization, while the previous two stages (agricultural and industrial) are slowly receding, then Italy is one of the best examples of the difficulties and dilemmas that arise from this triple impact. For here, in a relatively small country inhabited by less than 60 million people, these three ways of living rub elbows constantly, each vociferously demanding its rights, fighting for its laws, trying to survive at all costs.

Agriculture is still one of Italy's more important activities, and tradition, religion, culture and climate are all elements that favor the farmer and make him feel a part of the community, needed and loved. Industry, on the other hand, represents an admission ticket into the modern world, a world that became real to Italy less than 40 years ago; and this overwhelmed the country with its promise of progress and opulence. A strong Communist party and even stronger labor unions were instrumental in this rapid development, but Italian businessmen and enterprising managers can be second to none.

In the last few years the conflicts between these two models, along with the rising prices of raw materials—of which Italy is notoriously poor—and with the expense of maintaining the public apparatus (for Italy is nothing if not a mixed economy), have produced a worrisome rate of inflation, a significant rise in unemployment, as well as economic stagnation. And all of the above, added to a strategic geographic position, and a tradition of fierce infighting, have resulted in a wave of terrorist killings and kidnappings that soil the headlines of newspapers around the globe.

But in spite of all this a new civilization is slowly forming, even if the signs are still difficult to see with the naked eye. Some youngsters are going back to the artisan trades, uniting Italian taste and sensibility with modern merchandising techniques in order to make a decent living and live a civilized life. Sports are gaining in popularity, too. Ever since Italy won the World Soccer championship in 1982 it's patriotic to ride a bicycle, or swim, or fence. Young men take their dates and even their wives to watch soccer games, in yet another attempt to end the ancient separation between the sexes. Alternate sources of heat and energy are beginning to enter Italian homes and some of the old taboos are dissolving under the influence of mass distributed books, magazines and newspapers.

It has been said that in Italy things are done either with the Church or against it, which is the other face of the same coin. No doubt the presence of the Vatican has had enormous influence in the country's cultural, political and even economic life. But the world is changing, and Italy is a lively, vital country that often sythesizes the conflicts of Europe. So while the Communists and Christian Democrats remain relatively stationary, and even loose an occasional one or two percent of their votes, the area in between, the so-called "small, lay parties" such as Republicans, Liberals and Social Democrats, have been gaining strength. It seems a sign of growing independence, a need to create a democratic alternative to the old struggle between Guelfs and Ghibellines.

To the foreign visitor, Italy is still one of the most engaging, interesting and varied countries in the world. A wealth of art and architecture, splendid panoramas, marvelous food and wine, and lovely things to buy for prices that are, once again, very reasonable. Beginning in the late seventies, a renewed sense of pride in its splendid artistic patrimony has induced the administrations of cities, provinces, and regions to concentrate on the restoration and conservation of these priceless monuments. Thus, we hear of an ambitious project for saving Venice from its rising water; Florence is fixing the *Giotto Tower* and redoing the inside of *Bernini's Cupola;* Milan is delicately restoring Leonardo's *Last Supper;* and the *Roman Forum* is full of metal scaffolding meant to protect the old ruins until they are once again able to survive the ravages of modern man. An infinite number of statues are in the care of experts and specialists who know all about marble and bronze; an infinite number of paintings are undergoing cleaning and retouching; and new discoveries such as the magnificent *Bronzes of Riace* are being placed in museums that are especially designed for displaying them to the best advantage.

While we've spent enough space on places to visit and a separate section tells of Italian cuisine, it might be useful to say a few words on the newest developments in shopping. By the time this book goes to press a remarkable change will have taken place in Italian stores—shopping hours. Shopping hours have changed! As of summer 1982, a new government regulation allows shopkeepers to stay open continuously, up to a maximum of 50 hours per week, and all large chain stores modified their working schedules accordingly, while many smaller operators are also adjusting their business hours to the demand. It is still hard to tell what will happen in many small towns and villages, where family-owned stores have been traditionally open from 8:30 or 9:00 A.M. to 1:00 P.M. and in the afternoon from 4:00 to 7:30 P.M. This allows all concerned to have the proverbial siesta, of course. Probably, some will adjust to the new system, and some will not. But the department stores and supermarkets, especially in Rome, Milan and Florence, have rapidly taken advantage of the new law, and are open either continuously or with only one hour for lunch. This means that tourists can buy essentials almost any hour of the day.

As for *what* to buy in Italy, there is the proverbial *'embaras du choix',* with leather goods, clothing, straw goods and ceramics plus other items. We feel safe in saying that shoes, handbags and wallets are better here than

anywhere else. The experienced shopper in a large American city will probably counter that the choice is greater at home. But since the good quality
items will surely be Italian, and if it can be found here in Italy the price will
more than justify the shopping effort. Rome for shoes and straw items; Florence for knits, handbags and ceramics; Milan for gloves and jewelry; and
Venice for glass. This is only a very superficial summing up of the goods
available in each Italian city. Famous designers such as Roberta de Camerino,
Ferragamo, Feudi, Armani, Ferre, Missoni, Gucci or Krizia are sold in every
town, sometimes in their own private stores. But many smaller firms make
equally attractive items at more reasonable prices. The clever shopper will go
home with many satisfactory bargains in tow, if shopping in Italy is deemed
important. If your trip includes one or two medium-size towns such as
Ravenna, Padova, Lucca or Taormina, keep in mind that shopping is easier
in a small center, and often more rewarding.

The Cultural Scene

Much of the Mediterranean basin was inhabited by primitive man, and Italy was no exception. There are findings on the peninsula that go back 40,000 years, and some scientists have said that they are not the oldest. Later, when utensils were being made of metal, many tribes lived on this boot-shaped land. The northwest was occupied by the *Liguri,* down into Tuscany and across the sea to Corsica. At the center, the *Umbri* were present but the *Etruschi* dominated the coastal areas. Further south there were Greek colonies, plus the *Volsci,* the *Sabini,* the *Irpini,* the *Lucani,* the *Messapi* and, in Sicily, the *Siculi.* This large mosaic of tribes that spoke different languages and had different customs slowly got blurred, and generated a fairly uniform ethnic culture.

The Etruscans were the first to evolve into a nation. They are still surrounded by the mystery of their undeciphered language and are best remembered for their splendid tombs; the lovely jewelry made with imported gold; the highly developed engineering techniques; and an unusual religion based on the interpretation of birds in flight and the liver of sacrificed animals. They were a nation of merchants, and their well-established sea routes brought them into close contact with Oriental civilization. This fact may explain their rich clothing, languid ways, and vivid paintings.

While the Etruscans were working peacefully at their arts and crafts, a small tribe that lived just south of them was developing a simple, almost frugal way of life, based primarily on military discipline and achievement. In a relatively short period of time the *Latini* conquered all the surrounding tribes, defeated the more sophisticated Etruscans, and became the strongest and most powerful group on the peninsula. Their captial, a conglomerate of seven hills, was named Rome. It was strategically located on the Tiber River, its bridge an unavoidable passageway for all goods coming from north to south and vice versa.

During its rise to power Rome was first a monarchy (with seven Etruscan kings), then a republic, finally an empire. At the beginning of the Imperial Age, under Octavian Augustus, a great poet named *Publio Virgilio Varone* wrote an epic poem that told the origins of his nation. It was written at a time when the hardy Romans were becoming more reflective and when an intellectual, rather than participate in active politics, could begin a search for his roots.

L'Eneide tells the story of a Trojan prince who escapes his burning city with his father, his son, and some possessions, after many adventures, on Italian soil. The son eventually marries a local princess, and together they give birth to the Latin people, and thus to Rome itself. Enea's mother is Venus, providing divine origins and giving Rome its patron goddess.

As the world entered the Christian era the Roman Empire was at its most glorious moment. Within the next two centuries it reached its greatest territorial extension (A.D 117 under Trajan), and built its most impressive monuments. But the first signs of decay were beginning to show.

Many of the emperors that ruled during those years tried to avoid the inevitable. It befell *Constantino* to accept a new religion and change the location of the capital. Between them, these two decisions insured another thousand years of continuity for the Roman Empire, and almost two thousand years of life to the city of Rome.

With the Edict of Milan (A.D. 313) the Christians came out of their catacombs, and Rome as capital was moved to a lovely site on the Bosphorus which took the name of Constantinople. This lovely site was originally called Byzantium, a Greek town named after its founder, a Greek sailor called Byzas.

Meanwhile, north European and Asiatic tribes were coming through the Alpine passes to ravage the rich peninsula. Visigoths, Ostrogoths, Vandals and Huns came in successive waves, and found it easier and easier to besiege, sack and occupy the weakened Western provinces, and finally to take Rome itself. The Western Roman Empire fell in A.D. 476, the last emperor, a mere boy, bore two of the most illustrious names in Roman history: Romolo Augustolo.

With the division of the Empire, a vacuum was created in the city of Rome. But within a short time that space was filled by the leaders of new Church, the popes. There are many examples of papal power and influence throughout the early Middle Ages. One of the most significant is the armistice (A.D. 599) that Pope Gregorio Magno was able to arrange between the Longobards (a Germanic tribe that had occupied a large part of northern Italy), and the Byzantines who still had a claim on Italy (they were the *Romans* of the Eastern Empire). In fact, for the next thousand years—until Constantinople fell in 1453—Italian civilization was a conglomerate of East and West, with the Church acting as the judicious guardian over this delicate operation.

Another important service rendered by the Church to Italian culture began around the 6th century A.D.—perhaps even earlier. *S. Benedetto di Norcia* (480-after 546)-was a noble Roman who chose to lead a humble life. He developed the rule *ora et labora,* which means "pray and work." Following this inspired principle, many monks began to go among the people, working anonymously to bring both the message of Christ and assist the needy. Monasteries and abbeys were built along the main roads that connected Rome to north and south. Some monks were on secluded mountaintops. These buildings became centers of general assistance, schools, hospitals, and resting places for the tired traveler. But one of their most significant activities was the copying of manuscripts. The barbarians fought and burned their way through the land while the monks patiently saved, copied and preserved the written word for posterity.

The centuries that follow witnessed the consolidation of the Church into a powerful organization, and the establishment of the feudal system throughout Italy, mostly at the hands of the Longobard nobility. Unfortunately, this industrious tribe did not accept the dogmas of the Church, but worshipped according to the Arian heresy, whereas another northern tribe that occupied what now is France and most of Germany, was devoted to the Roman Church.

Thus, when *Charlemagne* fought and defeated the Longobards, Pope Leone III revived an old title and crowned him Holy Roman Emperor on Christmas day in 800. With this great king, the center of European cultural life shifted to his capital *Aquisgrana,* where he surrounded himself with teachers, philosophers and scientists. One of the lasting achievements of this revival was the introduction of small or lowercase letters, appropriately named "caroline writing." (Before Charlemagne all writing had been done in capital letters.)

The newly created empire did not outlive its founder, and in the 10th century was marred by conflicting interests of kings and kings, nobles and kings, nobles and nobles, and everyone against the plebeians. The 11th century dawned upon a confused and divided Europe, and an even more confused and divided Italy. The peasants lived miserable, hungry lives. The nobles fought each other at the least provocation, even the authority of the Pope was questioned, and many small heresies appeared.

But two energetic reform-minded popes, an inspired saint, and a mass movement that distracted the warring nobles long enough to restore Italy to civilization, opened the way for increased growth that was to come later.

The first of the reforming Popes was a rugged Tuscan who became Pope Gregory VII. He established the superiority of the Church in areas where it was being challenged, and invented the Crusades. The Crusades were an uneven and sometimes very disorganized attempt to liberate the Holy Land, but they polarized the attention of Europe's aggresive nobility and distracted them from petty squabbles. The saint was *Francis of Assisi,* a young nobleman who, after a serious disease changed his ways and went barefoot among the people, preaching a return to poverty and nature. In a short period of time he acquired many followers, and another reforming Pope, Innocent III, accepted his preaching as part of the Catholic dogma.

So while popes and saints were striving to bring order and stability, the Crusaders brought change. They brought back new interests and new information, and changed the Italian way of life, the cultural outlook and even the landscape. Sugar, rice, almonds and spices were added to the dull Medieval fare. Beds were made comfortable with silks, brocades and multi-colored rugs. Clothing became colorful and delicate. Even castles were built differently. And last but certainly not least, Greek philosophy filtered back into Italy, brought by the Crusaders who had studied in the East, with teachers who had maintained the Greek tradition.

As a result of all this the next two centuries were significant. On the one hand the Church became stronger and asserted its power, on the other the emperor also wanted his share. Into this squabble—which in Italy acquired the name of Guelfs versus Ghibellines, where Guelfs were those that sided with the Church and Ghibellines were the supporters of the emperor—came a third factor: the growth of free cities, the "comune."

The Renaissance really began in the 13th century. New methods for working the fields brought better and more abundant crops (the crusaders introduced the use of manure from the Orient), and more food meant an increase in population. More people needed more goods, a need that was rapidly met by enterprising craftsmen and merchants. This increase in activity required a central place in which matters could be discussed, and thus the birth of the market place. And around these grew villages, towns, and cities. The populations in these new towns were no longer serfs and peasants. They were now more informed, more independent, and had much to defend: their freedom and liberty and their newly acquired wealth. Thus the "comune" became a small free state, with its own laws, its own taxes, its own justice.

Meanwhile, the Church had found its new identity in St. Francis. His humble and reflective attempt to bring believers back to the original teaching of Christ was met with hope and joy. Religion once again was identified with spiritual guidance. St. Francis was not only a great leader but a fine poet as well. One of the side effects of *francescanesimo* was a new musical form, the *lauda*. In the climate of a fervent mysticism that descended on Italy, the 13th century witnessed the growth of this simple and lively song, first sung by one voice and later dialogued, telling the story of the Saint's preaching. Before the lauda all singing had been *liturgical*, all subjects purely religious, such as those in the Gregorian chant.

The greatest poet of Italian history was writing toward the end of the 13th century. *Dante Alighieri*, a Florentine, wrote a splendid, long poem in the Italian vernacular (rather than Latin), that combined in one work the best in Medieval teaching with new thoughts that were beginning to rise on the horizon of Italian culture. His *Divine Comedy* is not only an outstanding poem that tells of his wanderings through hell and purgatory (led by Virgil) and through Paradise (led by others), but is a pungent pamphlet of Florentine life and a philosophical discourse on the relationships of man and God, of Church and State. It introduced the modern concept that man *can* choose freely. Dante's work shows a remarkable knowledge of the sacred scriptures, Aristotle's philosophy, and the theology of St. Thomas Aquinas. And it inspired a vision of the world that sees man as the center of the universe. Over and above all this, the poet sensed the need for the use of everyday Italian. His treatise also proposed a moral structure for society that would allow men of goodwill to work and produce. His great work is both the last of an era and the first of a new one.

The 14th century was a time of turmoil, of wars and pestilence, but it was also a time of greatness. Especially in Florence other great writers followed Dante, some his contemporaries. The father of humanism, *Petrarca*, wrote of sublime love, of patriotism, of God and woman, in verses so delicate they are still considered among the best in Italian. His *Canzoniere* is a series of lyrical poems that symbolize man's acute awareness of himself, his country, his feelings. We should be mindful that all this was as startling and new in his time as the theories of Freud and Darwin were for the puritanical 19th century. Almost simultaneously, another Florentine wrote in a totally different style. With his *Decameron, Boccaccio* of *Certaldo* brought realism into literature, and invented the novel. He also celebrated man, but while Petrarca indulged on the finer emotions—such as love and conscience, Boccaccio glorified shrewdness and quick wit, exhalted rowdy sensuality and man's capacity to outsmart others; and left spirituality to fend for itself.

Stimulated by the writings of these three great men, predecessors of modern literature, Florence also developed a new musical style, the *Ars Nova Fiorentina,* a profound, polyphonic song that introduces two or three voices, sometimes played instrumentally. The expressive maturity of this music has led specialists to speculate that previous, undocumented experiments had taken place. The *Ars Nova* opens the way to music as we know it, no longer flat and uniform, but lively and interesting.

Enter the 15th century, and with it comes the definite end of the Middle ages. Not only did the visual arts, painting, sculpture and architecture vie with each other for supremacy in good taste and refinement, but the writings of Petrarca and Boccaccio and Leonardo's daring experiments in every field of science contributed to the impulse that led to a new age. Curiosity was the byword—man was no longer the object of God and fate, but saw himself as the center of the universe and wanted to know how things worked. Thus, there was renewed interest in nature and the search for laws that regulate natural phenomena. The poetry of *Lorenzo de Medici,* justly known as *Il Magnifico,* is indicative of this rediscovered love of life.

Politically, the 16th century brought a renewal of Italian court life, with splendid *signorie* in almost every city. All of the foregoing are the foundations of that well known historic moment—the *Renaissance,* which means rebirth; but in reality it was simultaneously the splendid ending of an era and the beginning of a modern outlook on the world, an outlook that led to changes in almost every field of human endeavor.

Throughout the Italian peninsula the democratic *comune* made way for the opulent *signoria,* which provided a fertile terrain for poets and philosophers. The most significant writing was done in Florence and Ferrara by *Poliziano, Macchiavelli, Ariosto* and *Tasso.* Poliziano invented the *pastoral poem,* which led to a musical version (Tasso's *l'Aminta*), that eventually developed into the musical melodrama or *opera.* Macchiavelli was a brilliant historian who produced one of the most valid essays ever written on political philosophy: *The Prince.* Ariosto, the greatest Italian poet after Dante, wrote the *Orlando Furioso.* The poem contained just about every literary aspect of the Renaissance. (The story was inspired by the Medieval conflict between the Moors and Charlemagne's armies, a theme that had already been sung in French by an anonymous poet.) Ariosto's splendid work glorifies beauty, intelligence and love in all its natural aspects; everything is enhanced by imagination, and his characters float from one incredible situation to another, glide from one unreal landscape to another, with a total disregard for space, time and reality. For the modern reader the most interesting part of this poem is Astolfo's trip to the moon, a precursor of science fiction. The other important novelty is the freedom of Ariosto's characters, liberated from all moral and social conditioning.

Meanwhile, the invention of the printing press made an impact on Italian life and Venice installed the first model. But the *Reformation* began to change the political climate and the Spanish wars of conquest disrupted the peninsula. At the end of the 16th century *Torquato Tasso,* working in Ferrara, wrote a poem called *la Geruasalemme Liberata,* celebrating the liberation of Jerusalem by the First Crusade. Here, Renaissance ideals so purely sung by Ariosto were modified to include a religious subject—the sacred city is conquered only after God sends Gabriel to inspire the men and unite them for the purpose of reaching their goal—no longer man acting as free agent, but by divine intervention.

With the 17th century cultural and intellectual supremacy passed from Italy to France. Great playwrights such as Corneille, Racine and Molière reflected the splendors of Versailles. Not only did they entertain the king and his court, but they also established stable theaters with permanent actors and new styles of acting, thus laying the basis for the excellent French National Theater.

For the next two centuries Italy declined culturally not only because wars were being fought on its territory, and in its bickering cities, but also because the commercial routes shifted from the Mediterranean to the Atlantic, Baltic and North seas. It was no wonder that the 17th century was static. Art and literature needed form and words rather than creative models. The one positive aspect of this century was the attempt to reach a greater public, even if that attempt was made with the intention of amusing rather than teaching. There was widespread interest in music in Venice, science in Pisa, and art in Rome.

Toward the end of the century the return to humanism boomeranged to Italy from England and France, where Locke and Montaigne were writing and influencing society. At the beginning of the 18th century, Italy showed some tendency to embrace *Illuminism,* and noted Milan lawyer *Beccaria* published a pamphlet against the death penalty: *Dei Delitti a Delle Pene.* The most original thinker of the early part of the century was *Gian Battista Vico,* who claimed that the only science accessible to man was history, which he forges as he goes along.

The two most significant Italian authors of this period expressed the conflicts and changes of 18th-century society in two diametrically different ways. *Carlo Goldoni,* the great Venetian who raised the Italian theater from its infancy, has been called the "Galileo of Italian literature." Before his time the *Commedia dell'Arte* was practically the only type of performance known to Italians. Groups of wandering actors interpreted a few well-known characters, such as *Arlecchino* or *Colombina,* and followed a loose text that allowed them to improvise according to the spirit that moved them. Earlier theater works were complete, but their performances were not adequate because the actors weren't prepared for the task. With Goldoni, Italian acting became modern. Scenes, choreography and text were integrated and plays written as complete entities. Goldoni's comedies, written in French, Italian and a Venetian dialect are still performed today, to the everlasting delight of audiences and critics. His characters are often simple *plebeians,* described with wit, charm, malice and great humanity.

Unlike Goldoni, *Parini* wrote about the aristocracy. He concentrated on Lombard gentlemen and his long poem *Il Giorno* underlines, with biting irony, the lack of content in the lives of such men. Luxury and pleasure do not mature the human soul, is the moral message.

With the failure of the French Revolution and Napoleon's ambiguous politics (with the Treaty of Campoformio large portions of Italy reverted to Austrian control) an end to Illuminist hopes brought on, once again, a return to spirituality. The first writer to sense this crisis was Piemontese *Vittorio Alfieri,* with his abandoning of reason and his concentration on personal dramas of historical characters, whose tormented lives usually led to suicide.

But the intellectual evolution that took place between the end of the 18th century and the beginning of the 19th is best perceived in *Ugo Foscolo,* a Greek who moved to Venice at a very early age and whose poetry is neoclassical in style but anticipates Romanticism in content. A great admirer of Alfieri, Foscolo dedicated several verses of his masterpiece, *I Sepolcri* to the Piemontese writer, who was especially important for the patriotic fervor of his dramas.

In all of Europe the post-Napoleonic period is characterized by the Romantic movement. England led the way with Dickens; in France there was Madame de Stael who theorized and Victor Hugo who fictionalized, and in Germany Goethe and Schiller gave a nationalistic approach to their rediscovered classicism. All of this filtered down into Italy, but there was an additional element to Italian romanticism: the lack of national unity provided Italian romanticism with a patriotic soul. This is clearly apparent in the writings of two most important 19th-century authors: *Alessandro Manzoni* and *Giacomo Leopardi.* In *Adelchi,* a tragic play, Manzoni tackles the subject of patriotism in an attempt to return to the roots of his land, before the invading Franks defeated the Longobards (8th century). It's important to note that at this point in Italian history Manzoni was not alone in his search for national roots; many others were awakening to this need. Serious thinkers and writers encouraged the nation toward an awareness that foreign masters and invaders had been present on Italian soil since the fall of the Western Roman Empire in A.D. 476. *Mazzini* and *Gioberti* were the two most significant exponents of this movement, called *Risorgimento.* Other artists felt the same way. *Verdi* was another important figure of the Risorgimento. His music was not only Romantic but also nationalistic and avid patriots often used it in that context. To this day there are some who would like to make the chorus of *Nabucco* Italy's national anthem. It eventually led to the unification of the whole peninsula which, before 1848, was divided in many parts: The Savoia reigned in Piemonte, Liguria and Sardegna; the Austrians ruled in Lombardia, Veneto, Friuli-Venezia Giulia and Trentino-Alto Adige; Toscana was still a Grand duchy governed by Lorraine; Emilia-Romagna was divided into a clerical state: the Ducato di Modena and the Ducato di Parma. This clerical entity also included the Marche and Lazio, and from Campania downward the Reign of the Two Sicilies was ruled by the Borbone dynasty.

Manzoni is known for his masterpiece, *I Promessi Sposi,* considered by many to be the first modern novel. It contains every aspect of 19th-century culture. Deliberately, the novel takes place in 17th-century Lombardia, when the region was dominated by the Spanish (at the time it was written, Lombardia was still under foreign domination, no longer Spanish but Austrian). The religious element is ever present: the humble who stand up against the powerful, man's life "vis-á-vis" God's Will or divine Providence. In the end, the young couple marry and live happily ever after not because the hero kills the villain, but because it is willed by God.

The other great representative of Romanticism in Italy was Leopardi, born in *Recanati,* a small town in the Marche. It is not a coincidence that this sensitive thinker and poet came from a region dominated by the Church. His work is a blend of illuministic teaching and the reactionary attitude of the clergy. Leopardi felt this conflict within himself, he synthesized and overcame it, and with his lyricism represented a deep reflection of man's unhappy condition, as well as his own sadness and pain.

On March 17, 1861 the Reign of Italy are proclaimed. the unification involved several wars, including the famous landing of the *Thousand* in Sicily (1860), led by *Garibaldi*. The last city annexed was Rome, where the Pope, defended by French soldiers, resisted the Piemontese Savoia dynasty. Finally, in 1870, Rome fell and the peninsula was unified. With World War I the small addition of Friuli-Venezia Giulia and Trentino-Alto Adige was made, and they, too, became Italian.

The last decades of the 19th century witnessed a change of attitude in the writings of several authors. This was partly due to the influence of English positivism and partly a sign of the times. Italian realism had its most important exponent in *Giovanni Verga,* who described his Sicilian countrymen with stark simplicity and naturalistic overtones—a combination that produced a book reminiscent of a choral Greek tragedy, *I Malavoglia.*

But literature and art responded to changing times, and the turn of the 20th century breathed an air that no longer suited the realistic approach. Intellectuals no longer thought science was the answer to everything, and literature swung back to a personal point of view, different for every poet. *Giovanni Pascoli* researched the language and its sounds, while *Gabriele d'Annunzio* concentrated on the superman myth. Both evade reality. *Luigi Pirandello* and *Italo Svevo* were also a part of this general scene, but their work concentrated on a search of the *ego,* almost sensing the dawning age of analysis. Pirandello's theater was a precursor of the absurd, underlining the eternal counterpoint between reality and illusion, especially in *Henry IV* and *Six Characters in Search of an Author.* He received the 1934 Nobel Prize for literature.

But no cultural story of Italy, however short and incomplete, can ignore the more than 20 years of fascist rule that covered the country with a soft, dark cloud between the two great wars. At the end of World War I Italy was on the winning side, but was not represented at the conference table; nor was Italy allowed share in the spoils of war. And soon Italians began to feel that the costly victory was a "mutilated victory." The result was a nation torn by social conflict and ravaged by struggles of various kinds—between classes as well as different interests. Mussolini and his men looked like the solution. Thus, with the reluctant complicity of liberals, Church and monarchy, and after reaching a precarious understanding with industry and agriculture, a fascist state was born.

A dictatorship is seldom conducive to creative activity, and the 1920s and 30s in Italy were no exception. Still, the European literary scene did filter back to Italy to some extent. Writers such as Joyce, Kafka and Proust, who represented the conscience of man at that time wrote about the hardships of living in a changing world, which was read, and deeply felt and discussed by Italian intellectuals. Alongside the abovementioned Pirandello and Svevo there are several poets, such as *Ungaretti, Saba, Quasimodo* and *Montale* who began their activities under fascist rule, but became full-fledged artists after World War II. On the narrative side of literature, *Alberto Moravia* and *Cesare Pavese* began to publish. They stressed, each in his own way, the hopeless decay of society and the pathetic condition of man. The latter, a brilliant translator of Anglo-Saxon authors as well, unfortunately committed suicide at an early age. Moravia, now in his 70s, is still an interested and interesting critic of Italian society who occasionally writes an essay of acute insight and perception about his country.

After the fall of fascism and with the close of World War II, Italy found itself a part of Europe, with all the attendant advantages and disadvantages. Squeezed between the two great blocks of East and West, with a strong Communist Party on the one hand and a still powerful Church on the other, intellectually Italy became a restless country.

Meanwhile, the industrial complex was growing, and in 20 short years Italy was to enter the modern world. Even if the so-called "economic miracle" has turned out to be less than perfect, the country did live in comfort and prosperity from about 1955 to 1977. The economic and political crisis that descended on all Western nations after that hit Italy with an even greater impact, probably because its new industrialism wasn't stable enough, and because its new democracy has not found a permanent political formula.

But Italy's cultural and artistic genius is still at work. In the last 30 years this genius has given the world the movies of *Fellini, Germi, De Sica, Visconti, Pasolini, Antonioni* and *Bertolucci,* to mention only those that are known best. Each is a master in his own way, Fellini may well be the Michelangelo of our time. They operate in cinema (even if most write as well) because, blessed with Italian perception of what is new and important, these great artists feel that this is the best means of expression in this confused and rapidly changing 20th century.

Food and Drink

Every Italian region has its own traditional dishes, just as it has its own dialect, customs and local saints.

Oversimplifying, we can say the following: The north favors rice and *polenta* over pasta, butter over oil and beef and veal over lamb. The pasta of central Italy contains eggs, but the pasta of southern Italy contains water. Toscana has the best bread in Italy, and Napoli makes the best pizza.

NORTHERN ITALIAN COOKING

A closer look at Italian regional cooking tells more. While the cuisine of Lombardia and its provinces is as varied as its territory, Piemonte and Valle d'Aosta present a more unified picture.

Piemontese Cooking

The traditional ingredients of Piemontese cooking are six: rice, butter, garlic, milk, cheese and truffles. At least one and sometimes as many as four of these basics are in most preparations. It should be underlined that milk is not used for drinking but milk or cream is very much a part of the excellent sweets made in this area. The superb wines, also made here, are for drinking.

As for pasta, the Piemontese hardly ever buys the ready-made product and only occasionally makes it at home. It's for a special occasions; the dough contains eggs and is used for dumplings called *agnolotti*. They are filled with a hearty meat stuffing and served with a good meat sauce.

The most popular meats are beef and game, with chicken and veal as alternatives. One of Piemonte's favorite dishes, *brasato di bue* (beef stew), uses full-bodied *Barolo* wine and is a worthy cousin of France's famous *boeuf bourguignon.* There is a very good traditional recipe of *lepre in salmi* (marinated hare in a special sauce) and a delicious *fondua ai tartufi* (truffle fondue), both of which could easily win a gastronomic contest. A hot garlic and anchovy dip, *bagna caoda,* is used with raw vegetables, and rice is served in every possible form, from soups to dessert, but never as a *risotto,* a dish that brings us to Lombardia.

Gnocchi alla Fontina, semolina dumplings rolled in cheese, are heavenly

314

Lombard Cooking

Lombard cooking is varied and excellent. This Italian region has given the world several great recipes, the aforementioned *risotto,* veal cutlets, famous *panettone* and *zuppa pavese.* Risotto is rice that has been, first, fried slowly in abundant butter with chopped onion, then, slowly boiled in good meat broth. An old-fashioned version requires saffron as well, so that the risotto comes out very yellow. The veal cutlets are Milanese and Viennese, and who gave it to whom is an open question. But it's a known fact that during the 15th century Milano was addicted to frying most foods, for it was believed that the golden hue produced by frying foods dipped in eggs and bread crumbs was beneficial to digestion. The origin of panettone is lost to history. It was eaten on Christmas eve by a united family; a patriarchal father sliced thick slices and gave one to every member assembled. Originally it was only a very large bread (*pane* means bread); the raisins and candied fruit were added later.

Lombardia produces good butter and several of the best cheeses in Italy. Other favorite foods are *minestrone,* a thick vegetable soup that uses lard as a base; *ossobuco,* a delicious dish made with slices of veal leg; *cazzoeula alla milanese,* a combination of pork hocks and ribs, sausages and cabbage; and *Faraona alla creta,* a Guinea hen baked in clay worthy of the most demanding gourmet.

Other of the region's infinite gastronomic treats include various recipes for cooking snails, a marvelous veal roast, tripe done with beans and served with grated cheese, asparagus with butter and cheese and beef pot-roasted to perfection.

A note to remember is that while Milano is the gastronomic capital of the region, *Mantova* is a frontier town that unites the three cuisines of *Lombardia, Veneto* and *Emilia* into a very interesting style of its own.

[handwritten margin note: Lombardy is the home of both gorgon- zola and Bel paese]

Venetian Cuisine

Venetian cuisine is the third great cooking tradition of northern Italy. For centuries the rich and pleasure-loving merchants of the Most Serene Republic brought the best new products such as rice, *polenta* (corn meal mush) and beans to their fair city and incorporated them into the local gastronomy. Conversely, when forced to go abroad, wealthy Venetians took their cooks and habits with them, and the result was that many of their dishes influenced other Italian regions.

The four most important staples in Venetian cooking are rice, beans, polenta and *baccalà* (codfish). Not one of the four is Italian in origin or even Mediterranean.

Rice was brought from the East, and if the Western world now eats it regularly, it is a result of Venetian enterprise. Rice was introduced into Europe by the Arabs in the 8th century and was made known in Lombardia somewhat later by the Spaniards. The early Viscontis gave it a certain amount of popularity.

Originally its high cost forced this digestible grain to be used only for the sick or in expensive desserts. But the Venetian sailors had been familiar with rice even before the Lombards, and while they were in the Orient they investigated this simple and satisfying food. More and more Venetian ships brought cargoes of rice back to Italy, and as its use became wider and found favor, attempts were made to plant and grow it on Italian soil. The first successful rice cultures in Europe were achieved in the Verona area during the first part of the 16th century. From then on the preparation of rice in savory and appetizing dishes was a favorite pastime for Venetian housewives and nowhere today is rice cooked in so many different ways.

When making a list of Venetian rice specialities, the very first is usually *risi e bisi,* a combination of rice and peas that is both light and delicious. Other combinations are rice and chicken livers, rice and sausage, rice and tripe, rice and eel, rice and partridge, rice and shrimp and rice and spinach.

Polenta, the other great Venetian staple, is now made primarily from corn. Originally it was a gruel made with wheat or buckwheat flour, and a dark polenta is still popular among the Veronese and Paduan peasants. Corn was brought from the Americas in the mid-16th century, and active cultivation started around 1630 after a very bad crop of other cereals; the yellow flour then took over and polenta became synonymous with corn meal.

The thick, yellow gruel, used almost as a substitute for bread, is eaten hot, warm or cold, with sauces or as a side dish to meat or beans, with milk or cheese or just sliced and fried.

Just like the people of most seagoing nations, Venetians have a great predilection for vegetables. The reason is simple: When on board ship sailors are forced to eat packaged and dried foods so that fresh greens become the biggest luxury. When back on firm land, fruits and vegetables are in enormous demand and are eaten in such quantities that a Venetian doctor once said the salad eaten in his city was enough to generate more diseases than any other single cause.

Another Venetian favorite, beans, is an American plant. It was introduced in Italy by Pope Clement VII somewhere between 1528 and 1532. He received some sample seeds from the Spaniards and gave them to Tuscan friends and to a humanist scholar from Belluno, Pierio Valeriano. When the successfully grown legume arrived in Venezia it was rapidly baptized as Turkish, obviously a frequent error in those days because corn is also called *grano turco.* Apparently, to Venetians, America and Turkey were one and the same thing.

Pasta e fagioli is a traditional Italian food. There are versions of it in almost every region, but the best and most elaborate is made here, in the pearl of the Adriatic. Other ways of eating beans are also popular from one end of the region to the other. They include beans in various sauces, several bean soups, and beans with polenta.

The last staple we will discuss is *baccalà* or codfish. No seaside community has been able to resist the practical dried cod, and Venezia had developed such a good recipe that it has passed into culinary history: *bacalà mantecato.* The well-known fish became part of Venetian cuisine only two centuries ago and is therefore the newest of the four ingredients we've mentioned. Venetians love it and eat it with a passion. In fact, one of their 19th-century poets dedicated a long composition of 36 verses, eight lines each to the delicious concoction. Naturally, the most Venetian way of eating it is with polenta on the side.

Trentino-Alto Adige Cooking

The three remaining northern regions are Trentino-Alto Adige, Friuli-Venezia Giulia and Liguria. Of these, only the first has a marked cooking tradition of its own. Friuli cooks are influenced by the Venetians on the one side and Trento on the other and, for good measure, by nearby Yugoslavia. The one thing that strikes us as totally local is the use of a tuberous root, the *topinambur*. It has a pleasant flavor reminiscent of artichokes. Liguria, on the other side of Italy, has a cuisine that resembles that of its neighbor Toscana and is famous for a cold sauce made with olive oil, garlic, basil and cheese, all chopped up and ground together: the *pesto*.

By looking at a map of the North it can be easily seen that Trentino-Alto Adige is the continuation of Lombardia that borders on Austria, no wonder its cuisine is a combination of Lombard and Austrian influences with some German and Slav thrown in. Unfortunately, here as in several other regions, the traditional dishes are rarely served in restaurants, and you may pass through the area and scarcely know them. The one place where this is an exception is *Bolzano*, a city that has very good restaurants and *trattorie* interested in keeping local traditions alive. The only newcomer is the ubiquitous spaghetti, which has traveled north and can be found everywhere in Italy.

(handwritten: A local favorite is lepre alla Trentina (jugged hare))

When learning about this region it is important to remember that the great Council of Trento was held here, and many important churchmen lived in the city for 18 years. Thus, several dishes were introduced to the population from outside and have remained. The various forms of *gulasch, canèderli* (from the German *Knodel*) and *strudels* are delicious. But the one item that exists only in this area and is of outstanding flavor is *speck,* smoked pork lard that is very good and difficult to duplicate. Salting and smoking this piece of meat is a delicate operation, and the Alto Adige experts have been doing it for generations.

CENTRAL ITALIAN COOKING

Central Italy is as varied as the north, and its cooking is just as interesting. Outstanding and as different from each other as any are the cuisines of Tuscany and of Emilia-Romagna. Next to these giants, the cooking of Marches is less important but it does have some unique dishes. Lazio has traditional and thrifty recipes and Umbria specialties are combinations from several other regions.

Tuscan Cooking

Let us begin with Toscana, which has a sober, balanced, ageless cuisine that matches its simple and harmonious countryside. Here, olive oil, good wine, vegetables and bread make up the modest base for some of the best food in the world. High-quality, fresh ingredients and a minimum of manipulation give splendid results, and the justly famous *zuppe*—vegetable soups served on bread—or the Florentine steak are still the region's best answer to a meal. Texas pride and tradition notwithstanding, this is the region that invented the T-bone steak (albeit smaller, because Valle di Chiana animals did not have

Texas dimensions). The best olive oil is also from this part of the world, and Tuscans use it on everything: soups, salads, boiled fish and even plain bread.

Tuscan bread is hard crusted, compact and saltless. Still baked the old-fashioned way, it lasts several days and is tasty to the end. Lack of salt means that it does not get moldy. In fact, old Tuscan bread gets hard as stone but has no trace of fungus growths. This region hardly has a pasta tradition, and like Piemonte, the Tuscans seldom make pasta. When they do, it is usually thicker than the fine product of Emilia. Tuscan *tortelli,* similar to *agnolotti,* are large dumplings with a good meat filling and are made for special occasions.

For all its simplicity, Tuscan cooking is full of marvelous scents from the many fragrant herbs present in almost every dish. Basil, rosemary, sage, thyme, mint and oregano are the most common; parsley is added frequently and tarragon is amply used in Siena. Both black and red pepper are used a lot; red is more digestible. Another specialty is the *insaccati*—several varieties of cold cuts prepared the Tuscan way using fresh ingredients, wisely dosed and mixed. A Tuscan sausage is one of the best in the country, and special items such as *biroldo* or *soppressata, finocchiona* or *rigatino* must be tasted locally for they defy description.

Some excellent fish dishes are part of the Tuscan tradition since the rivers and the sea provide such tempting varieties. From Livorno we have the famous *cacciucco,* a fish soup made with at least five varieties of fish; from Pisa comes the splendid *cieche* (also known as *cee*), which are baby eels cooked with olive oil, garlic and sage.

Toscana is also famous for its infinite, and infinitely tasty, dishes prepared with game of all kinds. A special sauce made with hare is used to flavor pasta that is typically Tuscan, a wide noodle known as *pappardelle alla lepre.* A stew made with wild boar is served with a very interesting sweet and sour sauce that comes from the Middle Ages, and pheasants, quails and partridges are roasted to perfection.

Tuscan wines, cheeses and sweets each has a tradition of its own. Wine is mostly red for this is the region that makes *Chianti* and the famous *Brunello di Montalciuo;* these two names alone tell the story. Cheeses are dry and savory and made mostly with goat's milk. Sweets are interesting, with some Arab influences (during the Middle Ages the caravans that came from the East stopped at Siena.) A local specialty is *castagnaccio,* a flat cake made with chestnut flour, rosemary, raisins and olive oil.

Emilia-Romagna Cooking

In terms of physical distance, Toscana and Emilia-Romagna are close, but the traditional gastronomies of the two regions couldn't be further apart. The food of Emilia-Romagna, the fat and wealthy region divided from the Tuscan hills by a wall of mountains—the Appenines—is rich and buttery, full of good cream and eggs, juicy hams and abundant pork cold cuts. Bologna, capital of Emilia-Romagna, is also the capital of that best-known little dumpling, the *tortellino.* Its ham and cheese filling is enclosed in a fine egg dough, which is rolled to perfection by experienced *Bolognesi* women. They use long rolling pins that are passed down as heirlooms from mother to daughter. This little item is eaten by the dozen, and contests of *tortellini* eaters are held

Fritto misto alla Fiorentina is not made with fish but with brains and sweetbreads

Sometimes cream is added to the ragù

regularly with unbelievable results. On one occasion a gentleman was known to eat, in only 90 minutes, about 6 pounds of these beloved dumplings.

Emilia-Romagna is renowned for its egg pasta; other types of noodles such as *tagliatelle, lasagne* and *maccheroni* are also eaten there. The standard sauce that goes with the meat and tomato combination called *ragù;* the meat is often seasoned with only butter and cheese, both of which are delicious here.

Cheese is one of the region's bywords, for this is the region that produces *parmigiano.* The splendid *prosciutto di Parma* (Parma ham) is also world famous. Less known but worth looking for is Ferrara's goose ham. In addition, the city has a large Jewish community, and several interesting dishes that follow the Jewish dietary laws are made here.

Another cold cut that has Bolognese origins that seem to go as far back as 1376 is the exquisite *mortadella.* It is so good that its name has become synonymous with Bologna, so much so that Americans have been eating a modified version of it for years, calling it *boloney.*

Two things Emilia-Romagna does not have are good bread and good wine. The only wine produced there is *Lambrusco,* slightly bubbly, slightly sweetish white wine that is exported in large quantities to the United States. The wine, however, is not as important to the average *emiliano* as to other Italians, and an old joke says that if you want to know where Emilia ends and Romagna begins, walk into a peasant's house and ask for something to drink. When they give you water, you're still in Emilia, but if you get wine, you've crossed the border into Romagna. As for bread, it's just plain white, fluffy and soft inside, with very little flavor.

Marches Cooking

After Toscana and Emilia-Romagna our culinary trip takes us to *Marches* on the Adriatic coast. This coastal region has the usual fish dishes, from codfish to anchovies. But its cuisine's two distinguishing items are a wide variety of fish broths and the *vincisgrassi,* a local version of *lasagne* considered by some the prototype of this well-known dish. The broths are interesting and tasty, and two are worth describing: The *Ancona* version is made with garlic, onion, olive oil, tomato, parsley, salt and pepper, plus several types of fish; the *brodetto allo zafferano,* uses olive oil, onion, white wine, saffron, salt and pepper and lots of fish. Both are served with toasted bread and both are delicious.

One speciality we cannot overlook is fried olives; they are large, green olives stuffed with a good meat filling, rolled in flour, egg and bread crumbs like a cutlet, then fried in boiling olive oil and served with lemon. The wines of the region are white mostly. *Verdicchio,* a light, dry, greenish wine is very good.

Lazio and Roman Cuisine

In the introduction to Central Italian cooking we mentioned that Lazio has a tradition of thrift. But Lazio means Rome, and Rome is not only the capital of the nation, but also the city that holds the Vatican as well as an extremely important crossroad of Mediterranean and international traffic. Therefore, we must distinguish the cosmopolitan, rich and elegant cooking that can be had in Roman homes and restaurants from the old-fashioned, traditional cooking of Lazio and the simple Roman's Rome.

More than others, this region's favorite dishes reflect the poverty of the 19th century when meat was not as available as it is today and the average family had to use imagination to make ends meet. Roman women used all parts of the animal, and one of the best recipes made there, to this day, is a dish that uses the small intestine of veal, *pajata*. Other interesting dishes are sweet and sour beef's tongue and fried brains and sweetbreads. Even though these dishes do not use meaty pieces of beef, they remain great favorites with the local population.

Spices have been a part of Roman cooking as far back as can be remembered, and cloves, cinnamon and pepper are used generously. Equally popular are garlic, onion, basil, bay leaves, sage, rosemary, marjoram and parsley, which testify to the Mediterranean tradition in Roman cooking. Celery was a late arrival but is now eaten along with the other greens and herbs. Lazio and Rome use little butter; lard and olive oil are the fats used most.

Pigs are bred and eaten in great quantities, equaled only by lamb. Even if lamb is popular in almost every Mediterranean country, few people can roast, grill or fry it the way Romans can.

Here is where the reign of good pasta begins, with every simple restaurant and elegant home boasting its own recipe for *spaghetti, bucatini, gnocchi* and *maccheroni*. Sauces are made from tomato, cheese, eggs, meats, vegetables, spices and herbs, oil and wine, garlic, onion, mushrooms—everything.

One special dish is worth mentioning, Ox's tail and celery, otherwise known as *coda alla vaccinara*. The humble tail, cut into pieces and panfried in olive oil and lard with chopped up onion, carrot and garlic, is cooked in white wine, a few tomatoes and basil. After about 1 hour, large chunks of celery plus raisins, *pinoli* nuts and a small spoon of grated bitter chocolate are added. Very little salt and pepper is put on and off to the table.

Local wines are white rather than red, dry and fairly light, good with fish, fowl or lamb. They are produced mostly around Frascati.

Umbria Cooking

Our last central region is Umbria, a small, green portion of Italy that lies between Toscana and Lazio, west of Marches. The cooking habits of these three regions are reflected in Umbrian dishes, sometimes to the advantage of Umbria. For example, pork is particualrly good in this area, and sausages, hams and cold cuts are as delicious as can be. Another specialty is grilled meats: They may seem simple to prepare, but a well turned out roast or barbecue is rare and requires experience. Furthermore, Umbria serves unexpected grilled meats, such as sweetbreads and innards, all seasoned to perfection with black pepper, anise seeds, cloves, olive oil and wine.

Two vegetables characterize the region: olives and truffles. The latter are black, have their season from November to March and are served in many preparations including eggs and spaghetti. Olives provide the population with an excellent oil, are used to season meats and vegetables or are chopped into a creamy paste that can be spread on bread—a poor person's savory caviar.

a good local dish is carciofi alla Romana, artichokes stuffed with herbs

SOUTHERN ITALIAN COOKING

Unlike the north and central Italy, southern Italy can be described as one unit. There are, of course, a few individual dishes in each region. The basic similarities are everywhere however, and one of them is so obvious that it cannot escape the most unobservant tourist. Its name is *pasta* and/or *spaghetti*. How pasta came to Italy is an object of frequent and heated debate. Modern researchers assure us that it is *not* a Neapolitan invention and that it was *not* brought from China by Marco Polo. The evidence points to Sicilia as the starting point of this popular food, probably a by-product of Arab civilization. It would seem that pasta originates from the same mixture of flour and water, with no yeast added, that has been used in the Mediterranean for centuries and has produced the flat breads of Arabs and Jews. The flat disk, cut into strips either before or after baking, has produced noodles; different manipulation of the dough has resulted in spaghetti.

Abruzzo, a region known for an excellent pasta called *alla chitarra*— the dough is pressed through a gadget that has thin strings, like a guitar—also makes a thick round strand using an old system called *manate.*

Other unifying factors of southern Italian cooking are the abundant use of tomatoes, a preference for lamb and pork, the many fish recipes present in every region, the love of spicy foods livened by *peperoncino* and a preference for *pecorino* and cheeses made with *pasta filata* as opposed to *pasta granulosa.* Pasta filata cheeses are oval in shape and usually hang.

Sicilian Cooking

As for the differences in the regions, let us begin with *Sicilia* cooking. The sunny island has a cooking tradition that goes back several centuries, but the dishes cannot be easily found in local restaurants. Sicilians are very closed about their traditions of which food is a part.

Sicilian cooking can be very complicated or slightly complicated. In other words, the dishes can be prepared for a rich person's or a poor person's diet, both with as many ingredients as can be had. Take the *caponata.* The simpler variety is made with eggplant, celery, a small octopus and a sweet and sour tomato sauce. The fancy version adds anything from capers and olives to lobster and wild asparagus. There is truly opulent caponata, covered with a rich chocolate sauce, toasted almonds and slices of hard-boiled eggs; we can't say who makes it now, probably no one.

The sunny island is full of splendid fruit trees, and the oranges, lemons, figs and almonds are responsible for the famous candied fruit, one of Sicilia's most important industries. Another Arab legacy are the tacky, sticky sweets made with almonds, honey, spices, and eggs and so on. Ice cream is also a Sicilian invention, and the simple *granita* is a reminder of the ancestor of this popular food. A granita is just chopped ice with a flavored syrup poured on top—very refreshing.

Campania Cooking

Tomatoes were brought to Italy by the Spanish who took them from Peru. Napoli and its region, *Campania,* became a natural habitat for the red and sunny fruit, and the best *pomarola* is made there. The tomato is also responsi-

Ask for Sartu, a rice-meat-vegetable casserole, covered with cheese ble for that great Neapolitan invention: *pizza.* Covered with tomato and *mozzarella* cheese and spiced up with *oregano* and whatever else you wish to add, a flat pancake of simple dough becomes the most widely eaten food in the world.

Puglia Cooking

Puglia is, gastronomically speaking, a unified region that eats pasta, bread, cheese and fish. Good bread and oil are made here, and the area is called Italy's cellar because its wine production is very large: 10 million hectoliters per annum. The one item that is eaten in different proportions in southern Italy is garlic—as you travel south in the region its use gets smaller and smaller until at Gallipoli it makes room for onions. Sauces for pastas are made with fish; meat is either lamb, pork or horse, with an occasional small bird such as thrush.

Calabria, Molise, Basilicata Cooking

Calabria, Molise and *Basilicata* share with Campania a love of spaghetti and fish, plus tomato, eggplant, the ever-present little red pepper and pork. All types of fruit, both fresh and dried, are present on Calabrian tables, and a surprisingly large amount of mushrooms and artichokes are eaten. As mentioned above and in tune with other southern Mediterranean cultures, the South of Italy favors spicy food, but an occasional recipe has sweet and sour overtones, reminiscent of the Middle Ages and perhaps of Nordic visitors or conquerors.

Sardegna Cooking

The last region in this quick trip through Italian gastronomy is *Sardegna,* the island west of Toscana and Lazio that still has some of its old-fashioned habits, including ways of cooking and eating. The area is relatively poor, and much of the population lives off the products of the land or are shepherds. Thus many Sardinian recipes contain cheese; meat is often roasted on a spit; and bread is a flat pancake.

Here, more than in any other part of Italy, possibly of Europe, an old civilization has survived. While fashionable, jet-setty Costa Smeralda enjoys its villas, swimming pools and other types of fun, other parts of Sardegna live an almost primitive existence where the fight for survival is a daily reality.

There is a tendency among sophisticated Italian gourmets to revive some ancient Sardinian dishes, and in the larger cities a few restaurants have catered to this taste. These places offer genuine Sardinian food and even import some of their ingredients from the island. Fashionable Romans and Milanese are perfectly at ease with such items as *angiulottus, impanadas, lepudrida, malloreddus, pane frattau* and *porceddu furria furria,* to name only a few. This interesting cuisine has been influenced by many others: Genoese and Sicilians, Arabs and Spaniards, Tuscans and Piemontese, each modified by the ingredients available on the island.

Such changes and novelties in modern Italian cooking are the result of many cultures, plus the ingredients available, plus the interest that Italians have in eating, plus the genius of the great cooks.

ITALIAN NOUVELLE CUISINE

Italians are extremely conscious of good taste, they consider refinement to be their own gift to modern civilization. The result of this is that the informed, the creative, the more energetic and resourceful restaurants have changed their whole approach to cooking. Some openly specialize in the so-called *nouvelle cuisine;* some create an Italian version of it, which they prefer to call *cucina moderna;* some merely improve on their traditional menus.

At present, the situation is still changing, and it will probably continue to do so for some time to come. So while a definitive word is not possible, what we can do is bring the information up to date.

In fairness to Italian cooks and chefs, the first thing to remember is that the traditional love and care are still present in the preparation of food in Italy. Whether you go to an elegant restaurant, a simple *trattoria,* or a private home, the food you get will be fresh, tasty and well presented. The changes are in the cooking methods: Less oil is used, cooking times are shorter, quantities of pasta are smaller, wines tend to be lighter (lower alcohol content). The second thing to remember is that the basic eating pattern is still the same: small breakfast, a major meal either midday or in the evening and a dinner that depends on whether you eat at home or out. If you eat at home, dinner is usually a secondary meal. The major meal consists of a substantial first course, which can be *pasta,* rice, *polenta* or a thick vegetable soup, followed by a second course of meat or fish, one vegetable and a dessert that is often fruit or fruit salad or sometimes a *crostata* (fairly dry fruit pie) but seldom cake or pudding. All of this is washed down with wine; of late the wines are younger and lighter.

The new trends are divided into two groups. The strictly *nouvelle cuisine* approach, with definite French influence, can be found in several excellent restaurants such as *Gualtiero Marchesi* of Milano, *San Domenico* of Imola and the *Antica Osteria del Ponte* at Cassinetta de Lugagnano near Milano. Here the *conauisseur* can enjoy new combinations of meat, fish, fruit and vegetables, done with attention to detail that is as delightful and beautiful as any in the world. The second group, led by the modern *Locanda dell'Angelo* of Ameglia (La Spezia) and the *Enoteca Pinchiorri* of Firenze, with *Guido* of Costigliole d'Asti, *Boschetti* of Tricesimo (Udine), *La Pergola* of Bergamo, *Il Sole* of Maleo, and many others, follows an approach that can be defined regional, seasonal or both, with modern variations of old local recipes and a careful search for the best seasonal ingredients: peas and cherries in May and June, peaches and tomatoes in July, figs and grapes in August and September, cauliflower in October, mushrooms in fall, artichokes in winter, asparagus in spring and so on and so forth. These restaurants offer the best food possible in their specific location and for the particular time of year. They follow a pragmatic, practical philosophy that is not only Italian but universal.

If your main interests in Italy are Roman ruins and Romanesque churches, you will still find that the majority of restaurants and *trattorie* serve good traditional dishes, with an occasional touch of novelty supplied by a lighter sauce or a new ingredient. All restaurants listed in this book are run by serious professionals who prepare their food with good fresh ingredients and serve it with pride. But if your main interest is food, we suggest the following itinerary that concentrates on the exceptional restaurants.

A GOURMET'S ITINERARY OF ITALY

Even though most Italian food experts feel that there are no great restaurants south of Firenze, we begin our itinerary in Roma where you won't be disappointed in either *Alberto Ciarla,* a very good fish place in Trastevere, the *Pergola* at the Cavalieri Hilton or *Checchino al Mattatoio.* The latter is one of the best, truly Roman restaurants and still serves authentic Roman food, while the Pergola tends to favor a *nouvelle cuisine* approach.

When leaving Roma you have two choices. Either take the fabulous *Settebello,* an express train that will take you to Firenze in 3 hours or drive on the *Autostrada del Sole.* If you go by Autostrada, a good stop for lunch is *Badia* at *Orvieto.* Badia is recommended not only for its good food—eat grilled meats, preferably lambchops, they are exquisite—but also for its atmosphere and beauty; it is an old abbey that has been transformed into a hotel and restaurant. For those with time to spare and a desire to see Umbria, we suggest a good restaurant in the city of *Spello* called *Il Molino* or an excellent one in the outskirts of *Perugia* (see the restaurant section of central Italy). Going north from *Todi,* You'll pass a place called *Torgiano,* and a restaurant called *Le Tre Vaselle di Lungarotti.* Lungarotti was the name of the owner —good restaurants in Italy are often known by the name of the owner or chef —it is now run by the widow. Neither *Badia, Il Molino* nor *Le Tre Vaselle* are five-star restaurants, but they all have the best food in their respective areas and will satisfy the most demanding palate.

At this point we assume you have reached Firenze, whether by train or car. Here the *Enotecua Pinchiorri* is a must, not only for its food but for its wine cellar, considered the best in Italy. You may also try *Sabatini,* one of the best traditional restaurants in the country or drive to Lucca for half a day and eat at *Solferino* (slightly out-of-town, at S. Macario in Piano) for an old-fashioned Tuscan meal.

From Firenze two itineraries are possible, both enticing from a gourmet's point of view. One itinerary goes east to *Bologna* and *Imola* with stops at the *Cordon Bleu* of Bologna, a very new entry into the Olympus of great Italian eateries, and the *San Domenico* of Imola, which has been listed in every gastronomic guide of Italy and is considered among the finest *nouvelle cuisine* temples in the land. From Bologna continue north, passing *Parma* and *Piacenza,* both blessed with at least one great restaurant.

About 25 miles out of Parma is a town called *Busseto;* a suburb of the town, called *Samboseto,* has a restaurant named *Cantarelli,* where a rich, Emilian meal awaits you. It's a great experience not meant for dieters. If you drive straight on to Piacenza, stop in town and eat at the *Antica Osteria Teatro,* which is altogether different. It's a sophisticated city restaurant with good services and the new approach to cooking. But both of the above are stops on the way to *Milano,* where two of the best restaurants in the country

[handwritten margin note: On try Falchetto, in Perugia]

are located. There is *Gualtiero Marchesi,* a modern, fascinating, expensive, creative, restaurant where the chef of the same name is the unquestioned king of Italian chefs. Slightly out-of-town at *Cassinetta de Lugagnano* there is the *Antica Osteria del Ponte,* a small, charming and very unique restaurant where you eat a *menu degustation* that will delight the most refined of gourmets. Service is exquisite, elegant and dignified.

The other itinerary goes north from Firenze. It takes you toward the sea, where on the road to Genova, right after *Carrara,* a small place called *Ameglia de Sarzana* has a country inn called *Locanda dell'Angelo,* that is presided over by another great Italian chef, *Angelo Paracucchi.* Here you can also stop for the night, where the rooms are modern and comfortable. But eating in the spacious restaurant will be unforgettable. With luck the *maestro* himself will prepare your spaghetti, manipulating his chafing dish, right in front of your admiring eyes, with the concentration of an orchestra director wielding his baton. From here you can cross the *passo della Cisa* in less than 1 hour and reach Parma by following the *Autostrada* to Piacenza and Milano, as in the previous itinerary. Or else, if you have time and a special place in your heart for truffles, drive north into Piemonte and *Castigliole d'Asti* where *Guido* will provide the best food and wine in the region.

It is not far from here to Milano; it's about 100 miles east, and your gourmet tour should finish in the great northern city, where good restaurants are the order of the day. Besides the well-known *Marchesi* and the *Antica Osteria* mentioned above, there is enchanting *Scaletta* and a new place called *Altopalato.* This last is an entirely unique gastronomic experiment; since it is open only three evenings a week you must book in advance. The restaurant may offer a Renaissance meal, a regional meal or an international meal; it changes according to the host's guests. Altopalato, which is not intended for the average tourist, can be very interesting for the gourmet, but the visit must be planned ahead.

The above are only a few of Italy's excellent restaurants. Many others provide very good food and wine, but an itinerary must follow a geographic design, and we have deviated enough from the central road. Out-of-the-way cities such as *Verona, Mantova, Bergamo, Cortina d'Ampezzo, Merano* or *Tricesimo di Udine* are all blessed with excellent restaurants. As a last word on gastronomic travel, we hope that you will try your own luck, and if you are successful, please let us know.

Index